DATE DUE

AUG 15 2010	
SEP 22 2011	
NOV 15 2011	

WANTED—
CORRESPONDENCE

DISCARD

WANTED—
CORRESPONDENCE

Women's Letters to a Union Soldier

EDITED BY

Nancy L. Rhoades

and

Lucy E. Bailey

OHIO UNIVERSITY PRESS

ATHENS

Ohio University Press, Athens, Ohio 45701
www.ohioswallow.com
© 2009 by Ohio University Press
All rights reserved

Printed in the United States of America
Ohio University Press books are printed on acid-free paper ⊗ ™

16 15 14 13 12 11 10 09   5 4 3 2 1

Library of Congress Cataloging-in-Publication Data

Wanted, correspondence : women's letters to a Union soldier / edited by Nancy L.
Rhoades and Lucy E. Bailey.
    p. cm.
Includes bibliographical references and index.
ISBN 978-0-8214-1804-8 (hc : alk. paper) -- ISBN 978-0-8214-1805-5 (pb : alk. paper)
    1. United States—History—Civil War, 1861–1865—Women—Sources. 2. United
States—History—Civil War, 1861–1865—Social aspects—Sources. 3. Ohio—
History—Civil War, 1861–1865—Women—Sources. 4. Ohio—History—Civil War,
1861–1865—Social aspects—Sources. 5. Women—United States—Social conditions—
19th century—Sources. 6. Women—Ohio—Social conditions—19th century—
Sources. 7. Letter writing—Social aspects—United States—Sources. 8. United
States—History—Civil War, 1861–1865—War work—Sources. 9. Lybarger, Edwin
Lewis, 1840–1924—Correspondence. I. Rhoades, Nancy L., 1915–2007. II. Bailey,
Lucy E. III. Lybarger, Edwin Lewis, 1840–1924.
    E628.W368 2009
    973.7092'2771—dc22
                              2009000022

For my sisters:
Davida Margaret Lybarger Wilke
and
Mary Finney Lybarger Collins
who were too young to know our grandfather
and whose heritage this is,
as well as my own

—*Nancy Rhoades*

Contents

Illustrations

Preface

THE BALLAD OF DEAD LADIES

Tell me now in what hidden way is
    Lady Flora the lovely Roman?
Where's Hipparchia, and where is Thais,
    Neither of them the fairer woman?
    Where is Echo, beheld of no man,
Only heard on river and mere,—
    She whose beauty was more than human? . . .
But where are the snows of yester-year?

Where's Héloise, the learned nun,
    For whose sake Abeillard, I ween,
Lost manhood and put priesthood on?
    (From love he won such dule and teen!)
    And where, I pray you, is the Queen
Who willed that Buridan should steer
    Sewed in a sack's mouth down the Seine? . . .
But where are the snows of yester-year?

White Queen Blanche, like a queen of lilies,
    With a voice like any mermaiden.—
Bertha Broadfoot, Beatrice, Alice,
    And Ermengarde the lady of Maine,—
    And that good Joan whom Englishmen
At Rouen doomed and burned her there—
    Mother of God, where are they then? . . .
But where are the snows of yester-year?

> Nay, never ask this week, fair lord,
>> Where they are gone, nor yet this year,
> Save with this much for an overword,—
>> But where are the snows of yester-year?

—François Villon (1450); translated
from the French by Dante Gabriel Rossetti

FROM THE DIM and misty past, François Villon calls to mind the names of heroines long gone in his "Ballad of Dead Ladies" and repeatedly asks, "But where are the snows of yester-year?" The snows covered the "dead ladies" until they were cast almost into oblivion, before the obscuring snow itself melted away. Who were these chaste and ardent women whose names speak of valor, intrigue, joy, and tragic endings? Villon, who could have heard their stories from the bards, suggests: their names are not forgotten, because he wrote them down and left us to puzzle over their fragile memories. We hear his plaintive grief over time and tales long told.

In the frantic bustle of centuries later and having no great learning, we do not recognize Bertha Broadfoot, mother of Charlemagne, who guided her son to create the country France from the warring tribes of Franks and Saxons. We do not recognize Thaïs (there were so many), but we see the glamour of the courtesan who went with Alexander the Great and his army. We should know Queen Blanche, queen of Castile, mother of Louis IX, religious and energetic, who ruled the realm with a firm hand until her son attained his majority and continued to influence his government. We should remember Joan of Arc too. Yes, the snows of yesteryear have melted away and left the names all but vanished with the snow.

But where are the snows of our time and clime? Ken Burns, in his notable television series on the Civil War, produced a visual record of the individuals and events. He often quoted Mary Chesnut, gracious Southern belle and hostess. Intelligent, well educated, informed, and opinionated, she left her imprint on the record of the war. Her written journal does not sleep beneath the snows of yesteryear but enlivens the events, the gossip, the humor, the scandals, the machinations of the South, the Confederacy, and the agony of defeat. Her voiced consideration of the position and plight of the Southern woman, her voiced emotions about slave women and slaveholding culture, her ideas and feelings we have today in her printed journal.

But who were the girls the soldier left behind at home? The Union letters gathered and printed here are a rare inheritance. The lives and loves, the social manners, the literature and music, the fears and grief of those days become a living legend that we can share and appreciate today. The wartime emotions that arose from the tragic separations evident in these letters from "the girls he left behind" convey a realistic picture of home life in the North not touched on elsewhere and rescue the names of these women from the oblivion of other "snows of yesteryear," 1862–67.

There was a small green wooden chest in the attic that was Grandfather's (although how I knew it was his, I don't remember). When I broke up my parents' household and moved my mother to live with us, I moved Grandfather's chest as well. Years later, when I sold my own house and moved to a retirement home, I moved Grandfather's chest besides. The chest was an officer's dispatch box, probably the original issued to him.

This time, having the leisure, I took time to examine it. The leather hinges were broken. The clasp and sealing hinge was broken as well. Inside were treasures, Grandfather's Civil War accouterments: a silver flask; a brass candlestick weighted at the bottom so it would not blow over in a gust of wind; his sash, yards long, now faded to a pale magenta; his lieutenant's bars. And wonder of wonders, I discovered a file of letters, closely packed and filed upright in neat order. How wonderful to read his thoughts of his experiences today, to know this man anew!

Grandfather, Edwin Lewis Lybarger, was a tall man (whom I remember as six feet plus in height) with a neatly clipped beard. He wore a GAR (Grand Army of the Republic) button in his lapel and had a huge gold chain draped across his chest to the thick gold watch in his vest pocket. He walked with a cane. When we went to his house for Thanksgiving or Easter, we usually found him sitting in his huge brown leather chair before the fireplace, cane at his side. His eyes twinkled when we came to greet him politely.

The *important* thing about Grandfather, we were told, was that he had been in the Civil War and had marched through Georgia with Sherman. For my brother and me, aged three and five, the *real importance* was that he had been wounded at the battle of Corinth. He had a hole in his knee. Really! His eyes twinkled as he averred that this was so. Yes, the hole went straight through. Yes, you could see it. Yes, we could feel it. So the four little hands stroked and poked and explored that knee, round and round, and up and down. But we couldn't poke a finger through a hole. Then we figured if we went up the trouser leg we'd get to it in the flesh. The striped trousers were tight at the bottom with a strap under the instep, so success was far away. Our small fingers creeping up his leg tickled him and he grew fidgety, so Mother reprimanded us: "Children, come away, don't annoy Grandfather." This put an end to the search but not to the wondrous speculation about the hole, a real hole.

When we were older, we were sent upstairs to Daddy's room to find books to read. There in the closet were piles of books, picture books of the Civil War. Huge, quarto, Mathew Brady photographs of battle scenes. Lying flat on our stomachs, we turned the pages, viewing the carnage. Soldiers lying still and stark, soldiers braced behind stone walls, rail fences, horses and cannons in confusion, tattered flags, swords flashing, noise and thunder, shouts and imprecations, officers astride, wounded cries for water, battle at its worst and glorious. As the pages turned, we learned the names: Antietam, Spotsylvania, the Wilderness, Bull Run, Shiloh, Gettysburg, and as an afterthought, Corinth. We learned them all. I cut my eyeteeth on the Civil War.

So now we come full circle to the letters. There in the bottom of the little chest was a whole file of letters neatly packed, one by one, in the smallest of envelopes. Some had no stamps (they had been torn off). Some were hand-canceled. I assumed these treasures from the past would let me learn more about Grandfather as a young man and as a soldier.

As each letter was lifted out, carefully unfolded, bent edges uncurled, and read briefly, then salutation and signature noted, then filed by date, I gathered that these were not letters that Grandfather had written. These were letters from GIRLS! What a cache! Letters and diaries of soldiers are abundant, describing their camp life, battles, impression of strange countrysides. Where does one find the thoughts and feelings of the homefolk—not parents, but girls who knew and loved the soldiers? The snows of yesteryear! My quest was on for the girls he left behind.

Soldiers saved the letters from girlfriends even when letters from parents were not that important. Girls were friends: one's own friends, peers, pals, loves, avenues to connect with past years and another life beyond the boredom of camp life and terror of battle. Girls gave them stature among their buddies; girls gave them rapport with others in the company.

These girls, growing into womanhood—meeting the grief and heartbreak of fathers, brothers, childhood playmates, and school chums stricken down in battle—have left their thoughts as soft, paper petals falling upon the muck and dirt, the monotony of drill and march. These are the words that touched and "dressed his wounds of mind and spirit after battle, and kept him whole." These are the treasures he kept and savored. Grace given, and grace received.

Nancy L. Rhoades

ORGANIZATION OF THE BOOK

The editors' primary purpose is to preserve these historical documents and make them available for wider use. To this end, the book is divided into two sections. The first section provides a detailed introduction to themes that arise in the Lybarger letters and the context in which they were produced: the nineteenth-century culture of print, the varied functions of letters during the Civil War, shifts in women's access to and engagement with education, and events on the Ohio home front. These themes are not meant to be exhaustive but are intended to synthesize diverse events and topics that emerge in the collection and to provide a framework for approaching these topics. Primary and secondary source materials are used as the foundation for this framework. The second section provides the letters in their entirety, organized chronologically by letter date.

The introduction first provides an overview of the "culture of print" in nineteenth-century America and the value of letters within this context. New writers and genres of writing emerged throughout the nineteenth century amid literacy changes and the rise of the common schools. Writing as a civilizing force in the midst of disorder and women's emergence as public writers are key elements of this context. The introduction then discusses scholars' varied approaches to letters as material artifacts and their "private" and "public" functions historically. During the Civil War, letters were utterly central to maintaining community, family, and romantic ties between the home front and the war front. They offered writers an outlet of expression and functioned as a form of "war work" and "romantic work." Women often viewed letter writing as a tangible service they could provide to the war effort in addition to nursing, teaching, procuring needed goods, and sustaining families and farms in the wake of men's enlistment. Third, the letters are framed in changing patterns of women's education and the transformation of teaching from a primarily male- to a primarily female-dominated occupation during the nineteenth century. Women's writing reflects the spread of literacy, women's increasing access to formal education, and their engagement with print culture. The final section provides context for Civil War events, political issues, and tensions that arise on the home front. Examples from the letters are woven throughout the introduction. We hope that the letters and the contextual information in which they are framed provide useful additional information concerning women's experiences and the Northern home front during these tumultuous years in the nation's history.

EDITORS' NOTES

We have chosen to preserve the original spelling, grammar, and punctuation of the letter writers wherever possible without the intrusive use of [*sic*] to indicate mistakes. We have at times added words and punctuation to enhance clarity. Ellipses are used for illegible words in the letters. Each of the letters in the collection has been assigned a number, 1 through 168, and the letters have been arranged chronologically. Throughout the editorial introduction, references to quotations and examples from individual letters are indicated by the number of the letter in parentheses: for example, (63). Readers can thus turn to specific letters for further perusal. Each letter is also identified with the date of the letter, the name of the letter writer, the area where the letter was postmarked, and the address to which the letter was sent (when this information is available). Because the troops were frequently in motion, this information indicates the military postal avenue, not necessarily the place where Lieutenant Edwin L. Lybarger was encamped. References to events in the letters can thus be more easily followed and ascertained in Civil War histories. References throughout the editorial introduction to primary and secondary source materials are included in endnotes. Although historians often write in the past tense, we have chosen to refer to the letters in the historical present to allow readers to follow women's thoughts and experiences as they unfold through the war years.

Lucy E. Bailey and Nancy L. Rhoades

Acknowledgments

MANY FRIENDS and relatives deserve recognition and heartfelt thanks for their encouragement and helpful suggestions. I would especially like to thank the multiple members of the staff of the Columbus Metropolitan Library, who have been most helpful with their prompt service, as well as the staff of the Ohio Historical Society Archives Library. Thanks is due also to Fern Hunt, professor emerita, Family Resource Management, Ohio State University, who provided information about the music of the period, and Linda R. Hengst, director of the Ohioana Library, for contributing initial information about soldier advertisements.

Jay Kegley, reference coordinator, Hilliard Branch, Columbus Metropolitan Library; Robert McGovern, professor and chair of English, Ashland University; and Barbara McGovern, associate professor of English, Ohio State University, Mansfield, read initial drafts of the manuscript and made critical and welcome suggestions, and I am most grateful for their evaluation and encouragement.

Last but not least, I wish to thank Bruce Ronk, Dave James, and Herb Griffith of InfoPro, Inc., who talked me through the computer snarls in the initial drafts. Kathy Callihan and Beth Marsh, whose widespread knowledge of "computerese" produced the initial printout copy, have earned my warm personal gratitude. I hope that this long-lost collection of letters will expand our understanding of the home front of the North during the tragedy of our fratricidal war so long ago.

Nancy L. Rhoades

Many people have contributed the labor and support necessary for this collection of letters to become available for public use. First and foremost, this project would not have been possible without the commitment, effort, and integrity of Nancy Rhoades, the coeditor of this text and the granddaughter of Edwin Lewis Lybarger. I gratefully acknowledge her efforts to make these rich family documents available to a wider audience and her graciousness in welcoming me to the project. I wish that she could have seen the evolution of the project and her grandfather's collection in its final form. Mrs. Rhoades died on April 9, 2007, at Friendship Village in Dublin, Ohio. She leaves a lasting gift to Ohio's and women's history.

I would also like to express my gratitude to David Sanders, director of Ohio University Press, for his guidance and his efforts to make this project a reality. The project has benefited from the work of Mrs. Rhoades's niece, Jennifer Wilke, who has contributed both research and resources in its years of development. The knowledgeable and professional research staff at Ohio Historical Society and Ohioana Library in Columbus, Ohio, whose work is vital to making a range of projects on Ohio history possible, provided key resources and professional direction. I am also grateful to my school head at Oklahoma State University, Bert Jacobson, for providing essential research support. Thanks to Larry Shawn Bassham for his good humor and diligent research assistance.

I am indebted to the years of mentorship I have received from Patti Lather, Valerie Lee, and Cynthia Burack at Ohio State University, as well as Mary Margaret Fonow at Arizona State University, whose scholarship and support continue to influence my work. I would also like to thank colleagues and friends who read drafts of the manuscript and facilitated the development of this project both directly and indirectly: Betsy Breseman, Michele Elnicky, Jill Lynch, Diana Moyer, Stacy Otto, Virginia Worley, Ed Harris, Christie Hawkins, and Mary Jo Self. Thanks to my family for their understanding as I negotiated multiple roles during the course of this project. Finally, I would like to express my gratitude to Lin Distel for years of support.

Lucy E. Bailey

WANTED— CORRESPONDENCE

Introduction

BOLD SCRIPT AND WAR WORK

Lucy E. Bailey

with Nancy L. Rhoades

> Follow the soldier to the battlefield with
> your spirit. The great army of letters
> that marches southward with every
> morning sun is a powerful engine of war
>
> —"Gail Hamilton," 1863

"VOLUNTEERS! Volunteers!" bellowed the headline in the *Mount Vernon Democratic Banner* on November 5, 1861. "Apply without delay," Colonel J. L. Kirby Smith commanded from the page; "I hope to raise one of the best companies in the State. . . . [T]he 43rd is designated to be one of the finest Regiments in the service." Twenty days later, Edwin Lewis Lybarger, the twenty-one-year-old son of the former Amelia Crum and James T. Lybarger of Knox County, Ohio, answered the colonel's call to service and was mustered into Company K of the "fine" Forty-third Ohio. Like thousands of other young Ohioans, Edwin Lybarger enlisted in the wake of President Lincoln's calls for 500,000 three-year men following the Black Monday of Bull Run. The *Ohio State Journal* declared "Ohio's Quota Full" with 61,000 men on November 12, 1861. At a payrate of $13.00 a month, Lybarger joined the blue throng preparing to push South to subdue the secessionists in what many believed in the first year of the war would be a short-lived conflict rather than the "cruel war" of unparalleled scale it soon became. Ohio sent more than 300,000 men to the Union army—more per capita than any other northern state—and Knox

County, Ohio, provided more than 3,000 of them. At war's end, Ohio had lost over 34,000 men to battles and disease, with 6 officers and 250 enlisted men of the Forty-third Ohio among them. Lieutenant Edwin Lybarger was one of the fortunate ones who returned relatively unscathed.[1]

Enduring sentiment about this conflict, which spanned four bloody years and involved millions of Americans, is that it was a Man's War. It was indeed a Man's Funeral, as more than 600,000 men lost their lives in the war's hospitals, camps, and battlefields—a death total that nears the combined losses of Americans for all other wars with U.S. involvement. At times, men sought to shield women from reports of war or viewed the fairer sex as uninterested in its details.[2] "Ladies, God Bless you!" the front page of the *Banner* implored the day after Lybarger enlisted. "Don't complain if you don't find stories, poetry or light reading in the *Banner* this week.... The details of the war news are too important and interesting to be omitted or curtailed."[3] Letters in this collection indicate that Lybarger, too, at times steered women away from the particulars of battles and marches in correspondence. "I assure you," a young woman responded to an 1864 letter from Lieutenant Lybarger, "you shall not be bored with sentimental talk about battles again from this source. Battles, indeed! Knoxville, indeed!" (63).

Yet as women at the time asserted, postwar historians detailed, and contemporary social historians have underscored since those years, the war had profound social, economic, and political reverberations that shaped women's lives as well as men's and left a sobering legacy that American people still struggle to understand nearly one hundred and fifty years later. The breadth of popular and academic work published on the Civil War testifies to the continued intrigue and perplexity these historical events inspire. Historian James McPherson identified this conflict as by far "the most written about event in American history."[4]

Social historians have long since responded to M. A. Vinovskis's 1989 query, "Have social historians lost the Civil War?" as well as Gerda Lerner's finding that only 2 percent of manuscripts produced in women's history in the 1980s addressed this significant historical event. In recent years, historians have reached beyond the military machinations of the war to explore its social and cultural aspects more fully. Those efforts have included analyzing the war's varied effects for American women and the integral role both Northern and Southern women played in its evolution and aftermath. Women in the slave-holding South, plantation mistresses, freedwomen, as well as Northern abolitionists, "dauthers of the union," and hospital workers have emerged in sharper relief against the backdrop of their social and regional contexts. Researchers have coaxed women's personalities and convictions from the pages of their diaries and letters and sketched their daily lives in the midst of war.

Others have sought to temper the often romanticized view of the Civil War era in public memory and to deepen attention to the ways in which race, class, gender, and region shaped women's experiences and investments. Although women's stakes in war could be both ideological and physical, the daily lives of freedwomen, "contraband" women, and white middle-class women living states away from the bloodshed were radically different. Women grappled with different challenges and forged new identities in their respective spheres. Exploring these key differences helps to thicken our understanding of diverse women's roles and lives, thus building on the foundation provided by Agatha Young's and Mary Massey's early studies of Northern and Southern women.

Scholars have also analyzed the gendered aspects of war, detailing how the war both reified and disrupted gendered beliefs and shaped soldiers' and citizens' experiences in gendered ways. The demands of the war necessitated that women perform traditionally masculine roles, and although some embraced such opportunities with relish, others found little liberation in the responsibilities they shouldered as men trudged to war. Civil War–era letters often describe economic and physical challenges of the home front and women's wistful hopes for men to return home. Recent research focusing on Northern women has explored how the challenges women faced and their civic engagement during war increased their awareness of their subordinated status and fueled their political activism in later years. This body of scholarship helps broaden our understanding of the war as a gendered phenomenon as well as its enduring meaning in American history. Much is left to mine in the social terrain of Civil War history and the letters, diaries, papers, and pamphlets that literate nineteenth-century women left behind.[5]

Tracing individual women in the archival record is rarely a straightforward enterprise; girls and women are often subsumed under their fathers' and husbands' names, and countless records relevant to women's history wither in obscurity in dusty trunks, private collections, and local historical societies nationwide. Some researchers have negotiated scattered resources concerning women's roles in the Civil War by identifying individual women who served the war effort and slowly amassing documents that detail their activities and accomplishments. The intent of these scholars has been to build, portrait by portrait, a fuller and more nuanced understanding of women's contributions and experiences. Owing to the prodding of genealogists, Civil War connoisseurs, and academics, numerous "women worthies" have emerged from the archival record with their tales of clandestine military service, compassionate nursing, and solemn fortitude as the battles waged around them.[6] On an individual level, women's "behind the scenes" work provided solace to soldiers laboring for the cause. On a social level, this work provided psychological and spiritual reinforcement to help sustain the war effort over its four-year span.[7]

This edited collection of letters offers additional perspective on individual Northern women's experiences during the war and their work to sustain the war effort. The collection contains 168 letters written to Lieutenant Edwin L. Lybarger of the Forty-third Ohio Volunteer Infantry during the years 1862–67. The majority (158) of the letters in this collection were written by women—three-fourths from women the lieutenant knew, and the remainder from women who responded to newspaper advertisements he placed that solicited correspondents during the war. Through the eyes of thirty-six writers, the collection offers glimpses of the Ohio home front during the Civil War years and the effects of war events on women living far from battle lines. Lieutenant Lybarger selected these letters from an unknown number of originals, carried them through more than three years of active military service, preserved them throughout his life, and left them to be discovered by his granddaughter Nancy L. Rhoades in an officer's dispatch box more than 125 years after Lee's surrender. Such romantic origins seem the very essence of history.

Like many other Americans left grappling with the effects of the Civil War decades after its end, Lybarger may have felt a need to reflect upon that tumultuous time in the nation's history and found the letters a ready vehicle for doing so. Indeed, the letters may have been potent reminders of the losses and loves of his youth. Patriotism and pride were undoubtedly factors; the letters may have enabled private, periodic returns to the triumphs and losses of that significant period in his life—service that shaped his identity and years thereafter. Other factors may be socioeconomic class and race; McPherson notes that native-born middle- and upper-class men were more likely to write and preserve letters than were their working-class or foreign-born counterparts. Whether shaped by personal motivations or cultural factors, Lybarger's decision to preserve the collection and Nancy L. Rhoades's discovery, transcription, and exploration of the letters' content have enabled this piece of Ohioana and Civil War history to be available for wider public consideration. Together, the editors are pleased to provide these primary documents along with an examination of key themes in the letters and elements of the historical and social context in which they were produced.

The women whose letters constitute this collection were primarily "Union loving girls," although some letters hint at Rebel sympathies and tensions between Peace Democrats and Republicans in this region of Ohio. The majority of the women lived in Knox County, in north-central Ohio, writing from such townships as Union, Howard, Butler, Brown, Monroe, and Clinton. Over three-fourths of the letters were written by acquaintances, childhood friends, love interests, and family members known to the soldier before he entered the army. Many women wrote from Lybarger's hometown of Millwood, Ohio, in Union Township, named after the first mill in the area; others wrote from Monroe Mills, Jelloway, and Amity; some came from Mt. Vernon and Danville. The lively Lib Baker sent her letters from varied parts of the county as she dashed about following her whims. Lybarger's cousin, Rozaltha

Crum, wrote steadily and earnestly from farther away in Bainbridge, Ohio, in Ross County. One informative man, Benjamin Stone, whom Lybarger apparently met while recovering from battle wounds, wrote from Macon City, Missouri, where he returned to convalesce after sustaining an injury during war service. A few relatives wrote from Indiana and Missouri. The surnames in the letters—Critchfield, Darling, Hawn, Welker, Sapp, Rightmire, and Shrimplin—reflect some of the earliest families that settled Knox County.

Another forty letters in the collection were written by people originally unknown to the soldier and are the source of this text's title: *Wanted—Correspondence*. This intriguing group of letters from strangers is grounded in the practice common during combat periods in which soldiers actively solicited correspondence from "fair and patriotic" damsels through social networks and newspaper advertisements. The heading of such advertisements commonly read "Wanted: Correspondence," followed by lighthearted and patriotic requests to correspond with the soldiers. Sometimes women placed similar ads. Around the time of the battle of Gettysburg in 1863, Lybarger apparently placed such an advertisement in newspapers in southern Ohio and northern Kentucky using a pseudonym. Women who responded to the advertisement and friends' requests wrote from Nelsonville, Mt. Gilead, and Brandon, Ohio; from Mt. Sterling, Kentucky; and from Marion, Indiana, among other areas. Although young women's practice of corresponding with strangers prompted some public concern, many viewed writing to soliders as a patriotic act. The women wrote for novelty, to while away the time, to establish and develop relationships, to perform a visible act of patriotism, to follow social etiquette, and to cheer the soldier in his duty. These varied letters also demonstrate ways in which young men and women negotiated courtship circumstances during the war.

Men's letters and diaries abound in Civil War history, but less readily available are comprehensive collections of letters like this one from middle-class and rural women that survived the weathering of marches, camp life, and battles to emerge unscathed from men's knapsacks at war's end. Some soldiers sent bundles of letters home for safekeeping, and others, like Lybarger, had dispatch boxes that may have protected some items from weathering. Just as letters were vital sources of connection from the home front to the front lines during the war years, so too can letters provide connections from the past to the present. Readers interested in the Civil War, Ohio history, women's issues, and education may find different strands in this collection useful for extending their understanding of events and experiences during the Civil War. Researchers and genealogists can draw elements from the letters to enhance and pursue their own historical projects.[8]

Readers seeking tidbits of Ohio history can follow the flurry of oyster suppers, political rallies, and brewing tensions between "Copperheads" and Unionists as Ohioans chose their allegiances during the war. Women's descriptions of singing schools, socials, and sledding offer a compelling portrait of small-town Ohio in the nineteenth century in which everyday life is central and women carry on at times as if disconnected from events in the South. Descriptions of local politics and fleeting comments about race speak to the presence of these topics in wartime conversations. Those interested in women's issues can read about Rosa Crum's domestic labors in the wake of her mother's death, Sophronia Rogers's distaste for teaching, and Lib Baker's passion for painting and literature as she flitted from school to school soaking up "book larnin'." Readers interested in gender issues historically will note the social norms guiding men and women's roles, relationships, and letter writing during the Civil War years, the domestic ideology that shapes Americans' understanding of home and war, and the gendered forms of representation that appear in correspondence.

Readers interested in romance will also find much to appreciate. Pen and ink helped women and soldiers alike develop and sustain relationships through the war years. Traditional courtship practices across race and class were disrupted dramatically by the war, and letter writing was one of the only viable, if inadequate, methods of pursuing romantic relationships amid the uncertainties of future and nation.[9] Indeed, the epistolary genre has had long associations with romantic love between the sexes. The Civil War called many men of courtship age to the front lines: eighteen-year-old men were the largest group of volunteers during the first year of the war, and the average age of Union soldiers at enlistment was 25.8. Only 30 percent of Union enlistees were married at the onset of the war.[10] The loss of young men to the war front and the battlefield (25 percent of Southern men of military and thus courtship age had died by war's end) shaped how young women experienced their courtship years. Such demographics also had implications for women's economic futures in an era in which marriage contributed to financial security. The promise of romance as well as its uncertainties and tensions are thus undercurrents in the letters. All the drama of youthful romance marks single women's writing: women vie for Lybarger's affections; occasional bouts of "he said, she said" dominate interchanges; some relationships flourish while others mysteriously dissolve; writers exchange photographs with fanfare and flirtation; and the lieutenant emerges in the end, in the words of one writer, "the hero of a thrilling romance." In 1867, one month before the date of the last letter in the collection, Lybarger married one of the letter writers.

Another feature of the letters is the flavor and personality of the young women's writing, offering glimpses of the women as flesh-and-blood beings. Writers move among stilted prose, smooth wit, patriotic rhetoric, and easy familiarity as they negotiate etiquette and individual preoccupations to find an appropriate letter-writing voice. Four women wrote for multiple years: Rosa (Rozaltha) Crum from 1863 to 1866, Phrone (Sophronia) Rogers from 1862 to 1866, Lou Pearl Riggen from 1863 to 1867, and Lib (Annie E. or Lizzie) Baker from October 1863 to January 1867, although less frequently than the other women.[11] Readers may track the epistolary relationships these women developed with Lybarger as well as certain distinguishing characteristics of the women that remained constant, such as Rosa's earnestness, Phrone's steadfastness, Lou's intelligence and depth, and Lib's vivacity. For example, Rosa writes steadily over the course of the war even as she shifts from a young woman of fourteen seemingly enamored with her handsome cousin and overburdened with housework to one with beaux of her own who dreams of teaching school. Lou, who enters the correspondence with a pseudonym and seeking "novelty" and "nonsense," leaves it twenty-five letters later pondering the relationship of letters to identity. Lou's musings and witty repartee are a gift to read and will leave readers nodding in understanding at Lybarger's decision to sustain their correspondence after the war ends.

The collection commences with sixteen-year-old Fannie Meredith's brief epistle of September 14, 1862, dated a few weeks before Lybarger was wounded in the battle of Corinth, Mississippi. Fannie's letter is a fitting introduction to the collection. In a mere two pages, she refers to activities on the Millwood home front, mentions the tendency for community members to discuss soldier letters publicly, expresses fear that a young soldier and mutual friend has been killed, laments the loneliness of Millwood without the soldiers, contextualizes her schooling within war events, criticizes her own letter-writing ability, and closes with an urgent plea for Lybarger to "write soon, very soon" (1). From the self-abnegating trends of letter-writing convention to the details of small-town life, the themes that appear in Fannie's letter surface throughout the collection. This stream of information conveys more than comforting details to a soldier miles from home; it captures the centrality of the Civil War to young women's consciousness and the contour of their everyday lives in a small town in Knox County, Ohio.

Given that many war events took place on Southern soil, the reverberations of the war for Northern women were strikingly different than for those Southern women who faced the perpetual material shortages and the looming threat of Union invasion and displacement. Northern women's understandings of the war were forged through newspapers, letters from the front lines, young men's dwindling numbers as they joined the Union ranks, and the changing character of their daily lives as the war continued. However distanced they might have been from the battlefields, Northern women were often preoccupied by events that occurred states away. They mobilize the language of war freely to describe social interactions and domestic matters. A newly married couple cannot "retreat" from their commitment; misunderstandings are soothed with a "cessation of hostilities"; love interests are characterized as "charming young ladies who 'present arms'" with "weapons" to "transfix" hearts (66). In weightier terms, Ella Rightmire, the twenty-one-year-old daughter of a Millwood farmer, writes to

Lybarger in 1863, "I don't know that I can [change my subject] for this Rebellion has its effects every where" (24). Ell Hawn, a school friend, expresses this sentiment more plaintively: "When O when will it cease" (13). Having lost her brother Marion to the cause in 1862 and with brother John still serving with Lybarger in Company K, Ell felt keenly the component of war that was common to Southern and Northern women's experiences: the absence and loss of men they loved.

A sobering theme that animates the letters is women's consciousness of writing to a man they may eventually mourn. Indeed, one of the ways the Rebellion "ha[d] its effects every where" was that a soldier's life might end at any moment, and writers seem to fluctuate between awareness and denial of this reality. Phrone Rogers, who was seventeen years old when the war broke out, confessed after Ed was wounded in the battle of Corinth, "It almost killed your mother when she heard you were wounded. I thought myself that we would never see you again" (5). Women sometimes shift abruptly in their writing as if shaking themselves from that very thought. After offering condolences for Lybarger's battle wound, Fannie Meredith comments, "O if this war would only close and you all be permitted to return to your homes well. But I fear that will not be the case. But do (most assuredly) hope that it will" (6). Without apparent consciousness of the potential effects of her words, this young writer awkwardly covers the page with her hopes and fears before she realizes that Lybarger, too, might become a casualty.

At times, women seem resigned as they assess the soldiers' chances, casting death in a patriotic and celestial glow. Rosa Crum hopes to see her cousin "once more on earth," but if they are not "permitted to meet here below," she hopes to meet him in "heaven where congregations never brake up and sabbaths never end" (39). Mary Collins, a Memphis resident Lybarger met when encamped in the area in 1863, supposes her draft-resistant brother would "go out there to die in 'the last ditch'" (54). Others write as if the soldier's return is far from certain. Lines such as "if you ever come home from the army" (41) and "if you should live to return home" (51) frequent the collection. In several letters, Lou Riggen struggles to reconcile her conviction that Lybarger had died in battle with the appearance of his most recent letter that testifies happily to the contrary. In the shadows of the losses at Chickamauga in September 1863, Lou writes, "I scarcely know how to commence writing to you, before I received your last letter you were probably included in the list of 'killed, wounded, or missing' of the last battle; the sad tale which follows either victory or defeat. I sincerely hope not however. I hope you are not among those unreturning braves whose deaths, thought glorious, 'makes countless thousands mourn.'" (43). Here Lou cites Robert Burns's "Man Was Made to Mourn," in which he laments man's inhumanity to man and the relief that death offers the weary and wanting. With the smooth prose and intelligence that characterizes her letters, Lou captures the amalgam of hope, dread, and patriotism that marks women's thoughts as the war progresses and they watch, wait, and write from the home front.

As with many other Civil War–era diaries and letters, death is woven through the lines of these letters. The opening letter forewarns of the first, and through the following pages, we read of unknown others who die during battle, from typhoid, from whooping cough, from impassioned and violent local tussles that mirror divisions of larger scale in the war.[12] Sometimes writers mention illness and death fleetingly. In 1866, Lou hints about a difficult loss that may have been her mother but offers no other information: "O how beautiful a face that has faded from my sight—a voice that was music which I shall never hear again" (163). At other times, women's descriptions are graphic. Ell Hawn describes "little Veloscoe Hildreth" of Union Township being killed "and since we learn that a part of his head was shot off and this only one of the thousands that have been mangled and crushed in this cruel war" (13).[13] Impending death is equally palpable. Phrone Rogers minces no words when she describes the failing health of Edwin's father: "[He] is . . . very dangerously ill. I do not think you will have a father long" (57). Brief epistolary reports indicate James T. Lybarger's continued deterioration until he passed away in April 1864 at age fifty-nine.[14] The traffic between home front and war front in grief, in patriotism, and in the rhythms of daily life are clear throughout this collection.

THE SCRIBBLING FAIR AND
THE CULTURE OF PRINT

> <u>If You Are Not a Man!</u> . . . Now will
> you inform me by what mysterious and
> to me unimaginable chain of reasoning
> you arrived at this sage conclusion
> based upon the single accidental cir-
> cumstance that I make long handled
> letters or write in too bold a style for a
> lady. If I make my letters so delicate as
> to be barely visible to the naked eye I
> presume you will from the same mode
> of reasoning include that I am un-
> doubtedly a lady.
>
> —Lou Riggen (63)

When Lou Riggen dismisses Lybarger's apparent charge that she must be "a man" because of her "long handled letters" and "bold style," she demonstrates key elements of the nineteenth-century context that shaped this collection of letters.[15] Although the Civil War may have driven writers to put pen to page, elements of the nineteenth-century culture influenced what and how they wrote. The above excerpt from Lou's letter reveals social conventions that governed the epistolary form as well as common beliefs about gender and writing. It also exemplifies increases in women's literacy, changing relationships between men and women, and especially significant, the importance of the written word in nineteenth-century America. In the years before the Civil War, cultural and technological forces amplified the symbolic power of the written word, expanded the types of writing that people utilized and read, and facilitated the emergence of new writers. Against this cultural backdrop, letter writing became both balm and weapon for the machinations of war. Civilians and soldiers alike produced unprecedented numbers of letters and diaries during 1861–65. The sheer volume of writing testifies to widespread belief in its productive, creative power in the face of the war's destruction and loss.[16] Lou's lively challenge to Lybarger's conflation of gender and writing and her refusal to follow social convention for women through "faint script" are among many examples in the collection that reflect broader changes in cultural patterns.

Bold Script and War Work

One significant cultural pattern influential to the production of war letters was the changes that occurred in the value of the written word during the nineteenth century. The written word achieved a level of social currency and legitimating power in nineteenth-century America that gradually surpassed that of oral and religious traditions.[17] Although the public lyceum and lecture were a vibrant part of culture in the 1850s and 1860s and religious revivals continued to sway converts throughout the century, writing became increasingly valued in both practical and symbolic terms. As one popular female author observed, "of all the influences about us in the present age, perhaps none is so largely educative as that of reading: the press even distances the pulpit in control over the minds of men; the paper and the pamphlet go where the pastor and preacher cannot find their way."[18] Paper and pamphlet became powerful mechanisms for forging identities, developing relationships, and making sense of widespread social and political changes as the century unfolded.

Indeed, the war may have strengthened the cultural pattern of valuing the written word. Letters were front lines of communication during the war—physically slight but symbolically weighty vehicles—that tied soldiers and families and communities together. President Lincoln perceived the mail system of such importance to the war effort that he asked the U.S. postmaster general to appoint a special agent to oversee operations for the Army of the Potomac. David B. Parker, the agent who took command of this "powerful engine of war,"[19] worked to increase efficiency in mail transport and delivery, improve materials used to carry supplies, and develop a system to transfer soldiers' paychecks to money orders for use on the home front.[20] Despite the cost of paper, citizens and soldiers who otherwise kept few journals and records produced a vast number of letters during the Civil War era. Those who recognized that they were living through an incomparable time may have sought to mark the events as they lived them. Some may have been drawn to writing as a balm for anxiety and a tool to help process psychologically the often incomprehensible events of the war.[21] Others may have found writing a distraction from "the 99 parts boredom" surrounding the "one part sheer terror" said to constitute war. Beyond these individual motivations, the collective impulse to write the war emerged in part from a nineteenth-century culture that increasingly valued the written word.[22]

Varied technological, social, and economic forces coalesced to amplify the symbolic and tangible power of writing in the decades before the Civil War. Improvements in technology and changes in the structure of business transformed publishing practices and facilitated the quicker and cheaper production of periodicals, newspapers, and books.[23] By 1855, the company that published the popular periodical *Harper's Weekly: A Journal of Civilization* could produce thirty-five volumes a minute from a massive assembly line of machinery that required at least three hundred women to operate.[24] As rapidly as the women could churn civilization out, the developing railroad system could deliver it. During the middle of the century, thousands of miles of rail crossed the country with the capacity to move equipment, goods, and people cheaply and efficiently. The railroad stimulated economic growth and industry, improved mail delivery, and provided publishers access to a variety of regional and national markets. By 1860, Ohio was in the vanguard of this development, with the most miles of rail in the nation.[25] The telegraph system was in place by 1861, fostering the speed with which information could reach newspapers—and newspapers, in turn, could circulate to readers. In the 1840s and 1850s, the dollar value of books produced in the United States tripled and the number of daily newspapers increased from 138 to 387.[26] For 1860, the Eighth Census reported 4,051 papers and periodicals published in the country.[27] These developments ensured that the nation's primary conduit of communication, the newspaper, was well poised to chronicle the years following the fateful events at Fort Sumter.

The symbolic value of print rivaled its practical value as a source of communication and information. Over the course of the century, collecting, reading, and discussing texts became a symbol of middle-class identity, of erudition—indeed, of civilization itself. "A bookless parlor," a nineteenth-century writer warned, "is a howling wilderness."[28] To keep the wilds at bay, literary societies and reading circles sprang up in middle-class communities[29] and in military camps.[30] Soldiers clamored for newspapers from home, and editors urged their subscribers to comply. "Send Papers to the Volunteers," the *Banner*, among others, instructed.[31] Demand for materials stimulated the publishing industry. Textbooks became central components of school curricula and the vision of quality education.[32] Teachers began to supplement curriculum centered on rote memorization and basic communication skills with writing forms that highlighted sensibility and aestheticism. Drama, essays, and poetry were used to model individualistic style over formulaic ideals and the cultivation of "taste" over "eloquence."[33] Written admission tests were instigated in public high schools in part to symbolize the greater rigor of this level of schooling in comparison to grammar schools. Colleges such as Kenyon in Knox County, Ohio, began to use written admissions tests by 1860.[34]

For some, writing skills enabled more than effective communication: they signaled a writer's learned position and middle-class membership. One prominent citizen of Knox County suggested as much to his son in an 1855 letter: "[A]s many judge of a man's literary acquirements by his experience of writing[,] it is worth cultivating."[35] As this father modeled in his letters, writing increasingly replaced oral tradition as a means for literate individuals to demonstrate their refined taste and express their ideas. That his son absorbed the lesson from schooling as well is illustrated in one letter in which he practices his penmanship: "In a gentlemans education a plain free hand writing is a beautiful acquirement."[36] Such literate expressions preserved a modicum of civility amid the country's growing tensions and demographic changes.

In some ways, the Civil War might be considered a battle over the very thing writing symbolized: civilization. Links among literacy, class position, and the freedom of expression were not simply abstractions in a period in which four million Americans remained enslaved. The contrast between "slave society" and "free society" was one of the many rallying forces that became rooted in geography as Americans forged their allegiances. The notion of civilization was fluid and contested; Confederates sometimes classified Northerners as "a low degraded set of people" and "the lowest and most contemptible race upon the face of the earth."[37] Abolitionists and Unionists, in turn, often posed the South as the locus of idleness and barbarism against the North as the hub of progress and civilization. The industrial strength of the North, its railroads, patents, educational institutions, and literacy rates—95 percent of New Englanders were literate in 1850—only strengthened these associations for Northerners. At a fundamental level, the ability to read and write symbolized a level of self-sovereignty and agency that was unattainable for millions. To pick up a pen, to read a book, to turn the pages of a newspaper—these activities were often the privileges of free Americans. Although Northern blacks sometimes exceeded Southern whites in educational attainment, full access to the promises of democracy remained elusive for people of color and for other women throughout the century. As war casts peace into sharp relief, the meaning of human liberty and the freedom of expression are crystallized against the sobering backdrop of slavery.

Slavery, immigration, and westward expansion left citizens and newcomers alike grappling with questions concerning liberty, freedom, and the meaning of being "American," and many turned to print to debate these questions.[38] Abolitionists William Lloyd Garrison, Frederick Douglass, and Harriet Beecher Stowe put their pens to work to condemn slavery as antithetical to democracy, while Protestant nativists with similar passion defended American institutions from imagined papal threats. Although the American Naturalization Act of 1790 granted citizenship to "free white persons"—a requirement echoed in Ohio's voting qualifications in 1803—identifying which of the millions of newcomers qualified as "white" was left to lawmakers and common citizens to determine. Print became a vehicle for such considerations.[39]

From 1846 to 1855, three million immigrants entered the United States with diverse cultural, religious, and linguistic backgrounds. The primarily Irish and German newcomers who comprised this first wave of European immigration were farmers, peasants, and unskilled laborers whose eagerness to work was insufficient to sooth the anxieties of some native-born citizens experiencing rapid demographic change. Tensions sometimes ran high, both in urban centers and in print, as diverse people vied for citizenship rights and economic ground. The Know-Nothing Party rose in the 1850s to protect nationalism and American identity from perceived foreign threats, and the Republican Party rallied to protect the republic from the governmental support of slavery. Racial and ethnic violence broke out in multiple cities in the Northeast, foreshadowing the greater conflicts to come in the latter half of the century. When Protestant Germans and Irish Catholics collided in Cincinnati, the largest city in Ohio in midcentury, Protestant presses contributed to the fray by publishing a spate of anti-Catholic literature that championed Anglo-Protestantism.[40] The need for immigrant labor and the uniting power of the Civil War helped temper, at least temporarily, this discord.

Women added their own voices to both the social issues swirling in print and the creative power of the written word as the country moved toward war. The mass emergence of women as public writers had profound implications for expanding their professional opportunities in the nineteenth century. It also changed established understandings of "authorship" and contributed to reconfiguring the literary canon. Between 1820 and 1860, women writers emerged onto the publishing scene in unprecedented numbers and, with pens flying and morals flowing, produced a variety of texts for the increasingly literate public. The scope of women's informal and published writing in the nineteenth century was extensive. In terms of nonfiction, women wrote letter after letter, village chronicles, memoirs, religious tracts, editorials, cookbooks, travel books, and textbooks. They published etiquette and household manuals with tips on topics ranging from cleaning carpets to managing finances. They translated texts from German, Italian, and French for English readers. They wrote advice books, edited newsletters and literary magazines, and recorded community and national histories with a Protestant, patriotic, and nationalistic voice.[41]

Their output of fiction was equally strong. Women used polemical novels, short stories, and sensationalist fiction to express opinions on domestic and social issues. They debated equal rights for women, abolition, race relations, temperance, religious reform, labor conditions, and suffrage. They sculpted heroines who stretched social boundaries and conformists who defended those same boundaries. The range and popularity of women's writing during the 1800s led literary scholar Nina Baym to claim that "authorship in America" became established as "a women's profession, and reading as a woman's avocation."[42] Similarly, Mary Ryan names this period "the Empire of the Mother," a phrase that highlights the extent of women's cultural production and women's roles as moral guardians of culture during this time. From

1820 until the close of the Civil War, the public consumed these domestic texts as quickly as authors could produce them: whereas publishing 5,000 copies of a single book was considered successful prior to the 1850s, authors commonly sold as many as 50,000 or 100,000 copies in the 1860s.[43]

The appeal of the domestic novel, much like that of reading a letter from the home front, stemmed in part from its focus on the daily activities and interactions of home life in middle-class America. Encountering details of home and hearth in novels, newspapers, and household manuals could comfort readers as they recognized elements of their lives in fictional events and envisioned other possibilities as well. Print culture seemed important to the women who wrote to Lybarger. Some writers quoted Shakespeare and Tennyson, referenced lyrics from sheet music popular in the period, and mentioned reading dime novels with adventuresome and romantic themes. Phrone experimented with writing drama and poetry, as well as an informal newsletter titled *The Evening* that contained jokes, poetry, and brief moralistic messages.

The ideology of "home" that was prominent in nineteenth-century print culture and in women's writing in particular also was key to soldiers' experience of the war. As Lewis Rowe of the Twenty-seventh Ohio expressed to his father in 1862, "the memories of home with its thousand endearments still linger in my mind."[44] Reid Mitchell argues that the Civil War was in essence a conflict over the meaning of home and community. Domestic ideology and mythology were central to soldiers' accounts of their experiences. Soldiers referred to dying as being "called home," adopted rituals from the home front into their camp lives, and often conceived of their service as fighting for those in their home communities.[45] "Home" is a frequent theme in the Lybarger letters. "At home," Jennie Hall writes in 1863, ". . . you can again bask in the sunny smiles of loved ones" (51). Ell Hawn underlines and capitalizes the word "Home" eight times in one letter (13). Although she wields the term circuitously to convey an array of different meanings, it captures themes of family, women, and community that were missing from men's daily experiences. The symbolic power of "home" threaded through books, letters, and hymns, carried in soldiers' memories, and, promised at war's end, was one factor among many that motivated men to fight.

The letter—a powerful symbol of home—was an important ingredient in the brew of women's writing and the culture of the written word. Literate people in the eighteenth and nineteenth centuries took letters seriously.[46] The cost of writing materials, the time to compose, and the pace of mail delivery meant that letters were often written with forethought and were prized when received. The postal service adopted the stamp in 1847 and required prepayment of postage in 1855, which reduced the expense of letter writing. Envelopes sent to Lybarger from 1862 through 1866 bore three-cent stamps, about a third of the cost of a dime novel in the 1860s, or the line cost for an advertisement in a local newspaper.[47] A Knox County newspaper urged readers late in 1862 to save "paper rags" and economize in paper use as the scarcity and price increased. Editors advised, "[W]hen writing a letter, let half a sheet answer instead of a whole one. Never waste a sheet or an envelope."[48] Writers to Lybarger often used paper fully, writing on both sides of the paper and sometimes sideways in the margins. One writer mentions that she "could not get any other paper" in January 1863 (13).

Yet, for many in the North, the cost of ink, paper, and stamps was a small price to pay, given the centrality of letters to sustaining connections among soldiers, civilians, and family members living at a distance from one another. For husbands and wives separated by the call to duty, the frontier, or the promise of the gold mines, letters were often the only source of information about one another's lives for years at a time.[49] Letters could enrich relationships and deepen intimacy as well as keep cherished ones informed about health, losses, and the daily minutiae of human lives. Although busy homesteaders in the west, for instance, often had to dash off letters when circumstances permitted rather than mull over their contents in a middle-class parlor, such haste did not compromise the value of these letters to loved ones: "[W]rite often, telling everything," pleaded one woman in southern Texas.[50]

Women's letters also helped to sustain middle-class women's friendships. Historian Carroll Smith-Rosenberg's classic study of thousands of letters women wrote during the nineteenth century emphasizes that letters helped create a "female world of love and ritual" across the miles and the years when women became separated. Women used letters to process life events and forge intense emotional bonds with one another.[51] Women sometimes commiserated about health concerns and offered home remedies from their own experiences.[52] Letters also had the power to forge familial, community, and social connections as well as "networks of spiritual support."[53] The common social activity of reading letters aloud to enjoy their merits collectively suggests the power of writing to bring relatives and community members closer together.

Order and Convention: "As Letter Writers Always Say"

Because letter writing was an aesthetic form and symbol of civilized interaction, it was often highly ritualized and ruled by convention. Writing conventions provided a modicum of order that may have been particularly comforting during a time of social disorder in which fissures in the nation were deepening and men began fighting to preserve their competing visions of government. At different points in history, writing has been seen as an instrument of social control and a method to create order out of the chaos of daily life. Mastering the skill of letter writing required writers to adhere to certain rules while also maintaining the appearance of originality. As early as 350 BC, philosophers stressed the importance of form, practice, the absence of artificiality, and the use of models in epistolary convention. Their tenets on the epistolary form remained prominent in the instructional literature on letter writing in the centuries that followed. Letter-writing manuals became increasingly popular in the seventeenth and eighteenth centuries. They contributed to creating a community of writers who constructed letters with common expectations concerning style and content.

Manuals demonstrated the fundamentals of appropriate form and address, clarified proper wording, and provided models for imitation and practice. Patterns for writing business letters and love letters were provided.[54] Just as letters were a standard component of curriculum in Renaissance Europe and English boarding schools, letter writing was often included in writing instruction in the American common schools as a vehicle to learn composition skills.[55] Children sometimes sought additional resources to refine their skills. Knox County's Daniel Van Buskirk asked his father to send him relatives' letters, "as it is a satisfaction to hear from my relations in the west and it also gives me an example in letter writing."[56] Parents, too, worked to inculcate their children with the epistolary arts. In 1873, Martha Wellington chastised her son for poor penmanship and mechanics, for using common phrases, and for insufficient detail in his letters. She modeled in her own response the elements she expected to see, urging him to write only with dictionary at hand and with sufficient time to develop his thoughts.[57] Adequate time and space helped create the appropriate atmosphere for the endeavor. Writers may not have always met expectations, but convention—and sometimes mothers—provided guidance.

Letters from the battlefield sometimes reflected epistolary conventions even though the amenities of home were few and far between. Soldiers, particularly in the South, had difficulty at times finding paper and pen. Some used elaborate stationery, while others tore pages from army record books to compose their letters home.[58] Sometimes men asked their correspondents to send stamps. Time, privacy, and conditions to write could be limited amid weeks of marching and fighting. Bell Irwin Wiley, the historian noted for his detailed accounts of Confederate and Union soldiers, notes that soldiers wrote in a variety of challenging conditions. One soldier described writing "by the light of a candle stuck in a pine stick, setting on the ground leaning against Bruce Wallace who is asleep." Others used knapsacks, "tin plates, books, cracker boxes, or drumheads for desks."[59]

Despite these privations, letters from writers of different competencies often seemed copied from the same letter-writing manual. A soldier in the Twenty-seventh Ohio writes, "Dear Father, I seat myself this morning to write you a few lines to let you know that I am well."[60] Another soldier struggles with spelling but conveys the same basic sentiment: "My old friend Milt, I fer the first time take my pen in hand fer the purpose of writing you a few lines to inform you that I am well."[61] Letters to the battlefront began with similar salutations. In the Lybarger collection, Rosa Crum begins a letter, "Always prompt to do my duty

I am seated again for the purpose of talking to you a few moments through the silent medium of the pen" (145). Similarly, Fannie Meredith once more "grasp[s] the pen eagerly to trace you a few lines in way of an answer" (100). Although consulting manuals was likely occasional rather than routine practice, writers recognized and often followed commonly understood conventions. The Lybarger letters reflect formulaic salutations of "Friend Ed" or "Lieutenant Lybarger" and complimentary closings of "your friend" and "respectfully yours."

Writers were often well aware that they were following established codes of correspondence. Lib Baker writes on November 2, 1866, "Yours of Oct. 1st was duly received (as letter writers always say) and its contents perused, with no little degree of interest" (161). Lou Riggen ponders whether she should begin her letters by discussing health first or the weather. Ell Hawn contains her letter length because "it is time according to Ediquet that my letter was brought to a close" (15). A particularly visible trend in letter-writing convention is women's entreaties to readers to overlook flaws and imperfections. What might be read as a painful degree of gendered insecurity that at times consumes precious writing space is in fact an expected convention in letter writing. Edith Welker apologizes, "I believe I have written enough for fear of worrying your father with this poorly written and poorly composed letter, but I have such a very poor pen that I can hardly write at all. I hope you will overlook all mistakes and blots" (11). Similarly, Deal Shroyer expresses, "I fear this will be anything but interesting to you. . . . Over look all mistakes" (10). These critical descriptors—mistakes, blots, poorly written, uninteresting—were pervasive among writers. Criticism of penmanship and writing style seemed to appear regardless of how well letters followed established norms.

Yet the gendered codes seemed fluid and shifting depending on the personality of the woman writer and the degree of familiarity between writer and reader. Lou Riggen dismisses convention repeatedly and pokes fun at the apologetic patterns adopted in letters. Failing to send a photograph with her third letter, Lou opens with a feigned apology for the letter's lack of substance. She writes, "Excuse this empty letter. I have not the slightest doubt that it will be so excessively timid so utterly overcome with its own insignificance that it will occupy just about a month in reaching its destination" (63). She declares that she despises deception and teases Lybarger about the mundane details of health and weather. In her twentieth letter, Lou calls attention to the self-abnegating codes for letter writing by including an apology in quotation marks: "I'm hoping," she writes, "you will 'excuse all bad writing and mistakes'" (149). Other women are similarly cavalier in adhering to propriety. In assessing a letter composed to a friend, Lib Baker confesses, "I wrote him such a nonsensical letter the last time that I suppose he thinks me a rather unprofitable correspondent. Well! So I am. I do wish I was more dignified, but it's no use to try. I'm Lib Baker and no body else" (99). Dignity and propriety, perhaps not—but this writer displays charm in abundance.[62]

Although men also apologized for their real and imagined epistolary flaws in Civil War letters, the men whose letters appear in this collection did so less frequently than women. For example, in Ben Stone's five letters, Stone apologizes for his writing in only two. The strongest apology consists of five words added in a postscript: "Excuse my awkwardness and carelessness" (69). Millwood physician and friend T. B. Campbell shirks propriety altogether, offering no apology at all in his two letters to Lybarger and throwing in a few colorful words for good measure (23, 73).

Public Letters: "Doubtless You and Captain R. Would Have Compared Letters"

Although broader social conventions shaped how people approached letter writing, many have viewed letters as an "emblem of the private" world of an individual.[63] As such, letters have been considered key vehicles to access a writer's "consciousness,"[64] to study women's lives, and to understand how women have constructed and performed their identities historically. The sometimes-limited availability of public records of women has heightened the value of letters and diaries for women's historians as a reflection of women's realities.[65] Unlike many forms of writing associated with a male literary tradition, the practice of letter writing has long been linked to women. Olga Kenyon, in fact, suggests that a cross-cultural "tradition" of women's letter writing has existed for "at least eight centuries."[66] Sally L. Kitch extends this argument when she suggests that before the nineteenth century, "the letter was all but synonymous with *woman,* not because men wrote no letters, but because literate women were permitted to write little else."[67] Although what women have been permitted to write has depended on their race, class, and context, the conception of women's letter writing as a "private" endeavor has allowed women more freedom with this genre than with forms of writing considered more public, political, authoritative, and appropriate to men.

Whether men or women held the pen has determined at times whether letters were deemed public substance or private scribbling. Whereas men's letters have often served historically as government edicts, testimonials, and literature, women's letters have often been viewed as an intimate form of communication intended to foster personal relationships. Women's letter writing has thus seemed a harmless activity consistent with their sphere and appropriate for their "natural" expressiveness and sentimentality.[68] Even when women have intended their letters to spur political changes—as Abigail Adams did when she reminded her husband President John Adams not to "forget the ladies" —they generally have not been perceived as threatening to the boundaries between the social roles of the sexes. Indeed, women's letters have more often been "stuffed away in old drawers" without visibility or regard than considered a threat to social norms.[69]

Certainly, the Lybarger letters provide perhaps the only glimpses available into the thoughts and feelings of their writers over one hundred years ago. They also offer additional windows into the past experiences of literate Northern women from the perspective of women. Yet to approach these documents only as mirrors of their writers' private thoughts and feelings is insufficient for understanding the varied functions of letters during the Civil War. As feminist researchers have argued, letters have not been static in form, purpose, or effect but have varied widely across writer, historical period, and cultural context. Considering the conditions in which letters are produced, circulated, and read offers additional insight into their content and the limits and possibilities of what the documents can reveal about their authors and women's lives in that context. The epistolary form is shaped inherently by its direction to particular correspondents and particular audiences and the writer's awareness that it will be read by those audiences. Through persuasive rhetoric, strategic silences, and genre compliance, letters create realities as well as reflect them. For example, in her study of a nineteenth-century women's commonwealth, Kitch found that letters among community members not only sustained women's relationships but also served as policy statements that shaped community norms. Letters were private and public, individual and relational.[70] Similarly, female missionaries throughout the nineteenth and twentieth centuries wrote letters from the field to testify to those who supported them financially that they were fulfilling their duties. These community letters were written with overt consciousness of the pious duty and self-denial that were expected of female missionaries working to spread the word of God.[71]

Michelle Farrell posits both private and public functions in the letters that the famed Mme. de Sévigné wrote to her married daughter in seventeenth-century France. Farrell suggests that because members of the upper class commonly composed and read their letters in public salons, Mme de Sévigné wrote her letters with particular liveliness and flourish in anticipation that they would be read publicly. Thus, while her letters provide the only possible glimpses into her thoughts and feelings that are still available centuries later, her intent for the letters to provide entertainment in upper-class social circles was a factor that influenced which thoughts and feelings she chose to express. Audience and purpose act as mediating forces in what writers include, exclude, highlight, and shadow. From this perspective, Mme de Sevigne's letters had both private and public functions. They helped sustain a relationship with her daughter across a twenty-year span. They also entertained, advanced her reputation as a skilled writer, and allowed her to experiment on paper with a public persona. These public functions were among the few available to women in Mme de Sevigne's elite but constrained social position.[72]

Scholars have argued that women's letters contributed to the development of the epistolary novel in the eighteenth century, facilitated women's development as professional authors in the nineteenth century, and contributed to women's political activism throughout the American women's movement. Letters connected women and built momentum for action during the abolition, suffrage, and temperance movements. This overlap between the "private" and "public" function of letters has led some to refuse the public/private distinction altogether as gendered, artificial, and politically motivated. Activists and writers Dale and Lynne Spender argue that women's activities, like men's, function in both public/political and domestic/private ways. Separating them conceptually not only glosses over their common functions but also can minimize the value accorded to the "private," whether symbolized through letters, childrearing, or home life. Drawing from language common to the American women's movement of the 1970s, the Spenders argue that "personal" issues have always been "political" for women. They entitled their compilation of letters *Scribbling Sisters*, perhaps to offer commentary on the historical practice of dismissing women's letters as trivial, private musings.[73]

Yet many writers do not intend for their letters to circulate widely. The symbolic importance of print to middle-class writers and its perceived permanence shaped what some writers chose to inscribe into blank pages. Civil War soldiers often confessed feelings or trespasses specific to the correspondent that they may not have wanted shared with others.[74] In Wiley's extensive study of "Yank" and "Reb" letters, he suggests that Yankee soldiers with more education and a greater "sense of delicacy" and convention than their less-educated counterparts were "more inclined to pass over the seamy side of camp life" in their letters home.[75]

A remnant of the eighteenth-century belief that circulating one's letters widely was an indecent practice for both men and women surfaces in the Lybarger letters.[76] Although some women choose to respond directly to a public advertisement for correspondents, they question in their letters whether writing to a stranger is appropriate. Others caution Lybarger to keep their confidences. Jennie Hall requests that her letters be kept "strictly confidential," perhaps because she fears their implications for her reputation (58). Phrone Rogers follows her list of local members of Knights of the Golden Circle "and all such trash" with the plea, "please keep these things to yourself. It might make a fuss if it was known I told it" (14). In another letter, Phrone asks him to destroy her letter: "This is intended for your eyes alone therefore I hope you will destroy it after you are through reading it" (121). The plea seems more hopeful than realistic, given the common tendency for soldiers to share letters and Phrone's knowledge that Lybarger had already sent some letters home with a fellow soldier, Oliver Taylor.

Sometimes writers choose silence altogether rather than risk misinterpretation, betrayal of confidence, or the permanence of inscription that renders writers accountable for their words. In 1864, Lib Baker mentions that an "interesting incident" occurred "that if you were here I might relate to you." Yet she chooses not to elaborate. "I do not wish to write it with pen and ink," she explains, "for as Mr. Smith says that will stand law" (99). The power of print, Lib suggests, lies in its permanence. Phrone echoes this sentiment in a series of letters written that same year. Bristling with anger at a remark Lybarger reportedly made to Lib, Phrone writes on May 13, "you seem to think that 'it will do me good when I get you' do you?" (84). Phrone seems infuriated with Lybarger for implying that she was chasing him. For a short time, volleys of "he said, she said" mark their correspondence (84, 86, 87, 95, 98).

When Lybarger attempts to smooth things over by explaining that he "did not remember all [he] said as [his] head was buzzing from the affects [of] Quinine," Phrone tosses his excuse aside. She writes, "I suppose the emphasis on 'all' implies that you do remember some things you said—but it matters not whether you remember some things or not—they are written. I hope you will at least grant me the same privilege you wish to enjoy—that is of choosing and using my own words" (98). To Phrone, like Lib, writing is an authoritative and powerful act that must be undertaken carefully. "The moving finger writes; and having writ / moves on: nor all your piety nor wit / shall lure it back to cancel half a line, nor all your tears wash out a word of it."[77] How Lybarger viewed the incident in question is unclear. However, his decision to save letters throughout his life suggests that he too believed in the power and permanence of the written word.

CORRESPONDENCE AS WAR WORK

> I feel that I would be willing to talk and
> write of nothing else, could I by this
> means contribute one mite toward the
> closing of this insatiable war. . . . I <u>will</u>
> forbear and I only hope that if you con-
> sider this a useless expenditure of words,
> you will not trouble yourself to read it.
>
> —Lou Riggen (90)

The significance of correspondence between soldiers and civilians extended beyond the solace and joy it offered individuals. Letter writing
during the Civil War functioned in both private and public ways: as a
gendered form of war work, as romantic and economic labor, as a tool
to sustain family and community, as a coping mechanism for feelings
of impotency as the war continued. Letters from individual soldiers
also functioned politically and symbolically when newspaper editors
published them to memorialize individuals and bolster patriotic sentiment for the war. As the editors of the *Banner* argued in publishing
"Colonel Broadhead's Last Letter," "such a letter belongs rather to
the nation at large than to relatives or friends, and should be chronicled
in the nation's annals, as showing forth the calm, heroic soul of one of
her best and most devoted sons."[78] The editors thus asserted the letter's
public value for the nation and for Civil War history.

Lybarger, too, had a letter published in the *Mt Vernon Republican*
in 1863 that highlighted the public function of testifying to political allegiances. He wrote to challenge circulating rumors that "most" soldiers are "dissatisfied with the war" and publically proclaimed his
commitment to preserving the Union. Serving as an authoritative
voice from the field, the soldier condemned "damnable" and "traitorous" Northern Copperheads who opposed the war and were thus
intent on "destroying the best government the sun has ever shown
upon." In the wake of the Conscription Act and increasing support for
Clement Vallandigham in Ohio, this public testimonial not only conveyed to local war opponents that their beliefs were an affront to the

service and sacrifices of Knox County's own sons but affirmed this soldier's and his company's devotion to the Union cause. As the war entered its third year, such ardent patriotism championed from the front lines via a Knox County native may have firmed resolve for the battles ahead.[79]

The practical and symbolic purposes of women's letter writing were as varied as the writers themselves. As historian Mary Massey argued, women's reactions to the war and their engagement in it (exemplified by the letters in this collection) display both human frailties and strengths.[80] Letter writing provided an outlet for women to express their vulnerabilities, needs, and desires. It offered opportunities for women to adopt personas on paper. It signaled their patriotism publicly. It testified to their relationships with soldiers. It strengthened their composition skills. For some, it facilitated vital connections to those on the war front (71). For others, it offered novelty, entertainment, and a method of whiling away the hours (39, 40, 51). Some noted war events only in passing; others filled their letters with exuberant patriotic rhetoric. Northern women's letter writing during the Civil War was variably personal and public, perfunctory and meaningful.

The Lybarger letters clearly were meaningful to the man who preserved them. As Nancy Rhoades explains in the preface to this collection, the circumstances in which she discovered her grandfather's letters envelops them in an aura of secrecy and privacy that speaks to their personal value: 168 folded letters, 125 years old, unknown to descendants and placed carefully at the bottom of an officer's dispatch box. Lybarger chose to preserve only a portion of the letters he received during the years 1862–67. The volume of letters that some soldiers wrote and received suggests the potential number he received during the war years. One source estimates that one thousand men in their first months of service could send out an average of 600 letters a day. One soldier's tally of his 1863 mail revealed that he received 85 letters and wrote 164 others, 37 of which were on behalf of other men. He sent 109 to folks at home and 55 to other friends.[81]

Lybarger's writing patterns were not as dutifully recorded, despite the rigorous correspondence he maintained with many on the home front. He mentions six times in his 1862 diary and twice in 1863 that he wrote letters and twice in his published 1864 diary that he received them. Sixty-seven dates in his 1862 diary—days he spent in the hospital after the battle of Corinth—contain no entries for any activities, letter writing or otherwise. Yet the collection contains 12 letters from 1862 that overlap with his time in the hospital, 45 letters from 1863, 53 from 1864, and 29 from his months of service in 1865: a total of 139 letters during the war years. Of those 139, 100 state that the writers are responding to letters received from Lybarger. In addition, letters include references to communication with many community members whose letters are not included in the collection. For example, several women note taking turns with their fathers in writing (18, 41). Phrone mentions mailing letters for women in the community (9). Most significant, the collection contains no letters from the soldier's mother, Amelia Crum Lybarger, even though a letter of February 22, 1863, indicates Amelia had already written six letters to her son after he had rejoined his regiment (14). Lybarger may have chosen to discard letters from his mother and any that existed from his father if they offered sad reminders of his father's failing health.

Some of the lieutenant's letters may have been lost along battlefields and roadsides, as were so many young men's lives during the war. Some may not have survived the marches, relocations, or years following his return to civilian life. Others may have deteriorated from frequent handling and sharing. The space in knapsacks was not boundless; sheer necessity would have required soldiers to limit the letters they saved during active service. Soldiers carried most of their belongings on their backs and sometimes shed their knapsacks, canteens, overcoats, and other items to lighten their loads.[82] Some ate their rations to avoid carrying extra weight. Lybarger's position as an officer, eventually with a horse, perhaps facilitated preservation because some belongings were likely hauled for him. Nevertheless, calculating with cumulative weight or inconvenience in mind, he may have deemed some letters worth the journey and others as fitting to let go. With the war's end in sight, Lybarger apparently worked to preserve what letters he had retained by sending them home with a fellow soldier, Oliver Taylor, for safekeeping (121).[83]

Scholars have emphasized the significance of war correspondence for soldiers as a source of connection, motivation, and diversion. Mitchell argues that letters provided constant "reassurance" amid the vicissitudes of war to "stay in the army day after day, year after year." Letters boosted morale and assured soldiers that "those back home approved of one's service." Wiley suggests that the constancy of letters made camp life "tolerable." Correspondence was certainly well received and appreciated: as one soldier put it, "the 'sojer' boys answer no call with a greater zest than [letter call]!" Soldiers asked home folk to write again and again: "A soldiers cup of joy is full when he finds a letter among the package for his company." One soldier's concise but fervent plea captures common feelings of urgency: "FOR GOD-SAKE RITE." Lybarger was equally enthusiastic. On December 18, he expresses, "received a mail . . . oh lord how glad we are!"[84]

Letters may have become more meaningful for Lybarger as the war progressed. The first letter in the collection, Fannie Meredith's of September 14, 1862, bears a date nearly ten months after he was mustered in. Lybarger entered the service on November 25, 1861, as a private and remained at Camp Andrews in Mt. Vernon, Ohio, while the regiment gathered its forces. His company left camp on February 21, 1862, to travel south through Cincinnati, Louisville, and across Illinois to Missouri, where on February 27 company members joined the Twenty-seventh, Thirty-ninth, and Sixty-third Ohio regiments in assignment to Colonel Fuller's Ohio Brigade at Commerce. Aside from the time he spent recuperating from illness and battle wounds, a thirty-day furlough home, and a temporary stint in command of Company A, Lybarger served in Company K throughout the war and attained the rank of first lieutenant. He was mustered out with his company on July 13, 1865, along with seventy-eight other men.[85]

Although the date Lybarger began saving letters is unknown, several events may have prompted him to begin the collection: the death of friends and acquaintances from Millwood, the Union man's own brush with mortality, and the period he spent recuperating after he was wounded in battle. Fannie's letter mentions the first of these events.

Her letter portends the death of a friend of Lybarger's, Newton Shroyer, who was a private in Company K and mustered in about a month after Lybarger. Fannie wrote, "[T]hey feel very bad about Nute, did not get any letters yesterday. . . . They do not know but what he is dead" (1). Indeed, Newton died of disease in Jackson, Tennessee, a week after this letter was written. The loss of this eighteen-year-old and member of a Millwood farming family likely hit the soldier close to home. Two letters in the collection are from Nute's twenty-one-year-old sister "Deal" (Adelia) Shroyer, who expresses her grief about her brother's death and reminisces about the "pleasant hours" she spent with Lybarger in years past (10, 55).[86] Letters in the collection mention another sibling, Washington, as well.

Another event significant for Lybarger that occurred within a few weeks of Fannie's letter is the battle of Corinth, in which Fuller's Ohio Brigade was engaged. Lybarger was wounded at Corinth on October 4, 1862. The battle of Corinth (October 3–4) marked the last rebel offensive in the Mississippi region and the first major action of the war for some members of the Forty-third Ohio. Lying at the intersection of major railroad lines connecting portions of the Mississippi Valley, Corinth, Mississippi, was considered a vital point for the Confederacy to control and from which Northern troops could access central cities in the South and in western Tennessee. On October 3, a memorable day on which temperatures soared to 90 degrees, Confederate forces of 22,000 men attacked Union troops on the outskirts of Corinth and drove them back two miles. After days of marching, Fuller's Brigade was assigned to defend Batteries Williams and Robinett, located northwest of the railroad depot. The Confederates renewed their assault in the early hours of October 4, and by midmorning rebel forces had advanced to the batteries in full force with heavy musketry fire and hand-to-hand combat. Lybarger remembered the enemy making an "impetuous and almost simultaneous attack" along the entire line of Union defense. Rebel efforts to capture Robinett led to "desperate" fighting. Members of the Forty-third Ohio jumped to man the guns when the infantry became disabled.[87]

Although Confederate sharpshooters, scorching heat, and thick underbrush assaulted Union forces as the rebels steadily advanced, by

12 noon on October 4, Commander William S. Rosecrans was able to thwart the Confederate drive and retain control of the region.[88] During the battle, both sides sustained heavy losses, including the death of over three hundred Union soldiers and injuries of close to two thousand more. Decades afterward, Lybarger described it as "one of the most terrific scenes of blood and carnage that it was my lot to behold during the war." Ohio's Brigade "literally mow[ed] men down by the hundreds."[89] On October 14, the *Banner* announced "serious" losses for "our side"; the final tally of casualties in the Forty-third Ohio included the notable Colonel J. L. Kirby Smith, a talented twenty-six-year-old soldier from a line of military men, who died eight days after being shot in the head.[90] An hour before the battle ended, Lybarger was shot in the knee. One source notes that seventy-five were wounded in his regiment. Eight men from Company K lost their lives, including Van Buren Shrimplin, the twenty-three-year-old-son of a Millwood farmer. Writers do not refer to these losses, but they refer to the Shrimplin family in other contexts. The war was costly for the Shrimplins: the *Banner* reports that Van was the third son Sarah Shrimplin had lost during the war.[91]

The months Lybarger spent recuperating from his wound also facilitated saving letters. Lybarger probably received the first twelve letters of the collection during his hospitalization in Paducah, Kentucky. They were likely welcome distractions from nearly three months in a hospital bed. After he was shot around 11 A.M. on October 4, Lybarger was removed from the field. Along with the other wounded, he was attended by hospital workers, transported temporarily to a hospital in Corinth, and then moved north to St. John's hospital in Paducah. Although similar wounds prompted amputation, doctors were able to preserve his leg, and he remained in the hospital until December 26, 1862. From a practical perspective, St. John's might have provided more stable conditions for collecting letters and a foundation for the practice Lybarger continued when rejoining his regiment on December 31. Personal losses and recuperative time may have left the soldier keenly aware that he might not outlive the war and wanting to preserve reminders from his service years in case he did.

Lybarger occasionally tracked his correspondence as the years passed and the collection grew. He sometimes marked dates of receipt on envelopes. He sometimes noted that he had answered a letter or the date he responded (84, 92, 102, 104–6, 108, 111). For example, the envelope for Letter 84, dated May 13, 1864, reads "Received Aug. 23/64; Answered Aug. 31/64." The inconsistent notations suggest the soldier may simply have tried to track mail delays or his responses to specific letters. However, like many a soldier, he may have imagined a peaceful future in which letters would serve as instruments of memory and lifelines to the past, and recorded dates with that vision in mind.

"Some Fair Unknown"

The majority of the letters in this collection, three-fourths, are from acquaintances, childhood friends, family members, and intimates.[92] The lieutenant knew two of the primary correspondents—Phrone Rogers (who wrote forty letters), and Lybarger's cousin from his mother's side, Rozaltha (Rosa) Crum (who wrote eighteen letters)—prior to the war. However, the third primary correspondent, a lively woman from Kentucky by the name of Lou Riggen (who wrote twenty-four letters as Lou after writing her first under the pseudonym Fannie Jerome), was unknown to Lybarger originally. Like a handful of others in the collection, Lou's letters are grounded in the historical phenomenon common during combat periods in which military men actively solicit correspondence through social networks and newspaper advertisements. This practice was common during the Civil War, although it was viewed with varying degrees of approbation. Excerpts from period newspapers capture patterns illustrative of this form of solicitation:

> Wanted: Correspondence—Three gay and festive young gents, between the ages of 20 and 24, having served Uncle Sam three years are desirous of opening correspondence with an unlimited number of the fair damsels of Ohio. Object fun and mutual improvement. Address, J. N.—M.C. or L.M. Box 56, Newark, Ohio.

> Wanted: Correspondence—Two of Uncle Sam's gay boys, who wish to correspond with as many neat and gay young ladies as wish to respond. Object—love, fun, and improvement, and to pass away

the lonely hours of camp life. Come, ladies, do not wait to be drafted to this.

Wanted—Correspondence!

Two of Uncle Sam's boys from the good Sucker State who have seen the elephant in all his moods, but who are unfit for duty at present on account of wounds from which they have not fully recovered, are very anxious to correspond with a number of the fair damsels in illinois. Object—fun, love, or anything that might arise from the performance. Now girls, we will think most of her who writes first.

Address W.H.M. or J.F.S., Medical Department, Convalescent Camp, Chattanooga, Tennessee

WANTED—CORRESPONDENCE—Two of Uncle Sam's gay boys wish to open correspondence with any number of Union ladies. All letters answered promptly. Address I.B.D. and L.C. ward 19, Camp Dennison, Ohio.

WANTED—CORRESPONDENCE—

> Writing, Many people say,
> Is good to drive dull care away;
> It makes men social, drowns their care,
> To correspond with ladies fair.
> Now ladies, if you choose to write
> To boys who for their country fight
> Two vets in the army you will find
> To writing very much inclined,
> Who like to write for love or fun,
> Or anything that's well begun.
> Address: W.S.S. or J.J.E.
> Company I, 8th O.V.V.O.
> Phillippi, West Virginia[93]

Perhaps gaining strength in numbers, these anonymous co-conspirators advertise primarily in pairs and trios. The similarities in the ads suggest that, as with letter writing, soldiers modeled their work on the examples of others and created informal standards for soliciting correspondence over the course of the war.

The ads share a number of common characteristics. They pose correspondence as harmless fun with patriotic overtones and an enticing aura of romantic possibility. Soldiers' careful linguistic choices of "the draft" and "lonely camp life" seem intended to incite women's sense of gendered responsibility to the war effort. Indeed, just as the draft should not be necessary to coax real men to their patriotic duties, these ads imply, mandates should not be required to enlist women of moral fiber to this corollary service. Women can have "fun" with "gay" soldiers and "improve" them in the process. The lighthearted tone that soldiers employed might have been intended to soothe any uneasiness women felt about the propriety of corresponding with strangers. The additional enticement of "improving" soldiers might have been designed to appeal to women's sense of moral duty and uplift. These understandings of wartime correspondence—patriotic duty, harmless pleasure, and romantic possibility—are echoed in the blend of gaiety and duty that infuse the Lybarger letters.

Sometimes women also advertised for correspondents. For example, an advertisement slipped between the pages of Lybarger's 1863 diary reads as follows:

> WANTED—CORRESPONDENCE—
> Four of Uncle Sam's nieces, both loyal and true,
> Correspondence desire with his nephews, in view
> To friendship or fun, or what else may arise,
> From acquaintance that's formed by us in disguise;
> Our standing is good, reputation is fair,
> As for beauty we boast not, we are free to declare;
> Our ages from eighteen to twenty-two years,
> We tell this in truth, to dispel all your fears.
>
> Address KATE TENYON, FRANCES J. BYRON,
> JENNIE A. HOWE and IDA MAY, Box 33,
> Wooster, Wayne County, Ohio.[94]

This advertisement, like those of the soldiers, hints at the possibilities of romance and uses patriotic terms to imply common cause with correspondents. Kate and her chums refer to their "good standing" and "fair reputation" to dispel any fears concerning their character. Paradoxically, they adopt pseudonyms but claim the advertisement is truthful. A notable difference between the women's and men's advertisements is women's denial of physical beauty. References to physical appearance are primarily absent from men's advertisements. In addition, the women use family metaphors (nieces and nephews) to inflect a wholesome air in their bold request for correspondents and to suggest writer and recipient alike are members of the American family.

Lybarger clearly participated in this practice of advertising for correspondents and seemed to do so at least once using the pseudonym of Frank Wharton (28, 31).[95] The first letter indicating a response to the ad is dated July 24, 1863. Lou was the most prolific writer who responded, and she also used a pseudonym before tiring of the subterfuge and revealing to her correspondent what she wryly calls her "pleasant," "musical," and authentic name (43). Lou's writing relationship with Lybarger began after a friend of Lou's apparently answered an advertisement that Lybarger placed in a local paper (31). In a flurry of personas, Lou's friend used the pseudonym of "Fannie Jerome" in her letter to the imaginary "Frank Wharton," while Lou claimed she wrote as "Irene Livingstone" to another soldier in Lybarger's company. Lou's friend was apparently reluctant to continue after penning the first letter, and Lou took over the job of writing on September 5, 1863 (40). The twists and turns of this romantic story reveal the elaborate plotting and camaraderie that could accompany wartime writing relationships.[96]

Lou's first letter sets the spirited tone that would mark their correspondence throughout. Writing as "Fannie," she states, "You wish an 'agreeable, interesting and useful correspondence.' Precisely my object in writing to you. I wanted novelty—or in other words—*fun*. And you most fortunately can write nonsense. You speak of this faculty rather deprecatingly. But, as 'a little nonsense now and then is relished by the best of men'—and women. I am happy to know that you can" (40). Relishing "nonsense" and craving "fun," Lou writes from September 5, 1863 (40), until February 26, 1867 (168). Nothing in the letters indicates that Lou and Lieutenant Lybarger ever met. Her last letter is dated about a month after he chooses to set sail on what Lou had earlier called "the sea of matrimony" (66). It is also the last letter in the collection. Lou's reflections on human nature and the relationship of letters to identity provide a fitting conclusion to the collection and to their three-and-a-half-year correspondence. The final lines of her letter read, "Write right soon and if you don't write a longer letter next time won't that be terrible!" Readers wanting more of this dynamic epistolary relationship over one hundred years later might agree that it is.

The sometimes lighthearted content of letters such as Lou's masks one of their weighty functions during the War Between the States. Women's letters from the home front can be considered a gendered form of "war work," tangible vehicles through which Northern women could contribute directly to the war effort. Whether penned by strangers or loved ones, letters often represent white, middle- and working-class women's sustained labor to bolster the spirits of enlisted men, to champion their service, to entertain and distract, and to sculpt enticing visions of home and hearth during a devastating civil conflict that fractured notions of nation and citizen. Although Wiley notes that the lack of censorship in the mail system meant that soldiers received gloomy epistles detailing home front hardships alongside cheery ones, the letters in the Lybarger collection more often reflect single women's efforts to "cheer the soldier" and report the "news of home" rather than catalogue scarcity and trial.[97]

Women were called to this labor repeatedly in popular periodicals of the day. The assertive journalist "Gail Hamilton" (the pen name for Abigail Dodge) urged white, middle-class Northern women to such action in a popular essay entitled "A Call to My Country-Women," published in the *Atlantic Monthly* in March 1863. This publication had wide circulation in the Northeast and was advertised freely in Knox County newspapers.[98] Hamilton insists that women should not focus their energy in sewing for soldiers' aid societies—as "stitching does not crush rebellion"—but should seize their pens with "passionate purpose" and channel their "soul of fire" directly to the front lines through letters. She writes, "Follow the soldier to the battlefield with your spirit. The great army of letters that marches southward with every morning sun is a powerful engine of war." Even though women cannot don uniforms and take up arms, "the issue of this war depends quite as much upon American women as upon American men—and depends, too, not upon the few who write, but upon the many who do not."[99] During a speech in the same month Hamilton's essay was published, one lieutenant colonel expresses the same sentiments: "If you wish success, write encouraging letters to your soldiers, tell them that they are engaged in a good and glorious cause. . . . Do not fill the ears . . . with tales of troubles and privations at home, caused by their absence."[100]

These warnings may have been ominous for women whose energy had been directed into Union aid societies and sewing circles. "The war," Hamilton reminds her readers, "cannot be finished by sheets and pillow-cases." She charges women to drop their needles, straighten their shoulders, bear up under the stress of men's absence, and begin to write. Letters should "hearten him, enliven him, tone him up to the true hero-pitch." Women should avoid sharing trifling concerns and petty details and instead "tell every sweet and brave and pleasant and funny story" possible. Women should remind soldiers that their labors, their sacrifices, their service, "this warfare" in which the nation is engaged, "means peace."[101] Hamilton argued, as Mitchell underscores more than a century later, that letters from home reminded soldiers that they were fighting both for their national home and for their families and communities.[102] The culture of print takes on new meaning in Hamilton's vision.

On the surface, letter writing has none of the heroism and intrigue that accompanies other services that women provided during the war. Great figures abound in Civil War history, men and women alike whose service, compassion, and labor contributed to shaping individual lives and historical events. Clara Barton nursed hundreds of men, orchestrated the delivery of medical and food supplies directly to battles such as Antietam, Fredericksburg, and Second Bull Run, and contributed to identifying 22,000 unknown dead from the 50 percent of Union men left unnamed at war's end. Abolitionist Harriet Tubman, renowned for ushering hundreds of escaped slaves to freedom through the Underground Railroad, nursed the sick and the wounded and served the Union army as a scout. Knox County, Ohio, native Mary Ann "Mother" Bickerdyke worked to improve the operations of military hospitals, nursed those in tent hospitals close to battlefields, procured supplies, and outraged many a military man when she dismissed social convention to accomplish her goals.

Some fiery notables, such as Confederates Belle Boyd, Belle Edmonson, and Rose O'Neal Greenhow and Unionist Pauline Cushman, served as spies and smugglers for their respective sides. One of the little-known but remarkable female figures woven through the folklore and history of espionage in the Civil War is Mary Elizabeth Bowser, an African American woman who had been released from slavery. Her intellect and skill at subterfuge allowed her to live in President Jefferson Davis's house as a servant during 1863 and slip messages to Unionists. Sarah Emma Edmonds and Albert D. J. Cashier (Jennie Hodgers) donned male clothing, enlisted in the army, and fought, primarily undetected, for the Union cause. Less-known women did the same; Malinda Pritchard Blalock is the only woman known to have fought alongside her husband in both the Confederate and Union armies, dressed first as a man and then later without disguise as a guide for Union recruits, a raider, and a guerrilla fighter. Others such as Kady Brownell and Annie Blair Etheridge became "Daughters of the Regiment," living alongside soldiers in camp and striving to inspire them. "Daughters" nursed men, shouted encouragement during battle, and sometimes carried regimental flags.

Other roles women performed lacked the romance of the smuggler and flag bearer but were instrumental in the administrative operations necessary to war. Mary Rice Livermore served as a leader in the United States Sanitary Commission, and Dorothea Dix furthered her contributions to the profession of nursing in her controversial role as a recruiter and organizer of Union nurses. Mary Todd Lincoln, Julia Dent Grant, Ellen Ewing Sherman, Varina Howell Davis, and Jessie Benton Fremont, like other women married to significant American leaders and military men, bore the pressures of their husbands' prominence and supported the men's political activities amid the ebb and flow of public opinion.[103]

African American women, both free and enslaved, worked to raise their children, support the war effort, and sustain their communities both spiritually and economically. Some free Northern blacks used activist skills developed before the war for abolitionist causes, raising money to aid the poor, and teaching reading skills to freedmen and women. Susie Baker King Taylor, a former slave who was literate, taught African American soldiers in a South Carolina regiment to read. She contributed one of the only known memoirs of a young African American woman's life on the front lines—a key service given the dearth of documents that enslaved and contraband women were able to leave behind. Some women sheltered soldiers, while others supplied information and sustenance. Thousands of "contraband" women fled slavery during the course of the war to join Union regiments and perform needed labor with little to no compensation and at times received horrific treatment from the very soldiers fighting to liberate them. Women washed soldiers' clothes and cooked their food while scavenging to provide for their own families. For some women, survival during the war years may have been their ultimate contribution.[104]

Women also flocked to form soldiers' aid societies across the North and the South. This work may have done little to "crush rebellion" in Gail Hamilton's eyes, but it contributed an enormous number of supplies to soldiers during the first years of the war. Knox County newspapers called for "loyal women and children" to sew shirts, provide winter clothes, and scrape lint for bandages for "those who fall in defence of their rights and their homes."[105] Sewing machines became "weapons of the home front."[106] Women sewed uniforms, collected supplies, scraped lint, raised money, made bandages, and procured every conceivable item perceived to be of need to soldiers and hospitals. Urgency interfered with many a straight seam, and Northern women sometimes misjudged what men at the front needed, sending butter, fried chicken, and an unfortunate headgear called the havelock—which had little relevance in the field and men promptly used for rags. Yet the work of soldiers' aid societies fell firmly within women's sphere, and they rose to the challenge. One tally from the Ladies' Aid Society of Mt. Vernon, Ohio, totaled "17 new hospital shirts, 14 pairs of drawers, 32 pads, 60 rolls of bandages, 12 sacks lint, 10 part worn shirts, 28 towels," in addition to linen coats, pillowcases, sheets, and neckties. Letters contain passing references to suppers and public parades to raise money, and to buying expeditions on behalf of soldiers' aid, particularly during the first years of the war (4, 7, 17).[107]

Providing goods became particularly difficult for Southern women as the war progressed and supplies dwindled. To procure material goods for soldiers while supporting their families created desperate circumstances even as it bolstered women's feelings of competency and independence.[108] LeeAnn Whites cites one Southern woman's assessment of her wartime circumstances: "'Pshaw! There are no women here! We are all men!'"[109] Many women struggled to find food for their families and keep their households and farms running while also facing invasion and occupation by Northern troops.[110] Women taught, nursed, spied, served in the military, provided needed goods, and maintained farms, families, and businesses in the wake of men's enlistment.

Women also served as physicians, a role seldom detailed in historical and popular accounts and often overshadowed by women's valuable contributions in nursing. Although the role of medical doctors and the grisly wounds, amputations, nudity, and death they encountered were considered sharply at odds with the proper sphere of middle-class women in nineteenth-century America, several hundred women had graduated from medical school by 1860, and a small number of both self-taught and school-trained women fought for the right to use their skills for the war effort. The colorful Mary Walker, for instance, petitioned repeatedly for a hospital commission, worked at times without pay, and traveled strategically to hospital and battle sites where need for her medical assistance sometimes took precedence over struggles to uphold gender norms. Although considered radical at the time, her actions may have paved the way for women's increasing presence in the medical profession in the postwar years.[111]

These wartime activities seem heroic compared to the scratch of a quill on paper. Indeed, many women serving on the front lines may have perceived few similarities between nursing the wounded and wielding a pen. As hospital worker Hannah Ropes expressed in 1863, "Mercy! What do the women at home know of work? *We never* stopped till the whole house were pronounced doing well."[112] Front-line workers sometimes referred to themselves as "soldiers."[113] Yet, perceived as little or great, letter writing was one of many forms of service women provided to the war effort. Some women took their "epistolary duties" quite seriously (99). One took pen in hand "to perform what I consider . . . to be my duty" (45). Another promises, "I will sympathize with you in your loneliness" (11). Still another strives to meet whatever informational needs arose from afar: "[I]f I have failed to say anything . . . you want to know about Millwood let me know and I will be very happy to inform you" (14). Grace Nello wishes only to provide a few moments of pleasure. She pledges, "I am a true friend of the Soldier, and if a kind word once in awhile will afford any pleasure I am satisfied" (72). Mollie affirms the "pleasure the union loving girls have is in writing to the soldiers . . . [to] cheer their hearts with words of comfort" (37). Letters in the collection written after Hamilton's call to action seem intended to comfort, entertain, and distract in the ways the journalist envisioned.

Women's letters sometimes reflect their struggle to describe activities on the home front likely to "enliven" and "hearten" the soldier while also honoring his contrasting circumstances and the tangible effects of his absence. This epistolary balancing act may have been important for maintaining men's belief that things were "right" at home —a belief that bolstered, historian Reid Mitchell argues, their sense of masculine duty to the war effort.[114] A letter Ell Hawn wrote in 1862 offers glimpses of this balancing act. "Your Folks allso are well," she assures Lybarger, "[and] the helth of Millwood is rather good." Yet she clarifies that "the pleasures of it are few. . . . We seek not for pleasure while trouble surrounds us as it does" (2). Similarly, Phrone witnesses little joy while the men are away: "The folks here do not enjoy themselves any better than you do in camp—They have very few parties" (5). To desire merriment during war might seem disrespectful of the soldier's service. Mollie Ward suggests as much in her distress over soldiers' privations: "Whilst [soldiers] are fighting the bloody battles of our country we are at home enjoying its comforts and pleasures" (45). Writers shift from assurances that soldiers' service is valued and their absences mourned to reports of the sledding and social visits that comprise the small-town life of soldiers' memories.

Women often attempted to oblige with information they believed men wanted to hear: "But a noughf of this as you wants the news of Home" (13). Writers report parties, weather, marriages, baptisms, illnesses, tensions among townfolk, and local events and gossip. Some letters respond directly to the soldier's requests for information. "You inquired about Foulks and Jenkins," Rosa writes in one letter (18).

"You desire me to tell you about Cousin John Gibson. . . . You wished me to remind your Uncle and Aunt Sarah of you," she writes in another (20). She delivers a steady stream of information concerning their relatives. Correspondents sometimes functioned as intermediaries between townsmen drafted into different regiments. Louise Welker informs Lybarger, "You requested me when I wrote to tell you where the 65th was" (12).

Some women characterized letter writing as both duty and pleasure. Jennie Hall, a twenty-two-year-old resident of Nelsonville, Ohio, who answered Lybarger's advertisement, thought it would be "novel" to correspond with a gentleman unknown to her. She also wanted to "cheer the souldier who has gone forth bravely to fight the battles of this our 'beloved country'" (51). Another writer describes correspondence in similar but more subdued terms. She writes after Lee's surrender, "Your very kind . . . letter . . . was read with interest as all 'soldier letters' are. Guess we will soon be relieved of the task of writing to the army though it was not an unpleasant one" (130). Conscious that she is participating in a particular genre of correspondence, soldier letters, she seems careful not to portray letter writing as unpleasant in the face of men's sacrifices. Yet, the word "task" implies an undercurrent of duty in "writing to the army."[115]

"Soldiers [Are] a Living Wall of Human Flesh Standing between [Us] and Destruction"

Women's letters also reflect their efforts to remind soldiers that they are cherished and valued.[116] Phrone's prose on this topic is powerful: "I could not . . . forget thee, for I hear you spoken of so often by the many friends you left behind you. Ed, your name is too deeply engraven on the pages of memory to ever be obliterated" (9). A resident of Howard Township, Emma Moody, praises the soldier as brave and loved: "Not that I had forgotten a brave sholdier Boy who was once with us an ornament to society and loved by all who knew Him" (33). Similarly, Deal Shroyer assures Ed that her delay in letter writing is not a reflection of his value: "I suppose you have felt as if you were forgotten by me, but quite to the contrary. In memory I am with you and would much rather you were here tonight than to be writing" (55). Other writers grow patriotic as they reminisce. Ella Rightmire, a descendant of a Knox County settling family,[117] reflects, "For my part I can never forget those that were once my associates in society and are now enduring hardships that the pen can not discribe for the liberties that we now enjoy" (24). Through nostalgic and at times embellished rhetoric, women assured soldiers that their lives and their service mattered.

Honoring soldiers' sacrifices often inspired fierce language. "The people here at home," Mollie Ward writes, "look upon the soldiers as a wall of human flesh standing between [us] and destruction" (32). Ben Stone, one of the few men whose letters appear in the collection, reflects on soldiers' service in reverent terms: "I believe our government has a high destiny and will yet live many ages undivided and unbroken in peace, that our Soldiers are performing one of the most sacred duties that can be performed by man" (19). Lybarger's published letter in 1863 shares similar sentiments. Stone's detailed letters reveal his opposition to enlisting African Americans and his belief that democratic principles will transcend the temporal flaws of any given administration (19, 29, 47, 69, 112). Stone insists, in the heady terms of glory and sacrifice, that Union soldiers must persevere "until . . . the last dollar is expended and every man has enriched the soil of freedom with his blood" (47). Rosa's message from her father is more concise: "[G]ive the Rebels Hell," she pens on May 24, 1863 (18).

Writers frequently linked patriotism and war service with honorable masculinity, an association as common in the South as the North. Volunteerism was seen as the pinnacle of honorable manhood. Emma Moody writes confidently, "I know you would much rather go a Volunteer than a drafted man" (3). Rebel Copperheads earn Ell Hawn's greatest scorn: "I hope they will take every man of them," she asserts, "and put them in the Service and make them fight and they will then apreciate the laws of the government they are disobeying" (22). As if issuing a proclamation, she follows this ardent rhetoric with her signature: "Ell Hawn." When the draft drew near in Missouri, Ben Stone criticizes those who refuse to serve: "It does seem strange to me how any man can feel himself an honorable man, while seeking to evade plain duty" (69). By some accounts, earnest patriotism surpasses in value more conventional determinants of masculinity. A Knox County newspaper asserts that "genuine recruits" with "pluck" tend to be "medium men" and not the "large, muscular" sort.[118]

Corporeality can nevertheless intrude on fulfilling the social dictates for honorable manhood. Stone struggles with feelings of inadequacy because his war-torn body prevents him from reenlisting. "Ed," he confesses on October 20, 1863, "I hardly feel like I was a man. Could I only be with you, my comrades in battles. It looks like cowardice, it makes one feel mean, to be at home, while there is a war in the land. . . . I do feel a contempt for those of us who are home with our aches and disabilities, exempting" (47). In this passage, Stone mobilizes a common construction of home as a "feminized" realm and war as "masculine." He links respectable masculinity for men with action and service and "home" with cowardice and impotency. Soldiers may have felt buoyed by the belief that their service epitomized ideal manhood.[119]

At times, women wrote as if a torrent of words might wash soldiers home. After Ohio's Brigade saw action in a string of battles in the spring of 1864,[120] Lou Riggen unleashes her frustration in an emotional letter that spoke to the war's prominence in her consciousness: "When I think of the wide-spreading gloom which hangs like a pall over all this once happy country and which is deepened by every battle, I cannot control my feelings. I feel that I would be willing to talk and write of nothing else, could I by this means contribute one mite toward the closing of this insatiable war. . . . I will forbear and I only hope that if you consider this a useless expenditure of words, you will not trouble yourself to read it" (90). Words en masse might not contribute even a "mite" toward ending the war, but Lou felt equal to the task if it would. Letters involved a modicum of action that may have helped Lou channel her rage and impotency as the war dragged on. "I'm for peace, peace, *peace*," she writes in exasperation in April 1865 (110), betraying what might be Democratic sympathies in the process. While writing may have seemed at times an insignificant contribution in the face of human loss and national upheaval, Lou felt willing to "forbear" if it mattered in the life of her correspondent.

By Lybarger's account, it did. At the end of the war, after his regiment had participated in forty-six sieges and battles, and after he returned to begin experiencing the nation as Unionists believed it "should be" rather than as Peace Democrats preferred "it was" before the war, Lybarger apparently wrote to thank Lou for her letters. Their spirited correspondence was a force that helped sustain him in his duty. As a token of his gratitude, he sent flowers from President Washington's grave acquired from his visit at the end of the war. Lou's reply is formal and circumspect. "I am . . . very glad," she writes, "that I have succeeded in making pleasant a few hours of your last two years of danger, toil and privation. . . . [My letters] have fulfilled their object, that of rendering a little less monotonous the time of a federal soldier and of bringing interesting replies" (129). Although sometimes modest in aim, this war work may have been mighty in consolation.

Letters offered comfort at both ends of the postal route. Letters from soldiers were discussed publicly, described in other letters, published in newspapers, copied in diaries, and exchanged among soldiers and civilians alike. This "kinship work" connected community members and eased family members' minds about absent loved ones.[121] However much the Union and Confederate governments worked to achieve an efficient mail system, the sometimes erratic delivery of mail meant that families and soldiers awaiting word from home or battlefront were never certain whether death, fading interest, or lost mail was responsible for silences. Some letters never arrived; some took many weeks to reach their destinations; other letters took months (62, 84). At one point General John Hunt Morgan invaded Kentucky and Ohio and "set all eastern Kentucky in an uproar," capturing mail, horses, and supplies, leaving residents without mail for weeks (90).

Given vicissitudes inherent to war, letters urge soldiers to share information of others when they write. Having received a letter from her brother John, Ell Hawn expresses with relief that this is "the first we have had for five long weeks. We were quite uneasy about him but this tells us he is well. He spoke of you which he never fails to do when writing Home. I wish you may both speak of each other for very often your Folks get letters when we do not and sometimes we get when they do not. So this would be a satisfaction to us all" (13). Because she lost one brother to the cause the previous year, John is foremost in her mind.

Even fleeting mention of other soldiers could offer families solace and tie Northern community members together in their uncertainty during a war that was consuming psychically but distant geographically. At one point, Deal Shroyer encounters Lybarger's brother and says she "told him I received a letter from you; he was very glad to hear from you. . . . He was afraid that you was in that Battle fought near Chattanooga" (55). Sometimes silences confirmed a family member's greatest fear. In the first letter that foreshadows Newton Shroyer's death, it is the absence of letters that strikes Nute's family as ominous. They "did not get any letters yesterday. . . . They do not know but what he is dead" (1). While silence in correspondence could occur for any number of reasons, letters confirmed life.[122]

Soldiers' knowledge that letters were discussed publicly also reminded them that the eyes of the community were upon them as they served the Union cause. "I read the letter you wrote to Mrs. Israel," Phrone writes in 1863; "it was very good indeed" (9). Military units during the Civil War were often raised by local leaders in villages, cities, and counties and consisted of lifelong friends and acquaintances. These ties, Mitchell argues, meant that the "community never entirely relinquished its power to oversee its men at war."[123] Many of the men in Company K were from the southern and eastern parts of Ohio, and some were friends, acquaintances, and brothers who served together throughout the war. Smith's history of *Fuller's Brigade* reports that the largest number of men in Ohio regiments who reenlisted in December 1863 were in the brigade, including 436 men from the Forty-third Ohio.[124] One letter reports similar groupings in Mt. Vernon, Ohio: "William Mitchell, former Superintendent of our high school raised A company [of the 96th Ohio]. Some twenty or thirty of his company were formily his pupils in the high school" (7). In the case of Company A, the eyes of the community were not only upon them from afar but accompanying them in the form of the superintendent.[125]

Community members conveyed their expectations that men would represent their country well through praise for their sons' bravery and cautionary tales of local men's cowardice. "Let me tell you," Mollie

Ward writes in disgust, "the men here at home are not noble, brave Soldiers like those in the field, but cowards and afraid to defend even themselves" (53). Emma Moody reminds Lybarger that his service "will be an honor to you when you come home. How much better you will feel than if you had stayed at home and done as some are doing" (33). Contrasting bravery with cowardice reminded men of the public yardstick measuring their behavior. Even soldiers' manners fell within the bounds of public commentary. Local newspapers report the "good impression" and "gentlemanly deportment" of the "sturdy" soldiers in the Forty-third Ohio when they were encamped at Mt. Vernon.[126] Similarly, Phrone chastises Lybarger indirectly for failing to respond to others' letters. "Joss think it was quite strange that you do not write to her as she has writen to you a second time. . . . Mrs. Israel wants to know why you do not answer her letter she wrote to you" (17).[127]

Women sometimes critique the behavior of other soldiers as well. Lou writes of "inexperienced boys" who "forget their mothers' prayers and warning words" and are idle, play cards, drink, curse, and then plunge into battle unprepared for their calling. She attributes battle losses to such shameful behavior (103). Another writer's complaints are more particular. She grumbles that she has not received a "single letter from John Hawn since he left home" and she "don't know why he don't write" (12). John had more than one woman telling him what to do. His sister asked Lybarger to convey her concern: "tell [John] to take good care of himself and write Home often" (13). John apparently did his best; this twenty-two-year-old Millwood son who enlisted on the same day as Lybarger in 1861 was mustered out with his company at the end of the war.[128] Leaving the hospital too quickly, letter length, delays in responding, and correspondence with others all inspired writer commentary on soldier behavior. The message to soldiers seemed to be that no detail was too small to be beneath the attention of a Union man.

Also significant in the war work of letters was family members' belief that loved ones were receiving their missives of care and concern. "Your mother was crying about you," Phrone confides in 1863. "She said she had writen six letters to you since you had joined your regiment, and that you had writen home you had received but one letter in three months" (14). Other letters sought information from soldiers. Deal asks for details about her brother, Phrone probes for information about other soldiers, and Mrs. Samuel Israel expresses curiosity about the reputation of Colonel J. L. Kirby Smith (who died at Corinth). "I want to know," this prominent Mt. Vernon citizen demands, "how Collonel Smith was liked by his men. . . . Some reports say he was very much disliked and called him a perfect tyrant" (7). The traffic of information seemed to flow freely between the home front and the war front to cheer soldiers in their duties and to remind them of their roots and their responsibilities. This war work was of no small consequence. As McPherson argues in *For Cause and Comrades,* the soldiers' belief in their families' and communities' support was a central force that sustained their will to fight.[129]

CORRESPONDENCE AS ROMANTIC WORK

> If boys don't come back soon the girls will be obliged to take widowers, lame men, or any kind they can get, fir you know it won't pay to be an old maid, you know how cross they are.
>
> —Phrone (5)

Although many women wrote with patriotic fervor to "cheer," direct, and distract the soldier (51), these purposes were often accompanied by more-personal hopes. Women at times betray starry-eyed visions of romance, courtship, and marriage as they communicate with men outside their social circles or whose familiarity is recast in the rosy glow of patriotism. Letter writers vie for Lybarger's attention while he juggles multiple writing relationships. Newspapers hint at the promises of wartime romance, while advertisements for correspondents state the desire for love, fun, "and anything that's well begun." Letters clearly nourished the flurry of Knox County marriages that took place in the spring of 1864 when a local company returned on furlough. Writers report that soldiers in Company A of the Sixty-fifth Ohio were struck with "matrimonial fever" (77) and began "getting married 'with a vengeance'" (75). Many a romantic letter would have set the stage for such unions.

Negotiating propriety with the courtship circumstances of the war left women in a quandary. On one hand, letters were a central vehicle for women and soldiers to represent themselves and to pursue romantic relationships through the war years.[130] They functioned as one tool in the work of wartime romance. On the other hand, women's letters could symbolize their chastity and character. Thus, circulating their letters and photographs—and symbolically their favors—could threaten their reputation. Lou Riggen recognizes such social expectations for women when she admits in a wry tone, "a few conscientious qualms occasionally arise to remind me that I am 'entirely out of sphere'" (81) in writing to Lybarger. In a more solemn tone, Mollie Ward states that she consults her own judgment and that of her parents before responding to Lybarger's first letter (32). Pursuing the romantic work of letter writing required women at times to couch their lively personalities and imaginative minds in the restraints of gentility expected in the age in which they lived.

The romantic threads woven through the letters had both individual and cultural significance. In deeply divisive times, with state mobilizing against state and neighbor turned against neighbor, romance kindled a spirit of reconciliation, peace, and hope. One member of a ladies committee reportedly sent a pair of stockings to the front with the following note: "Brave sentry, on your lonely beat, may these blue stockings warm your feet; And when from war and camps you part, may some fair knitter warm your heart." The writer emphasizes the welcoming image of a fair knitter beckoning at war's end. Ben Stone hopes for a fair companion so that his "native state will be the home of the brave and the happy" (69). Lib Baker expresses with excitement and relief, "Have you heard of the marriage of Temp. Darling? *Union! preserve the union.* Joy be with her!" (60). This enthusiasm for united souls increases in significance when another letter reveals that Miss Darling married "the renowned butternut Jack Butler" (41). "Butternut" was a term used to describe both Southern soldiers and Southern sympathizers in the North who favored a negotiated peace over war. Whether Lib felt genuine pleasure concerning Miss Darling's choice or was offering a Republican commentary on marrying a Southern sympathizer, she conveys the appeal of marriage as a uniting force in troubling times. One marriage announcement read, "First Union of Hearts, Then Union of Hands. . . . Oh when will the North, And the South [be] side by side." Marriage offered a vision of peace, tranquility, and partnership that could help "preserve the union."[131]

Attaining this vision of peace was by no means guaranteed for women reaching courtship age during the Civil War. Because traditional courtship rituals and the pleasures of social interaction for single men and women were disrupted dramatically by the war, letter writing was one of the few methods for pursuing romantic relationships with young men who enlisted. Considered in this light, letter writing was neither trivial nor peripheral to women's economic well-being. Women in the nineteenth century often depended on marriage to ensure a secure future. As the Civil War progressed and the death toll mounted— 620,000 American men and 34,591 Ohioans are estimated to have died in this conflict—the safe return of community members, beaux, and loved ones became less certain.[132] Estimates of battle casualties fluctuated wildly; some young men's bodies were never found; some community members died while others returned safely home. The perpetual feelings of uncertainty such circumstances created underscore the importance of what may seem obvious functions of correspondence during the war—connection and courtship—but have significance for women's economic futures and identities that might be less recognized elements of wartime epistolarity. The sometimes-impassioned nature of war correspondence indicates that writing may have served as a vehicle for channeling courtship energy that in peaceful times may have been spent socializing with men, seeking a mate, and preparing for roles as wives, companions, and mothers.[133]

Women certainly perceived the numbers of men on the home front to be dwindling. Fannie Meredith observes in 1862, "I was at church today. . . . Was a great many Ladies there, not many Gentlemen for they are pretty scarce here these war times" (6). Jennie Hall describes in more-sentimental prose the loss of men in her community: "As I look around me here and there I see a vacant place. A Mother's hope and a Father's pride taken away from their fond embrace no matter how dear" (38). Phrone worries that Lybarger's absence will become permanent: "I thought myself that we would never see you again" (5). Deal Shroyer, with her brother's death ever present in her thoughts, remarks, "I do not enjoy myself as I used to, not by any means. There are too many vacant seats, too many absent ones, ah loved ones" (55). Each vacant seat signified another potential loss.

The death tallies reported in newspapers throughout the war may have felt particularly ominous to young women contemplating their futures. Northern and Southern newspapers used the tolls of dead and wounded for the propaganda war that accompanied the military war. After the battle of Corinth, the *Banner* noted that "the loss is serious for our side but bears no comparison with that of the enemy." Northern newspapers proclaimed "terrible destruction" of the male population in the South. Indeed, nearly 25 percent of Southern men of military age were dead at war's end. Although the public did not yet know the final tally of approximately 360,000 Union men and 260,000 Confederates who died during these bloody years, the varying figures that were available were undoubtedly staggering for citizens trying to grasp the human costs of the war. Young women may have felt the losses of so many Americans on personal as well as human and patriotic levels.[134]

Early in 1863, Phrone conveys women's growing awareness of the links between war casualties and their own futures in stating that they "will be obliged to take widowers, lame men, or any kind they can get" (14). Although she presents this catalogue of supposedly substandard manhood with humor, her comments reflect keen awareness that a scarcity of men means fewer choices for women. To avoid becoming cross "old maids," women will be forced to turn to "lesser" men. Many young women coming of age in Phrone's time, familiar with the common ridicule of old maids in popular culture, would have wished to distance themselves from that unhappy fate. The term "old maid" was frequently used to deride women who stepped out of their sphere, such as suffragists and advocates of dress reform. References to abolitionists as "old maids" and older women who, alone and pensive, dream of the missed opportunities of youth abound in nineteenth-century print culture.

Although historian Drew Gilpin Faust argues that the sheer losses of Southern men sometimes required Confederate women to "embrace their anticipated spinsterhood" rather than indulge in fruitless marital aspirations, and other letters historically indicate some women's preference to remain single, the letters from Ohio women suggest that they felt few celebratory impulses for a future without matrimony.[135] Lib Baker jokes of Lybarger's anticipated marriage as a transition from "Single Blessedness" to "Double Wretchedness" (166), yet scattered references to her own relationship woes belie this as her stance on romance. In February 1863, Phrone sets her sights on a hopeful future in which Lybarger will be one of the soldiers who "will have their pick and choice of the young ladies" upon his return to Millwood; "I feel certain you will be one of the fortunate ones that will be permitted to return home. How glad do we welcome the day" (14). Jennie Hall seems similarly intent on a rosy future and, with the privilege of youth and beauty on her side, ridicules single women in even stronger terms than Phrone. Striving to dispel Lybarger's concern that he is "corresponding with an 'old maid,'" she writes, "Ha ha! its rather funny to be sure. Well I can't blame you for they are detestable beings (as the men say). . . . I don't want you to think me so decidedly frightful" (44). Although women clearly developed significant relationships with other women in the postwar years and led meaningful lives without men, writers' harsh words regarding spinsters indicate their intent to avoid that role if they could.[136]

Some young women were convinced that whether one became an unwanted aged maiden or a cherished lifelong partner depended on the vagaries of the war. "[They] will make a match," Lib asserts of one couple's future, "if the Lieut. gets safely through the war" (60). If men survive, they might hold the upper hand in marital decisions. Rachel Blakeley reports sharing with other women Lybarger's comment "that the soldiers would not need any wives when they got home" (109). Some promptly choose mates rather than taking their chances on the whims of returning soldiers (109). Phrone predicts dwindling options for the Millwood fair at war's end. After listing a string of local pairings in February 1863, Phrone jokes that "the girls will have to take old men or non at all. This is a great consolation to the boys who expect to get home," for they will be able to pick and choose among the young ladies, of whom "there seems to be more than ever" (14). Whether in jest or in earnest, Phrone hints at the costs of the war for women's agency, marital options, and accordingly, economic health.

Patriotism and Romance: "Any Amount of Drunk Men Shouting for Jeff Davis"

The economic implications of marriage for nineteenth-century women do not tarnish the luster of the romantic ideals they express in their writing. Karen Lystra's study of period love letters indicates the widespread use of playful, candid, and romantic expressions in couples' epistolary exchanges. Consistent with larger cultural shifts throughout the nineteenth century that increased women's options in social roles, employment, and childbearing and expanded how they imagined their identities, women often expected far more than a secure match in marriage; they desired partnerships that would provide happiness. The dominant ideal of romantic love rose in the nineteenth century to rival economics, religion, and political alliances as factors in marriage choices. Jennie Hall captures the yearning quality of this romantic spirit: "[I] have yet to find the one to whom I could safely confide my happiness for life" (48). While Jennie's letter hints that a strapping young soldier just might be able to provide that safety, it also reflects the broader cultural ideal that "happiness" was increasingly central to women's matrimonial vision.[137]

The emotional intensity of the war stirred this romantic cultural brew, and letters often became its receptacles. Judith Harper suggests that the letters couples exchanged during the war sometimes surpassed in intensity and passion that of prewar and courtship correspondence: "The greater the threat of danger, the more intense were the expressions of love."[138] Emotional investment, in turn, may have intensified the potential satisfaction letters offered their writers.[139] Emotional zeal is occasionally apparent alongside more-cordial and circumspect missives to Lybarger both during and after the war. "My love to you will never fail," one complimentary close reads (74). "My Darling Pet," reads the salutation of another (156). Cousin Rosa's letters practically brim with adoration: "[F]or Edwin I love you as the dearest friend on earth. I think of you by day and dream of you by night. You are continually in my mind, but if the lords will be done I hope the time is not far hence when we will meet again" (39). Soldiers might have appreciated these effusive feminine epistles in the masculine arena of camp life for their reminders of tender normalcy in tumultuous and abrasive wartime.

Although Phrone's willingness to open her heart seems to waver throughout the four-year correspondence, romantic intensity and its corollary issues are at times palpable. Her most striking letter consists of only one line. She asks, "Why don't you answer my letters?" (133). Phrone's terms of address shift distinctly in February 1864, after Lybarger returns to service from his brief furlough in Millwood. She addresses him as "My Dearest friend," and closes with the word "love" for the first time: "With much love I am yours in haste." She writes openly of her feelings and confides that she cried after reading his letter: "[I]t made me feel so badly. I hope you will cheer up and remember there is one living for you alone" (64). Phrone retreats to the safer territory of friendship and mentions other suitors in subsequent letters, however, when Lybarger's writing patterns and affections become unpredictable (57, 75).

The spirit of romance may have inspired soldiers to juggle multiple epistolary relationships. While Phrone was "living for [him] alone" on February 21, 1864, the lieutenant was professing his love to Jennie Hall. After a string of letters, an exchange of photographs, and a promise to visit her in Nelsonville, Ohio, on his return from furlough, the soldier apparently confesses his love to Jennie in a letter dated February 27 (67). He pens this love letter a mere ten days after leaving Phrone in Millwood mourning his absence (64). Jennie returns his affections in a letter dated March 9. She opens with exuberant prose on the glory of spring and its "green fields, sweet birds and bright flowers," which "seem to whisper of happiness and Love." As the letter unfolds, Jennie confides, "I am quite as highly pleased with your (dear letters) and Photo as you could possibly be with mine. Don't you think they have captivated my heart as well as mine have yours? Certainly" (67). She envisions climbing "yonder lofty hill" with Lybarger and "whil[ing] away the hours" reading poetry after the war.

Whether they climbed and whiled may never be known, as this romantic letter from their eight-month correspondence is the last available. Letter 128, dated over a year later, provides the last reference to Jennie by way of a friend: "Jennie desires to see you and explain her long silence that you may have termed 'night'" (128). Perhaps Jennie had a change of heart after sealing her last letter. Perhaps Lybarger destroyed additional correspondence. Perhaps he discovered the suspicions about Jennie to which the final letter alludes were all too true (67). Their writing relationship ends in mystery, and the soldier continues his correspondence with other women throughout the war and beyond. Indeed, some believed that this was any soldier's due. One enlisted man asserts in a letter home, "Clemmie she must learn that a soldier has the right to write to all the ladies they can."[140]

Both Northerners and Southerners recognized the novelty and promise of wartime romance. Prolific diarist Mary Chesnut wrote that "flirtation is the business of society . . . spurred on by idleness and a want of any other excitement." One woman of her acquaintance believed "war leads to lovemaking. . . . [T]hese soldiers do more courting here in a day than they would do at home, without a war, in ten years."[141] Romance was one arena in which conspiring with the enemy—at least for men—was sometimes an acceptable practice. Ben Stone, making the best of troubled times, seems willing to engage in dalliances with Southern women and encourages Lybarger to do the same. "The Secesh girls are quite nice and very friendly," he writes in May 1863; "I dont believe they would very seriously object to have a kiss or a hug from a 'fed' as they call us. I have heard that Memphis is a great place for pretty women. I guess you know" (19). For Lybarger, a Unionist and lifelong Republican, Stone's friendly coaxing may have held little appeal. While some suitors view congruent political allegiances as a requirement for romance, Stone considers politics to be irrelevant to a little wartime flirtation. These varying stances toward romance parallel scholars' arguments that civilians and soldiers had varied levels of investment in the political positions of their respective sides.[142]

Some women were not as understanding as their male counterparts about romantic traffic across political borders. Some writers espouse Union identification as a prerequisite to their interest in a man. Women pose the masculine appeal of "true" Unionists against Abolitionists, Copperheads, and "home cowards." "O Ed," Phrone expresses, "tell Frank Hogston that all the girls around are in love with him for his true patriotism. He acted so manly at the Ballet Box when all his friends were Copperheads—he waved a Brough ticket and said that was his vote, and we all respect him for it" (4). Hogston's support of Governor Brough heightened his appeal, just as Copperheadism rendered others unattractive. "It is a disgrace to the 4th of July," Emma Peterman writes of local men's behavior, "[to have] any amount of drunk men shouting for Jeff Davis" (25). Mollie Ward similarly dismisses the "deep dyed Copperheads" in Brandon, Ohio, who are "traitors to their country and their God," insisting that "they are not patronized a great deal by the Ladies and not at all by me. If I have anything to do with the gentlemen I want them to be lovers of their country, not traitors or cowards" (45). Emma Moody concurs. "Ed," she writes in 1862, "if you ever hear of me maring an Abolition or a home coward you will please tell me of it for if there is any I dispise it is these two classes of men" (3). Military rank sometimes intensified the allure of a Union man. One woman comments, "It is grand to get a Colonel" (33). Phrone jokes, "You know those shining appeletts will captivate" (5).

At times, distance and nostalgia may have fueled the romantic imagination and reframed the romantic possibilities of the home front. Millwood women sometimes express surprise on hearing from Lybarger, a pattern that suggests soldiers might have sought varied contacts to encourage a steady stream of correspondence and to keep romantic options open. Ella Rightmire writes in 1863, "I might say that I was rather surpized when I received your letter. But I am pleased to know there yet exists one spark of remembrance which has caused you to spend a few moments of time endeavering to converse with one that I thought you had forgotten" (24). Nineteen-year-old Ella, who was reputed to have a fondness for dancing, attracted the interest of at least one other member of Company K. Private Samuel Williams apparently proposed to Ella, probably in jest, via the mail (17).[143] Perhaps striving not to be outdone, Lybarger wrote to Ella within a month of hearing this news. Ella's solitary letter suggests that "a spark of remembrance" was insufficient to sustain correspondence on either side, and by December of that year, John Hammond had claimed her attention (57).

In a culture of romance sustained through script and the power of imagination, a full mailbox had implications for identity and social reputation at home and at camp. Public discussion of letters, the details of enclosed photographs, the number of letters, and the duration of correspondence all could testify publicly to the recipient's ability to attract and sustain attention from members of the opposite sex. Receiving letters from soldiers gestured to women's patriotism, femininity, and desirability as a correspondent. The fragility of such perceptions is evident, as many a writer attributed men's delay in responding to waning interest rather than the obvious demands of the battlefield. Jennie Hall expresses as much: "So long a time had elapsed since I wrote you that I had almost come to the conclusion I did not perhaps come up to your idea of a Lady correspondent" (44). This concern seems disproportionate to the mere month passing between letters during wartime but may be a common experience for beaux hovering near mailboxes. Phrone is uncertain how to explain similar lapses in correspondence. After a two-month gap between letters in the fall of 1863, she expresses her disappointment to Ed "that you have neglected or forgotten me—perhaps both. You have not answered my letter, although I wrote to you so long ago" (52). "Darn you," she responds more fiercely in 1864 to his claim that he answers all his letters, "You tell a story. You do not write me as many [letters] as I do you, let alone answer them" (105).

Phrone may have had reason for concern. Between her letter of September 25 and her next on November 27, Lybarger likely received eight letters from four different women and exchanged photographs with at least one of them. Two additional letters from other women, dated November 28 and December 3, followed shortly afterward. Yet these epistolary entanglements clearly did not occupy all of Lybarger's time. On October 18, 1863, Fuller's Brigade began a twenty-six-day march from Memphis to Prospect, Tennessee, with the intent of relieving the Army of the Cumberland. They marched between eighteen and twenty miles a day, experienced a week of rain while camped on the Tennessee River, and trudged into Prospect on November 13. Although December and January letters indicate that the lieutenant related details of the march to multiple correspondents (54, 58), remaining dry and finding food undoubtedly overshadowed letter writing in importance.

Just as romance blossoms through the pages, so does jealousy. Women perceive Southern belles' proximity to Union soldiers as one source of threat. Rosa rebukes Lybarger: "Edwin dont get to deep in love with those secesh Ladies down there for if you do you will have me on you" (39). Phrone delivers harsher words on the same topic: "If I was close to that sesech lady you are in love with, I think her stay in this world would be very short—as I feel exceedingly jealous" (4). Romantic skirmishes emerged in imagination and in print.

Knox County sometimes seems a hotbed of romantic tensions, as women write of social visits, flirtations, and Lybarger's varied textual ties. "I am aware," one writer remarks, "that you have quite a number of correspondents that will keep you posted" (55). Although the writer offers this comment in passing, it indicates the public discussion of correspondence that contributes to shaping how letters are perceived, circulated, and received. Louise Welker also recognizes the lieutenant's other epistolary commitments but dismisses their importance: "I dont care, I want to hear from you anyhow" (12). Phrone is not so accommodating. "I do not allow any one save myself to love you," she writes in June 1864, "but allow every body to respect you as deeply as they please" (92). Despite Phrone's possessive tone, she peppers her letters with references to socializing and flirting with other men.

The tensions that arise among women reveal the complexity of pursuing romantic relationships through letters. First, Ell Hawn and Phrone compete for the lieutenant's attention (13, 26, 34), and later, Phrone becomes angry over a series of statements Lybarger allegedly made to Lib Baker (84, 87, 92, 98). "Do you and Ell correspond yet?" Phrone challenges late in 1862. "Don't think me impudent but I just want to know for everytime I receive a letter from you she gives me one of those snearing laughs as much as to say that you are no friend

of mine. I know that she is not my friend although she pretends to be"
(4).[144] Friction intensifies in Millwood while each woman writes to the
soldier states away. Ell eventually bows out of the correspondence in
August 1863, with Lybarger's encouragement. Her final letter's circuitous style and bewildered tone indicate her dashed hopes for their
relationship (34). Her comment, "[I] close by subscribing yourself ever
my friend. But no longer my Lover," remains potent today. Phrone
quotes that line a year later as if she has read Ell's letter (68). Conflict
between the women surfaces again in 1865 when Ell apparently reads
some of Phrone's letters that Lybarger sent home to preserve and feels
insulted by their contents (121).

Phrone's epistolary anger later shifts to Lib Baker. Following a
series of mysterious interactions, she charges Lib with lying and issues
Lybarger an ultimatum: "If now you would rather correspond with
her than with me you can do so, for as true as I write it you can not
under the circumstances write both of us at the same time" (87). She
repeats her warning a month and a half later: "[Y]ou had better cease
your correspondence or else I can not certainly think you the kind of
a friend that you have professed to be to me" (98). Regardless of
Phrone's position on the matter, Lybarger continued to write to Lib
over the following two years as she rushed from painting class to literary society to schoolroom (97). Whether Phrone knew of their contact is unclear, but the soldier clearly valued his relationship with Lib,
as they exchanged letters until 1867. Lybarger also risked Phrone's
displeasure on other occasions. Once he asks Phrone for information
on "his lady friends," at times he seems "cool," and as already noted,
he apparently lapsed in corresponding with her for weeks at a time
(105, 142, 150).

Writing and Reputation: "Blush to the Faces"

The propriety of correspondence between the sexes had long been a
matter of public debate, given its historical association with romantic
love. In the eighteenth century, private letters between men and women

were associated with "seduction" and with man's "encroachment on a woman's chastity" through "encroachment on [her] consciousness."[145] To write to a woman was viewed as an act of pursuit; to write to a man, an indication of receptivity. The intrigue of women's written intimacies apparently led one Ohio postmaster to violate post office laws by opening and reading their letters.[146] The occasional misgivings about corresponding with the opposite sex, particularly strangers, that women express in the letters indicates the practice remained a delicate matter in the nineteenth century. "As you say," Jennie Hall admits, "there is a great deal said and written against replying to these army correspondents, and if what were written were true and the argument plausible it would put the blush to the faces of we who may have answered the same" (51). In true ladylike form, Jennie's reference to a blushing response undermines any accusation of questionable character that a critic might level against letter writers.

Writing about worry—and worrying about writing—were understandable reactions given the social norms women were negotiating in epistolary relationships: propriety, reputation, concern for their economic futures, and the courtship circumstances of the war that bound romantic labor primarily to the pen. Jennie Hall expresses hesitantly the notion that "a gentleman" might not "form a very exalted opinion of a young lady who would reply to an advertisement but I sincerely hope that no such thoughts have entered your mind" (51). Adherence to gendered propriety in a well-crafted letter was a primary form of self-representation for those who wished to create a good impression from afar. Mollie Ward writes that a letter's "contents impressed me deeply . . . from the fact that it bore the marks of having been written by a gentleman of more than ordinary intelligence" (32). One writer suggests that epistolary quality is sufficiently powerful to assuage concerns about behavior. After questioning Captain Rhodes's choice of lady companions, for example, Phrone uses his correspondence to reevaluate his character: "The note he wrote me shewed for itself that he was not only gentlemanly, but also very intelligent" (57). Attention to epistolary etiquette may have been particularly important when writing to strangers.

Correspondents struggle with the limits of what pen and ink can reveal about their authors. Just as pseudonyms can hide the "real" identity of letter writers, so too can letters shield and falsely assert any number of qualities of the writer such as age, physical attributes, and marital status, depending on the perceived interest of suitors. At times writers seem suspicious and at others quick with assurances. "If . . . you . . . doubt the truth of what I may have told you . . . *time* will remove them *all*," Jennie Hall insists (51). Although Lou describes her letters as her "thoughts" (103), claiming a degree of synthesis between embodied writer and her product, she also acknowledges that writers ultimately retain control over which elements of an authentic self appear in their writing. "I know you only as a letter-writer," she admits in 1864; "if you are anything less than a gentleman your letters do not discover the fact to me, and you have the same method of forming an opinion of me" (66). Because letters are superficial, they are limited vehicles to access truth. Lou later returns to the same subject: "you wrote some time ago that you did not know who I was which was very true. Do you know anything more now? How can an unknown correspondent be more interesting than your intimate friends[?]" (96). Lou's questions indicate her awareness that disrepute or connivance might lurk behind the pen, and a letter will not betray it. Letters thus facilitate "knowing," but they cannot ensure it.

Lib rejects altogether the idea of letters as adequate testimonials to character. She declines to correspond with Lybarger's friend and company member Captain Rhodes, despite the distinction of his title and Lybarger's praise. "His was a good letter," she assures her friend in 1864, "[but] knowing that a nicely written and composed letter is not sufficient proof of a man's respectability I refrained from writing" (70). Indeed, the use of pseudonyms in letter writing, the tendency for pairs to place advertisements, and soldiers' occasional practice of having friends write letters for them suggests that Lib's concerns were well grounded.[147] That writers could control what they included and omitted made letters potential vessels for deception.

Despite this potential, some correspondents imagined letters as extensions of the living, breathing individual who penned them and as proxies for the writer's physical presence. The threats inherent to war may have intensified the power that letters held in this regard. In Karen Lystra's study of love letters, couples often anthropomorphized letters from their amours as if the slip of paper were an extension of the absent intimate. They read letters in private, kissed them, carried them around, and conversed with them. One lover wrote to his wife, "I kissed your letter over and over again . . . and gave myself up to a carnival of bliss before breaking the envelope."[148] While such fervent reactions do not surface in the Lybarger collection, Phrone does describe letter writing in anthropomorphizing terms and claims to compose her letters alone. Over the years, she writes by moonlight, by candlelight, on porch steps, in empty schoolrooms, and at her kitchen table while the relationship between her sister Joss and Frank Israel blossoms in the next room. On a snowy night in March 1864, she shares her feelings about writing: "I am alone tonight yet not lonely. My thoughts are very pleasant companions, but my pen is my best friend, for by its means I can hold sweet conversation with my absent friend" (71). The pen enables "sweet conversation" with the lieutenant as if he were sitting beside her. Writers sometimes grant the page the power of embodied personhood.

Similarly, as if Lou's slips of paper were veritable pieces of her body and soul, she tries everything in her written power to impel her correspondent to return her letters and photographs. She takes Lybarger to task for failing to comply despite repeated requests. In one of the most remarkable letters in the collection, Lou delivers two potent lines in 1866 and then fades from the page: "I cannot drive from my mind the haunting anxiety [that you] have possession of [the] letters I sent you. Therefore, will you [have] the kindness to [return] them, if they [are still] in existence, and *particularly* and *especially* and *certainly* the photograph" (147). Although some words in the letter are illegible (and are filled in here with the most likely text), Lou's "haunting anxiety" is sufficient to reveal her investment in these written offerings. Moreover, Lou's fierce underlining for emphasis in an age in which convention deemed the practice improper for genteel writers suggests that the photograph's elusiveness was of particular concern for her.

PHOTOGRAPHY, LIKENESSES,
AND SHADOWS

A thousand thanks to you for that
splendid photograph! It is nothing more
or less than *Edwin-ning.*

—Lib (88)

Please send me your picture taken in
your uniform.

—Rosa (18)

Photographs played particular roles in the romantic work of war correspondence. Like letters, photographs had both cultural and individual significance during the War Between the States. Cousin Rosa's
request, "Please send me your picture," was common among correspondents. Fifty-six letters in the collection refer to photographic portraits, likenesses, and shadows; many refer to them multiple times.
These references speak to the increasing cultural importance of photographs during this historical period as well as their importance to
individuals as tangible reminders of friends and loved ones during the
war (54). Had the war erupted a mere fifteen years earlier, such portraits would not have been readily available to provide this comfort. A
shift from the earliest form of photography, daguerreotypy, to mechanically reproducible photographs in the 1850s ushered in new possibilities for imagining identity and relationships in the latter half of the
century. For the first time in history, photographic images could be re-
produced and distributed en masse, offering opportunities for sustaining allegiances in new and different ways.[149] The 35,000 photographs
that Mathew Brady snapped during the war indicate the increasing use
of this visual medium, particularly in the North, where photographic
technology and use developed more rapidly than in the South.[150]

As Shawn Michelle Smith argues in *American Archives*, the techni-
cal power to reproduce photographic images enabled Americans to
think of themselves and others in new ways by linking individuals in
an "imagined visual community."[151] The potential for photographs to

foster personal relationships as well as American identities had particular importance during the Civil War. Part of this power stemmed from the meanings that viewers attributed to photographic images as their circulation increased. Terms that appear in the letters such as *likeness, shadow,* and *photographic portrait* are often used synonymously to refer to the same basic object, a photograph, once images became reproducible mechanically after 1850. However, some photographic artists distinguished between mere photographic "likenesses" and artistic "portraits." The term *likeness* referred to an image that reflected a person's physical features whereas a portrait or photograph captured a more artistic rendering of the character, depth, and essence of a human being.[152] Correspondents' descriptions of photographs in the Lybarger letters suggest that they often viewed images with these greater character elements in mind (49).

Photographs fostered American identities by inviting civilians to imagine their destinies linked with men in far-off battlefields and reminding soldiers for whom they were fighting. Indeed, starry eyes may have motivated Rosa Crum's request for her handsome cousin's photo "in uniform," but his patriotic image also had the power to color her gaze with glints of red, white, and blue. The "rituals" of "photographic self-representation" became "increasingly standardized" as the practice of photography expanded so that subjects posed and adorned themselves according to established norms. These familiar features signaled viewers to imagine connections with those represented in photos and read bodily cues for a sense of interior "depth" and "essence." During the Civil War, these features could inspire nationalistic spirit. Such exterior elements as a uniform and a sober expression in the photograph of a soldier could intimate an "honorable" and "patriotic" interior essence, evoking sentimentality in the viewer and reinforcing a sense of shared nationalism. A stranger examining Lybarger's photograph felt inspired to write him in March 1865 because she "considered the face . . . an honest looking one and . . . we were both friends to the same cause" (120). As civilians and soldiers gazed into photographs across the miles, they sometimes imagined patriots in the images.

Photographs fostered personal relationships in varied ways, from providing comforting reminders of loved ones to nourishing budding romances. At a basic level, photographs functioned simply as likenesses, reminding individuals of familiar features and expressions of absent friends and family members. Thanking her cousin for his most recent photograph, Rosa comments, "I was delighted indeed to get your Photograph as I knew that other one did not look like you with those large eyes" (79). Similarly, a young woman who had grown up with Ed but had not seen him for a while reported after seeing his likeness that "although you have changed still I could tell it was Ed" (33). More significantly, photographs could tie individuals together in a "cult of remembrance."[153]

As with letters, correspondents sometimes imagined photographs as actual physical extensions of their beloved, standing in as objects to view, kiss, and touch in their absence. This function as intimate placeholder was sometimes quite explicit. Jennie Hall expresses, "I think friend Edwin your picture is sweet enough, and so sweet, that I shall be tempted to . . . k[iss it]" (48). Though her writing is illegible here, another letter from the Civil War era hints to the sentence's possible closure. As a wife reads her husband's letter, she writes, "I pressed to my lips over and over the spot that yours had touched and tried to imagine I could feel your own precious lips & that dear moustache."[154] Rosa seems more resigned to the inadequacy of photographs and letters to substitute for the soldier. She writes, "I was proud to see I had such a handsome cousin, but would [be] better pleased to see the original" (79). She personifies her own photograph: "I am going to have my negative taken tomorrow and next time I write look out for me. I often come down that way. Went down to Memphis last week and expect to go that way . . . again" (132). This perception that photographs retain traces of their embodied subjects may explain Phrone's concern at one point that Ed had given her photo away to John Hawn. It seems to raise the question, is her photo and personhood of so little value that it could be bandied about? Photographs, however inadequate, helped to hold the place of loved ones.

For correspondents engaged in the tenuous work of building romantic ties through letter writing, photographs also fueled the romantic imagination. For unknowns, photographs could hold great sway. Rosa shares a friend's reaction after seeing the soldier's image: she "sends her best respects to you. . . . [S]he would like to be acquainted with you for she knows you are all right" (94). Jennie describes her re-action to his photograph in more animated terms: "If you could have been an unseen observer of my countenance as I opened your letter and beheld the 'Photo' my eyes certainly did sparkle with delight. The frank open countenance, the intellectual forehead, the bright expressive eye—how was I going to say—burned my hand, and if, you will allow me the expression, made a complete conquest" (48). No soldier could have been disappointed with this enthusiastic endorsement of his image. Jennie's romantic imagination springs to life as she ascribes depth, essence, and character to the flat black-and-white image of a man she has never met: the forehead that is "intellectual," the countenance that is "open" and "frank," the eye that is "expressive." The photograph, in lieu of the man himself, "made a complete conquest." Also notable is Jennie's claim that Lybarger's photograph evokes a physical reaction. Women described their physical features only occasionally in this col-lection and more rarely used corporeality as a vehicle to express enthu-siasm. Jennie's gushing description of her "sparkling" eyes and her "burning" hand invites photograph viewer and owner to dissolve miles in their imaginations, conjure images of their correspondent's physical features, and experience photographs as physical extensions of the per-son represented.

Photographs, like letters, fostered personal relationships by testi-fying publicly to connections with a given soldier. Not only were pho-tographs frequent topics in social and community gatherings, but these interactions were often relived on the pages of personal correspon-dence. "I shant tell you the compliments my Painting teacher past on your 'photo,'" Lib writes in the summer of 1864, "'twould flatter you too much I fear" (88). In her enthusiastic thanks for his visage she also alludes to its public and romantic role. She writes, "a thousand thanks to you for that *splendid Photograph*! It is nothing more or less than *Edwin-ning*. Don't wonder much that Miss Phrone found place in her Album for 'three' similar ones" (88). With a witty flourish, Lib affirms the power of the photograph—or three in Phrone's case—to testify to affection. Indeed, requests for photographs sometimes held a competi-tive and urgent air. After seeing a photograph sent to his mother,

Phrone chastises him: "Ed, I think you might have some Photographs printed and send me one in return for the one I am sending you" (21). Similarly, Rosa closed with the "expectation of seeing your picture soon" (20). A matter of etiquette and an emblem of connection, portraits helped to sustain relationships during the war.

As steps in the dance of romance, women sometimes used photos as tools of flirtation and as symbols for their own favors. Spunky Lou exchanged banter with Lybarger for nearly seven months before acceding to repeated requests for her image. Once she enclosed audaciously in its stead "as good a likeness of myself as I can draw" (50), a gift that provided much sport in subsequent letters and among members of Company K (63). Jennie used photos to quickly establish the boundaries of intimacy. She declares in her second letter, "Of course, I should not feel at liberty to send my shadow until I have received yours. Therefore you know the terms by which you can receive mine" (38). Her third letter reflects greater daring in her promise of something "sweet" in exchange for the lieutenant's portrait: "I promise that you shall have mine by and by. So please send yours in your next letter and then I have something sweet to tell you which is worth knowing— something real interesting—something that will do to dream about. I might forget to tell you unless you send the shadow" (44). Such teasing seems intended to entice Lybarger's interest and encourage his attentions. Similarly, Phrone uses photographs to remind her correspondent that her social life has not fizzled away in his absence. Hoping for his promised photograph to arrive, she writes, "I have quite a fine lot of pictures and I would be so proud to have yours among them" (35). Through references to her collection of photos, Phrone reminds Lybarger that he is vying with other men for her affections.

Although members of both sexes exchanged photographs, the photographs of women carried different meaning than those of men. Certainly, like letters, photographs could symbolize men's and women's appeal as companions and correspondents. A soldier with more mail and more photographs might garner esteem among his company members, while photographs of soldiers might attest to women's desirability and patriotism. However, women sometimes believed that the manner in which their photographs, unlike images of men, were exchanged mattered for their reputation. As if woman and photograph were the same, women voiced concerns that circulating their image would expose them to the gaze of strangers and threaten their social standing. "You will allow," Jennie Hall writes, "that with gentlemen it is different. There will be no impropriety in your sending a Photo" (44).

The letters provide support for Smith's argument that mechanical reproduction contributed to a woman's anxiety about the "inability to control the reception of her photographic portrait as it circulates beyond the bounds of intimacy."[155] "To be candid with you," Jennie observes, "I don't think any gentleman would have a very exalted opinion of a Lady who would send a picture to a stranger" (44). Another writer jokes, "I have [no photos] at present, presume I could not induce one to go if I had, as they have a great antipathy of going into the Army" (127). Sharing a photograph too liberally might sully a woman's reputation.

Writers expected a certain degree of etiquette in exchanging photographs that, if violated, inspired judgment and censure of the woman herself. In response to Lybarger's apparent request for her likeness, Mollie Ward declines to comply. "I should consider it very imprudent for any *lady* to give her picture to a person she had never seen although it is no uncommon thing in this fast age. Should we become better acquainted and should we both live to meet here on earth and then if I deemed you worthy of my thoughts your request should be granted but for the present the matter will have to remain as it [is]" (32). Mollie emphasizes the word *lady* as if to distance herself from other women whose photographs (and perhaps morals) flow more freely "in this fast age" than decorum demands.

Even forthright Lou held fast to social norms in this regard, indicating that she perceived photographs as more intimate offerings than letters: "If you are [married] however you are perfectly welcome to the fun [of correspondence], but not to my shadow" (50). Later, she asks Lybarger repeatedly to return the photographs shared in their early writing years. "I disapprove," she states reprovingly, "of the practice which many ladies have of giving their photographs to gentlemen, do not think it is proper, and never did give my photo to any gentleman—never gave it to you—now will you return it" (90). To Lou, the offering of a woman's photograph seemed equivalent to inviting an improper degree of intimacy. As if the object contained elements of her soul, character, even body, a woman was sometimes judged through the way in which she bestowed or withheld her photographic image.

With or without photographs, women at times created "snapshots" in their letters that speak to the social norms governing standards of attractiveness for women and the role that physical appeal played in the romantic work of letters. Superlative authorities on middle-class femininity such as *Godey's Lady's Book* alerted women to social norms needed to fashion their bodies and behavior. "The graces accommodate themselves little to labor, perspiration and sunburning," espouses one *Godey's* author, "severe and long-continued labor . . . deforms the . . . cellular substance which contributes to the beauty of their outline, and of their complexion."[156] Men and women alike absorbed such norms. For some soldiers, Wiley claims, "femininity" was highly regarded, "robustness" was "objectionable," and "big feet were almost disqualifying."[157] With such clear dictates, little wonder that Jennie Hall claims a brunette complexion and graceful figure (38); yet Grace Nello acknowledges outright her "homely" physical features (72), and Lou Riggen poses briefly as a large-nosed, red-haired, freckle-faced girl to toy with Lybarger (40). Jennie, too, expresses some preference for "manly beauty" and the character elements that "fill the bill" of masculine perfection (48).

Grace seems to recognize the importance of women's attractiveness given that, unlike other writers, she announces immediately and without solicitation her perceived feminine inadequacies: "I am a 'Buckeye' girl, and as homely as a 'hedge fence.' I am 19 years of age, five feet four inches in height, and—and—as I said before, homely! But, notwithstanding all this, I am a true friend of the Soldier" (72). That this "true friend's" letter is the only one in the collection indicates that either her claim of "hedge-fence" homeliness or her barrage of requirements that men neither chew tobacco, drink liquor, nor use profane language may have deterred further contact. This is the last we hear of forthright, plucky Grace.[158]

Correspondents relied on epistolary aesthetics, descriptions, and enclosed photographs to evaluate a writer's physical appeal. Lybarger sometimes requested descriptions from correspondents, to which Lou responds with characteristic flair and Jennie with a degree of feigned humility. "Complete description indeed," Lou writes as Fannie Jerome, "red hair, freckled face, nose more prominent than any other feature—unless it be the mouth, eyes squinted—O horrible! You have thrown the letter down" (40). She follows this dramatic description with a flippant reference to women who wear size ten gloves before revealing herself to be a "very plain girl" with "gray eyes." In contrast, Jennie offers a feminine disclaimer and a bevy of superlatives: "Well really [a description] is something I have never attempted, and I fear I shall make a terrible blunder if I attempted such a thing—but here goes" (38). She then lists black hair that curls beautifully; a round face; a slender, neat, and graceful form; and her "kind, generous, warmhearted, confiding, social, lively and very talkative" spirit (38, 44).

The letters following Lou's and Jennie's submission of photographs to Lybarger suggest that attraction mattered in the epistolary work of wartime romance. The soldier seemed to react very differently to the women's images. Jennie writes in 1863 that she wishes him to "allow me to return you many, very many, thanks for the flattering compliments you have so wordily passed on my shadow. I was not vain enough to imagine you would admire it for it's only a plain looking picture" (51). Her writing becomes more effusive as she warms to the soldier's praise. In contrast, after Lou at last relents to requests for her picture (81), it seems to evoke a much different response (85). The letter Lou writes two weeks later suggests that after Lybarger received her picture, he wrote quickly to dispel any misunderstandings about their writing relationship. Her response is brief, sarcastic, and firm. It reads, "You 'hope I will not deceive myself in regard to your intentions!' Thank you. I hope you will attribute to me at least a modicum of common sense. That you should be so solicitous for the state of my mind as to devote a whole sheet to the purpose of preventing my being deceived about—I don't know what—is really magnanimous. My gratitude is unbounded" (85). Her indignant tone and the soldier's clarification of relationship boundaries does not impede their correspondence; Lou and Lybarger's "interesting and interested" relationship survives throughout the war and beyond (103).

These examples reveal that building relationships through letter writing was a tenuous undertaking fraught with maneuvering, performance, and hope. Letters and photographs functioned as inevitable but inadequate proxies for their writers even as correspondents recognized the limits of what writing could reveal. Letters protected writers with distance and offered avenues to experiment with epistolary personas. For soldiers, letters offered interest and intrigue to "pass away the lonely hours of camp life." And for women, letters offered a concrete avenue by which to forge and sustain connections across the miles that for some might increase the possibility of attaining a secure economic future. Indeed, as is revealed over the course of the letters in the collection, one correspondent attained that security with Lybarger after he returned to Millwood in 1865.

WOMEN AND EDUCATION

> I intend commencing my school next Monday. *O! horror*, how I hate it. I would just as soon go to my grave the first week.
>
> —Phrone (52)

The "horror" that Phrone expresses at the idea of walking into a schoolroom points to the complex relationship that individual women have had with the teaching enterprise since the profession first cracked, then threw open its doors to admit them. While many teachers have found joy and empowerment in seizing the reins of the classroom, others (such as Phrone) have found trudging to the podium little cause for enthusiasm. Perhaps hoping for the lieutenant to whisk her away from it all, Phrone characterizes teaching as a burden rather than an opportunity to attain personal liberation or to facilitate the moral development of youth.[159] These feelings, however, do not prevent her from laboring in the role and passing her skills to her sister. She writes in December 1863, "Joss is coming up this afternoon. I think I will show her how to teach a spell" (57).

Whether with reluctance or relish, Phrone, Lou, Lib, and other writers were among the thousands of women whose presence in schools contributed to changing formal education and the teaching profession over the course of the nineteenth century. A remarkable demographic shift that occurred in the history of American education was the feminization of teaching. In the early 1800s, men constituted the majority of teachers in the country. By the close of the century, those figures had been completely reversed: women held 70 percent of teaching positions in America's schoolrooms and as much as 90 percent in cities. That women were excluded from formal education and the teaching occupation almost entirely before 1800 makes the breadth of the change from males to females, and its longevity, even more noteworthy.[160] In the letters, teaching is the only form of professional work that women mention performing (66).

Scholars have attributed this shift in teaching demographics to a variety of factors. Some interpretations point to positive forces spurring women's presence at the lectern: the development of common schools; increased educational access, literacy, and print; increased opportunities for women in the public sphere; and women's leadership in the benevolence, abolitionist, and women's rights movements. Other interpretations of women's rise to numerical dominance in teaching paint a less progressive picture. The low cost of women's labor, the comparatively low status of teaching, the perception that women's maternal and moral "nature" was ideal for guiding youth, and the exigencies of hiring women once the Civil War drained the teaching ranks of its men are additional explanations scholars offer for the rise of the female teacher. These explanations point to economics and essentialism rather than to progressive social ideas as key forces. The war was certainly a powerful engine of change for Ohio women. During the war years, Ohio women gained numerical parity with men and achieved the majority in the teaching profession, which they have held since then.[161]

Women who wrote to Lieutenant Lybarger clearly benefited from increased educational access, the stretching of social boundaries, and the greater occupational choices that developed over the century. One complex effect of the war for some of the nation's women in both the North and the South was that it propelled them into social roles, material circumstances, and identities that they may not have imagined previously. As a hospital worker reflecting on her service expressed, "are we not all soldiers?"[162] To different degrees and in varying ways, women rallied to perform duties previously deemed men's domain, which included slipping into schoolrooms that soldiers left vacant.[163]

Women's varying facility with prose, mechanics, and erudition suggests the "mere smattering of education" some Knox County girls received in the common schools and other obstacles they may have faced in their educational pursuits.[164] Rosa's, Lou's, and Phrone's attention is often claimed by domestic work that must be negotiated with schoolbooks and war work: laundry, sewing, cooking, and caring for ill family members (33, 106). "Don't I know how to boil & bake & fry & stew & roast beef & biscuit & pork & light bread & 'season to taste,'" Lou writes in 1864 (106). Mollie Ward has similar responsibilities that interfere with reading: "[Mother] has been sick over three weeks and the principal part of the care of the household rested upon my shoulders. . . . I have been so busy I have scarcely found time for reading the news" (53).

Socioeconomic class, family circumstances, and geography affected women's household responsibilities and their ability to pursue formal education consistently. Rosa, for example, mentions the daily responsibilities of washing, sewing, cooking, and caring for her younger brothers. As a teenager whose mother had recently died, she bears significant responsibility for sustaining the household. Washing alone would have meant a full day of work hauling water from a spring or well, heating it over a wood or coal stove, maintaining the heat source, and using a hand wringer to shift clothes from thirty-five-pound washtubs to rinse tubs. School lessons may have seemed delightful in comparison to this arduous labor. The 1860 census reflects fifty-six women in Millwood over the age of twenty who could not read or write and others of school age who did not attend in the previous year. Even those who did attend, as seven of eleven children did in Ell Hawn's family in 1860, might have done so erratically, given the need for their farming labor. Erratic school attendance may explain the struggle with writing mechanics and expression evidenced in Ell's letters. Indeed, families would have needed young women for any number of farm tasks, as Ohio continued to be heavily agrarian and a major producer of corn, wheat, and wool even as industrialization began in the state in the 1850s. In 1860, Knox County was one of twenty-three counties in the state with a cash value in farms of over $10,000,000 and nearly 200,000 improved acres of land. In Millwood, farming is listed as the primary occupation in 1860.[165]

Despite some unevenness in letter writers' skill level, the letters document a literate group of writers who seem by and large to have benefited from print culture and basic education. Women refer to schooling, teaching, singing schools, and literary societies. Some letters demonstrate a writer's facility with basic skills. Others display more sophisticated command of the written word, including lines from canonical texts, poetry, and war hymns to articulate feelings about the war. Women's letters also reflect evidence of an aspect of wartime correspondence beyond its war, kinship, and romantic work: letters as an educational force. One writer characterizes letter writing as an act of "improvement." Several women's letter-writing skills improve over the course of the war. Some use letters to summarize their fondness for novels, poetry and particular authors. "I can't read about the greatest men nor the most stirring incidents," Lou admits, "unless I like the author" (106). These examples suggest the varied ways women seized educational opportunities and benefited from educational changes in an age in which women's intellectual capacities were deemed inferior to men's and their education considered of secondary importance to their other roles and responsibilities.

"The People Seem to Want a School"

The development of a tax-supported system of common schools during the 1820s expanded girls' educational opportunities and provided a skill base for teaching.[166] The growth of common schools helped communities offer more-consistent access to basic education, which aided girls of all classes. Private academies and seminaries had been available to girls from upper-class families since the late 1700s, but rural girls commonly did not attend these institutions because of cost and the need for girls' labor at home. In the early 1800s, seminary education could cost four to five dollars per term in addition to room, board, and specialized coursework. In 1861, the Mt. Vernon Female Seminary charged $110.00 per year for boarding, fuel, and instruction in Latin and English. In addition, the girls were required to perform domestic labor for a half hour per day in the home in which they boarded. At a time in which a local singing concert could cost a dime, a hardback book between fifty cents and $1, and gold watches $75, over $100 for schooling may have seemed a hefty sum to pay. Many citizens resisted secondary and higher education for girls and young women and continued to echo the sentiments of a *Godey's Lady's Book* author that "the education which is suited to the male, is not calculated to render the female available and useful in society."[167] Yet as print culture spread, as New Englanders moved west with their conviction in the value of an educated citizenry, and as the number of common schools increased, gender and socioeconomic class began to fade as definitive barriers to girls' educational pursuits.

Ohio was swept up in the common school movement and the democratic spirit of equal educational opportunity. As a Knox County native and Ohio state representative expressed in 1849, "the peculiar form of government under which we live requires an enlightened population to impart those blessings to future generations . . . and whatever can be done we are bound by every motive of philanthropy—by every moral consideration—to do."[168] What this official said of the common schools, Philander Chase, founder of Kenyon College in Gambier, Ohio, had said of colleges more than twenty years earlier. Chase considered colleges to be key vehicles for preparing citizens of all classes for their self-governing roles in a democracy. Although citizens and legislators grappled with how best to actualize—and fund—such ideals, progressive reforms in tax laws, teacher training, and school organization in Ohio (and elsewhere in the country) testify to the prominent place that education held in public thought by midcentury. Lib Baker, who alongside Temperance Darling and Edwin Lybarger received her teaching certificate from the Knox County Board of

School Examiners in March 1861, encountered this spirit in Spring Mountain, Ohio: "[I] would remain during the winter as the people seem to want a school" (161).[169]

Ohioans faced controversial issues related to school reform as they honed their vision of the government's role in forging an educated citizenry. In particular, governing agents struggled to find ways to pay for schools that many taxpayers supported in theory but not always with their pocketbooks. Citizens at midcentury had difficulty following frequent alterations in school laws, and they sometimes objected to paying taxes for schooling other people's children, for schools outside their locality, or for "public" schools saturated with Protestant doctrine when "private" parochial and denominational schools could not receive such funds.[170] Graded schools, school libraries, compulsory attendance, minimum school sessions, tax levies, school board versus township control, and curriculum all surfaced as key issues in public debate. The Ohio School Act of 1853 established a state school tax and designated local townships as the administrative unit for rural schools, which nudged schools closer to fulfilling citizens' educational ideals. At the start of the Civil War, Ohio boasted 13,192 common schools that served 364,000 boys and 322,000 girls.[171]

Although Ohioans did not seem to enroll their girls to the same extent as their boys in any year from 1837 to 1875, and educational opportunities remained circumscribed, females became an increasing presence in private, public, and higher educational institutions throughout the century. Ohio's common schools reflect steady growth in girls' enrollment in nine of eleven years following the 1853 School Act. Gaps in enrollment between girls and boys range from over 40,000 (1852) to 12,000 (1864). Gaps in attendance between girls and boys for the same years decreased from 23,000 in 1852 to 2,500 in 1864.

Several letters in the collection reflect these erratic attendance figures. "I havent went to school any this winter yet," Edith Welker admits in 1862; "I dont think I will like the Teacher very well and therefore I am not in a very great hurry about starting" (11). The next summer she dispenses with the idea altogether: "I do not believe that I will go any more ... for I never could content myself in the school House in the summer" (89). Fannie finds the war too distracting for lessons: "Mae Lydick is at Danville going to School. I intended to go but geve it up. There was so much excitement about war that I could not think of going" (1). Later she seems more certain about her plans: "Our school commences week from tomorrow. I expect I will attend" (6). The war may have diverted many from attending. Although 346,147 girls were enrolled in Ohio schools in 1862, the daily attendance figure for that year was 189,972, with school in session an average of 24.6 weeks.[172]

Private and parochial schools also thrived alongside common schools and expanded women's educational options. In 1859, 135 of these institutions were serving over 16,000 Ohio youths.[173] Female seminaries operated in various areas, including Delaware, Urbana, Cincinnati, and Cleveland.[174] Spring Mountain Academy, opened in 1855 by James Loudon Drake less than twenty miles southeast of Danville, was one such institution near Knox County, calling to Lib and Phrone with painting and music classes and later coaxing Lib with instructional responsibilities (78, 97). High schools were also developed in the 1850s—amid much controversy—and by 1854 grew in number to at least fifty-seven. By 1860, the number of these institutions had reached 161 across sixty-six of the eighty-eight Ohio counties, located primarily in urban areas.[175] Despite perceptions of high schools as "educational luxuries" and public concern that they might instill superior attitudes in their pupils, their growth expanded girls' opportunities. After midcentury, girls constituted the majority of high school students in the country, a pattern true of some Ohio schools as well.[176]

Ohioans also developed dozens of colleges throughout the nineteenth century to serve their growing population and educational vision. By 1860, Ohio had established more colleges than any other Union state.[177] Ohio University and Miami University were two of the first institutions in the state, with Oberlin, Kenyon, Denison, Mount Union, Otterbein, Wilberforce, and others opening between 1820 and 1860. Knox County's Kenyon College, which did not admit women until 1969, was Lybarger's school of choice before the Union cause lured him away. Some of these institutions attracted attention and controversy for their progressive policies of admitting African Americans and other women.[178] Antioch and Otterbein accepted women in the 1850s, and others (such as Ohio Wesleyan) developed companion colleges for women to attend.

Oberlin became the first coeducational institution in the country in 1833 when it admitted women to a "ladies course." It solidified that status in 1837 when four women enrolled in the full collegiate course of study.[179] Although inequities existed in the treatment of Oberlin women, from prohibiting female graduates from participating in graduation exercises to requiring the women to launder male students' clothes and clean their rooms, the college produced an array of social reformers who worked to change the prevailing racism and sexism in society underlying such schooling inequities. Women's rights activists Lucy Stone and Antoinette Brown Blackwell were two such notable pupils.[180]

"I Like to Go Middling Well"

By midcentury, basic education was sufficiently commonplace for Ohio's middle-class women that correspondents seem to relish or begrudge attending school as any young person might, rather than remark on its singularity for women. For instance, Phrone's delight with her male teacher's errors betrays no hint of feminine intellectual inferiority. "You would die laughing if you could hear some of the mistakes he makes in grammar," she discloses, "but he keeps very good order" (14). Schooling pleases Edith for other reasons: "I like to go middling well. I have [a] couple of new studies which keep me pretty busy. I am studying algebra, Rays Higher Arithmetic, Grammar, and Cornell's Geography, beside my reading and spelling" (56). Edith was enjoying texts and subjects commonly taught in Ohio schools at this time.[181] Rosa, perhaps relieved to escape her family responsibilities, takes Latin in the winter of 1865 and appreciates "the study very much" (113). In contrast, Emma Peterman breathes easier when her term ends. "Our school is out and I am most awful glad," she expresses in July 1863, "for me it is to warm to go to school" (25).

Both students and teachers participated in "boarding around," the practice of living with community members while in school. Lib boarded for a few weeks while taking painting lessons (98). Students at Mt. Vernon Seminary boarded with families in exchange for a fee and domestic chores.[182] Phrone reports that she boarded for a time with Mr. Reaghs while teaching in Martinsburg (148). Amelia Lybarger, Edwin's mother, takes a singing teacher as a boarder after her husband dies in April 1864 (78).[183]

The population of Ohio was over 2 million in 1860. With 27,735 residents in Knox County, 1,104 in Union Township, and 870 in Howard Township, teachers in rural areas were mobile and schools were often small.[184] Writers mention class sizes of between 18 and 40 scholars (126, 146). Reflecting a common pattern in the nation overall, many taught on a term-by-term basis and viewed teaching as a temporary occupation. More than one-third of teachers in Ohio's township schools in 1866 were under twenty years of age.[185] Writers' use of teachers' names when referring to schools indicates that some thought of schools less as fixed institutions and more as extensions of those at their helm. "I go to school to Henry McElroy this winter," Phrone writes of her grammatically challenged instructor (14). "I have been going to school to Fannie this summer," another informs Lybarger (89). Another indicates that teachers negotiate multiple roles and community responsibilities: "We have such a good minister at the Presbyterian church now. . . . [He] has a very good school there" (16). Although teachers entered and left the field regularly, writers mention individual teachers in relation to schooling as often as the physical structures in which lessons are conducted.

"Nothing Would Be So Pleasant as to Be a School Maam"

Women's opportunities to become educators blossomed alongside their educational opportunities.[186] Although standards for teachers were erratic, school growth stimulated demand for teachers, and women's increased educational access provided them with a necessary skill base to perform this role.[187] This demographic shift had regional variations. By the 1830s in some New England cities, women had replaced men in the primary schools. The trend in hiring women gained momentum in

Ohio during the 1830s. Although male teachers outnumbered female teachers in Ohio during every year for which figures were available from 1837 until 1862 (some years by the hundreds and other years by as much as four thousand, as in 1842 and 1849), in 1837 women teachers numbered 3,205 in Ohio schools in comparison to 4,757 men. By the time the number of female teachers increased to 5,168 across the state in 1850, one nostalgic Ohio educator reflected on the changes in his institution and remarked that it "could not prosper without a woman."[188] Some Texans, in contrast, resisted this form of "prosperity" in the 1860s and went without teachers for months at a time while school boards continued to seek men.[189]

Teaching may have offered nineteenth-century middle-class women their "first great public profession."[190] Certainly, American women worked before schools opened their doors; indeed, planting and harvesting may well have been women's first great "profession." Women sustained the frontier household; harvested and sold crops; operated mercantile interests with their families; bound shoes; performed "outwork"; and laundered, sewed, and canned for others. Women of color and immigrants often helped white women with their domestic work. Factories welcomed women to their assembly lines as the Northeast began to industrialize: textile, shoe and clothing manufacturers, and later, printers and publishers all employed women.[191] Hiring women was fiscally appealing to factory owners because of women's willingness to work for lower wages than men. By 1860, women numbered 270,000 of such workers, comprising as much as 65 percent of New England's factory labor. In that same year in Ohio, nearly 10,000 women were employed as seamstresses, tailors, milliners, and laborers in the laundry, garment, and paper-box industries, among others. Ohio women taught in nearly the same numbers: 9,693.[192]

Teaching was accorded a degree of middle-class respectability in comparison to other forms of labor, particularly if economic necessity or a husband's death propelled women to step into the role. Some influential educators, such as Emma Hart Willard, Horace Mann, and Catharine Beecher, considered teaching a "natural" extension of women's moral and nurturing qualities. Mann held that, despite women's intellectual inferiority, their gentleness, patience, and tolerance were instrumental for nourishing youth. Beecher spurred lasting changes in education and achieved national prominence in advocating for women as teachers with a similar argument. Beecher argued that women were ideally suited to cultivate future citizens. Teaching is, Beecher said, "woman's natural profession. . . . It is ordained by infinite wisdom, that, as in the family, so in the social state, the interest of young children and of women are one and the same." Through patience, order, and thrift, women had unique power to elevate teaching to a noble profession capable of shaping the very character of the nation. This work, she argued strategically, would elevate the status of women in the process.[193]

Education accrued urgency in this view. Alice Freeman Palmer, who became president of Wellesley College in the 1870s, suggested that uneducated women who did not take their role as moral leaders seriously could damage American youth. "Little children under five years die in needless thousands," she declared, "because of the dull, unimaginative women on whom they depend. Such women have been satisfied with just getting along, instead of packing everything they do with brains, instead of studying the best way of doing everything small or large; for there is always a best way, whether of setting a table, or trimming a hat, or teaching a child to read. And this taste for perfection can be cultivated."[194] Formal education and household manuals became an avenue for "imaginative" women to develop and express such "perfect" skills.

Although the classroom seemed to hold no such imaginative appeal for Phrone, Beecher's vision coaxed others to teaching and contributed to the "culture of professionalism" that emerged among middle-class Americans over the course of the century (68).[195] Managing classrooms provided women a modicum of autonomy, a sense of professionalism, and a broader role in the public sphere. Rosa longs to teach for these very reasons. "I am placed in a situation that is very confining," she admits, "I am all Father has to look to" (152). After sewing since daylight one day in 1865, she confides, "I almost envy you to think you are teaching school. I wish I was there to help you. I would then be in the occupation I have so long desired. It seems to me nothing would be so pleasant as to be a school maam" (145). Phrone also experiences autonomy amid the trials. Although she is often home-sick and laments in 1866, "I get so tired of the noise. I do not feel as if I could live another minute," she enjoys many opportunities Rosa cannot access (148). Phrone lives independently from her family, manages her own classroom, teaches in various locations, and attends social events.

Rosa imagines the teaching occupation as a promising escape from the washing, canning, and sewing that consumes her hours (152, 157). To better prepare for this occupation, she vows, "I will study hard and learn all I can" (141). Phrone and Lib continue to take spelling, writing, and music lessons while teaching (146). Some comments in the letters portend shifts later in the century in which teachers, like lawyers and doctors, began training in their respective fields and adopting markers of expertise to signal their competence and separate themselves from laypeople. The development of normal schools, teaching institutes, rules of conduct, certification and professional associations provided authoritative weight and practical aid for building teaching as a profession. Educators and legislators advocated for funds and facilities to train teachers in Ohio as early as 1837, but few institutions were established until late in the century. By the 1850s county examination boards were in place, and forty-one teachers' institutes trained 3,251 teachers in 1851. Examinations varied in difficulty: for example, in 1871, the Knox County Board of Education accepted all but 3 percent of its certification applicants while Muskingum County evaluators turned away a full 55 percent of its applicants.[196]

"Am Not Much of a Believer in Free Loveism"

Other social forces facilitated women's presence in teaching. Ohio women caught glimpses of activists who were working in visible, collective ways to reform society and advance women's rights.[197] Amelia Bloomer, activist and architect of the controversial "bloomer" costume, published her newspaper *The Lily* in Mt. Vernon in midcentury. Prominent activists such as Catharine Beecher, Frances Dana Gage, and Ernestine Rose lectured locally on social issues. Salem hosted the first Ohio women's rights convention in 1850, and Sojourner Truth gave her famed "Ain't I a Woman" speech at an Akron convention in 1851.[198] The signing of the Declaration of Sentiments in neighboring New York in 1848 marked the beginning of the women's rights movement in America and over seventy years of organized activism to expand women's rights and opportunities. Although the onset of the Civil War diverted the nation's attention to other social and political struggles, activists had gained visibility by midcentury and had established a foundation for the temperance and suffrage efforts that marked Ohio's later years. Women's rights activists worked to raise awareness, change existing laws to better serve women, and establish organizations such as the Ohio Women's Rights Association.[199]

Ohio's women primarily channeled their energies to social causes considered congruent with women's proper sphere. Using the idealized feminine tools of moral suasion, thrift, and sacrifice, women worked to alleviate hunger and poverty in urban areas, to improve conditions for the mentally ill, to spread the gospel, and to advocate for temperance and social purity. Although many Ohio women working for moral reform were indifferent to the percolating spirit of discontent that in time erupted into the women's rights movement, their work to empty whisky barrels and to feed the poor contributed to expanding women's social roles. The presence of even sometimes-reluctant teachers such as Phrone in Ohio's schoolrooms contributed to this expansion as well.

Women also agitated for social reform in more-threatening ways —through the lectern, pulpit, petition, and press—calling propertied men to deliver on the promises of democracy that had thus far been available to only a portion of Americans. Reformers worked for women's right to speak publicly without condemnation, for better working conditions and wages, for temperance, for abolition, for changes in inheritance, property, and divorce laws, and for suffrage. Seneca Falls activists protested the denial of woman's right to an education and to "nearly all the profitable employment." The final declaration addressed this issue: "Resolved, that the speedy success of our cause depends upon the zealous and untiring efforts of both men and women . . . for the securing to woman an equal participation with men in the various trades, professions, and commerce." The first Ohio women's rights convention in 1850 was highly publicized and drew an estimated five hundred people. As in Seneca Falls, women expressed their grievances and resolved to improve women's opportunities. Among these was the goal to "open state endowed colleges to women."[200] Lib's dogged pursuit of education, teaching, and her forthright communication style— "I'm Lib Baker and no body else" (99)—gesture to women's changing social roles.

Lib's remark that she is "not much of a believer in free Loveism" (97) indicates that utopian communities and women's rights issues were sensationalized sufficiently in the press to have caught Knox County women's attention and engendered their disapproval. Activists, who were a minority of Ohio's women, were accused of behavior antithetical to true womanhood, such as practicing "free loveism" and acting like "men women." "A true woman," the *Banner* explained, is one who can "comfort and counsel . . . reason and reflect . . . feel and judge . . . assist [a man] in his affairs, lighten his sorrows, purify his joys, strengthen his principles . . . educate his children."[201] Lybarger's pen pals seem to have understood these norms. These young women may have tromped through the snow, attended Union rallies, climbed onto sleds, caught fish, picked cherries, read sensationalist novels, pursued educational opportunities, and exchanged spirited banter with any number of acquaintances, but they said little in the letters that contradicted norms of "true womanhood."

The letters do reflect women's awareness of the differences between men's and women's spheres of activity and influence. Lou refers directly and repeatedly to gender norms in writing, dressing, eating, and travel (65, 106, 159). Rosa mentions her father's preferences concerning appropriate behavior for women: "Father does not desire me to commence teaching while so young" (145), and she supposes that she "will have to stay home a while longer" (152). However respectfully Rosa couches her comments, she recognizes that both household responsibilities and her father dictate her choices. Similarly, Ell Hawn recognizes that Election Day holds a different meaning for Lybarger than for her: "Today is quite an exciting time for Millwood as you are a male that this is Election day" (15). More than fifty years would have to pass before Ell could legally cast her own vote. Another writer expresses envy for Lybarger's opportunity to visit President Washington's grave, which newspapers report being "thrown open just at the time the grave closed upon Lincoln."[202] She writes, "I should like much to visit the hallowed spot, but as I cant be a soldier suppose I will never have that pleasure" (130). Lou also recognizes the limits of what women can experience and contribute politically: while men are at war, "the ladies, poor things, stay at home and 'hurrah for the Union'" (43). To Lou, mere cheering seems a paltry contribution to a nation at war. Gender limitations evoke fiercer sentiment in Edith Welker. Frustrated at what she sees to be Butternut cowardice and draft dodging, Edith declares, "If I was a man I would stand my ground. If I died by it I would not expose my cowardice that way anyhow. It makes me so mad when I think about it that I wish I had the power" (56). The passage reflects her desire for the agency and power that were available to many men.

Edith's outrage concerning Butternut behavior provides an example of historians' arguments that war circumstances spurred some flexibility in gender norms, yet the line drawn between inappropriate and appropriate female behavior was a fluid and shifting one. Edith's patriotic stridency may have been a welcome, even laudable, quality, but channeling similar passion for the cause of women's rights may have raised eyebrows. Union General William Tecumseh Sherman considered his wife's management of sanitary goods appropriate to her sphere but admonished Ellen for selling such goods in public. "I don't much approve," he wrote in 1865, "of ladies selling things at a table. So far as superintending the management of such things, I don't object, but it merely looks unbecoming for a lady to stand behind a table to sell things. Still do as you please." Modeling feminine ideals might have been particularly important for the wife of a general.[203]

Conceptions of idealized womanhood sometimes followed battle lines and sometimes shifted to reflect new demands the war placed on women. Mary Chesnut marveled at women's perseverance, endurance, and patriotism[204] just as Northern women praised Union women's service in sanitary commissions and hospital work. One Northern hospital worker's assessment of women's labor at the front lines reflects her belief that hard work and sacrifice exemplify the ideals of womanhood during war: "mercy! What do the women at home know of work?"[205]

When Mary Chesnut pointed out the socialized passivity of Southern women to members of her social circle, a friend countered with a critique of the "loud" and "shrill" ways of Yankee women who are quick to fight and divorce.[206]

Gender norms governing women's lives in the nineteenth century are legible throughout women's letters, and women work to align themselves within and sometimes against such mores. Writers laud earnest, competent women and question the character of others who "flit away the hours in idleness and vanity" (27). Phrone characterizes marriage between a seventeen-year-old man and a twenty-five-year-old woman as "one of the awfulest things I ever knew of" (104). Another hints that women's dancing and tobacco use are problematic (16). Teaching seems sufficiently commonplace and consistent with women's "natural" role that it garners none of the commentary that letter writers offer for behaviors deemed less respectable for women (16, 57). Lou highlights the disjuncture between the demands of women's working lives and social ideals of (upper/middle-class) femininity in a flippant response to Lybarger's question, "can I eat my share of a dinner?" Lou queries in return, "could a young lady who ate nothing but white roses and drank the sparkling dew from the delicate morning-glory be guilty of burning her face over a cooking stove[?]" (106). Domestic labor, Lou suggests, demands that women consume more substantial fare than rose petals. Although changing norms throughout the century and war circumstances may have stretched boundaries of acceptable feminine behavior and incited women to new forms of political and social engagement both during and after the war, the degree to which women absorbed and acted upon such beliefs inevitably varied.[207]

"Father Is Away at Work at the Rate of $25.00 a Week"

Cost was another reason school boards turned to women to mold young minds.[208] The gradual increase in hiring women that occurred in the 1830s in the Northeast expanded in other parts of the country in the 1840s and 1850s, in part because employers realized that they could pay women between one-half and one-third of the amount they paid male teachers. Such prospects were welcome in school districts struggling to make ends meet. Reformers justified the common practice of paying women lower wages than men on several grounds. Catharine Beecher argued that women did not have the responsibility to support a family and could afford to work for lower wages. Others believed that women were interested only in teaching temporarily until they married to rear children of their own. Some argued that women's primary interest in teaching was to contribute to the social good rather than make money. Lou's, Lib's, and Phrone's letters bear evidence that contradicts such claims, but these explanations for pay differences were nevertheless common.[209]

Historian Thomas Woody reports that low wages contributed to women's outnumbering men two to one in Massachusetts schools by 1842. At the start of the Civil War, some Ohio women earned $16.25 a month while men earned $27.81 to teach in the common schools, with higher wages at the high school level. In Knox County, where women obtained the majority of teaching certificates in March 1861 and April 1862, women earned less than half of what men earned. For example, the board of education in Mt. Vernon's township, Clinton, noted payments to male teachers ranging between $25.00 and $30.00 per month in 1861. In contrast, Mary Ewalt, Eliza George, and Emma Brown (among other Knox County female teachers) were paid between $10.00 and $12.00 per month. A year later, Ann V. Scott earned the odd amount of $16.66 per month, while Mary E. Turner and Mary F. Parmenter each earned wages of $18.00. Others did not fare even that well. In November 1862, Annie M. Irvine was paid only $10.25 for her month's work. Given that board members were paid $1.00 a day for attending meetings and workers $1.25 for a day of repairs on a schoolhouse, the remuneration of $.33 to $.58 a day for running a schoolroom was comparably quite low.[210] In contrast to these figures, Rosa Crum's father earned the robust wages of $25.00 per week for what may have been construction labor (94).

Knox County wages were remarkably better than the $4.00–$6.00 per month that some Ohio teachers earned and the $6.00–$8.00 per month that seamstresses earned in the 1850s. In addition, Mary Turner's and Mary Parmenter's earnings in Clinton Township exceeded the $15.00

per month that the male teacher at Sand Spring School in Guernsey County, Ohio, had earned a few years earlier. Wages for teachers were frequently less than for unskilled laborers and significantly less than those of male principals, whose salary could top $1,800 per year. However, Ohio teaching wages were comparable to other areas in the North: a teacher in Michigan was paid $4.00 per week while one in Vermont could earn $3.00.[211]

The Civil War was an influential force in the demographic change in teaching in Ohio. An estimated five thousand teachers joined the service, taxes became diverted from schools to war efforts, and college enrollments dropped. School boards turned to women more aggressively to meet the needs of the common schools. In 1860, women constituted 25 percent of the nation's primary and secondary school teachers. By the 1870s, more than half of the nation's teachers were women.[212] By 1880, they constituted 60 percent. Although women were a strong presence in Ohio schools before the war, the shift from male to female teachers occurred during the first years of the war. In 1861, Ohio men outnumbered women teachers by 740; in 1863, women outnumbered men by 3,890.[213] Women held the majority thereafter. Momentum for hiring women increased gradually nationwide until women's presence in the primary and secondary schools became normative rather than exceptional.

Correspondence as Educational Work: "Interchange of Thought"

Women's letters reflect traces of a collateral effect of wartime correspondence beyond its war and romantic work: letters as an instrument of education. Women discuss their reading preferences and learning in letters, use letters as vehicles of improvement, and weave lyrics, poetry, and prose into their writing. Their letters reflect women's engagement with print culture and use of the epistolary form to demonstrate and accelerate their learning. Edith's striking comment on December 19, 1862, hints to this sometimes subtle aspect of correspondence for Northern women distanced from the front lines. She writes, "the Rebels have possession of Frederickburg. I suppose you knew where that is. It is in Virginia" (11). In a brief paragraph, Edith describes Burnside's actions in the battle of Fredericksburg that she gleans from conversation and newspaper reports. She whittles down Burnside's tactical errors and the horrific loss of Union troops to a few lines about the rising river, Rebel possession of the town, and her hopes for Union triumph.

In reality, the battle followed only a few months after agonizing losses at Antietam in September 1862 and a month after President Lincoln removed McClellan from command of the Army of the Potomac. The overcautious McClellan was well loved by many, including Ohio Democrats, but was resistant to Lincoln's orders and maintained a healthy sense of his own importance. Burnside took over as commander of the Army of the Potomac and headed the drive to Richmond. With ribbons of river to cross, Burnside was delayed in advancing, his orders were confusing, and his officers were sluggish in responding; Lee's troops had time to gain a protected position with a clear field of fire. On December 13, 1862, Union men in fourteen brigades were shot in waves as they advanced on Confederates "loading and shooting so fast that their firing achieved the effect of machine guns." Although the *Banner* initially claimed "no real victor" in the battle with Burnside "repelled from across the river with 200,000 men," this battle was one of the worst Union defeats of the war, with 13,000 Union casualties and 5,000 Confederate losses.[214] It occurred six days before Edith penned her letter.

Although the details and nuances of Fredericksburg are absent from Edith's letter, her brief comments glimmer with her new learning about war events through informal educational tools. Edith's language, "I suppose you know where [Fredericksburg] is. It is in Virginia," suggests that reports of war events had the power to open up a geographic world to young women as it did for many a soldier traveling states away for the first time. As noted previously, print, war work, and the losses of men they loved were primary avenues by which many Northern women experienced the war. Print propelled Northern women to imagine and learn about distant locations that were, until this point, perhaps unimaginable and irrelevant to the contours of their daily lives. Edith reads about this place called "Frederickburg" because a battle took place there. She then relates information in a letter to do her part to keep soldiers informed about war events elsewhere.

Correspondence has functioned as an educational force in other ways. Scholars have described the epistolary form as a "long arm of education" because of writers' elaborate rhetorical work to establish connections with the subjects to whom they are writing.[215] Successful communication requires writers to choose their words, content, and writing tone carefully, as they imagine correspondents' reception and interpretation of their words. The act of writing is itself a catalyst for learning; Bell Irwin Wiley and James T. Brenner both note marked improvements in soldiers' writing during the war in the letters they studied. Soldiers who "maintained a considerable flow of correspondence, despite their handicaps," Wiley asserts, "showed decided improvements in style during the course of their service."[216] Writers inevitably mold and hone their products as they accrue experience, encounter new models, and anticipate new recipients.

Women's letters in the Lybarger collection suggest similar improvement. Rosa's first letter in 1862 reads, "Papa received a letter from you daybeforeyesterday stating that you was well and getting along well. As pappa has not time to write I will have to write in behalf of him" (1). In contrast, her final letter, written four years later, reveals mastery of the epistolary form and the flowery prose of period literature: "I have just come from the concert and while all the rest of the family are wraped in sweet repose and perchance having pleasant dreams, I am here this cold still night all alone writing to my cousin with naught to disturb me save the ticking of the old clock" (165). Rosa's diligent approach to her studies, her emotional maturation, and her development as a student likely nourished her writing skill. Yet writing letters to her cousin, other soldiers, and family members undoubtedly contributed as well.

Some women viewed the act of letter writing as a strategic method and informal educational tool to improve their communication skills, literacy, and facility with language. One writer declares self-improvement a specific aim in corresponding with soldiers: "I am a school girl, and the greatest desire of my heart is a good education. I come to the conclusion that by interchange of thought I should be enabled to obtain usfull knowledge" (36). Many criticize their own letters' content and penmanship with promises to improve in future. Women's use of quotations from canonical texts, battle hymns, and poetry reveals their engagement with print culture and use of letters as a vehicle for "interchange of thought."

Lybarger and Lou participate in such interchanges by sharing opinions of literature, poetry, and novels, and comparing and contrasting their authorial and genre preferences. She likes Sir Walter Scott's romances of Scottish life, the *Waverly* novels, and Longfellow's epic poem *Hiawatha*, on the legends of the Ojibway people: "I think of none I like better than Longfellow. His Hyperion has something rare and beautiful on every page and Hiawatha I dearly love" (106). Lybarger seems to think otherwise, and Lou rises in defense of her beloved texts in a letter penned two months later, insisting that "the words flow so musically and the thoughts are in such charming unison with them" (110). Lou lists novels she likes (*Rutledge*) and those of "everlasting" length that she does not care for (*Great Expectations*). She has little interest in Sylvanus Cobb's and Emerson Bennett's dime novel adventure tales and finds Pollock's mammoth religious poem, "Course of Time," "not animated enough" for her tastes (110). She sometimes threads favorite lines and stanzas into her letters. For example, she uses John Keats's epic poem *Endymion* to characterize her photograph: "a thing of beauty is a joy forever" (81) and expresses her pleasure in Tennyson's description of smoke: "the warm-blue breathings of a hidden hearth" (163).

Some writers reflect on themes of sacrifice prominent in Civil War battle hymns to empathize with soldiers in their patriotic duty. Phrone mentions learning the melancholy ballad, "Bingen on the Rhine," which Caroline Norton wrote to capture a dying soldier's dream of his homeland on the Rhine River (57). Writers also refer to such hymns as "Just before the Battle, Mother" and "O Wrap the Flag around Me, Boys" that glorify sacrificing one's life for the noble cause of country. Women learned these poignant hymns, played them in family and community events on the home front, and discussed them in letters.

Other writers also draw freely from canonical literature and poetry to express their thoughts without discussing the obvious formative role that the texts play in their intellectual and aesthetic development. Jennie Hall quotes lines from Shakespeare's *Midsummer Night's Dream* to convey her status as an unmarried female (44), Lib draws from an amusing song by the Hutchinson Family Quartet to describe herself as a "fickle wild rose" (99), and Phrone uses Edward Young's poem *Night Thoughts* to capture her yearning for sleep: "nature's sweet restorer" (14). These examples suggest the common role that print culture played in writers' lives and in the genre of "soldier letters" written during the war. They also hint to the varied ways in which some rural and middle-class women seized and expressed opportunities for learning, for interchange of thought, and for skill development during the Civil War years.

OHIO'S CIVIL WAR

> We heard last night that Morgan was intent on making another raid through Ohio. If such should be the case . . . —the national guard being away Guess the women will have to "buckle on their armer" & march to the front.
>
> —Lib (88)

The rumor that Confederate general John Hunt Morgan was planning another raid surfaced nearly a year after the Kentucky cavalryman sprang across the border in July 1863 and led several thousand men through southern and eastern Ohio to wreak havoc on territory previously untouched by Rebel invasion. The raids of Morgan's men, which lasted forty-six days and stretched over one thousand miles overall, was one of varied ways in which the "Rebellion ha[d] its effects every where" (24). What began as a military initiative evolved with every horse and bolt of calico seized in a looting frenzy that lasted two weeks in Ohio and eventually cost the state one million dollars. Morgan had threatened similar exploits in Ohio the previous summer but turned south at Cynthiana, Kentucky.

In the 1863 incursion, Morgan disobeyed Confederate General Bragg's command to confine his movements to Kentucky and led his band of marauders through a string of Indiana and Ohio counties. Reports of Morgan's whereabouts circulated wildly; concerned citizens rushed to protect their property; Governor David Tod mobilized citizens into a militia; Unionists accused local Copperheads of aiding the Rebels; and the exploits of Morgan and his men were recounted until the raid became "magnified to the proportions of a legend." Morgan intended to unsettle Northerners, divert Union troops from military initiatives expected against Confederates in Tennessee, and rally discontented Southern sympathizers to join their ranks. In the end, local informants seem to have overestimated the degree of support Morgan would encounter as local men—numbering fifty thousand—rallied to protect property and pursue the invaders. Morgan's efforts to pillage and elude capture thus quickly eclipsed any intent to recruit.[217]

The raid had little military significance but was mightier in its effects on some Ohioans' sense of security and eventually on Ohio lore. Whether locals considered Morgan a danger, a colorful diversion, or a mere horse thief, his exploits brought Confederate action to Ohio soil. Morgan's success in eluding pursuers for weeks before surrendering on July 26, 1863, in Columbiana County, highlighted some vulnerability in Buckeye borders. Women in southern Ohio counties may have felt vulnerable as men departed to join the militia. The unpredictable route Morgan's men followed created temporary unrest and confusion. Morgan divided his forces, bypassed large cities, and scrambled to avoid citizens mobilized to apprehend him. He raced through nineteen Ohio counties in all. As Morgan sought a strategic place to re-cross the river and shake the troops on his heels, he and his men stole food, goods, and horses, engaged in skirmishes, and burned bridges and buildings. Morgan was forced to end his exploits in surrender to Majors W. B. Way and G. W. Rue. He was imprisoned in the Ohio penitentiary, escaped a few months later, and was shot on September 4, 1864, in Tennessee as he tried to escape Federal soldiers.

The governors of Indiana and Ohio called men to arms when the raid commenced, and they responded in droves. Lib Baker expressed little confidence that women, even if pressed, would do the same. Although Lib jokes that if Morgan returns "women will have to 'buckle on their armer and march to the front,'" their efforts would have little effect: "if [the women] should all prove no more brave when in battle, than I thought I did when in Dreamland last night, they would do nothing more than to retreat after the first volley" (88). Lib sprinkles her indirect praise of men's bravery with humor, but her comments reveal a degree of gendered consciousness concerning the event's implications for women despite her distance from Morgan's path. Rosa's account of the 1863 raid echoes this concern: "[We] were almost scared to death for as there was no men" (30). Morgan's invasion and surrender remained an active topic of conversation long after the raid ended in 1863 (88).

Southern Ohioans may have felt some vulnerability well before the Morgan raid in 1863. In September 1862, Confederate General Edmund Kirby Smith advanced toward Ohio, entered Lexington with twelve thousand armed men, and instructed General Henry Heth to invade Covington, Kentucky, and Cincinnati. The extent of Smith's forces and the threat to Cincinnati spurred Governor Tod of Ohio to call immediately for "squads of men" to protect the Queen City. The *Mt. Vernon Democratic Banner,* the *Mt. Vernon Republican,* and the *Ohio State Journal* were among the Knox-area papers that disseminated the call in the first two weeks of September. Regiments seeking to fill quotas used the threat to promote enlistment: "The Rebels are upon us!" declared an announcement for recruits for the 113th Regiment; "they are about to tread the free soil of Ohio."[218] Fannie Meredith's account of Smith's invasion is brief. "The rebels are near Cincinnati, they are expecting a battle there," she writes on September 14, 1862. "[T]hey will commence drafting here Tuesday" (1). A draft was not needed for this initiative; approximately fifteen thousand armed citizens from across the state seized weapons, hopped aboard locomotives at the state's expense, and joined forces in southern Ohio.

Lybarger knew a number of the Knox County "Squirrel Hunters" who responded to the call: Dr. Emanuel Mast; Frank Israel; Frank's father, Samuel; Deal Shroyer's brother, Washington; and one of Phrone's admirers, Dawson Critchfield. Other men were members of local families: James McElroy, James Engle, Reason P. Britton, Harrison Fowler, John Hammond, Judson Hildreth, William Hawn, and members of the Welker, McGugin, Warden, and Vance families. Although newspapers continued to report Smith's approach as evidence of a shift from a "defensive" to an "offensive" war intended to "aggressive[ly] invade the Northern Border states," the immediate threat to the Ohio border passed when Confederate troops began withdrawing September 13. The Squirrel Hunters returned to their homes shortly thereafter. Men were offered official discharges, and decades later, consequent to U.S. Senate action, one month's pay of $13.00 for their services.[219]

Ohioans' eagerness to serve was apparent from the first days following Fort Sumter. Ohio was among the states swept by "war fever" in April 1861 that rallied quickly to meet President Lincoln's initial call for volunteers. Although the governor received a quota of thirteen regiments, he notified the War Department that "without seriously repressing the ardor of the people, I can hardly stop short of twenty." Such volunteer zeal is apparent in the reaction of an Oberlin College student: "WAR! And volunteers are only topics of conversation or thought. The lessons today have been a mere form. I cannot study. I cannot sleep, I cannot work." Over a year later, Fannie Meredith feels similarly distracted from her studies: "There was so much excitement about war that I could not think of going [to school]" (1). Even in the needy year of 1864, Brough was able to raise 35,982 "hundred days' men" in sixteen days. As the war continued, recruiting grew more difficult, however, and the governor had to implement the draft in many locations. Yet the draft was not used in Union Township, and the majority of the 300,000 Ohioans who fought in the war volunteered to do so.[220]

In October 1863, Mollie Ward reports continued enthusiasm for the Union cause despite more than two years of fighting, growing financial costs and casualties for the North, and the Confederate triumph at Chickamauga mere weeks before. Buoyed by the Brough gubernatorial ticket, she writes, "We are at present preparing for a great convention that will be held in Mt. Vernon. . . . [T]he union loving people are all up and doing. . . . Every person is alive with excitement" (45). This energy was channeled into the Republican Party's decisive victory over Clement Laird Vallandigham later that month. Ohioans' convictions undoubtedly ebbed and flowed with personal losses, military defeats and victories, tussles at home, and the steady march of time, but women's expressions of devotion to the cause appear throughout the Lybarger collection.

"Battles, Indeed! Knoxville, Indeed!"

Gender shapes writers' attention to political events central to Ohioans' experiences during the war. In addition to Morgan's raid, women mention Republican and Democratic tensions, African Americans' role in the war, soldier desertion, and draft resistance.[221] Key figures appear as well: Brough, Vallandigham, McClellan, and Jefferson Davis. The rallies, Union leagues, and community suppers by which women demonstrated their political activism in gender-appropriate ways are prominent in accounts, as are the conflicts among Democratic and Republican factions active on the Ohio home front. Yet, young women's glowing rhetoric often consumes more textual space than do political particulars, and their coverage of events varies. Attention to some events is fleeting and to others mysteriously absent. For example, women mention the battles of Vicksburg and Fredericksburg but do not discuss Gettysburg. Mere days after the smoke cleared from that battlefield, Emma Peterman writes, "we are having quite gay times in Mt. Vernon this summer" with festivals, ice cream, and cake (25).

Writers' erratic attention to events at the front also characterizes their discussion of President Lincoln's assassination on April 14, 1865. His death prompts remark in only two letters (122, 124), and brief criticism of his terms of peace emerges in an additional letter dated April 22 (123). Yet Lincoln collected 40,000 more votes than his contenders in the 1860 election and over 60,000 more votes in 1864. He was loved by many Ohioans, and Lincoln, in return, apparently respected Ohioans' power to influence the war at several key moments. For example, Brough's victory over Vallandigham at the 1863 polls coupled with Union triumphs boosted soldier morale and interrupted the peace movement's momentum in fragmenting support for the war. Lincoln's relief for the victory was clear in a message he allegedly sent the morning after the election: "Glory to God in the Highest, Ohio has saved the

Union." His funeral procession drew an estimated 7 million stunned Americans to railroad tracks and statehouses to pay their respects.[222] Yet the letters do not mention the funeral train's passage through Columbus and Cleveland or the ceremonies that marked its long trek to Springfield. On April 30, a cousin relates from Indiana that almost everybody "has gone to Indianapolis to see the remains of A. Lincoln ower most Beloved and Esteemed President" (124). She then shifts the subject abruptly to practical family matters.

Christie Blakely expresses greater sorrow and captures the complexity of experiencing a national tragedy of these proportions mere days after rejoicing Lee's surrender at Appomattox. Christie begins her letter with hope for restored peace and then writes, "Since commencing to write we have the sad, sad intelligence of the murder of our president. What can we say or think. It seems we can do neither, it is so sudden. So awful we hardly comprehend it. How thick the gloom it spreads over the bright light that was dawning." Christie seems unable to reconcile such discordant events: the Union's survival and the murder of its leader. Words seem inadequate to capture the amalgram of grief, elation, relief, and sheer exhaustion that mark the end of the war. She chooses to focus on Lincoln's vision for the nation: "But we will not be despondent. Believing that the death of no one man in the nation can work our overthrow. Trusting that the God who presides over the destinies of all nations will bring all things to work together for good. Though we may not be so near the end of the great struggle as we were supposing" (122). Christie's words portend the many adjustments awaiting Americans at war's end.

Women's varying attention to war events may reflect in some cases their conscious and careful war work, and in others, their personalities, preoccupations, or differing investments in the war. A passing remark of Ell Hawn's indicates that women's access to information varied because they relied in part on their fathers and brothers to provide news: "Pa did not stay [at the meeting] so I cannot tell you how it went off" (25). Women's facility with issues deemed political differed; while Edith queries Lybarger tentatively about the prospects of the war's end (101), Lou ponders the philosophical contradictions of fighting to preserve peace (110). Women's investment in the war differed as well. Just as scholars note that for some soldiers paychecks rivaled patriotism as incentives to serve, so too does documentary evidence from women's war letters reflect that their struggles with men's absence sometimes superseded conviction for either the Confederate or the Union cause: "What do I care for patriotism? . . . My husband is my country. What is country to me if he be killed?"[223] The absence of similar comments in this collection indicates marital status was another factor shaping letters' content.

Gender roles shaped political content as well. The ideology of *separate spheres* that surfaces in the epistolary realm reflects women's lives in the social and civic realms. Although gender norms were supple across the century and linked to race, class, region, and necessity, women's letters suggest that separate spheres ideology continued to guide men's and women's behavior during war. The term *separate spheres* is commonly used to capture both material and ideological shifts in men's and women's roles. The term refers to shifts in labor patterns from agrarian duties shared between the sexes to a general pattern of male employment outside the home and female responsibility within the home. Separate spheres also functions rhetorically to champion domestic roles as the "natural" domain of women, and business and political activities as the "natural" direction for men's strengths and abilities. Many nineteenth-century citizens operating within this guiding framework thus considered war matters primarily men's domain.

Individuals, service organizations, and newspapers were among the forces fueling the understanding that war was a deeply sex-segregated matter. Although women workers on the frontlines often fought these prevailing ideas, ladies aid societies sometimes framed their supply of material goods as "aiding" men's war efforts. Similarly, local Ohio newspapers often separated "ladies departments" from war news. A typical ladies section contained fashion tips, anecdotes, and advice on mothering and femininity, as well as light stories and jokes. For example, one newspaper separated the ladies section from regimental reports, an assessment of the South's strengths, and a Union colonel's dying wishes. The newspaper's apology early in the war highlights dominant gender ideology that was reflected and perpetuated in the realm of newsprint: "Ladies. . . . Don't complain if you don't find stories, poetry or light reading in the *Banner* this week. . . . The details of the war news are too important and interesting to be omitted or curtailed." Advertisements for hats, gloves, and other fashionable items, posed as women's concerns, create the momentary illusion that "generally all is peace, calm as if there was no war" (19).[224]

Trace evidence in the letters suggests Lybarger respected gender norms because he works to preserve lighthearted content and gender etiquette with some correspondents while discussing politics freely with others. In this regard, the small number of letters the soldier preserved from men offer telling contrast to those from women. Dr. T. B. Campbell details draft resistance that occurred in Holmes County in June 1863 and Ben Stone discusses the role of African Americans in the war. In contrast, Lou's flippant response in one letter indicates that previous battle talk may have elicited commentary from Lybarger: "O, ye battle! Ye wasted sympathies! . . . I assure you you shall not be bored with sentimental talk about battles again from this source. Battles, indeed! Knoxville, indeed!" (63). Despite this soldier's respect for intelligent, competent women, he, like other soldiers, may have preferred women's letters to distract him from the war rather than relive it on the page.

Other letters suggest that Lybarger apologized for sharing travel details and for discussing politics. Lou's wording in one letter seems intended to assuage his concerns, "I was not wearied, but interested in your description of the boat expedition, and I consider no undertaking 'insignificant' in which the lives of human beings depend on the uncertain chances of war" (81). Similarly, Rachel Blakeley affirms Lybarger's apparent decision to vote for Lincoln in 1864 as if he had apologized for introducing the topic: "You never need apologise for speaking to me on that subject, as it is my conviction every female should be interested enough in the cause of our Government to keep pretty well posted on politics" (109). Although Rachel's comments about politics concern information rather than activism, gender norms are clearly fluid for this erudite writer and former schoolmate. Phrone appears less willing to stretch gender boundaries in this arena. Before the much-anticipated political contest of 1863, Phrone writes, "I would tell you how much I think of old Jonney Braugh, old Abe, the Union, and so forth &c if that would not be writing politics, ha! ha!" (35). Whether she intends this passage to ridicule gender norms or comply with them, she refers little to national politics in her letters.

Lou seems to share her political opinions freely but with less detail than male writers and only after her correspondence with Lybarger is well under way. In an early letter as Fannie Jerome, she moves quickly away from the topic of war politics, asserting, "I am not writing a political letter" (40). In response to Lybarger's charge that she is a "counter-hopper" because she lives in the politically divided state of Kentucky, she describes herself as "simply Union very strong and conservative" (43). However, in later years she expresses disagreement with the capability of "military arbitrament" to settle the war (96), her support of McClellan, her belief in the union "as it was," and her desire for "peace, peace, *peace*" (110). These comments reveal her affinity for the ideas fueling the peace movement active in Kentucky (96). Her early letters demonstrate careful effort to avoid discussing politics so as to respect the service of her correspondent, and at least on paper, respect gender norms.

Geography was another factor that influenced women's epistolary attention to Ohio's Civil War. Ella Rightmire's discussion of Morgan's raid offers an example. Knox County in Ohio sits slightly north of the state's center, some distance from the Southern border most affected by Smith's threats and Morgan's travels. As a Knox County resident, Ella discusses the raid almost as an afterthought and as if Governor Tod's forces had Morgan on the run from the moment he spied the border. She remarks, "I suppose you have heard of Gen. Morgan's invasion of Ohio. I guess he has not accomplished very much. Gov. Todd is in persuit of him with 60 thousand me[n]. . . . Morgan is on the retreat thinking the Yankees are a little too sharp for him" (24).[225]

This dismissal of Morgan's exploits and the confident tale of Yankee ingenuity differs from Rosa's perspective from Bainbridge in Ross County, located mere miles from the dusty path of Morgan's cavalry. She captures the escalating confusion that many felt in southern Ohio as rumors spread. Rosa writes in July 1863, "We came very near having war at home. Old Morgan was within 6 or 7 miles and some say 4. . . . There was a very throng time here when the people thought John

Morgan was a coming through. . . . I was going to say you never seen such a time in your life but you have and worse to I suppose. The people of Bainbridge and the community were almost scared to death." Rosa mentions skirmishes, camp names, and the lack of protection for Bainbridge citizens. She finds conveying the dizzying order of events in a letter a difficult endeavor: "I will tell you the rest when I see you" (30). Rosa's proximity to the action may explain the presence of detail in her letter, which contrasts sharply with Ella's offhand treatment of events from her more protected position hundreds of miles away.

Women write with a degree of geographic consciousness that reflects how they often forged war allegiances and identities through geographic borders. Women sometimes saw themselves as "union loving girls" and at other times "Ohio girls" and even "Millwood girls." Lib declares on the eve of Brough's election in October 1863, "What if we should be disappointed [if he were defeated]!! I for one would feel like seeking a home in other parts and ever disowning that I belonged to the once glorious but now disgraced Ohio" (46). In this dramatic rendering, state allegiance seems to hang in the balance. Ben Stone similarly laments changes in his beloved Missouri, which he opines "has been cursed as never a state has been cursed before" (112), after having once coursed with the "arterial blood" of the Union. His remarks likely allude to General Sterling Price's invasion in 1864, the guerrilla warfare ravaging the state, debates over the constitution, and the abolishment of slavery in the area in 1865. Campbell meanwhile remarks from Knox County, "A man can't support his government in Ohio country without being branded an Abolitionist" (23).

The varying use of the category of "we" to capture family, community, state, and national allegiances speaks to the fluctuating ways in which writers imagined their identities and connections. One writer's geographic pride is concentrated in Millwood: "you ought to hav bin here last Saturday to hav seen Old Millwood respond to the call of patriotism. There was [a] Union meeting there that day. It is supposed there were 15 hundred people there" (24). Others sing the praises of Millwood's "one Grocery and plenty of whiskey" (26) while decrying other towns' exceeding Millwood in Union supporters (15). Phrone, too, remarks that "we have about as many secesh as union men" (14).

Knox County voted Republican in 1863 in the gubernatorial elections. Mere miles away, in bordering and staunchly Democratic Holmes County, which along with Crawford County had "the largest percentages of drafted men" in Ohio in 1862, voters decided the opposite.[226]

"Copperheads, Butternuts, Sircles or Traitors"

Diverging sentiments among Knox and Holmes County voters mirrored the experiences of families, church members, and neighbors across the South and North who turned against each other over issues foundational to the war.[227] Some family members fought for opposing sides and never spoke to each other again. Some Southern sympathizers left their churches when clergy espoused Union ideals. Even those fighting for the same cause disagreed about the methods of doing so. Lybarger and Ben Stone were at odds concerning the role African Americans should play in the war. While their disagreements seem amicable, other conflicts elicit fiercer sentiments. "To be a Democrat," T. B. Campbell insists in 1863, "a man must be a lawabiding union loving citizen. If he is not that in the present hour of our country's peril he must be a disunionist and anarchist—There are but two questions for the people of the Loyal States to decide" (23). Antiwar Democrats' "vociferous bleating" about conscription laws and constitutional violations is equivalent to "playing into the hands of the Rebbels" (23). Sharp divisions and ideological convictions fueled conflicts among Ohioans that at times seemed to rival in intensity those driving bloodier battles in the South.

Campbell's firm opinions reflect the centrality of political battles to some Ohioans' experiences during the war.[228] Ohioans aligned themselves and others with varying categories of "us" and "them" as the war progressed. Unionists, Butternuts, Peace Democrats, War Democrats, Black Republicans, Abolitionists, Copperheads, Loyalists, and Traitors all emerged as terms—and often epithets—to describe political allegiances meaningful to citizens' identities and understandings of the war. Writers mention Union leagues and antiwar "secret" societies such as the Knights of the Golden Circle (14, 23). They scoff at the disreputable behavior of local Copperheads and Butternuts. They recount Democratic and Union gatherings and volley attendance figures as if these were musket fire: "we had a grand Union meeting . . . there was over 2000 People presant" (26); "there was [a] Union meeting. . . . It is supposed there were 15 hundred people" (24); "We was down to Chillicothe to a big speech. . . . There was about 50,000 there" (39). Numbers were rhetorical tools wielded to substantiate continuing support for the war.

The tone some writers use to describe divisions among Ohioans conveys keen competition among political parties but belies the substantive issues underlying their alliances. Gender norms direct women's attention to the politics of their relationships and communities rather than nuanced debate of pressing national issues. For example, Rosa describes the competitive character of float making during one war parade: "Their wagon beats ours . . . I am sorry to say. . . . It is about 40 feet long trimed in cedar red and Blue and Buckeyes . . . [but at a later parade] we are a going to beat them all to pieces. . . . We are not a going to have the name of letting the butternut beat [us]" (39). This contest in ribbons and buckeyes gestures little to the issues of racial equality, state's rights, and constitutional fidelity that fueled party divisions, but it reflects the contours of women's daily lives.

Similarly, Phrone characterizes the subversive group Knights of the Golden Circle (K.G.C.) as an "infernal society" and their members as "trash" (14). This organization was more myth than substance, but newspaper accounts (combined with a healthy dose of gossip) fanned Ohioans' fears that the K.G.C. was infiltrating Union strongholds, inciting discontent, and swaying loyal volunteers to desert (23).[229] One local whom Phrone names as active in the organization, Joseph S. Butts, along with Isaac Baker, apparently deserted the Forty-third on February 21, 1862.[230] The popular claim that K.G.C.s would bring "civil war" to the state is echoed in Phrone's assessment, "we will certainly have war at home if [they] are not broken up somehow" (14). Others suggest that Copperheads interrupt the monotony of the home front: "I would say here there is nothing interesting a going on here . . . [and there] are no parties or amusements of any kinde except those, what shall I call them: 'Copperheads, Butternuts, Sircles or Traitors'"

(22). This writer attends a Copperhead fishing party by mistake and boldly asserts her support for the Union by refusing a piece of "Grand Velandingham cake" (22). Without the legal right to vote, this writer uses cake as a makeshift ballot. War dissenters appear here as a troubling group who drink and run horses rather than a formidable political force whose support grew sufficiently strong in 1862 and 1863 to rally 187,492 votes for Vallandigham during the 1863 gubernatorial contest.

Brough secured the election by 100,000 votes, yet hearty support for Vallandigham, "dissenter extraordinary," speaks to strong antiwar sentiment in Ohio. The cry of western Democrats, "The Constitution as it is, the Union as it was!" alludes to the reasons that many offered for their opposition to the war: constitutional violations in maintaining the war, conscription and taxation to support it, the contradiction of preserving the Union through bloodshed, and the elevation of African Americans to equal social status with Anglo-Americans, among others. On April 13, 1863, General Ambrose E. Burnside, who had been appointed commander of the Department of Ohio, intensified the strife when he issued General Order No. 38, which declared that expressing "sympathy for the enemy" was an act of treason that was grounds for arrest. Although Burnside intended this order to temper the expression of Southern sympathies, peace Democrats claimed it violated the right to free speech.[231]

Vallandigham's encounter with Order No. 38 and his prominent role in Ohio politics during the Civil War era are well known. An Ohio-born son of a Presbyterian minister, a studious lawyer and legislator, and a passionate peace leader, Vallandigham opposed the war on many ideological fronts. He viewed the ballot box, not the battlefield, as the arena in which diverging state interests should be settled. He championed western sectionalism, opposed abolitionism, and viewed African Americans as inferior to Anglo-Americans. Setting his sights on the governor's seat in 1863 but lacking strong support in a divided party, Vallandigham traveled the state espousing his political platform to marshal support and wrest it from the favored candidate, Hugh J. Jewett. Burnside's zealous order to suppress speech sympathizing with "the enemy" provided Vallandigham a well-timed opportunity to turn the tide of Democratic public opinion in his favor. He defied the order at a Mt. Vernon Democratic rally on May 1.

In a speech that stretched over two hours, Vallandigham added to his characteristic and deeply felt denunciations of Lincoln's despotism with the argument that Order No. 38 was a base usurpation of power and a constitutional violation of free speech. Vallandigham claimed that the order epitomized the Lincoln administration's tyranny. Events unfolded rapidly when the speech was reported to Burnside. Vallandigham was arrested on May 5, 1863; a military commission heard his case; he was found guilty and sentenced to imprisonment; and President Lincoln intervened in the aftermath of the decision to exile the Dayton Democrat to the Confederacy. Public outrage at the events intensified as press coverage increased. In June 1863, Vallandigham succeeded, via the martyrdom of his arrest, to secure the Democratic nomination. Continuing to fume and foment as he wove his way to Canada, he ran his campaign from his state of exile and attracted a strong following in a party that was by no means unified. Lib Baker was not among his followers. In 1863, she remarks, "How strange to think that men, good, honest, and to some extent intelligent men, can be so blinded by party spirit as to support such a vile traitor as . . . Valandigham!" (46). Lib seems mystified that supporters could not dislodge truth from rhetoric to recognize the peace leader's traitorous essence. Although "good, honest" and "intelligent" men followed Vallandigham's ideas and felt disillusioned with the war, Union victories at Gettysburg and Vicksburg overshadowed support for his campaign and rejuvenated soldier morale and the Republican party.[232]

The conscription act passed in March 1863 incited draft riots in New York City, fueled the growing peace movement, and set the stage for armed draft resistance in Ohio. Dwindling numbers of volunteers and the sheer need for men on the battlefield spurred Congress to pass the act that made all males between the ages of twenty-five and forty-five eligible for the draft. The vote was starkly partisan: all Republicans in Congress supported the bill, whereas 88 percent of Democrats opposed it. In addition, the loopholes the bill provided—drafted men could furnish a substitute or opt out through a $300 fee—angered those without ready funds to buy their way out of fighting in a war that many fundamentally opposed to begin with. When officials went to carry out the draft in New York in July 1863, the outrage felt by immigrant, working-class, and Democratic groups for an unjust act in an unjust war swelled into what McPherson called "the worst riot in American history." Four days of violence, looting, and property destruction left 105 dead. Although the draft prompted volunteerism and in that sense accomplished governmental objectives, McPherson characterizes the Conscription Act as "one of the most divisive issues of the war."[233]

The issue was certainly divisive in Ohio, and opponents near Knox County organized a brief resistance effort in June 1863. Antiwar sentiment led men in Holmes County, which abuts the northeast corner of Knox County, to attack an officer sent to enroll citizens for the draft. When the men responsible were arrested, a group of men forcibly released them from custody. Reports indicated that large numbers of men were organizing to attack enrollment officers. Governor Tod "ordered the malcontents to disperse" and sent more than four hundred troops to ensure that they complied. On the approach of the troops, resisters fired; during the troops' response, several resisters were injured and others fled. The rebellion was quickly quelled.[234] Campbell offers full treatment of "Fort Fizzle" in his letter of June 23, 1863, and names Knox area men who were affiliated with the affair: Sam Shrimplin, Calvin and Jess Winteringer, and Chaney Gamble (23). Holmes was one of the counties whose delegates to the Democratic convention in the spring of 1862 pledged opposition to despotism, the war, and governmental interference with slavery.[235]

Impossible to gauge from women's letters is how news of draft resistance so close to home struck Lybarger while he was marching toward Corinth, disarming Rebels, commandeering their horses and earning a promotion alongside his comrade Captain J. H. Rhodes. Lybarger had already penned his outrage at local Butternuts in the Republican newspaper in May. Frustration with antiwar efforts throughout Ohio may have solidified Brough's securing 94 percent of the absentee soldier vote in the 1863 election.[236]

Draft resistance was also afoot in bordering Harrison Township (15, 22, 101), and Campbell informs his friend of details (23). Although the *Banner* suggests that regions beyond Harrison and Jackson have equally "determined resistance," one tally of Knox County volunteers in 1862 noted Harrison as having the lowest number of volunteers (one). This figure compares with sixteen in Millwood's township, Union, and forty-eight in Hilliar.[237] In Harrison events, a marshal "was met by a party of 18 rebbels and ordered to leave . . . and not return under penalty of death." The Harrisonites swore that when the company of state militia arrived, they would "not leave a grease spot" in the militiamen's place. "They hastened home and marshaled their clans and started to meet and give battle to the invaders under cover of darkness. They stole stealthily up to them. They saw them. It was a reality. Here was 85 men. . . . How the Harrisonites could have fought. But now they saw them face to face and their hearts failed them. Their knees did tremble and their heands did shake." Campbell reports that coming face to face with armed troops inspired the men to lay down their weapons, and the uprising was over (23).

The ideological divisions fueling local draft resistance and rebellion affected community relations. The Union supporters who write to the soldier name draft dodgers and deserters, report Copperhead meetings, and describe snubbing those of opposing political positions. Phrone's words capture how political categories become tools of social organization that mattered for women's daily lives: "The secesh and union do not associate together very much. I think the time will come when they will not speak to each other at all, and I think this will be perfectly right for my part. I dont want to speak to a secessionist nor I dont want one to speak to me" (17). Such divisions may have shaped the Lybarger letters. Writers claim that the Gamble family is secesh (57, 99); although Ella Gamble corresponds with Lybarger after the war, no letters indicate that they communicated during the conflict.

Such national and community strife explain Lib's nostalgia for past days in which neighbors stood side by side rather than became "blinded" by party spirit: "would that the names Democrat and Republican could be lain aside until this cruel rebellion is entirely crushed" (46). Mollie Ward speaks of the loss of "peace and harmony" in Brandon: "Society is broken up" (37). Later, she writes, "I am sorry to say that the principal part of the young men now in our vicinity are deep dyed Copperheads:

traitors to their country and their God" (45). Events on the Ohio home front exacerbated previous tensions, birthed new ones, and echoed in minute local forms greater fissures between the North and the South. Local battles were primarily bloodless, but they shaped relationships central to women's daily lives.

"The Negroes Are Raising a Company to Go to the Army"

Rosa's letter of June 14, 1863, containing this statement marks a significant event in Civil War history that would shape the war's aftermath (20). The enlistment of black troops signaled, in the words of one historian, "the transformation of a war to preserve the Union into a revolution to overthrow the old order." South Carolina mustered in its first black regiment in January 1863. The same year, the War Department granted Governor Andrews of Massachusetts permission to raise the Fifty-fourth and Fifty-fifth regiments and Ohio to raise the 127th Ohio, later renamed the Fifth Regiment U.S. Colored Troops. Over 200,000 African American men served in the Union forces; 5,000 of them were Ohioans. Varied events created the conditions of possibility for these initiatives. Congressional mandates to enlist blacks in the service in limited capacities, the Emancipation Proclamation, the need for soldiers, shifting racial attitudes, and initiatives among free and contraband blacks to form units in South Carolina, Louisiana, and Kansas were among the forces underlying this historic change.[238]

Rosa's seemingly dispassionate response and informative tone concerning the mustering of black troops is at odds with the views of some of her fellow Ohioans. Although 25,279 blacks lived in Ohio by midcentury and strong abolitionist sentiment led some to desire the overthrow of what was considered a barbaric system, active abolitionists constituted a minority of Ohioans overall. Ohioans had declared theirs a free state, many were active in the Underground Railroad, and their congressmen primarily denounced the fugitive slave provisions in the Compromise of 1850. Yet the prospect of African Americans serving alongside whites for the Union was a troubling idea for some native-born white Americans socialized to believe that other races were inferior to their own. Characteristic of the nation's racist history, voting rights in Ohio were limited to "whites" in 1803; treaty by treaty, Ohio settlers had shuffled Native Americans off their land and nudged them to the west; and surges in immigration spurred xenophobic sentiment and incidents of racial and ethnic violence that increased in the latter half of the century.[239]

Northern abolitionists and free blacks anxious for citizenship rights rejoiced in opportunities to serve, but others found the idea of arming black men "as white soldiers," with "*no distinction made*" among the men unfathomable.[240] Such a prospect seemed to undermine the natural racial order. "American soldiers," the *Banner* insists, "will not allow them[selves] to be degraded by being marched in the ranks with negroes, and all of the officers of my acquaintance would resign rather than participate in such a brutal warfare."[241] This opinion, expressed in a Democratic paper, also surfaced among Republicans. As Benjamin Stone writes from Missouri, "we think we have patriotism and wisdom enough, bravery and capability of endurance enough, power and ability altogether sufficient to put down the traitors and crush out the last remnant of their power without the employment or assistance of the slave" (19). To Stone, the presence of African Americans in the military pollutes the noble principles for which (white) men are fighting: "[F]or very shame I would not use the slave as a soldier" (29).

Newspaper reports and Stone's language typify the conceptual conflation between "American" and "white" that was common in popular thought, espoused in education, and concretized in policy. Indeed, citizenship rights were initially granted to "free white persons" in the American Naturalization Act of 1790, conceptually rendering those deemed non-white as outsiders.[242] Letter writers participate in the enunciation and policing of racial borders when using the terms "our men" and "our patriotism" to refer to white Unionists.

Although few writers address racial aspects of the war explicitly, several references in the letters herald changes in rights for African Americans on the postwar horizon.[243] Indeed, the *Mt. Vernon Republican* assures Knox County citizens of the growing acceptance of African American soldiers and the need for their service. "The black soldiers are becoming quite popular here," one writer reports from the South. Praise for the soldiers' effectiveness, however, is framed in essentialist and racist terms: "they are soldiers by nature, they are fond of music, and it would do you good to see them march, they keep such good time."[244] While a Republican writer acknowledges that enrolling people of color as soldiers to "secure the existence of our state" is "not gratifying to our Caucasian pride," he reminds readers that Copperheads have taken full advantage of this discomfort to incite Northern prejudice.[245] Despite these beliefs, the need for Northern soldiers and the willingness of African Americans to take up arms on behalf of the Union led many to deem the growing number of enlistments as sensible.

Lybarger seemed to support the mustering of African American troops and to disagree with his friend Stone on the matter. This perspective surfaces in letters Stone wrote to Lybarger in 1863: "When you say we have the same right to put arms in the hands of negroes to shoot rebels as we have to turn the enemies guns upon him that we may capture I think you go farther back into the times of Barbarians for your rule of right" (29). Anticipating the day the nation will be reunited, Stone recommends that Northerners respect Southerners' "peculiar opinions or prejudices" concerning blacks. Stone exemplifies the perspective that slavery, abolitionism, and the rights of African Americans are peripheral (even irrelevant) issues in a war intended to preserve the Union and uphold its Constitution. Enrolling free or enslaved African Americans to fight reflects the government's eroding confidence in it's "own freemen" and degrades the patriotism Stone suggests only white men could embody (19).

Phrone's comments parallel Stone's racial investment in the welfare of white soldiers in the social, legal, and economic advantages linked with Anglo-Americans historically. A month after Lybarger was wounded at Corinth and several months after the president circulated the Emancipation Proclamation, Phrone writes fiercely, "Indeed now I am not much in favor of the war and more especially not in favor of getting our men slaughtered up for the freedom of negroes. This seems to be what . . . most are fighting for" (5). Northern women's empathies and perspectives were often forged by the press and pulpit rather than sown on the plantation. Phrone, living in a free state and in a town with no African American residents recorded in 1860, is distanced from the system of slavery central to Southern social and economic history that many considered "monstrous."[246] The issue that strikes Phrone close to home is Lybarger's safety. The threat to his life seems to rouse an instantaneous weighing of human lives and a ready pronouncement that "freeing negroes" is not worth the slaughter of "our men."

Phrone's suggestion that abolition "seems to be what . . . most are fighting for" alludes to a motivation to fight that was initially less common than some Democrats heartily claimed. "Abolitionist Republican Sentiment," one Democratic headline declares, "[is] the cause of the Rebellion and Disunion."[247] Democrats labeled their political rivals as "black" Republicans and the "African Brigade" to stir simmering fears of abolitionist radicals, racial equality, and amalgamation. Yet Lib ridicules the very perspective that Phrone seems to accept as factual. In 1864, Lib dismisses the "ignorance" of those who perceive the war as an abolitionist crusade: "Hadn't you better sheath your sword and come home 'quit fighting to free the Niggers' such was a sentence I saw written to a soldier not long since. How ignorant some people are" (99). Lib presumably interprets the forces propelling the war as multidimensional.

McPherson argues that although some Union volunteers fought initially to abolish slavery, the majority fought for other reasons. Soldiers were likely to cite such abstract concepts as liberty, duty, country, the founding fathers, and the Constitution as initial motivations to fight. Women's letters espouse similar abstract ideals but do not include abolitionist leanings. In fact, days after local newspapers publish the Emancipation Proclamation in 1862, Ell Hawn expresses regret for the president's coming action: "And Allas the President has ishued a proclamation that all the negroes shall be set free by the first of January if the Southerns do not go Back as they once were" (2). Whether Ell's disappointment stems from the president's change of heart, her concern that freeing African Americans might result in harm to Northern white "women and children" as some claimed, or a general sense of alarm that war events were instigating profound changes in the existing social order is unclear.[248]

What is clear from these snapshots of the Ohio home front is that Northern white women recognized they were standing on shifting racial terrain. However distant racial and citizenship issues may have felt to these Northern white letter writers, their discussion of blacks' role in the war, the mustering of black troops, and the Emancipation Proclamation indicate their awareness of changing roles and opportunities for African Americans. The women would witness even greater changes when the fighting ceased.

"PEACE, BEAUTIFUL, LIFE-GIVING, JOY INSPIRING PEACE HAS RETURNED"

The final letters in the Lybarger collection offer striking comparisons to those written during war. They capture the eagerness with which American citizens sought distance from years of bloodshed to regain a sense of normalcy. In June 1865, Lou celebrates the war's ending with the words, "*peace*, beautiful, life-giving, joy inspiring peace has *returned*" (129). At long last, the "cruel war" has ended and soldiers can relish the "peace and harmony" earned through their labor and sacrifice (75, 29). However, with four million Americans liberated and hundreds of thousands more dead, it was neither the same nation nor the same idea of "peace" that had been experienced before the war. Citizens nevertheless embraced the end with relief. Reports of demobilization and returning soldiers soon faded from the pages of newspapers. Letters in the collection decrease in length and frequency, whether from Lybarger's shifting investment in the collection or because social interaction began to replace correspondence. Efforts to mend political rifts were evident as Knox County residents planned "A Grand Union Democratic Celebration" at the caves near Millwood for the Fourth of July without "distinction of party."[249] The patriotic tone of earlier letters fades, and 1865 and 1866 accounts focus on teaching, visits, marriages, and family relationships. A Crum family farm in Missouri continues to evoke speculation; Rosa writes faithfully and looks to her future; Lybarger seeks new society with Ella Gamble; correspondence with Lou dwindles; and Phrone's increasing use of endearments suggests that her relationship with Lybarger intensifies. Salutations shift to "friend Lybarger" and "Ed," although Lou holds fast to "Lt. Lybarger," the identity by which she has known him throughout the war.

Relinquishing their military identities was sometimes difficult for soldiers. Regaining their footing on postwar soil meant adjusting to peacetime activities and relationships that had weathered multiple years of absence, loss, yearning, and change. In the letters, events unfold in rapid succession as the war draws to a close. Lybarger visits Washington's grave on May 21, 1865, in the company of Generals Fuller and Sprague and Colonel Park of the Forty-third Ohio. He sends flowers to several correspondents to commemorate what to Northerners signaled the preservation of the Union. To Lou, the flowers "breathe the very spirit of peace" (131). He participates in the Grand Review of the Army of the Tennessee on May 24; the Forty-third Ohio is mustered out on July 13, 1865; and Lybarger returns to Millwood on July 21. A proposed visit to meet his colorful Kentucky pen pal on his return journey never transpires, and Lou feels regretful: "[I] was anticipating your visit with any amount of pleasure. I had my best smile and bows in reservation" (136).

Lou's letters offer glimpses of Lybarger's postwar spirits. "I should think," she writes in 1865, "your happiness on returning home would be so exquisite that all congratulations would be dull and commonplace, but for the fact that you say you are lonesome . . . a returned soldier who has been longing for the pleasures of home [now tells] me how lonesome he is after his arrival there" (139). No doubt this "lonesome" veteran was experiencing what many veterans felt as they adjusted to civilian life: the daily regimen of army and camp life has vanished; the brotherly camaraderie of fighting for a common cause has dissolved; citizens faced reconstruction and rebuilding efforts; relationships once dear and familiar have been altered by four years of gendered and geographically separate experiences that were, in many ways, incommensurate. Moreover, his family and friends, as Lou remarks, expected him to be happy.

This soldier's decision to sustain correspondence with Lou—a figure known only through the page—speaks to the value of his identity as a soldier and his participation in a struggle that had profound consequences for the nation and its citizens. Letters remained ever-present avenues to access the romantic and noble aspects of his service. Lou is also reluctant to sever their epistolary bond despite the need for "soldier letters" having passed. She voices her qualms: "I expect I ought to quit. As I write, I stop, and think, and I realize just now, that I am perhaps doing wrong. Then again, what harm is there in reading your uniformly respectful and agreeable letters, and answering them? Thus I reason with myself, and continue to write" (129). Their mutual capacity for introspection may have provided a safe outlet for expressing postwar struggles and offered Lybarger a meaningful, private lifeline to his past. Lou's continued raillery as she sought the return of her elusive photograph may also have been a good tonic for cold feet. Lybarger wed Sophronia Rogers on January 27, 1867—more than four years after their initial wartime correspondence—and remained devoted to her for fifteen years, until her death of typhoid fever on May 13, 1882. The last letter from Lou is dated a month after their marriage.

Giving up the correspondence with soldiers that provided Lou the opportunity to entertain through the safety of distance may have been a particularly wrenching sacrifice for her to make at war's end. In an era in which "bold script" on a page rendered femininity suspect and women's political, educational, and occupational opportunities remained circumscribed, Lou's choice to launch independently into a correspondence of her own choosing may have been empowering. She, too, had her letters to savor in later years as reminders of her contribution to the war effort and to at least one soldier's comfort. In this regard, the letters women wrote during the war are valuable beyond the additional insights they provide into the effects of the Civil War on individual lives. The opportunity that letter writing offered women such as Lou to forge new relationships, contribute to the war effort, and sculpt personas on paper also portends greater social changes on the horizon for women in "the world's broad field of battle" (143).[250]

Edwin Lewis Lybarger, probably 1859–60, near the time of his graduation from Millwood Academy

Edwin Lewis Lybarger as a young man

Private Edwin Lewis Lybarger of the Forty-third Ohio Volunteer Infantry Regiment, Company K (photograph taken between November 25, 1861, when he was mustered in, and February 7, 1862, when he was promoted to sergeant before leaving Ohio for action in Missouri)

Sketch by Captain J. H. Rhodes of Sergeant Edwin Lewis Lybarger at Fort Hooker, Tennessee (made sometime between February 7, 1862, and April 27, 1863)

Second Lieutenant Edwin Lewis Lybarger (photograph taken between April 28, 1863, when he was promoted to second lieutenant, and November 17, 1864)

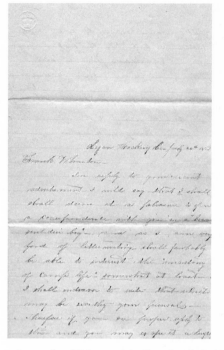
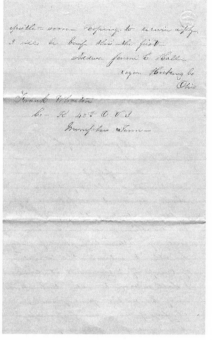

Letter dated July 24, 1863, from Jennie E. Hall of Logan to "Frank Wharton" of the Forty-third OVI, Company K, the pseudonym Lieutenant Lybarger used when placing a newspaper advertisement soliciting correspondence

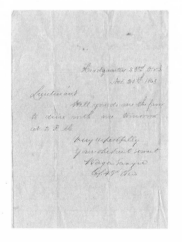

Invitation to Lieutenant Lybarger from Colonel Wager Swayne to dine with him on the first Thanksgiving, proclaimed by President Lincoln, November 26, 1863

Greenwood Glen.
Jany 23d 1864.

Lieutenant Lybarger.

Excuse this empty letter. I have not the slightest doubt that it will be so excessively timid, so utterly overcome with its own insignificance, that it will occupy just about a month in reaching its destination. I know the poor innocent paper will tremble and flutter at your righteous indignation, because it is not the bearer of that photograph instead of useless apologies,— which articles I always did despise.

I think I hear you say: "Pshaw! the girl does not intend to redeem her promise;" then you will enter into quite a logical disquisition, as follows;

The first page of a letter dated January 23, 1864, from Lou Pearl Riggen of Greenwood, Kentucky, and the envelope addressed to Lieutenant Lybarger in Prospect, Tennessee

Lieut E D Lybarger.
Co K. 43d Regt O.V.I.
Prospect. Tenn.

First Lieutenant Edwin Lewis Lybarger (photograph taken sometime after his promotion to first lieutenant on November 18, 1864)

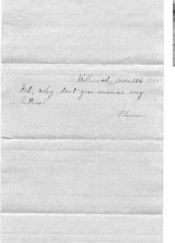

A one-sentence letter dated June 27, 1865, from Sophronia Warren Rogers of Millwood, Ohio

Two photographs of
Sophronia Warren
Rogers (Phrone),
probably taken in the
mid-1860s

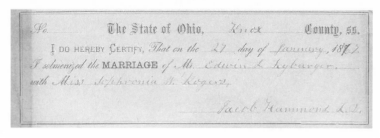

The certificate of marriage, January 27, 1867, for Sophronia W. Rogers and
Edwin L. Lybarger

Photograph of Edwin Lewis Lybarger, probably
taken after the war, possibly in 1867 at the time of
his marriage

Women's Letters to Edwin Lewis Lybarger, 1862–67

1862 LETTERS

$

letter 1

September 14, 1862. Postmarked Millwood, Ohio.
Fannie Meredith. Iuka, Miss.

At Home, Sept. 14/62

Remembered Friend Ed

I thought I would write you a letter today, although I wrote to you about two or three months ago, and have been looking for a letter from you, would have been looking yet, but Delia Schroyer told me that she had received a letter from you, and you said you had written to me but had not received an answer. I directed my letter to New Madrid, presume you had left there before the letter had gotten there. This is Sabbath Day and I am so lonely. Ria Welker has been here all day, has just gone home. I was out to Dunkard Church last night. Saw them eat soup, wash feet and take Sacrament. They had it in Mr. Ross's [?] barn, were a great many there.

I was over to Deal's last night, they feel very bad about Nute, did not get any letters yesterday. There were four or five letters came from the Regiment but none of them said anything about him. They do not know but what he is dead but think if he was dead some of you would have written it. Colwell Campbell is dead, was buried week ago yesterday, he was taken sick on Monday night and died on Thursday night. His disease was Tiphod fever.

Ed how do you like war by this time, not very well I presume. Have you been in any battles? I suppose you have heard the Rebels are near Cincinnatti, they are expecting a battle there. They will commence drafting here tuesday Oh! Isn't this war an awful thing, there is not much hopes of it ending. Every thing is so uncommonly dull here (all on account of this detestible war) that I scarcely know what to write. I was down to town last Sabbath to Sunday School and Church. It is about as lonely there as out here in the country.

Aaron Lybarger moved over to town last week. Mae Lydick is at Danville going to School. I intended to go but geve it up. There was so much excitement about war that I could not think of going.

It is getting late and I must close for I know you are tired of reading this poorly written and uninteresting letter.

Love to all I know. Goodbye.

Fannie Meredith

Write soon, very soon, your friend.

letter 2

September 27, 1862. Millwood, Ohio.
Ell Hawn. Iuka, Miss.

Millwood, Sept. 27, 1862

Friend Ed

I take this opportunity of addressing you a few lines, in reply to your last [letter] which was received sometime since & ought to have been replied to long ere this. But as you say procrastination is the thief of time you are aware it would not be <u>Ediquet</u> for me not to observe it as strictly as yourself & perhaps it [might] not have been so interesting to you had I violated this your rule. But as quite a length of time has elapsed since I received your worthy letter I have nothing to write you.

Tis true we have had news from the war department which are encourageing as we have gained many victories of which we have written to John & you will hear. And Allas the President has ishued a proclaimation that all the negroes shall be set free by the first of January if the Southerns do not go Back as they once were & obey the laws of thire Country. I would tell you more conserning this but its mail time & I must strike while the Iron is hot. Tell John we are all well, give him a Sisters love & tell him to write. Your Folks allso are well, the helth of Millwood is rather good but the pleasures of it are few. The Folks were all over & spent the Eve with us not long since. Twas then we thought of old times & of Brothers & friends & O where are they now. Some in their graves & others gone perhaps never to return. We have spoken of the pleasures being few. We seek not for pleasure while trouble surrounds us as it does. But enough of this, we must cease writing or the mail will be gone. Forgive all my imperfections since they are many & write soon.

Good morning, Ell

🕸

letter 3

October 12, 1862. Millwood, Ohio.
Emma A. Moody. [No envelope]

Millwood, October 12th, 1862

Friend Ed.

This beautiful afternoon I seate myself to answer your very welcome as well as interesting letter that came to hand last week. I was pleased to hear of your good health and that you are not dissatisfied and do not regret you went, had you no gon it is quite likely you would have been drafted and I know you would much rather go a Volunteer than a drafted man. 19 were drafted from this Township, 2 from Union, 31 from Harrison and 18 from Monroe. I suppose you have heard who most of them are and that your Brother Elijah is going as a substitute for Jo Ingle.

How much I wish there was no such thing as war but it appears that we as a Nation must drink of this bitter cup even to the dregs and that the Liberties purchased by the blood of our Fathers must be made more sacred by the blood of Husbands, Brothers, and <u>Lovers</u>, but I trust pease will be made before this once happy Land is made a dreary Desart. It looks strange to me that so much time has been spent, so many lives lost, and so little accomplished. Why is it that our bravest and best must die and the mean and dispised be left at home to enjoy the pleasures of a happy home. Ed if ever you hear of me maring An Abolition or a home coward you will please tell me of it for if there is any I dispise it is these two classes of men.

Well Ed I have nothing to write that I think will interest you. There is nothing going on. Everything is war and I expect you hear plenty of it down in Dixey.

I received a letter from brother John yesterday. He was still at Covington, said they had marching orders that morning (the 7th) did not know where they would go but expected to Lexington. I think from his letters he is tired of the buisness. I trust the day will soon come when you can all come home and be repaid a thousand times for the hardships and privations you have endured then you will see who will be honored and respected by all good men. I often think of the many pleasant hours I have spent in the society of some of the brave soldier Boys and the many times we have met at church and other places, but now your seats are vacant. Go where we will all is trouble and sadness, but when you all get home we will know how to appreciate the Liberties we enjoy.

Well Ed as I do not feel like writing today you will please excuse this short letter. You will have many imperfections to lookove if you correspond with me, I feel delicate about writing to one I know to be far my superior in almost every thing but if you can excuse all errors I will endever to make my letters more interesting in the future. Our folks all send their good wishes to you. I will close by saying I hope to hear from you soon.

Yours Truly, Emma A. Moody

letter 4

October 27, 1862. Millwood, Ohio.
Sophronia Rogers. Memphis, Tenn.

[Note: This letter is likely misdated; correct date
is likely October 27, 1863. See note 144.]

Millwood, Oct. 27, 1862

My Dear friend Ed

After beang very much disappointed at your not coming home,
I seat myself to answer your very welcome letter. Ed I had formed
quite a favorable opinion of Captain Rhodes. But when I tell you
what I know of him, you will know what any respectable lady ought
to think of him. When he came to Millwood he brought with him
Mary Wolf of Mt. Vernon, as I had known Mary when she was very
young and we went to school together I felt it no more than my duty
to call and see her. I have since learned from authority not to be
disputed, that she is a disgrace to her sex. I hope as a favor you will
tell Captain Rhodes <u>who</u> I am for fear he might consider me no
better than she. I do not wonder that he had no time to call on your
friends. Ed I have spoken very plainly to you, first because I consider
you a friend, secondly because I want every one that knows me at all
to know who and <u>what</u> I am. I am alone, but not lonely. I have plenty
to think of, or at least enough to occupy an <u>ordinary</u> mind.

Joss went to New Castle today, Ell Hawn went along. They are
going to stay three or four days. Ed do you and Ell correspond yet?
Don't think me impudent but I just want to know for everytime I
receive a letter from you she gives one of those snearing laughs as
much as to say that you are no friend of mine. I know she is not my
friend although she pretends to be. I have too much confidence in
you to think that you would betray friendship. But I will drop this
subject for the present. I hope you will have the luck especially if
you consider it a pleasure to stay at Memphis. If I was close to that
sesech lady you are in love with, I think her stay in this world would
be very short—as I feel exceedingly jealous.

Enclosed you will find the discription of different diseases and death of Copperheads friend. I just happened to see it when reading the Journal, and I thought if you do not take that paper you would enjoy it.

I feel pretty tired tonight, we have been cleaning house. I expect I will go down to New Castle tomorrow night, they intend having a jolification over the election. Rill Hammond and Oscar Welker have been married two weeks. They expect to go to house keeping in Millwood in a week or two. They are going to live in that house above the Methodist Church. Our "Union League" is prospering finally, we intend giving a supper soon for the benefit of the soldiers. I guess I have written all that I can think of now. Your father does not get any better. Your mother would feel much better if you were here to console her. She does not think your father will ever get any better. Please excuse this paper as it is all I have from the store. Remember me kindly to Oliver and answer soon. O Ed tell Frank Hogston that all the girls around are in love with him for his true patriotism. He acted so manly at the Ballot Box when all his friends were Copperheads—he waved a Brough ticket and said that was <u>his</u> vote, and we all respect him for it. I only wish I could see him to congratulate him on his own goodness.

Ever your sincere friend Phrone

Lieut. E.L.L.

letter 5

November 5, 1862. Millwood, Ohio.
Sophronia Rogers. Pedaukah Ky.

Millwood, Nov. 5th, 1862

My kind friend Ed

As I wrote to you about two months ago and received no answer I thought I would write again and see if I would not meet with better success. I have heard from you through other or different persons very often and was always very glad. I believe your mother has not heard from you for the last two weeks and she is quite uneasy about you. Ed I hope your wound is not serious yet I hope it will be the means of you getting home to stay. We all want you to come home very badly. It almost killed your mother when she heard you were wounded. I thought myself that we would never see you again. If I were you I would not walk a step until I got home if I could, you have stayed long enough anyhow. Indeed now I am not much in favor of the war and more especially not in favor of getting our men slaughtered up for the freedom of negroes. This sees to be what the most are fighting for. The drafted men will not stay in camp, those that are there and a greater part of them will not go at all. They have not furnished them (the drafted men) with blankets or tents and they swear that they are not going to stay.

The folks here do not enjoy themselves any better than you do in camp—They have very few parties. We had a large surprise at Lewis Critchfield's last Friday night. Almost every lady there had something [to] say about you. "Though absent not forgotten," a good motto, and I always keep it in remembrance. It always does me a great deal of good to know that my friends think of me. Amanda Israel told me to remember her to you Ed. They are such warm friends of yours. Jossie is up there visiting now and I suppose enjoying herself for we are having such beautiful weather—not quite enough rain to benefit us.

Captain Cassil is here recruiting. I do not know men or the ladies—they have all fallen in love with him. I suppose you heard that he has been promoted to Leut Col. Have you not. You know those shining appeletts will captivate—so if you boys don't come back soon the girls will be obliged to take widowers, lame men, or any kind they can get, fir you know it won't pay to be an old maid, you know how cross they are.

Ed I will close by hoping you will recover from your wound enough so that you can come home but not so you can join your reg—do come

Ever your friend Phrone

letter 6

November 11, 1862. [Millwood, Ohio] Fannie Meredith.
[No envelope]

At Home, Sabath eve. Nov. 11/62

Ever Remembered Friend Ed.

Some time has elapsed since the reception of your letter, and I once more grasp the pen to trace you a few lines in way of an answer. I would have written to you ere this but did not know where to write to until now, perhaps I am mistaken, but understood you were at Paducah.

I was at church today. Deal and I went down to Presbyterian Church. Was a great many Ladies there, not many Gentlemen for they are pretty scarce here these war times. Deal came home with me, stayed until this eve. They feel very badly about Nute. Ed how are you getting. I was very sorry indeed to hear that you were wounded. Hope you will recover. Where is John Hawn? Is he near you? O if this war would only close and you all be permitted to return to your homes well. But I fear that will not be the case. But do (most assuredly) hope that it will.

Millwood is very dull since you poor soldiers have gone. Although I know it is not the only place that is made lonely for it is so most everywhere, especially in the country, everything is beginning to look so dreary. Winter is fast approaching, we had a very deep snow here last week, did not last long. The leaves falling off the trees makes everything look so dreary and desolate.

Our school commences week from tomorrow. I expect I will attend. Do not know yet, but will go here or to Danville, Miss Baker is teaching in Danville, her school will be out week from Tuesday. Will have vacation two weeks then commence her winter school. Dan Campbell is going to teach over there. I presume you know him, he is a young man.

They have all gone to bed but me and guess I will have to close expecting to hear from you soon, very soon.

Good night, pleasant dreams.
Fannie Meredith

letter 7

November 30, 1862. Mt. Vernon, Ohio.
Mrs. [Samuel] Israel. Paducah, Ky.

Mount Vernon, Nov. 30th, 1862

My dear Young Friend

Edwin Lybarger I was much pleased with your favor of Oct. Twenty seventh. Glad to hear you are so well cared for. I fear all of our poor wounded soldiers cannot say as much, as we have much reason to fear many poor fellows die for the want of care and attention.

Well I suppose you have heard that Hon. Joseph Vance of our town is Collonel of the Ninety-sixth Ohio. William Mitchell, former Superintendent of our high school raised A company. Some twenty or thirty of his company were formily his pupils in the high school. Among that number was Charlie Warden. He is now lying very sick in Louisville, Kentucky.

The regiment have been ordered down the river, probably to Memphis, Tennessee. I fear they are destined to endure many hardships before they are home again.

Frank was up a few days since from Millwood. Nothing new except a wedding. I believe a Miss Ulry. The gentleman's name I have forgotten. I presume you will know better than I can tell you as I think it one long talked of.

Well I was down to Millwood I think about the tenth of October. Went on a buying [?] expedition in favor of the Soldiers Aid Society. Mrs. Rogers went with me. We crossed the creek below the mill and went up the creek. The first house we came to was your Mother's. We intended stoping but everything looked so quiet we concluded there was no person home so drove on, thinking we should return by the same road and call as we returned. But concluded we must make the best of our days werk came round by the way of Mrs. Shrimplins. We were quite successful, but I must say I felt very much disappointed not seeing your Mother as I had so much intended to see her when in Millwood.

Charlie Hawn started two weeks go tomorrow morning for Cairo to see his brother but arrived there just in time to be disappointed in seeing him as he had recovered sufficient to return to his regiment. So he had to return home without seeing him, as they would not permit him to cross the river.

Well I often think of you since the season for mince pies have returned. But [?] a review of my scribbling admonishes me to close as I fear you will be puzzled to read what I have already written. But a question comes up to ask you. I want to know how Collonel Smith was liked by his men generally. Some reports say he was very much disliked and called him a perfect tyrant. And how do you poor fellows feel about this war. Do you think it will close soon. I fear if it does not close soon our country will be ruined.

Winter is upon us and I fear our poor soldiers are not provided with half the comforts they should have. I will enclose a couple of postage stamps fearing you cannot obtain them very easily where you are, so I hope to hear from you soon again as we are all interested in your wellfare. Are there any of the Millwood boys with you, if so remember me to them.

Yours truly, Mrs. S. Israel [Elizabeth]

letter 8

December 8, 1862. Millwood, Ohio. Ella Hawn.
Paducah, Ky.

Millwood, Dec. the 8th, 1862

Friend

A few days since I received your <u>most perfect</u> letter & hasten to answer. But when I peruse your letter I know not how or who I am addressing. So you speak of answering in your awkward imperfect way and you allso say you hope that I will look over the errors of one whose misfortune it was to be born without those mental capacities which are so necissary but when all is taken into consideration we feel you should be very thankful. And again when we look back over memmorys page I feel free to write in my awkward imperfect way, then I know I am corisponding with one whome I have known allmost from his birth & know the advantages as well as disadvantages he has enjoyed over many. And when I reflect on days gone by I see my corispondent at Home, surrounded by friends & in friendship accompanied by those Dear Brothers of mine of which you spoke. But where o where are they now. You are not permitted to enjoy each others society and that of friends as you once was but are widely separated & one of those loved ones sleeps in death beneath a Southern Soil whilst the other wanders we know not where, exposed to all the hardships that a Soldier must endure. We sent for John but was disappointed as he had left just one week before Charlie got there & we have not heard from him but once since he was there in Tenn. at Grand Junction & was well with the exception of his Arm which was not quite well but not painful. We feel uneasy about him as it has been some two weeks since we heard from him & know not the cause of his not writing unless he is sick.

You gave your opinion of the war & spoke of its just commenceing. This is allmost discouraging, yet we fear it is to true as prospects are not very flatering now. We have not heard of a Battle for some time; all is quiet. But tis thought there will be a hard Battle near Richmond soon & some think if we gain it will be a desisive one which we hope it may as long [as] peace reigns triumphant.

But enoughf of this as you know doubt want the news of Home. I am sorry to say I have nothing of any importance for you. The folks are all well. Millwood is rather still, nothing going on. There is a protracted meeting commences here this week. I wish you & John was here to go and then I wish for Marion but this can never be. We have tried three times to get his remains but cannot untill the river raises and the gunn boats can pass up and down. As you know the rebels have Hamburg in their possession. We sometimes fear we will never get him & you know this was his last request & we should & will use every effort to get him & this is all we can do.

But Ed excuse my dwelling on this so long. When I get to talking of him I know not when to cease as it reminds me of many passed pleasures & of troubles & grief that now rests upon our once happy Home, forgive all imperfections since they are many & answer if this be worthy. My best wishes to you,

Ell Hawn

December 8, 1862. [Millwood, Ohio] Phrone Rogers.
Paducah, Ky.

Monday eve, At Home, Dec. 8th/62

Ever friend Edwin;

Another day has passed & gone and left me to think of the friends of the past—the greatest pleasure I have. But sometimes I grow weary of this when I think how they are separated from me. You seem to think I had quite forgotten you, I could not if I would forget thee, for I hear you spoken of so often by the many friends you left behind you. Ed your name is too deeply engraven on the pages of memory to ever be obliterated. I wrote you once before my last letter but received no answer but I suppose you never received it. I read the letter you wrote to Mrs. Israel, it was very good indeed. They all seem to think that you were blessed with very good discreptive faculties. I only wish you could have been a mouse or a spirit so you could have heard the many kindly words spoken of you; I suppose you have long since received a reply to your letter to Mrs. Israel, for I took it to the P.O. one week ago when I was up there.

You have heard long before this the John Wilkerson & K.J. Selery [Selby?] were married. They were married two weeks ago yesterday. They went on their Bridal Tour, to Oxford. I suppose John will soon become a "Camelite" as they have now commenced a distracted meeting. It is going to last over two sabaths. Ed you just ought to hear our new preacher, he is such a good one, I know you would like him.

Ed, I want to know if you correspond with Ell Hawn or not. She says you do. She said she received a letter from you last Saturday. I saw the envelope but it did not look like your hand writing. She says "I received a [letter] from Bygoshelmighty (that's what she calls you) and if Pap knew it he would row me up salt river." I thought what a pity.

Ed never tell this to anyone. There are three runaways from the rebel army here now, Dr. Landeckers' brothers. They came from

Kentucky, as I understand it, as were pressed into service. I have not seen them yet.

Ed I have had the tooth ache all day so if I make a good many mistakes you must look over them. I think I will visit Dr. Mc . . . or some other Blacksmith shop tomorrow. I hope your wound is getting along finally but I should think it consoling to be a criple (not a bad one) so that I could get home. I would stay in the Hospital and risk lonliness rather than bullets. I think you could amuse yourself nicely by reading as you always loved to read so well. Jossie send her love and says she would like to hear from you

Receive my kind wishes for your wellfare & write soon

(Phrone)

Your Mother talks of you all the time & very often cries about you. She is very uneasy about you.

letter 10

December 14, 1862. Millwood, Ohio. Adelia Shroyer.
[No envelope]

Millwood, Dec. 14th, 1862

Respected Friend Ed;

I was pleasantly surprised last evening on receiving a letter from you. I have been long expecting an answer until I at last came to the conclusion that you had never received mine. I am cincerely glad to hear that you are as well.

Washington received your sad letter imeadtly after Newton's death, but neglected to answer it not knowing exactly where you were. We heard at first that you were mortaly wounded and I mourned you as lost but I am rejoiced to hear that you are getting well and hope you may be able to go to your Regt soon as you wish to go, and also hope you may never get into another battle, for I shall ever respect you as a Brother for the kindness that you have bestowed upon my poor Brother who is gone although I cannot realize it. I cannot think it although it is too True.

John Conkle went after his Brother but did not get him. Excuse poor writing, my eyes are dimed with tears. We sent for Newton's clothes and they came.

O what a horrible sight to look upon and to think that was all that was left of the once merry-hearted bright eyed Boy, my <u>Dear Brother</u>, it is dreadful to contemplate, but alas how frail is life.

I have nothing of much importance or that will be interesting to you to write. I was invited to a party at Elijiah's last week but did not go. Your folks are all well as far as I know. I suppose you have other correspondents that write to you regular that inform you of all the particulars. There has been a great many weddings this fall and Deaths also but I suppose you have heard of news by some one of your Correspondent which would not be news to you if I should enter upon the particulars.

I saw two Cousins of yours, they were up at your house and at Elijiahs. Their names were Upton Lybarger and I furget his Sister's name, it was his Sister.

Well Ed I hardly know what to write. I fear this will be anything but interesting to you. You will please excuse brevity as I have several other letters to write yet today. I made a mistake in commencing on the wrong page. I was confused. Over look all mistakes. Wash sends his best regards to you.—You have my well wishes, in memory, I am often with you and often think of the many pleasant hours that we have spent together, hours that I enjoyed myself as agreeable [?] as any that I have spent since.

I will close, Good By Ed
I remain ever your true Friend Adelia

Mother requests me to ask you if Newton ever received his discharge as it is not to be found among his papers, and she wishes to know if he ever spoke of home or made any request, you will oblige me by writing.

Yours

letter 11

December 19, 1862. Monroe Mills, Ohio.
Edith Welker. Paducah, Ky.

Minroe Mills, Ohio, Dec. 19th/62

Respected Friend

I hail this favorable opportunity of answering your very kind
and interesting letter which reached its destination a few days ago.
It was a very welcome visitor I assure you. We are all well, and I
sincerely hope when this reaches you it will find you well.

I was sorry to hear of your being wounded; And glad to hear
that you are getting along so well.

I havent went to school any this winter yet. I dont think I will
like the Teacher very well and therefore I am not in a very great
hurry about starting. Erastus Cake is teaching our school. I would
much rather hear of your getting the school. I wish you were here to
teach. I think I could go with a free good will.

There was [a] big meeting at Millwood last week and partly of
this week at the Disciple Church. I attended partly of the time. I
went down on last Saturday and stayed until Tuesday, had a very
good time. I went over to school where we used to go. D.R.
Cambpell is Preceptor. He is a very good Teacher, not quite strict
enough. I will find no fault with him. If I only liked our Teacher as
well [as] I do him I could [get] along very well.

Well Ed there is not very much new news only the Rebels have
possession of Fredericksburg. I suppose you knew where that is. It is
in Virginia. Burnside had possession of it but had to recross the river
on account of the river raising. If it would rain it would wash all the
pontoon bridges away, and he could not retreat, so that he would be
compelled to surrender, that is if he could not master the Rebels;
which I hope will not be any trouble to do. From what I can learn I
guess there will be a pretty big force to contend with. I have written
you the news as I have gathered it.

I believe I have written enough for fear of worrying your father
with this poorly written & poorly composed letter, but I have such a

very poor pen that I can hardly write at all. I hope you will overlook all mistakes and blots, for I will try to do better the next opportunity I have of writing to you.

With an ever grateful Remembrance of you I am your ever true Friend.

Edith F. Welker

Please answer as soon as received. I will sympathize with you in your loneliness. I could hardly write on this envelope.

$

letter 12

December 24, 1862. Millwood, Ohio.
Louisa Welker. Paducah, Ky.

Millwood, O. Dec. the 24th, 1862

Respected Friend

I take this opportunity of replying to your letter which was received some time ago, and which might have been answered ere this but better late than never.

Well I have nothing of importance to communicate to you but I thought I would write you a few lines to let you know how we are getting along way up here in the north. First I will say that times are awful dry, there is nothing going on here at all worth mentioning except the protracted meeting at the Disciple Church at Millwood. It commenced two weeks ago today, and is going on yet I expect they will keep it up till Sunday. There has been six immersed. I will name them. James Rightmire and Wife, Harrison Rightmire's Wife and Daughter Lydia, and Pierce Crichfield's Wife and Mrs. Shelman. I guess they think they will get Liz and Ellen Rightmire, but I dont think they will for I think they like dancing too well. Well I believe this is all I can tell you about the meeting.

Tomorrow is Christmas. O how I wish you were all here to spend the holidays. There is nothing going on here that I know of. I hope you have not forgotten the party that we were at, at Aaron Lybargers. That will be two years tomorrow night. Little did we then think that you would now be where you are, but we must make the best we can of it, it is bad enough anyhow.

You requested me when I wrote to tell you where the 65th was. I guess the Reg is near Nashville, Tennessee. Osker is not with the Reg now. He is very sick at Louisville. He was taken sick at Nashville about 6 weeks ago and was sent to Louisville last week to the officer's Hospital. We received a letter from him yesterday, he is getting better slowly. I fear he will not stand the service very well.

I believe I will not weary your patience any longer. I cant think of any thing that would be interesting to you now. Ed I want you to write often for I love to hear from my good old friends. I know you correspond with someone else but I dont care, I want to hear from you anyhow. I have not rce a single letter from John Hawn since he left home but I dont know why he dont write but I suppose I am not worthy of his thoughts but I think I am. I will close hoping to hear from you soon. Please excuse this short and uninteresting letter and I will endeavor to do better in the future. I am well and enjoying myself as well as could be expected in this place. No more at present. I remain your affectionate friend.

Louisa Welker

1863 LETTERS

letter 13

January 29, 1863. Millwood, Ohio. Ella Hawn. Bolivar, Tenn.

Millwood, Jan. the 9, 1863

Friend Ed

Your kind letter came to hand on the 26th & I read it & reread it as I must say it suited me very much as it is booth free and friendly & remindes me of old times. You no doubt know that there is a change in the feelings of those at <u>Home</u> And when I received your <u>letter</u> previous to this I read its many apologies & formal ways I scarcely knew who I was writing to or how to write. In fact I did not feel to care whether I wrote a very acceptable letter or no. but when we take all things into consideration we know not why we should be offended. So this is the work of some who had it in view when we were all at <u>Home</u> together. Yes they made the attempt then & they have since accomplished their desires. But when we remember the past with its truest <u>friends</u> we feel this should never make any change in us, although we may hear many things which are untrue & unpleasant. Yet why heed them, were <u>you</u> not the choicest <u>friend</u> of that Dear Brother who with you bid Adieu to <u>Home</u> true to each other & we feel you done so until separated by death.

And now that we have but <u>one</u> left to share the fate of this <u>reached</u> [wretched?] <u>War</u> which we know not how long may last, may you treat each other kindly & cherish a <u>lasting friendship</u>, that if permitted to return you may come more firmly united, & if not you may relieve each others sufferings while no other friend is near.

We received a letter from John the same mail I rec <u>yours</u>, the first we have had for five long <u>weeks</u>. We were quite uneasy about him but this tells us he is well. He spoke of you which he never fails to do when writing <u>Home</u>. I wish you may both speak of each other for very often your <u>Folks</u> get letters when we do not and sometimes we get when they do not. So this would be a satisfaction to us all.

But a noughf of this as you wants the news of <u>Home</u>. Well the folks are all well & doing the best they can. There is but little enjoyment here this winter as the weather is very unpleasant. We have had some snow but it does not last long a noughf for us to get ready for Sleighing. I have had one little <u>Sleigh ride</u> & like to a not got that. We have had or have been invited to several <u>Parties</u> but did not attend. Last week we were invited up to Critchfields where you spoke of taking Het and I if you remember. And we were allso invited to Malhouse, this was a nice time they tell me. We were up to J. whites the night after Newyears, had a good time there. Was quite a number there. O yes, was invited to A. Whites but of course should be. You are gon & Lizzie is married no danger now, but no more of this glimmering through the past.

Ed you would like it here this winter on account of Church as we have very nice Church entertainments. Our Ministers are much

better than they were when you were Home booth at the Presbyterian
& Methodist. There will be a Protracted Meeting held at the
Presbyterian Church ere long; this no doubt will be very interesting.
I wish you & John were here to attend do you not; but this cannot be.

Give John a Sisters love & tell him to take good care of himself
& write <u>Home</u> often. Tell him we are very sorry you are compelled
to live on half rations. Would that we could supply the other portion
but this is not in our power. O Ed to think of the miseries of this
War. Just think last week the news came of little Veloscoe Hildreth
being killed & since we learn that a part of his head was shot off &
this only one of the thousands that have been mangled & crushed
in this cruel war. When O when will it cease is the language of all
at <u>Home</u>.

Ed I will cease writing. I could not get any other paper & I do
not know but it's a good thing as I have hardly room in this to write,
but you must forgive this lengthy letter & all imperfections since
they are many. My best wishes to all. Write if this be worthy of an
answer. So good night.

Ell Hawn

☥

letter 14

February 22, 1863. Millwood, Ohio.
Phrone Rogers. Bolivar, Tenn.

Home, Feb. 22nd/63

Ever Dear Friend;
    This quiet Sabbath I seat myself to pay an old debt which
no doubt you will think a long time coming. I should have answered
your letter sooner only Jossie wrote to you not long ago—and I
thought you would not care about hearing from us both at the same
time. I was down to your house yesterday and spent the afternoon.
Your mother was crying about you. She said she had written six
letters to you since you had joined your regiment, and that you had
writen home you had received but one letter in three months (if I

mistake not). You have a dear kind mother who cares for you. Indeed her whole conversation is about you—and you father. Why Ed you would not know his form—he does not show his grief like your angle mother but he shows it in his wasted form and sad countinence. Ed if you knew how your friends (I mean your true friends) mourn your absence I know it would give you a very cheerful heart. Think not that your mother has not writen to you because you received but one letter from home. I hardly ever go down but what your mother is writing to you—and cannot enjoy my visits on account of her grief.

If you have not received Jossie's letter please let me know and she will write again. She told you all the news in her letter so that if you received it little remains for me to say that will be new to you. But I will mention over some things which I know she did not tell you as it does not come under her "style." Something about our "dogries" as we style them. Landen Welker gets as drunk that he staggers when he walks. Milt Hawl too. Indeed I could mention a great many others that would supprize you equally as much. George Butler & Joe Johnston are just going it on the "oog" system. I dont know what our little village is coming to.

There are societies all over the country who call themselves The Knights of the Golden Circle. They absolutely refuse to give aid for the continuance of this war. We will certainly have war here at home if these infernal societies are not broken up somehow. Col. Cassil made a speech at the "Camilite" Church last night. There was quite a respectable crowd out to hear him speak. He gave it to these secret societies thick and thin—you had better think. He told them if they were for peace and they knew of any other means to bring it about beside fighting we were all in for it. I can give you a few names of these who belong. George Butler, Milt Hawl, Joe Butts and all such trash. Ed please keep these things to yourself. It might make a fuss if it was known I told it. But I can trust you and tell you what I please. Doctor Campbell is as perfect secesh as you will meet in rebeldom. He and Joe Butts and Peterman had quite a quarel about the matter as Will Hawn tell us (he was present at the time the conversation took place) Will said after he had got through talking he asked him if he had forgotten the Union speach he made in public. He said no but he had changed his mind. Will said it got him down a little. We have about as many secesh as union men.

I believe we have had one wedding lately which you will hear of with interest (I presume) Mr. Bazil Critchfield to Miss Julia Fields. We wish them all the good luck imaginable in this their new state. She had a wedding partie—part of them came through Millwood. Bob Critchfield and Miss Anderson (who lives at Dr. Masts in Amity) Emma Critchfield & Col. Cassil. It is reported that they will be married. I do no know how true this is, he seems very attentive indeed. I suppose the girls will have to take old men or non at all. This is a great consolation to the boys who expect to get home for they can have their pick and choice of the young ladies, and there seems to be more than ever. Ed I feel certain you will be one of the fortunate ones that will be permitted to return home. How glad do we welcome the day.

Jacob Hammond is not in Millwood now. He has been out west all winter choping cord wood. As I understand it he is in Rushville, Schuyler Co., Illinois so if you want to write to him put the letter in care of Henry Hammond and he will be sure to get it.

Frank Israel has left Joe Johnstons and gone to Jim Pyles to board. Mrs. Johnston called him a liar at the dinner table about a book that Frank had borrowed of her to read somebody a letter that was in it. He naturally got up from the table and left.

This day has been blustery and cold. We have enough snow now for sleighing. I have felt sad I cannot tell why all day. Daws Critchfield came home from church and stayed all the afternoon with me. You have heard I suppose that he has been my ascort for some time past. He is quite a nice little gentleman. He is going to school in Gambier and gets along nicely. He got the first honor of his class last year, but enough about him. I like him pretty well I guess, anyhow I will untill I meet with some one I fancy more. Dont laugh at my noncence if you please. I am just telling you every thing that I think of right along. I have a miserable pen not much better than a stick; if I make a hundred mistakes look over them.

Tis now 9 oclock and I am weary yet I will bid "tired natures sweet restorer" linger outside my room untill I have finished. Joss and Frank are in another room. Mother has gone down to your house and I am all alone. We expect another draft will come off soon. That will make some feel where they live. Ed if I have failed to say anything or left unsaid anything you want to know about Millwood let me know and I will be very happy to inform you.

Women's Letters to Edwin Lewis Lybarger

I go to school to Henry McElroy this winter. You would die laughing if you could hear some of the mistakes he makes in grammar but he keeps very good order. He hopes [to be] around a spell.

Write soon. From your true friend Phrone.

$

letter 15

April 6, 1863. Millwood, Ohio.
Ella Hawn. Fort Hooker, Tenn.

Millwood, Aprile 6'63

Well Ed

Sometime has passed since I received your worthy letter which I have delayed answering untill now for the purpose of getting something good to write you. But news are a scarce article here or at least on one side of the river and therefore I have nothing more interesting than if I had written the day after I received yours. But I would here say that today is quite an exciting time for Millwood as you are a male that this is <u>Election</u> day, & there are Union & Disunions for office. But the Sitizens feel bound that the Union shall win the day which I hope it may, for I was very much disapointed in its strength when I see these Copperheads come in & take possession of our most popular Church and there preach there Secesh doctrine. I must say I was discouraged to see those who have children & friends in the Army uphold such doctrine. I think it disgrace to our Town & those who have gone in defence of their Country.

Danvilles far exceeds Millwood in union. They applied there for a church but they refused & would not eaven permit them to preach in the Schoolhouse untill C. Wintringer broke the door open & then there was but a few little boys went to hear the Old Traitor. They now talk of putting the (little) man through for his trouble, which I hope they will & that <u>soon</u> for Ed I think it time they were doing something with them. Tis nothing uncommon for the Harrison Township fellows to [be] hollowing [hollering] for Jeff Davis & the southern Confederacy. This I think would not be allowed. There is talk of them taking those drafted men now soon & I hope they may & all the best (?) of the (Copperheads) with them.

We have had no war news for the last day or so but the people feel much encouraged [to] think this rebellion will soon be crushed. Many think it will not last six months. I hope it may not, yet this I fear is to good to be true (but hope) But Ed I supose you know more about this than I can tell you, & would rather here the news of home & it is time according to Ediquet that my letter was brought to a close. But I would here say the Girls are all doing fine & your moste favorite one down the river will be married if you dont soon get back & then O then poor Ed. So excuse all imperfections since they are many. So good night. O yes, Ed, Col Cassil has resigned & is at home. Give my love to John, answer soon do.

Ell Hawn

Ed there was quite a good letter come from the 43d last week & the Director [?] says he is going to take it to Town & have it Corrected & Published. Good for you. My best wishes to you all. Good night.

$

letter 16

April 16, 1863. Millwood, Ohio. Joss Rogers. Cairo, Ill.

Home, Thursday eve., April 16th/63

My kind friend Ed

I seat myself this evening to answer your letter again and I hope with better success than before, as you never, it seems, received the letter I wrote some time since. I guess there is nothing very startling in the events that have transpired around here lately. The opinion of almost everyone (except secesh) is that it will not be long before this rebellion will be crushed. Col. Cassil is home. He thinks he is not able for service in the army, while I think he *is*. The prevalent oppinion is that he intends getting married. I expect this what Ed is thinking of from what he said in Phrone's letter, about the girls in your part of Dixie.

We have a new landlord in Millwood, Mr. William Buck. Their introduction was a dancing party, about such as you spoke of, only the ladies do not chew tobacco I believe. I am glad to hear you have gotten into such a pleasant place. I hope if you like it there that you may be permitted to remain until the war is over. Your log houses are very pleasant and comfortable I presume.

Do you have any devine service in your camp? We have such a good minister at the Presbyterian church now. He lives in New Castle and has a very good school there. We have communion next Sabbath. Mat Collinse's school is out. She is coming up to stay over Sunday. She is going to teach in Warsaw this summer again. Osker Welker has been very sick but is some better now; they did not think he would get well. Loraine White has been very sick with a fever. Lizzie Millis has moved to New Castle. He (Mr. Millis) is a going to sell goods there. They are everyone (the whole White family) secesh.

Ed I hope you will excuse mistakes and write soon. I will close as I can not think of anything else to write. Your folks are very well. Your friend, Jess Rogers.

⚲

letter 17

May 22, 1863. Millwood, Ohio. Phrone Rogers. Cairo, Ill.

Home, May 22nd/63

Ever kindly remembered friend

I thought I would write you a few lines this morning before the mail goes out. Joss think it quite strange that you do not write to her as she has writen to you a second time. I was up to town a few days ago. Mrs. Israel wants to know why you do not answer her letter she wrote to you that I am aware of for I took her letter to the office.

There is a going to be a union meeting in Mt. Vernon the 29th of this month. Governor Tod is a going to address the meeting. I suppose from all reports there will be a very large crowd of people. I intend going. I expect to stay a few weeks.

We have nothing very exciting going on here except the two societies "The Union" and "Knights _____." The secesh and union do not associate together very much. I think the time will come when they will not speak to each other at all, and I think this will be perfectly right for my part. I dont want to speak to a secessionist nor I dont want one to speak to me.

The Ladies are organizing union societies. They have quite a large one in Mt. Vernon. They are going to march the day of the meeting and carry a flag. They have 32 little girls all of one size to represent the states dressed in white dresses with blue sashes. They will meet the speaker at the depot. They will also have a stage near the speaker decorated with flowers. "Hurrah for the Union League" If I had my will of the rebels here I would have them all hung.

Ed I received that portrait of you, think the position looked very natural. I intend having it framed. I expect to have some Photographs taken when I go to town, then if you will answer my letter I will send you one.

I received a letter from Oliver Taylor (directed by you) I answered it, did he ever receive my letter? I have often wondered. Give him my very best wish for his happiness. He writes a very good letter. Ed tell me all about Williams in you Co. He wrote Ella Rightmire a letter and proposed to marry her.

Excuse haste and answer soon. Your friend, Phrone Rogers

$

letter 18

May 24, 1863. Bainbridge, Ohio.
Rozaltha Crum. Memphis, Tenn.

Brainbridge, Ohio, May 24th, 1863
Dear Cousin

I take the pleasure this afternoon to write you a few lines. We are all well at present and I hope when these few lines come to hand will find you enjoying the same blessing. Papa received a letter from you daybeforeyesterday stating that you was well and getting along well. As pappa has not time to write I will have to write in behalf of him. He has been away at work all week and just came home yesterday evening and as Uncle Abram and Aunt Sarah was down he could not write so I thought I would write this time and let him write the next time.

You said you had writen several times but received no answers. We have received but one letter from you since you have been in the army and that we received day before yesterday. You said you had received no letters from us. I wrote you a letter in the winter sometime but received no answer.

You inquired about Foulks and Jenkins. They are all well or at least was two or three weeks ago. None of them are in the army. Bud Jenkins enlisted in Cousin John Gibson's Regt. But he was so green they gave him a discharge. I do not know what Regt Cousin John is in but can find out by writing to Missouri the next time I write. I will then tell you. That is all of our friends as far as I know that is in the army.

Pappa says for you to give the Rebels Hell and if he was their he would help you. Yes I guess you cannot hold the Copperheads in greater contempt than Pappa does.

Aunt Sarah sends her love to you and wants you to write to her and she will write to you. Aunt Sarah says her boy is the finest one in existence, I am a going to have it called Edwin. Aunt Sarah says she is a looking for you and your Ma and Pa & Alanda down this fall and I do hope you will come.

Well I have nothing of much importance to write this time but will try and do better the next time. Edwin take good care of your self and try and get back and see us once more. Pappa says for you to write soon again and tell us all of the news. Well I will have to close by sending my love to you. Write soon Dear Cousin pappa and all the rest sends their love to you.

Write as soon as you can. From your ever loving

Cousin Roȝaltha Crum

I send my love to you.
P.S. Please send me your picture take in your uniform.

letter 19

May 30, 1863. Macon City, MO.
Benjamin Stone. Memphis, Tenn.

Macon City. Mo., May 30th, 1863

Dear Friend

I received yours of the 18th Inst. Which I perused with much pleasure and interest: for I was really glad to hear from you. I shall always remember the times we had at the hospital. While they were in one respect disagreeable they were in another, in the friendship we found, very agreeable to me at least.

Your letter found me well but my arm it is not entirely. I am enjoying myself first rate and find agreeable employment in reading Blackstone, and occasionally a play of Shakespeare, or a page of Byron rests my weary head and then I read the news to see how "the boys" are getting along, go to town on Saturday, to church and see the girls on Sunday and so pass my days.

During my stay in the South persons and things have taken a change here at home and I find that Secession is about "played out" (to use a common phrase) and men whom I have heard to boast, in high flown language, of the glories of the glorious "Confederacy" are now like fawning dogs licking your feet, base flattery. Some sulk and say nothing. Their hopes have forsaken them. Generally all is peace, calm as if there was no war, untill some news of battles below breaks in upon their quiet when there is eagerness to hear who are the victors, who have friends, husbands, brothers, or lovers, killed or wounded in battle, then all is calm. But our people are not to be betrayed by their stillness. We have militia organized and organizing ready should any reverse of arms or any unforeseen circumstances require their assistance. Then their presence will keep down disturbers of the peace or any disaffected.

The political sentiment here generally is in favor of a vigorous prosecution of the war at all hazards and at whatever expense untill the rebellion is crushed and the flag of our country waves triumphant over all the land and the laws can be executed by even the lowest magistrate without molestation. We think we have patriotism and wisdom enough, bravery and capability of endurance enough, power and ability altogether sufficient to put down the traitors and crush out the last remnant of their power without the employment or assistance of the slave. But the Congress, the Administration have seen fit to insult our patriotism and confidence in the power of the government and to abuse our patience by the calling to war so base an ally. We will use our greatest energies to strengthen the hopes of the present authorities that they may put down the enemy meanwhile looking with an eager longing to the time when the people can elect men to high places who believe and trust in the ability of our government to defend itsself against all enemies everywhere by the patriotism and bravery of its own freemen. We have most confidence in those who have confidence in us.

I entirely agree with you that the first great object of the government should be to put down the rebellion and I have entire confidence in the power and will of its people to do it. I believe our government has a high destiny and will yet live many ages undivided and unbroken in peace, that our Soldiers are performing one of the most sacred duties that can be performed by man.

Allow me to congratulate you on your promotion. I was really glad to hear of that. Justice will come at last. I hope you every success and that the enemies ball will all miss you, that you will have plenty to eat and drink, (for I know one of the great blessings of mankind) and when you are out of service you will come and see me. There are plenty of pretty girls in this country and I am thinking well of them believing therefore they ought to think something of me. They have not given me the sack yet. The Secesh girls are quite nice and very friendly. I dont believe they would very seriously object to have a kiss or a hug from a "fed" as they call us. I have heard that Memphis is a great place for pretty women. I guess you know. I hope to hear from you often.

I am truly your friend.
Benjamin F. Stone

Lieut. E.L. Lybarger.

letter 20

June 14, 1863. Bainbridge, Ohio.
Rozaltha Crum. Memphis, Tenn.

Bainbridge, Ohio, June 14/63

My Dear Cousin

I seat myself this beautiful Sabbath morning to answer you ever welcome letter which it is needless to say I was very glad indeed to receive. We are all well at present and hope when these few lines come to hand will find you enjoying the same.

You desire me to tell you about Cousin John Gibson. I do not know his rank, neither what Rgt. he belongs to, but I have written to Missouri to find out.

You wished me to remind your Uncle & Aunt Sarah of you. I gave Aunt Sarah your address and she said she would write to you. But for Uncle Elijah, Strawder, & Harrison I have not seen them since I seen you consequently it will be impossible for me to do so as I have no correspondence with them at this time but will certainly do so.

I received a letter from your mother 2 or 3 days ago. They were all well. I have a letter that you wrote back to the editor. Your mother sent it to me. I think it is very good and so does all that have read it. They think you are one of the wright kind. Cousin I do not tell you this to flatter you but to give you some encouragement. I would be very much gratified to see you this fall but as you say you do not intend leaving the service it will be impossible for me to see you. Nevertheless it will be very pleasing for me to get your likeness.

Well I must close as there is nothing interesting to write about. The negroes are raising a Company to go to the army. There was part of a company left here the fore part of the week. They started for Massachusetts to go to their Regt.

Well I will have to close my letter with the expectation of seeing your picture soon. Papa and all the rest send their love to you. From your Cousin

Rozaltha

Write soon   Remember me

letter 21

June 20, 1863. Millwood, Ohio. Phrone Rogers. Memphis, Tenn.

Millwood, June the 20th/63

Kind friend

I have been waiting some time to receive an answer to my last letter, but have waited in vain. This time I am only agoing to scribble you a note.

This is Sabbath afternoon. Attended the Methodist church in the forenoon, and this afternoon I have been walking down the crick. Amanda Israel is visiting us now. Will Knight has preached once for us and once in Mt. Vernon. He is going to preach for us next Sunday, he does so well.

Ed I saw your picture you sent to your mother. It looks so good. Joss has fallen in love with Captain Rhodes. She says she is in hope that he is a bachelor or at least not married.

Ed I think you might have some Photographs printed and send me one in return for the one I am sending you. This is a very good picture of me every one says except the mouth which looks too large.

I received a second letter from Oliver Taylor. He is such a little gentleman I think.

How have you spent this day? I often wonder what you do with yourself all the while. I hope you will excuse haste and answer very soon.

Friend Phrone

letter 22

June 22, 1863. Millwood, Ohio. Ella Hawn. Memphis, Tenn.

Millwood, June the 22, 63

Ed

I read your letter sometime ago but as I had nothing good to write & I have nothing still. But I will not delay writing any longer for fear you forget you have written & think I am a new corispondent added to your list which I am not if you remember. But Ed the last Souldier or Sergent I wrote to I allmoste forgot I had written when the answer came & by this you can see how interesting such a corispondent is. But this is sufficient now & I will say more when I write again.

I would here say there is nothing interesting a going on here, all is still & dey no parties or amusements of any kninde except those, what shall I call them: Copperheads, Butternuts, Sircles or Traitors. You can choose the name you think most suitable. Well they are a Stiring People & had a grand <u>Fishing Partie</u> at the Caves & we were invited but did not know at the time that the company consisted of the above & they came up & invited us down to eat dinner with them & I am sorry to say I went & the refreshments were Grand Velandingham Cake & all other cakes. But can there be any good come out of _____. Yes there can for among all this they had <u>Colde Ham</u> & when they passed the Velandingham they insisted on me having a peace. But I thanked them, that I preferred the Colde Ham & shortly after I retired from the sceans of rebeldom, satisfied hereafter to stay at home on such occasions.

But this is but one of the many grand gatherings they are having. Just last Saturday they were all in Millwood & Frank Hurd was expected to address them. But I supose he thought the souldiers were to near as he did not come. W. Morton & J. Adams addressed them but tis said they done more harm to their own Partie than good. I guess the day was mostly spent in drinking whiskey, running hosses & fighting. So you can see their interest does not extend very far in the rebellion or the saveing of the government.

Last week there was some two or three companys of Souldiers came to Harrison & compelled them to obey the enrolling officer which they had refused to do, & tis said there has been a great many more Souldiers came. I hope they will take every man of them & put them in the Service & make them fight & they will then apreciate the laws of the government they are disobeying. Ell Hawn.

Write soon, if this be worthy of an answer & remember the lines near the last one on the first Page . . . Give John a Sisters love & tell him to write & that we are all well. Het sends her love & best wishes to the 2d Lieutenant of Co. K, & says she is glad he has lost his front tooth for she has to She says not get them put in untill you come home. She thinks it a great addition to her looks & sertainly improve the looks of you.

P.S. You spoke of you & John being warm friends, we hope you will remain so untill you get home. John ever speaks in the warmest terms of friendship of you.

$

letter 23

June 23, 1863. Millwood, Ohio.
T. B. Campbell. Memphis, Tenn.

Millwood, Knox Co., Ohio June 23d/63

Lieut. E.L. Lybarger
Dear Friend,

We received your very welcome, interesting and patriotic letter yesterday, and in behalf of myself I now attempt a reply. You speak truly when you say we still adhere to the <u>true</u> principles of Democracy—not this bogus spurious <u>cecesh</u> Democracy that is now cursing and disgracing the country and bringing an everlasting stigma upon that once honored name—To be a Democrat a man must be a lawabiding union loving citizen. If he is not that in the present hour of our country's peril he must be a disunionist and anarchist—There are but two questions for the people of the Loyal States to decide. The people of the rebble states as you are aware boldly and persistently proclaim that nothing short of an acknowledgement of a Southern Confederacy will ever meet their aprobation Any measures looking towards reconciliation or reconstruction have by them been spurned with contempt. Any man therefore or party who will thrust compromise under their noses where he knows or ought to know that they will be indignantly rejected is simply making an ass of himself and playing into the hands of the Rebbels

The question then to be decided is this: Shall the war be prosecuted vigorously for the restoration of the Government and Union as the only means by which it can be restored.—Or shall we ceace this strife for the maintainance of the Government and acknowledge a Southern Confederacy—These are the questions to be decided. Men may quibble and prevaricate as much as they will —they may call this a war waged expressly for the freedom of the Negro—they may wail over so-called arbitrary arrests—they may talk loudly of alleged violations of the Constitution and bleat vociferously about freedom of speech and freedom of the press— they may complain of the unfairness and unconstitutionality of Conscription Laws. But it amounts to nothing more and nothing less than an oposition to the government, and a playing into the hands of the rebels And the more these follish and imaginary objections are agitated, the more corrupt becomes the adjitators and the more corrupt becomes the minds of the people who entertain such false notions and speculative theories.

A man can't support his government in Ohio country without being branded an Abolitionist, as though that name had a terror that would frighten honest men from a support of their country—But the word Abolition has a terror to some honest but ignorant minds, and rather than be branded with it they will and do act with a party that in effect are doing everything to bring about an acknowledgement of a Southern Confederacy.

We have had a small foretaste of war here. We have had the objects and purpose of that treasonable organization known as the K.G.C. fuly verified in what is called the Harrison township and Holmes County rebellion. There was a Marshall sent to Harrison to enroll them. He was met by a party of 18 rebbels and ordered to leave the township and not return under penalty of death. The case was submitted to the State Authorities and a company of 85 soldiers were sent into Harrison—some of the Harrisonites were in Millwood when the word came. They swore they would annihilate the soldiers, that they would not leave a grease spot for a remnant of what was once 85 soldiers. They hastened home and marshaled their clans and started to meet and give battle to the invaders under cover of darkness. They stole stealthily up to them. They saw them. It was a reality. Here was 85 men perfectly willing to fight. Oh had the soldiers only staid in Mt. Vernon, how the Harrisonites could have fought. But now they saw them face to face and their hearts failed them. Their knees did tremble and their heands did shake, and some go so far as to say that they had to change their pantaloons when they went home. Thus ingloriously ended the Harrison township rebellion.

The Marshall went to work and without opposition enrolled the township. Notwithstanding the defeat of the Harrisonites Jackson township boasted of <u>their</u> valorous and good fighting qualities, refused to be enrolled peacibly. Killed some sheep for their loyal neighbours, destroyed ornamental trees, threw down fences and committed other depridations that went far to prove their valour and courage. So the immortal 85 had to [go] to Jackson even unto the City of Bladensburg to quell the Danivites. But the heroes of Jackson could not stand the sight of the blue coats. Sudently as if by magic they all became loyal and wonderingly said one to another "Why did these soldiers come here?" Enfield rifels and beyonets have a wonderful effect in making men loyal. It seems to work as well or better here than it does in the south. The rebellion in Holmes Co. near Nepolion was somewhat more extensive than in Harrison or Jackson. Four men stoned, shot at, and otherwise abused. The enrolling officer, the <u>civil</u> authorities (not military) arrested these four culprits.

The K.G.C. assembled in force and recaptured not only the four men, but the authorities who took them, disarmed, and parolled them. Five hundred soldiers were sent to quell the rebellion. The rebbels collected all their forces to the amount of six or eight hundred with two pieces of artillery. (Among the number before the soldiers arrived was Prince Calvin but when he saw there was danger his cowardly heart failed him) The soldiers came up, sent forward a Co. which fired on the rebbels, wounding one or two and taking one or two prisoners and causing the ballance to skeddle. It was finally arranged that the leaders should be given up to the Civil authorities and their poor ignorant and deluded followers were allowed to go home and ordered to attend to their own business.

All now is quiet in Holmes—and it is hoped that they have been taught a lesson that they will long remember. It would require more time than I can at present command to give you a minute history of the Holmes County affair. Report says that Calvin [?] Winteringer, Jess Winteringer, James Smith, Joseph Johnson, Sam Shrimplin and son Welters, John Carpenter and brothers, Chaney Gamble &c &c were among the rebbels aiding and assisting them as long as there was no danger but when they learned that the soldiers were coming, sure enough, the Union township delegation came home–

Rance Lydick and John Meridith and Chas. Pasco have volunteered in the six months service. If there was a good recruiting officer here a Co. might be raised in this neighborhood.

I made a short visit to Murfreesboro not long since so that I have had a peep at the great Army of the Cumberland. The visit paid me very well. I was gone about three weeks. I was in Nashville about ten days. Saw something of soldier life &c &c.

As the mail is about to leave I must close. Your father and mother and friends are all well. In fact everybody in Millwood is well. Write soon and often. There is nothing does me more good than to get a letter from my old and tried friend and schoolmate. Wishing you health, long life, and all the comforts possible for a soldier to enjoy, I subscribe myself your sincere friend and well wisher.

T.B. Campbell

(Please consider the names I have given you confidential)

letter 24

June 23, 1863. Millwood, Ohio.
Ella Rightmire. Memphis, Tenn.

Millwood, Ohio June 23, 1863

My friend,

I might say that I was rather surpized when I received your letter. But I am pleased to know there yet exists one spark of remembrance which has caused you to spend a few moments of time endeavering to converse with one that I thought you had forgotten. For my part I can never forget those that were once my associates in society and are now enduring hardships that the pen can not discribe for the liberties that we now enjoy. This I suppose you can say is true from experience. I would not wonder if you would rather I would change my subject.

I don't know that I can for this Rebellion has its effects every where. Our society is not as it was once. The name of party is all most forgotten. But it is my impression there would be a great change if our men would be as successful at a few more points as they were at Vicksburgh. The capture of Vicksburgh has produced a great excitement here with the so called Abolitionists. The Copperheads hav not much to say. You ought to hav bin here last Saturday to hav seen Old Millwood respond to the call of patriotism. There was Union meeting there that day. It is supposed there were 15 hundred people there. We had some very interesting speeches made, especialy one by the Honorable C. Delano of Mt. Vernon and a very good one by T. Cample of New Castle. They did not leave the Velandingham men but a very small space for there Platform. For my part I think the union men need not be discouraged.

I suppose you have heard of Gen. Morgan's invasion in Ohio. I guess he has not accomplished very much. Gov. Todd is in persuit of him with 60 thousand men. They have captured, killed and wounded a great number of his men. Morgan is on the retreat, thinking the Yankees are a little too sharp for him.

Well I suppose you have become tired of trying to read my

scribling and I will close by asking you to write soon.

Your friend
Ella Rightmire

$

letter 25

July 6, 1863. Mt. Vernon, Ohio.
Emma Peterman. [Bolivar, Tenn.]

Mt. Vernon, July 6th

Respected Friend

I received your short note some time ago and have neglected answering it for so long I am almost ashamed to do it at this late date. It is an old saying "better late than never."

Our school is out and I am most awful glad. For me it is to warm to go to school. It was out the 16th June. In the evening the graduating class [had] their exercises which were very interesting. As I had to stand up all the evening did not enjoy it very much. Commencement was not very good this year, all that graduated are going to study for the ministery but one. I send you a programme.

I suppose you would like to know how I spent the 4th. There was nothing going on in town. It was just like any other day only the stores were closed. I will not say there was nothing going on fore there was a horse race and any amount of drunk men shouting for Jeff Davis. For my part I think it is [a] disgrace to the 4th of July, men acting as so many of them do when our country is in such great danger.

There was a "Butternut" meeting in Millwood. Frank Hurd and other distinguished men of his kind were to speak. Pa did not stay so I cannot tell you how it went off.

We are having quite gay times in Mt. Vernon this summer. We have had two Festivals the past week. One was for the Methodist and the other was for the Presbyterian church. We had ice-cream, raspberrys and cake. How I wished the soldiers could have enjoyed it. There were several officers there

They are having some kind of a trial at the Courthouse today about a man in Bladensburg shooting Mr. Fawcitt horse. He was a Butternut and did it for revenge. He will have to pay for it dearly before it is all over.

As this is my first letter I will not write a very long one. All the family send their respects. Answer soon and tell me all the news and obllige.

Your true friend,
Emma Peterman

N.B. I am very much obbliged for the record of your company you sent me. Yours, Emma

Enclosures: (1) Second Annual Commencement of the Mt. Vernon High School, June 22nd, 1863. "Industry, Patience, Integrity, Success."

(2) Thirty-Fifth Annual Commencement of Kenyon College. Gambier, Ohio, June 25th, 1863.

letter 26

July 17, 1863. Millwood, Ohio. Ella Hawn. Memphis, Tenn.

Millwood, July 17, 1863

Well Ed

I read your worthy letter last mail and I have been deprived of answering untill late this Eve. But as you are misconstruing my letter I will write enough to give you its true meaning if I have but little time. But Ed I would hear say that you are getting to Cute. I think those refined Bells have rather turned your understanding as it appears dull of apprehension. You must remember we domestic girls of the north Speak and write as we mean. Therefore you will take me as I have written not as you would imagine. I will not say as you do, for I do not believe this your true opinion. You, I presume, fell that you have not been so interesting & claim this as an excuse. You, I would say, have excused yourself bravely. I should not wonder if you would soon be Promoted. Again. But if you are not I hope you will heareafter take me as I write, & let me not forget who I have written to as you have heretofore remembered, Ed.

I am sorry to say I have as usual no good news for you except from the Army which I supose you get as soon as me, they are good & have been for some time and hope they will still continue so until this cruel war is over! Which many of our leading men think will soon be over.

O yes, I will here tell you we had a grand Union meeting here last Saturday. There was over 2000 People presant. Mr. Dellino and Mr. Cammell addressed them. They were booth very interesting speeches, especialy Mr. Dellino which I wish you & John could of heard. He spoke in the best terms of the Soldiers. He gave praise to whom praise is due.

We allso prepared dinner for them & took it to the grove & we had all kindes of Music. We had a Brass Band and part of the String Band from Danville which you know is good, & a Band of vocal music. O it was cheering to hear the sweet voices of the Ladies proclaim the cheering praises of the Stars & Stripes and those in its defense, the Soldiers.

Ed, we are all good Union here as all that are worthy of being called good. We have both Gentleman & Ladies Union Leagues & are propering finely. Millwood possesses many other good qualities, has one Grocery & plenty of whiskey. But I will say no more this time, hope you will believe me much interested & ever mindful of my correspondent. The friends of Millwood are all well, your Folks I believe are well. Tell John we are all well & feel quite uneasy about him as your Folk recd a letter stateing he was not very well. I hope, Ed, you will do all you can for him if he is Sick & let us know as soon as you can. Give him a Sisters love & tell him to be careful of himself. My best wishes to you all.

Write soon if you can understand this which I hope you can.
From Ell.

Ed, since I last wrote to you I have spent three weeks in New Castle, had a very pleasant visit. Saw Will [K]night , he has become quite a Preacher, think he will do much good.

Good night, Ed.

letter 27

July 18, 1863. Mt. Gilead, Ohio.
Elizabeth Roberts. Memphis, Tenn.

Mt. Gilead, Ohio, Seventh Month, 18th, 1863

Respected Friend

E.L. Lybarger

About two weeks since I was a little surprised by the reception of a letter from an entire stranger, to which under some circumstances I should not feel willing to reply, but being confident that my friend Wm. Eccles would encourage no one to write whom I should consider unworthy of notice and respect, I feel it my place to acknowledge its reception although I cannot promise to make a correspondence very "interesting" or "agreeable" as I do not profess to possess any great talent for letter writing.

I feel grateful toward Wm. Eccles for entertaining so good an opinion of his unworthy scholar, but please remember it is sometimes easy for a teacher to overlook the failings and overestimate the good qualities of his pupils and perhaps it is so this case for it was in the capacity of teacher and scholar that our acquaintance was formed.

I hope I am not one of that class of young ladies who see in life no noble duties, but who are content to flit away the hours in idleness and vanity, as a butterfly among the flowers, who see less bounty in efforts of usefulness than in hands unsoiled by toil. Therefore if thou would choose a correspondent of that description perhaps it would be well to look farther.

I am now engaged in teaching and as a general thing I find real pleasure in the occupation.

We hear from my brother often. The last account from him, he had a prospect of leaving LaGrange and going to Memphis. I am afraid his health will not permit him to remain in the south long.

It is a satisfaction to know that you are enjoying yourselves, have plenty to eat &c. it is so distressing to hear, as we sometimes do, of the soldiers suffering from lack of provisions. If Wm. Eccles is still there give him my respects. My "Quaker" dialect may be something new and perhaps not very agreeable to thee, but it is the language which I have been educated to use and which I therefore for various reasons prefer, so please excuse.

Most respectfully, Elizabeth Roberts

☙

letter 28

July 24, 1863. Logan, Hocking County [Ohio].
Jennie E. Hall. Memphis, Tenn.

[Note: "Frank Wharton" was a pseudonym used in placing
advertisement; see letter 31 and note 95]

Logan, Hocking Co., July 24th, 1863

Frank Wharton

In reply to your recent advertisement I will say that I shall shall deem it a pleasure to open a correspondence with you as a "brave soldier boy" and as I am very fond of letter writing shall probably be able to interest the "monotony of camp life" <u>somewhat</u>, at least I shall endeavor to write that which may be worthy your perusal. Therefore if you see proper reply to this and you may expect a lengthy epistle soon. Hoping to receive a reply I will be brief this the first.

Address Jennie E. Hall
Logan, Hocking Co., Ohio

Frank Wharton
Co. K 43rd O.V.I.
Memphis, Tenn.

letter 29

July 29, 1863. Macon City, Mo.
Benjamin F. Stone. Memphis, Tenn.

Macon City, Mo., July 29th, 1863

Dear friend

I received your very agreeable letter a few days ago and I am truly glad that you are doing so well and are in good spirits, really all of us well may be so: For things have lately been accomplished to make us think that surely no one need to think of warring successfully against so good a government as ours, that violators of law and rioting need expect nothing less than punishment and traitors the just doom they merit. I am looking forward with pleasing anticipation when we can all enjoy in peace the fruit of our labors, that would be a living enjoyment to me though I should be barred [?] of many others. Understand me, the fruit of our labors must be the Union undivided, the laws executed. For this I think we can afford to be magnanimous to our enemies and tell them "go thy way but sin no more." I will not so fear fall out with the Administration that I would care to give it my support in crushing out the rebellion and carrying on the just purposes of the government. But for very shame I would not use the slave as a soldier. You assume in your position that it is proper to take all the property of the people of the Southern States by military power. I would prefer leaving private property as much as convenient, untouched by the military. When you say we have the same right to put arms in the hands of negroes to shoot rebels as we have to turn the enemies guns upon him that we may capture I think you go farther back into the times of Barbarians for your rule of right, than these times of civilization and humanity in their restrictions upon war will allow. And I think good policy will dictate to us to fight our enemies in war after such a manner as that some day we may best live with them in peace under the same government; and to this I think it would be better to yield somewhat to their peculiar opinions or prejudices, and leave the subject of Slavery or freedom to the Negro, to the decision of the wisdom of the people in each of the Slave States in calmer times. In thus acting we would show to the people of the South that we have determined to respect their political rights by our observance and obedience to the laws State and National and that our real objective was to enforce what was acknowledged by all to be the law of the land, in this manner we would show them that they were only fighting for a shadow occasioned by an intemperate discussion of Negro Slavery and, the criminal ambition of some of their leaders and thus by our manly obedience and real spirit of freedom our enemies would become convinced of their error, and demobilisation and desertion would eat up the Rebel army, it would melt like ice before the midsummer's sun. Do not [mis]understand me by holding forth this that I would for a moment discourage the use of the bayonet. Sometimes a little bloodletting is healthy, but rather, use all the energy and power of the nation. This in my opinion is the quickest, the shortest way to put down the rebellion. It will ultimately be put down anyhow. But as you say, enough to know that we love the same nation, the same flag. We are all quiet and enjoying peacible times here now. Secession ebbs low, patriots are jubilant over our recent Successes, they seem as a heavy load had been taken of their shoulders.

Crops look well, rather dry until recent refreshing showers. I hope you much enjoyment among the ladies, pleasure in your study and success in war. My parents and others join me in a "good luck" to you and would be glad to see you and have you visit us. We have a fine country in which all can have pleasure enjoyment and happiness. You will pardon my having written in haste and accept my well wishes.

Truly your friend
Benj. F. Stone

Lieut. E.L. Lybarger

letter 30

July 30, 1863. Bainbridge, Ohio.
Rozaltha Crum. Memphis, Tenn.

Bainbridge, Ohio, July 30th/63

(Write soon)

My Dear Cousin

I received your ever favored letter of the 20th inst. ready to devour its contents. I had begun to think you had gone away from Memphis before my letter reached you but I was glad to learn that you had got it. We are all well and hope you are still enjoying your camp life.

Well I must tell you that Uncle Elijah has got up a company of men for 5 years, he is the Captain as you understand and the people from around here say he makes a first rate one. They say he is one of the greatest war men they almost ever seen.

We came very near having war at home. Old Morgan was within 6 or 7 miles and some say within 4 but I dont think he hardly got that close. There was a very throng time here when the people thought John Morgan was a coming through here (you never seen) I was going to say you never seen such a time in your life but you have and worse to I suppose. The people of Bainbridge and the community were almost scared to death for as there was no men. I tell you if he had of come thro here he would of showed old Bainbridge sites. the Bainbridge Malicia was of course called out and it included all of the men over 18 and under 45 so of course there was not many left to protect this place.

Morgan and his crew camped at Locust Grove. I suppose you know where that is. His camp was between 5 and 6 miles long. Papa says tell you he was out on pursuit of John Morgan and his crew; he traveled 2 weeks every day and almost every night and at last they captured the old chap and all of his men. They had a couplil of skirmishes with him. One was at berlin, the other on Captenia Island. Papa arived at home day before yesterday. He says they was down right around the brow of the hill and Morgan on the top when the battle commenced, but as it happened the bombshells went far over them and bursted in their rear.

Well if you was here we would find a great deal to talk about but as it is I cannot put it all in a letter. I will tell you the rest when I see you, just step over this evening or tomorrow and we will have a little talk. Morgan and his crew are now in prison but the people are looking for another attack from old Breckinridge, but I think if he hears how Morgan fared when he was thro here he will not make the attempt.

I received a letter from Aunt Anna. They were all well. One also from Aunt Sarah. She said she was a going to write to you. I gave her your address. Very much obliged to you Dear Cousin for your picture. I have not had a chance to get my picture taken lately as the artist was out with the malicia but will get you a good one taken at some more convenient time. This photograph is not very good, notwithstanding it will do until you get a better one. Write to me often so I will be posted with your address if you should go away any time before you should get my letters. Write anyhow and tell me where to direct.

Cousin Rosa

$

letter 31

August 1, 1863. Mt. Sterling, Ky.
Fannie Jerome. Memphis, Tenn.

[Note: Envelope is addressed to: Mr. Frank Wharton, Co. K. O.V.I., Memphis, Tenn. Fannie Jerome is a pseudonym for Lou Pearl Riggen; see letter 43.]

Mt. Sterling, Ky.

Dear Sir;

Having ascertained that some of you Gentlemen wished to get up a mutual corresondence with the "Fair Sex" I though that I <u>would</u> comply with your good wishes.

Hoping you will respond soon.
I will therefore Subscribe myself
"Fannie Jerome"
"My Address is Mt. Sterling" Ky
August the 1st 1863

$

letter 32

Aug. 4, 1863. Brandon, Ohio. Mollie Ward. Memphis, Tenn.

Brandon, Saturday evening, Aug. 4
Mr. Lybarger

About a week since I rec'd a letter written above your signature, bearing date of July 18th. Its contents impressed me deeply, not more so from the usual tenor than from the fact that it bore the marks of having been written by a gentleman of more than ordinary intelligence. Not knowing upon its receipt, whether to let it pass unnoticed or whether to the best of my ability to favor you with an early response, I chose the latter, after first consulting my own judgment and then that of my parents. As far as exchanging photographs is concerned, I should consider it very imprudent for any <u>lady</u> to give her picture to a person she had never seen although it is no uncommon thing in this fast age. Should we become better acquainted and should we both live to meet here on earth and then if I deemed you worthy of my thoughts your request should be granted but for the present the matter will have to remain as it is: however if you feel so disposed you can send me your photograph and I will see how I like the looks and then return it: perhaps under those circumstances I might send you mine.

I was glad to hear you were all getting along so well in the army. Health is one of the richest boons bestowed by Heaven and certainly ought to be the most desirable whilst employed in the service of your country: although there are but few that know how to appreciate it rightly. Only think of the poor sufferers in the Hospital! Compare your lot with theirs and then judge of the difference. So be sure the people in this part of the country and those that are out of the reach and hearing of roar and all its demoralizing influences know but little about it in <u>reality</u> when compared with some whose farms have been laid waste and houses burned or otherwise destroyed & homes made desolate and all their property confiscated merely for the sake of this <u>unholy,</u> this <u>unjust</u> and <u>uncalled</u> for rebellion. And now you poor soldiers are called upon to do the fighting while those that have done the planning are quietly enjoying the good of their sofas at home. (I mean only Jeff Davis and his followers). The people here at home look upon the soldiers as a living wall of human flesh standing between them and destruction. They will ever be honored and respected by all. Oh may the soldiers in the field at the present time all live to once more enjoy the pleasures of home and the security of the dear ones now there anxiously watching and praying for their safe and speedy return. And oh may <u>you</u> although a stranger to me: may you be <u>one</u> among the "favored few" out of so many brave and self sacrificing men who have periled their lives for their country to return to the peaceful land among dear friends never more to be disturbed by roaring of cannon or the clashing of arms. By asking you to excuse this short and hasty letter I will close by signing myself yours with respect.

Mollie E. Ward

$

letter 33

August 7, 1863. Millwood, Ohio.
Emma A. Moody. Memphis, Tenn.

Millwood, Ohio, August

Friend Ed;

This sultry Sabbath afternoon I seate myself to try and offer an apology for not writing sooner. I have answered all your letters except one. That one I received last winter about the Willie was taken sick. During his sickness it was impossible for me to write. A few days after His death word came that my sister was quite sick, a few days more and news came that she too was dead. Mother was sick at the same time and being troubled about John it was impossible for me to write when I should, and then I thought you had correspondance more interesting and more punctual than I had been so I remained silent. Not that I had forgotten a brave sholdier Boy who was once with us an ornament to society and loved by all who knew Him, but I thought it best not to write after I had neglected it so long. But I hope you will forget and forgive the past and I will do better hereafter. I was pleased to hear from you but would have been much better pleased to [have] had a long letter in the place of that note but that was more than I expected and I am obliged to you for it. Your Mother made us a visit not long ago. We had quite a good time. She told me all about you and she had your likeness with Her, I think a very good one altho you have changed still I could tell it was Ed. I am pleased to hear of your getting along so well and being so well liked by all. It will be an honor to you when you come home. How much better you will feel than if you had stayed at home and done as some are doing. Ed you would be surpized if you knew how some are doing. Those we thought honorable men are proving themselves to be worse than nothing. I am often sorry that I am not able to whip some of them when they holl[er] for Jeff[erson Davis]. I wish we had a few of your soldier Boys here. I think they would know who to Hollow for then.

They are aresting traitors every day. Old Mr. Shiply and six or seven more was taken last week, Mr. Whites, are all butternuts. I suppose you have heard that my old friend Cal is a traitor. I cannot help thinking what different pathes you and He are treading, one to fame and Honor, the other to drunkenness and misery. Poor Cal, I pity Him and I am shure you do.

Well Ed I hardly know what to write that will interest you as nothing very interesting goes on here any more. I suppose you have heard that Talor Kenwood and Miss Tompson are married. I believe this is the only wedding that has been this summer. I think Colonel Capel and Em Crichfield will be married before long, but for my part I think I would prefer some one else. It is grand to get a Colonel but I do not envy her position. I think your Ella is waiting very patiently for you but you must remember you promised to invite me and I expect to be there.

Burr Bennett came home yesterday from the 20th. He saw John a few hours before He left Vixburg. Co. A of the 96th can only muster 19 men, John is one of that number. They saw hard times while following Jonson in His retreat. They came near dying for watter. How much I pitty the poor Boys. Bennett said the 96th would start for Tennessee in a few days, perhaps you will see him. Ed Dunbar is going in the service again. He was a Lieutenant in the 43rd, I expect you are acquainted with Him. They are getting up indipendant Com [companies] in all Townships where butternut officers were elected. The union boys will not drill under a traitor and I am glad of it. You will see what a hard crowd will be left.

Well Ed I will close for the present hoping the excuses I have given for not writing will be sufficient and hope I will have the pleasure of reading a letter from you soon. The family all send their good wishes to you.

Ever your true friend, E.A. Moody

$

letter 34

August 13, 1863. Millwood, Ohio.
Ella Hawn. Memphis, Tenn.

[Note: This is Ella's last letter to Lybarger.]

Millwood, August the 13, 1863

Ed

Your letter came to hand today & I have read it, & truly am surprised beont measure with what it contains; In the first place you say you must confess that my last letter was a greadeal more unintelagible than the one previous to it. Well Ed if I had not had the honor of your acquaintance allmost from my Infancy up to the present time I would believe you understood me as you write. It is true I must confess uniteligible, unintelligent & I supose uninteresting from what I have received.

But Ed I think this is a poor way of getting around or rid of my irksome imperfect relying. I will admit they were dull & not fit for an intelligent mind, but you was well aware of the knowledge of your friend when you engaged the coripondence & as a friend I should look over my imperfections rather than criticize or note them down' & Say as I request an answer, you conclude to answer.

Ed it has never been my intention to insult you, but I would here say there was no compulsion whatever. You are free to drop the corispondence without gathering those <u>Scored</u> & emphasised lines of which you spoke. You eaven refered to the Promotion & Cuteness & Say they were intended for a Slave, & allso say for the life of you, you cannot see what I am driving at. Say you have not the remotest Idea. It appears to me you think you have an idea when you take it for an <u>insult</u> & say there is an inconsistency in my last letter & that in the beginning of boath I imply that you were uninteresting & that I had forgotten to whom I had written when I received your last letter; & that I ment you well. Ed I <u>did mean</u> you. But as I have heretofore said I do not believe that you understand me as you say you do. & your father say that I have no confidence in you when you express yourself freely & confidently & say it seams strange that I have no confidence in a person with whom I have been corisponding for allmost two years & with whom I am so intimately acquainted. I must say it is truly strange that you who knew my conversation so well would misconstrue it as you have done.

I thought it uninteresting & wrote that I allmost forgot who I had written to when I read your letter but I spoke of the length of time that passed after writing before I received an answer & I must say I think you understood me this was did you not Ed. I believe the last previous lot those two uninteligible ones of which you spoke. It was three months ere I received an answer & I do not think this interesting however choice the friend my be & I see no other light in which you can view it.

You allso say you have never yet done anything to your knowledge to cause me to doubt your confidence. I rather think from what I can gather from your letter that your intention as you are undoubtedly aware is different as you truly know you have misconstrued my simple lines.

And you say you can see the point when I spoke of being mindful of my corispondent & think it not necissary to pursue the subject any further, that you do not desire to force a disagreeable corispondent on anyone & close by subscribing yourself ever my friend. But no longer my Lover. Ed by your language I feel that you are weary of your Old friend, this is all I can make of your letter &

do not wish to weary you with my unworthy efforts. But will congratulate you in the blotting out of boath friendship & love if you feel that I deserve the banishment as I am confident intentionly I have done nothing to merit your displeasure & have never asked your love nor can I seek it against your will, never. But will remain ever your friend & well wisher. Give Brother my love and tell him that the health of the family is much better than it has been, tell him to take good care of hisself & write often. The friends of Millwood are well, So good night Ed.

From Ell H.

Excuse my paper and my imperfections as they are many.

Now Ed I could have explained this long since. But suposed you were jesting when you requested an answer, never dreamed of insulting you. Know that you have done nothing to deserve sensuring. But I just mearly spoke because I thougt a more punctual corispondence pleasantier believe me this is all I had reference to. All I could have you say I can attribute your dullness to ignorance, or to your disordered imagination, or to those Southern Ladies, or whatever suits my fancy. Well Ed your first & second choice of which you gave me is a mear come off. As I have said a good way of getting rid of a friend of which you desire no longer & your third I would Answer by hoping I possess not a jealous heart of which this I believe you refer to. But O why should I write & tire you when I remember your last sentence. Ell.

letter 35

August 13, 1863. Millwood, Ohio.
Phrone Rogers. Memphis, Tenn.

Home, Thursday, Aug. 13th, 1863

Ever dear friend Ed;

My thought so naturally follow you this evening I concluded you must be either talking or thinking of me, and propose we try to establish a spiritual telegraph. Should we succeed in this we should (happily for me) do away with what is a great task, letter writing.

Ed I received your very interesting letter a few days since. I was away when it first came and therefore did not receive it as soon as I would have done had I been at home.

I was visiting Newcastle. O, I enjoyed myself so much while there. They have but two or three young gentlemen in the place that amount to anything. Lon Rich, Lon Henderson (and he is a cripple) and Will Knight. Maggie is at home this summer. I saw her intended husband, he is a Theological student at Alleghany Sem. Penn. His parents live in Massachusetts.

Ed you said perhaps I could tell you something about the folks across the river. I know you hear from them and write to them as often as you do me for Mary Hammond and I were at the P.O. not very many weeks ago and I saw a letter directed to you by Hett I supposed for Ell as she is the one that corresponds with you. She seems to appreciate your letters (as only she can) as of course she has a deeper interest in you than any one elce, if I had the same claim on you that she has I presume I would hear from you <u>oftener</u>.

Ed I have allways been a good friend of yours and hoped you were the same to me, but I would advise you not to occupy precious time in any amusement that will not benefit you as I am not at all fond of amusing anybody by mearly writing to me for greens a pass time, reality is what I am always seeking. Ed I hope you will construe the right meaning upon what I have said, for perhaps I have not expressed what I mean in the right manner for <u>any one</u> to understand. All I want to make known is that I appreciate your last letter, certainly I do entertain the warmest feeling of friendship for you and I am very happy to have the privilege of corresponding with you. I often imagine you

> "Within a country unknown and dreary
> A wanderer forlorn and weary"

I heard that you expected to visit home this fall. <u>Oh do come</u>. I would like to have you come for a good many reasons, one of the prominent reasons is because I want to see you so badly. I hope to see that promised Photograph coming very soon. I have quite a fine lot of pictures and I would be so proud to have yours among them.

If I have failed to make this letter as interesting as yours was to me, I hope you will not think the fault mine, as you know it takes material to make letters as nill as anything else. I would tell you how much I think of old Jonney Braugh, old Abe, the Union, and so forth &c if that would not be writing politics, ha! ha!

Wishing you a happy good time I close friend Phrone.

Beck Hawn has been very sick with typhoid fever but she is some better now but does not sit up a bit yet. It has been now three weeks since she was first taken, she is not entirely out of danger yet—but do not tell John. I guess they did not let him know how bad she was.

Joss is very much pleased to know that Capt. Rhodes is not married. Ed do not wait so long to answer this letter. Your folks are all well but Ligah is a Velandighamer, he votes the butternut ticket. You ought to talk to him a spell, come home and make them all right again.

Phrone

letter 36

August 23, 1863. Marion, Ind.
Hellen P. Hesler. Memphis, Tenn.

Marion, August 23rd, 1863

Respected Sir;

I seat myself to acknowledge the reception of your card, and send in return my compliments.

I presume you will think it strange that you should receive a note from the Hoosier state in answer to one sent to Buckeye. "But truth is stranger than fiction." The object of your corispondent is improvement.

I am a school girl, and the greatest desire of my heart is a good education. I come to the conclusion that by interchange of thought I should be enabled to obtain usfull knowledge, and also, sometimes to drop a word or two to cheer the dull monotony of camp life.

Now Lieut E.L. If you take interest enough in your unknown "friend or corispondent" to make further inquires I will answer with pleasure after you tell me something of your self.

I have writen this in candor and hope you will answer in the same. From a friend to all true Loyal Soldiers.

Hellen

PS. Address Hellen P. Hesler
Marion, Grant Co.
Indiana

$

letter 37

Aug. 28, 1863. Brandon, Ohio. Mollie Ward. Memphis, Tenn.

Friday evening, Aug. 28

Mr. Edwin Lybarger

Last evening I had the pleasure of receiving your very interesting and I might almost say <u>flattering</u> epistle. I do not mean to charge you with the crime of flattery, at all, for I should think (if I may be allowed to judge from the tone of your letters) that you were too much of a gentleman to humble your self to that position but it is merely my intention to state here that I greatly fear you will find my personal charms and attractions to number but few and my accomplishments (as the saying is) will come up "among the missing." I am not possessed of any of the graces which so often adorn the female character but am a plain hearted outspoken girl of seventeen summers. Pray do not consider me impertinent or rude for speaking thus plainly for as I have already told you I speak just what I think and trust you will do likewise in writing to me. It is not my desire or wish to morass a stranger in the cloak of deception any more than an intimate acquaintance and every one that knows me is aware that I never deceive any one. I have heard something of your character and standing in society from some of your associates and I find that no one speaks of you except in terms of the highest praise and regard not only as a soldier but as a citizen. We all have a faint idea of the fatigues the soldier has to endure of the hardships he has to undergo the wearisome marches through rain and mud, cold and heat but I will readily admit that none but those that have undergone its trials and temptations know exactly what it is to lead such a life. To be sure we enjoy the pleasures of a good home and the society of some dear friends but where oh where is the poor boy that was wont to fill that vacant chair that empty place at the table? Alas we know not. He may be lying on the bloody field of battle weltering in the agony of death or he may be in the Hospital under the care of some unskilled physician. There is hardly a person to be found nowadays that does not feel to symnpathize with the poor soldier. These northern copperheads come out boldly and say they don't care what becomes of the "Abolition boys" and I don't think some of them <u>would</u> care if the whole northern army would be surrendered to the Jeff Davis confederacy. We do not enjoy peace and harmony as we did formerly. Society is broken up and about all the pleasure the union loving girls have is in writing to the soldiers and endeavoring to administer to their wants and cheer their hearts with words of comfort, to endeavor to the best of our ability to make them as contented as possible during their long absence of three years. Three Years! Oh how the poor boys long and anxiously await for the expiration of that time which would pass by almost unheeded were they enjoying the pleasures of good society and the friendship of their former acquaintances. Every person and every thing will be changed so that they will not be able to realize greatly that they are free and at home and never again to rush to a bloody conflict for freedom and the constitution founded by our forefathers. It is a great mystery to the more intelligent class of persons to know how <u>anyone</u> after always having lived under the American government and its laws how they <u>can</u> expect to enjoy more privileges than they have been enjoying should the south gain her independence and so should lose the victory.—

We are going to make a party here at our house for the returned soldiers or those who are home on furlough and I should be very happy to receive you as one of the guests did I know it was useless to entertain the idea. However you can comfort your self by resting assured that although absent you are not forgotten and by hoping that the time is not far distant when all friends can be permitted to meet again never more to part until the sounding of the great trumpet that calls us from this earth to a higher and more holy place in that far off land above the skies. I will close by wishing you "God speed" and safe return. I remain yours in friendship.

Mollie Ward

$

letter 38

August 30, 1863. Logan, Ohio. Jennie E. Hall. Memphis, Tenn.

Logan, Hocking County, Aug. 30th, 1863

Lieut. Ed Lybarger
Kind Sir

This is a beautiful Sabbath morning. The warm sun is shedding his light over all the earth—now my ear catches the sweet sound of the church bells peeling forth, calling the people to the house of God. I perhaps should be on my way too but have concluded to devote this morning to letter writing—you shall have a portion of the time.

Perhaps my letter may bear a tone of sadness at this time. If so I hope you will pardon the same—I have just heard of the death of a kind friend of mine in the army—and a shade of melancholy has been thrown over my usually gay spirits. Oh the curses of this terrible war—I grow heart sick a[nd] weary when I think of them. How many hearts and homes made desolate. As I look around me here and there I see a vacant place. A Mother's hope and a Father's pride taken away from their fond embrace no matter how dear—go they must to sustain this union—and that dear old flag which so long waved so proudly in freedom over our once happy nation. Oh glorious old flag—with your thirty four stars and broad stripes you are a mighty old banner yet allthough you have held up your head on some occasions with much difficulty your brave stars will still float broadly over our nation. How many brave hailed you with shouts of harmony as you have triumphed over many a bloody battle field and your broad stripes & stars have cheered the fainting souldiers heart and nerved his arm for the contest. The dying souldier has taken

```
LESSONS 1.9-2.3
X.218     0        PAR 1103.1    16 D

LESSONS 2.4-2.7
X.218     0        PAR 1103.1    16 D

LESSONS 3.1-3.4
X.218     0        PAR 1103.1    16 D

LESSONS 3.5-4.1
X.218     0        PAR 1103.1    16 D

LESSONS 4.2-5.1
X.218     1        PAR 1103.1    16 D

LESSONS 5.2-5.5
X.218     1        PAR 1103.1    16 D

LESSONS 6.1-6.4
X.218     1        PAR 1103.1    16 D
```

) REMAIN ON RESERVE <<<<<<<<<

thee for his shroud and breathed his last breath within thy folds. You have gone around the world and made <u>all</u> nations tremble and acknowledge thee their superior—but alas! some of your power and greatness has departed your beautiful stars & stripes, once the radiant emblem of greatness, progress, unity, and power, now droops around the smoke of the conflict—your glory paled and many of your stars stricken out. Notwithstanding all this I hope soon to see you wave proudly again over these <u>United</u> States—upon every mountain and every plain.

Then the absent loved ones may return (Alas! many never will) You will say perhaps that I am very enthusiastic. Indeed I am on this subject. I am union out and out—as you will judge by my letters —but I have almost forgotton that you asked a description of your correspondent. Well really that is something I have never attempted, and I fear I shall make a terrible blunder if I attempted such a thing—but here goes—Height—5 ft -4 inches—slender form neat and graceful. Black hair which curls beautifully. Black eyes noted for mischievousness. Round face—Brunette complection. I am no beauty but passably good looking. Kind, generous, warmhearted, confiding, social, lively and <u>very</u> talkative. Does this description suit your fancy? I expect not. I have mingled much in <u>refined</u> society as I spent some three years in the great King City, New York, with my brother. I believe through that I enjoy a more retired life after all. This is a pleasant little village. I expect to go to Nelsonville, Athens County, to spend the winter and should you not write me before the latter part of September you will please address me at that place as I shall be there then.

I trust you will be too <u>generous</u> to criticise this effusion of mine. I may be able to do better in the future. Of course I should not feel at liberty to send my shadow until I <u>have received yours</u>. Therefore you know the terms by which you can <u>receive mine</u>.

Hoping that you are enjoying a degree of health & happiness and that you will write soon.

I remain Very Respectfully
Jennie E. H.

letter 39

September 5, 1863. Bainbridge, Ohio.
Rosaltha Crum. Memphis, Tenn.

[Note: Rosa refers to John Brough as "Governor"
although he was not elected until October.]

Bainbridge, Sept. 5th/63

Dear Cousin as I have just finished my Saturday's works and I had nothing else to do I thought I would reply to your ever welcome letter which came to hand one day last week. You will pardon me for not writing sooner for when I tell you I am so busy I hardly ever have time to set down and write, and when I do get the opportunity I have to dash it off in a very great hury.

Artenchor has gone home and I have the work to do for the preasant but notwithstanding I have a very nice time keeping house by myself, but I will not get to be housekeeper very long as school takes up week after next.

Papa gone to Athens on an 8 days drill. All of the officers of the Militia had to go. It is very lonesome here with out him. How I wish for your company now in my loneliness, nevertheless I would be very much gratified to see you once more on earth, but if we are not permited to meet here below I have a hope of meeting up in heaven where congregations never brake up and sabbaths never end.

Last Sunday evening I went to church to hear Bro. Kendrick preach his farewell sermon. He is going to his country's call and tho he is no kin to me yet I had to weep for to think he was going out on the tented field to [be] exposed to all the hardships belonging to solders life. You do not know how much we sympathize with the soldiers in the field, the soldiers is all our composition

Edwin dont get to deep in love with those secesh Ladies down there for if you do you will have me on you. I mean not to think to much of them in reality. Write often Dear Cousin for it does me so much good to get a letter from you.

Well I must tell you about the Union meeting, thats a going on. We was down to Chillicothe to a big speech daybeforeyesterday given by Gov. John Brough. There was about 50,000 there. We had a large car made with 34 little girls in it who were dressed in white with red and blue sashes on, and from Bournesville a fort called Sumpter, from Adelphia a large wagon about 40 feet long wheels 11 feet through the center and it had 100 horses to it all trimed in red, white and blue. Well I will close but still remain your affectionate cousin.

Rozaltha Cousin
Rozaltha Crum

Please excuse bad writing and mistakes for I have to write in a very big hury, you may well guess my circumstances as you know my employment.

P.S. this is sabbath morning and I seat myself to write you a few more lines and moreover to pass away time as I am by myself. The time seams so very long for the boys are hardly ever in the house. I have just come from sabbath school and now the church bell is ringing for preaching but I believe I will not go today as it is very wet as we had a very thunder storm this morning and last night. The weather is very pleasant here now notwithstanding. We have had some tolerable cool weather for the time of year. We have had two very large frosts this fall. They feel sometime during last month but it has turned warmer now. I hope we will yet have some pleasant weather.

Well I must not forget to tell you that the copperheads are going to have a grand time here tomorrow. They are going to Chillicothe tomorrow and have a secesh picnic. They had begun to make their wagon the day we had our picnic, and they have had all that time to fix on. Their wagon beats ours but I am sorry to say so far I told them it could not come up to ours but it exceeds all I have yet seen. It is about 40 feet long trimed in cedar red and Blue and Buckeyes [?] but we are a going to Greenfield the 16th and 17th of this month and then we are a going to beat them all to pieces. We are not a going to have the name of letting the butternuts beat. We are agoing to some expense this time but what we will get a head of them.

I have not heard from A's [?] for some time. I do not know the reason of it. I have written to them 3 or four times but received no answer. I received a letter from your Mother. They was all well excepting your father. He had been sick but is now better. Straines are all well as far as I know. You will please write often to me for Edwin I love you as the dearest friend on earth. I think of you by day and dream of you by night. You are continually in my mind, but if the lords will be done I hope the time is not far hence when we will meet again. Oh how I long to see you and have a talk about the war and soldier boys. Dont flatter yourself by thinking that photograph looks like me for it does not look like me now. It have been taken over a year. It looks like I did when you seen me but I will send you one by and by that does look like me and so big you would not know me. I am up to Papa's sholder. Well I am putting in a good deal of foolishness in this letter but am doing it to pass away time.

> *Your sincere friend*
> *Cousin Rosa*

Remember me my youthful friend
while oer this little piece you bend
for tis a love of truth to me
and in return I will remember thee
Remember me tho far away
for often we will stray
and round your heart a beggar be
whispering the wish remember me

Answer the first opportunity

letter 40

[Note: Fannie Jerome is a pseudonym for Lou Pearl Riggen;
see page 180, letter 43.]

Mt. Sterling, Ky. September 5th, 63

Lieut. E.L. Lybarger

Your letter of August 8th was received with pleasure. I am glad
to know that you entertain so favorable an opinion of Kentucky
ladies. Since the very great prevalence of secession proclivities in
some parts of the state had been the occasion of anathemas neither
few nor far between bestowed by brave soldiers on unappreciating
rebel ladies. Don't infer from this however that there is any scarcity
of Union ladies—not the least; But I am not writing a political
letter—

You wish an "agreeable, interesting and useful correspondence."
Precisely my object in writing to you. I wanted novelty—or in other
words—<u>fun</u>. And you most fortunately can write nonsense. You
speak of this faculty rather deprecatingly. But as "A little nonsense
now and then is relished by the best of men"—and women. I am
happy to know that you can—not claiming however to be one of the
best of women by any means.

This reminds me of your request—that I give a complete
description of myself. Complete description indeed: red hair,
freckled face, nose more prominent than any other feature—unless it
be the mouth, eyes squinted—O horrible! You have thrown the
letter down in the dust (I actually meant disgust) You are shocked.
"<u>Interesting correspondence</u> with such a fright! No ideas worth
reading can be penned by such a being; doubtless the hand that
writes these very words would fit No 10 gloves" Interest you-fun
nowhere-correspondence ceases. Ah me—goodbye—

Excuse me for shocking your sensibilities so much—but a
description was necessary since you were so kind as to describe your

handsome self with which description your ugly correspondent is decidedly pleased.

To be serious because in the <u>first place</u> I don't want you to think me so decidely frightful and second because I do detest deception. I am a very plain girl having gray eyes, brown hair, no freckles, and make no pretensions to beauty; height five ft. three inches—age—— ah when was a woman known to tell her age. Guess and I'll tell you in very next time.

Is your name really E.L. Lybarger? and do you really expect mine? I excused myself for the impropriety of writing to a strange gentleman by the fictitious name and I hardly know how to do otherwise. Answer if you think this worthy.

Fannie Jerome

I have been visiting & could not write sooner.

$

letter 41

September 13, 1863[?]. Postmarked Mt. Vernon, Ohio.
Emma Peterman. Memphis, Tenn.

Sept. 13th

Friend Ed

You may think I never intended to answer your letter as Pa and I both correspond with you I thought you would get tired of writing to one family so often. I am just recovering from a spell of the Chills. Almost every [one] on the street have had them. Sister Lou and I have them, that is enough for one family. In your last letter to Pa you spoke of having them. I should not think they were a very desirable thing to have in the army.

You spoke of forming the acquaintance of the young ladies in the South and think them superior to the ladies of the north. They might easily be superior to the young ladies around Millwood for some of them do not know how to treat a stranger with any kind of politeness let alone any thing else. If you ever come home from the army I don't think you will care about staying in Millwood long.

Since we have left I don't see how we ever lived there as long as we did but "Home" being there made it seem very different.

The "Butternuts" intend to have a meeting in this place the twenty-third of this month. I expect they will have a grand time as they always do. They are going to try to have a larger number than we did but they can't do it. I don't think the Butternuts will say very much if they don't happen to get Vallandingham for next Governor. Hope they won't. Pa don't think there is any danger. I suppose you have not heard that Temp Darling is married. I believe she used to be one of your ladie <u>loves</u>. She married the renowned Butternut Jack Butler of New Castle. I will close. The family sends their respects. Write soon.

> *Your Friend*
> *Emma Peterman*

letter 42

September 25, 1863. Millwood, Ohio.
Phrone Rogers. [No envelope]

Home, Sept. 25th 1863

Kind friend

This morning is delightfully cool so I am seated on the floor in front of the fire to answer your letter. Everybody except for myself has gone to the fair. This is the last day. I should have written sooner but we have all been sick. Emma is just getting better of Dyphthera, we did not expect her to live for about five days.

Ed my pen writes so badly that I thought I would finish with a pencil. Nothing new has happened since I last wrote you—only Geo. Welker is married. He got a right-nice looking lady. "A fool for luck" as the saying is—he has not a teaspoon of brains. Oscar Welker and Rill Hammond will be married in a few weeks.

I was so much pleased to receive that Photograph you sent me —it was splendid. I also appreciated your letter and would briefly say I return all you give.

Captain Rhodes was in Millwood yesterday—he did not call. He did not stay but a few hours which time was occupied in necessary calls, but as good luck would have it he brought one of my lady friends with him from Mt. Vernon, Mary Wolf. I called on her and got to see the Captain. He is nice looking but does not come up to Lieut E.L.L. in my eyes or anybody else. I liked his easy self possession very much.

Ed it is almost dinner time so that I will have to quit and get something to eat. I have not had any time to think so you will have to excuse this letter and I will try to do better next time. Your mother is well but your father is not. He has not been well for some time.

Remember kindly your <u>friend</u>, Phrone

Please answer soon and be sure and come home.

letter 43

September 30, 1863. Postmarked Mt. Sterling, Ky.
Lou Riggen. Memphis, Tenn.

[Note: This is the first letter in which Lou reveals her name;
see Letters 31 & 40 for pseudonym Fannie Jerome]

Lieut. E. L. Lybarger.

I scarcely know how to commence writing to you, before I received your last letter you were probably included in the list of "killed, wounded, or missing" of the last battle; the sad tale which follows either victory or defeat. I sincerely hope not however. I hope you are not among those unreturning braves whose deaths, thought glorious, and in a glorious cause, "makes countless thousands mourn" that among those left to rally once again round the flag is my pleasant correspondent—not I hope selfishly for the sake of that correspondence so pleasant, but for the sake of his mother, and sisters if he has any, for the sake of the Country waiting to be rescued by valiant arms and stout hearts from ignoble slavery and—for the kindly interest I have in all the soldiers. I wish they

could every one live to enjoy the place for which they are <u>fighting</u>
—While the ladies, poor things, stay at home and—"hurrah <u>for the</u>
<u>Union</u>."

xxxxxx You flatter me exceedingly. "Counterhopper! loafer!"
O, O how could I help laughing at the funny idea? What a pleasant
impression my letters must have made. I never had a very flattering
opinion of my letter writing ability until the reception of your
last. If you judge from my letters that I belong to one of the
aforementioned classes how can you be "very well pleased?"

You certainly do not expect my photograph though I have a
<u>decided curiosity</u> (the heritage of the world in general) to see your
photo. I shall certainly not take the initiative. Will it not be fair to
exchange and <u>return</u> them.

Your guessing proved that you are a Yankee. I am twenty past—
have just completed my 22d year two or three days since. I know you
expected "just 18."

I am glad to know that you are down on copperheads in
particular and traitors in general. In return I am <u>decidely</u> opposed to
the rebellion and all rebels, have no sympathy whatever for treason.
I am equally opposed to that other ultra party the Abolishionists.
Simply <u>Union</u> very strong & conservative. I am not a resident of
Mt. Sterling as you seem to think, but live in the country about five
miles from that little city. I should however be happy to see you any
time. My Post Office as you know is M—

Send your photograph and I will send mine, both to be returned.

No more of Fannie Jerome. I am tired of it already, don't like to
receive letters addressed to that young lady who is imaginary.
Especially when I can substitute, so pleasant and musical a name in
its stead.

Hoping that this will prove equally as interesting and pleasantly
suggestive of the writer as my last, I shall discontinue.

Respectfully
Lou Riggen
Greenwood, Ken

Wednesday, Sep 30th, 1863   "loafer"

letter 44

October 1, 1863. Nelsonville, Ohio.
Jennie E. Hall. Memphis, Tenn.

Nelsonville, Athens Co., Oct. 1st, 1863

My kind Friend unknown

Much obliged for your very interesting and "<u>patriotic</u>" letter of the 21st of last month. The contents were perused with <u>pleasure</u>. So long a time had elapsed since I wrote you that I had almost come to the conclusion I did not perhaps come up to your idea of a Lady correspondent. But I am happy indeed to know the contrary. I am grateful for the many encomiums you pass upon me but do not bestow too many as I shall be tempted to think you are a flatterer and you would not wish for me to think that—would you? Echo say "no"

I was considerably amust over one portion of your letter where you asked my age and said "who ever heard of a woman telling her age?" I suppose you are afraid of corresponding with an "old maid." Ha! ha! it's rather funny to be sure. Well I can't blame you for they are detestable beings (as the <u>men</u> say) Well now for the age—I suppose I ought not punnish you any longer by keeping your curiosity on "tip toe"—but I am going to serve you just as you served me—tell you part or rather near the right age—and as you seem to be so <u>good</u> at guessing—you can guess from 18 to 25. Don't you consider this a <u>very</u> satisfactory answer to your <u>very</u> civil question. Ha, ha, I almost imagine I hear you laughing heartily as you say "I knew she would not tell." Well then, kind sir, if you knew that, you are not disappointed in the least. I am glad of it. I do not like to disappoint any one. I'm noted for teasing though as this letter will indicate.

You flatter when you say I possess both beauty and intelligence. Indeed, sir, I must humbly beg your pardon if in giving a description of myself I gave you to infer that I was handsome. I meant for you to understand that your correspondent was only a plain looking girl. I would certainly be far from speaking flatteringly of myself and I am sorry if you took what I might have said in "that light" I have never heard any one say "that was posotively ugly" but this I hear almost daily "I love you Jennie for your nobleness of soul and your warm and generous heart I, too, love your bright black eyes which can flash with imagination or melt with kindness, and I almost envy those beautiful curls."

Mr. L. I like to hear you say "intelligence is preferable to beauty" —although both combined are not objectionable the least. I often meet with persons who are handsome as "Adonis or a Cleopatra." I have admired them vastly but alas have found on acquaintance that there was want of education and intellect. After I become acquainted with a person if they converse well I scarcely ever notice whether they have regular features or not. But enough of this for the present. My sheet is almost filled and I . . . not think of writing more than one sheet this time but there [is] something else I must not forget to speak of so here goes another page.

About my "Photo." You wish me to send it, do you? Now don't you know how <u>very</u> sensitive we Ladies are about sending our shadows to gentlemen? To be candid with you I don't think <u>any</u> gentleman would have a very exalted opinion of a Lady who would send a picture to a stranger. Perhaps I have not the most correct idea of the matter. There might not be any harm is so doing, after a little longer acquaintance I will consider it over, hoping in the mean time you will take no offense at my refusal. You know as yet we are perfect strangers to each other and have no way of as yet learning each other's character or standing. I am of a frank nature as you will learn. I write just what I think but indeed I shall be delighted to receive yours and sincerely hope you will send it. You will allow that with gentlemen it is different.

There will be no impropriety in your sending a Photo. Do you think there would now? I promise that you shall have mine by & by. So please send yours in your next letter and then I have something <u>sweet</u> to tell you which is worth knowing—something real interesting—something that will do to dream about. I might forget to tell you unless you send the shadow.

Well enough for the present. With a kind good night and a request to write soon—<u>very</u>

As ever I am

Jennie

N.B. no more apologies about your penmanship—You do fine.

letter 45

October 3, 1863. Postmarked Brandon, Ohio.
Mollie Ward. Memphis, Tenn.

Saturday Evening, Oct. 3rd

Mr. E. L. Lybarger

I was much pleased with the receipt of your kind epistle which was rece'd some days ago but as this is the first favorable opportunity I have found of answering it I hope you will pardon my seeming neglect. We are at present preparing for a great convention that will be held in <u>Mt. Vernon</u> on Tuesday inst. The union loving people are all up and doing making every preparation possible for the comfort of the great mass of people that will doubtless be in attendance. Every person is alive with excitement. The "<u>Copperheads</u>" held one in the same place about one week since but the day was poorly celebrated and the congregation small—

I prepared myself to go to church this evening and then the thought flashed across my mind that I had a letter to write to a friend in Fredonia and one to you (a soldier in the army) so I remained at home to perform what I considered to be my duty. I love to write at any time but it is a double pleasure when ones thoughts escape through this medium to distant and highly prized friends. How often does my mind revert to the conditions of <u>some</u> of our poor soldiers now in the army. Whilst they are fighting the bloody battles of our country we are at home enjoying its comforts and pleasures and more than that there are those that are blaming and censuring them. I am sorry to say that the principal part of the <u>young</u> men now in <u>our</u> vicinity are <u>deep dyed Copperheads</u>: traitors to their country and their God. One thing they are not patronized a great deal by the Ladies and not at all by <u>me</u>. If I have any thing to do with the gentlemen I want them to be lovers of their country, not traitors or cowards. Society is very dull in this part of the country at present owing mostly to the disloyalty of the citizens but when the soldiers all return (or those who will be spared) they will not be permitted to carry the day I trust. I am thinking we will then rule supreme. Do <u>you</u> not think so? I rec'd a call from my friend Miss Frank Robison this afternoon and she informed me that she was formally, personally acquainted with you and she gave me quite a lengthy narrative concerning you which was very favorable to your character as she spoke of you only in the highest terms. I like the looks of your photograph very much but I shall not attempt to send you mine in this letter but perhaps by the next time I write I will have it ready to send. This is a glorious evening. The moon shines in full splendor. Oh! how much I would like to take a ride of about six or eight miles to pass away the lonely hours but I think I can enjoy myself very well as it is although I must confess I do not feel much like writing tonight. It is now twelve o'clock and I am getting somewhat tired so I will have to make my letter as brief as possible. I very much doubt whether you can ever read what little I have written.

Please excuse me for this time and perhaps by the next time I write I will feel more in the humor. I will bid you goodbye for the present and retire for the night.

Yours in haste
Mollie E. Ward

letter 46

October 12, 1863. Gambier, Ohio.
A. E. Baker. Memphis, Tenn.

Gambier, Ohio, Oct. 12th/63

Lieut. Lybarger
Neglected Friend

Do not be too much surprised upon receiving a letter from one who has been silent for nearly <u>two years</u>. As I was sitting alone in my room this lovely evening, and thinking of my many absent friends, the thought came creeping into my mind that I was indebted to several of my correspondents. Lieut. Lybarger, I believe you now bear that title, [are] among that number. And now though at the "eleventh hour" I am going to write to you, although I will not be so presumptuous as to ask a reply, since I have been so cruelly neglectful in writing to you.

I know that I enjoy receiving true friendship letters from valued friends as much perhaps as any one, but when the time for answering comes I am too apt to think some other time will do just as well. And thus days lengthen into weeks, weeks into months, and months into years before many of my letters are answered.

How do you do now, & how have you been enjoying yourself since you last wrote, are the first questions with which you would be saluted <u>were</u> you <u>here</u>. I am well & am enjoying myself as well as I could wish to during these dark & troublesome times.

I was visiting our relatives in Indiana and Ky. during the earlier part of last summer and since my return (which was sometime in August) I have been here in this fair Eden, Gambier, taking lessons in Oil Painting & Perspective Drawing, both very pleasant studies I assure you. Our teacher, Mr. Heartly, is from Scotland & one of the most eccentric men I ever knew. He seems to be perfectly devoted to his work, & is "everybody" says a first class Artist. I have my third picture almost completed. My next will be a scene at our own Brillwood Caves, the Caskade, sketched by Mr. Heartly. By the way, we, i.e. our painting class, consisting of eight ladies, together with our teacher & several others of "<u>Kenyon's brave sons</u>, spent a day at those <u>famous</u> caves not many weeks ago. Had a most delightful time. No <u>quarreling</u> or disputing as has been the case at picnics that I have attended there.

Our term will close in about four weeks, after which I shall go (If a change don't come o'er the spirit of my dreams) to Spring Mountain & take lessons in Music, as they have a most excellent instructor.

Of course you are still a good Union man & as such are looking forward with <u>anxious</u> delight to the morrow when "John Brough" shall be proclaimed Governor! What if we should be disappointed !! I for one would feel like seeking a home in other parts & ever disowning that I belonged to the once <u>glorious</u> but now <u>disgraced</u> Ohio. How strange to think that men, good, honest, & to some extent intelligent men, can be so blinded by party spirit as to support such a <u>vile traitor</u> as Clement L. Valandigham! . I received a letter a few days ago from an army correspondent & while he denounced "Val" a traitor to his country, & all those who voted for him he wound up by saying that he had no doubt but that <u>Brough</u> would be elected as all the soldiers who would vote at all would go for him.

But for <u>himself</u> he did not intend to vote at all, as he would not support the traitor Valandigham, nor could not <u>think</u> of voting with the <u>Republicans</u>. Is that a <u>true</u> and <u>right</u> Spirit? I think not, & am going to tell him so too. Would that the names Democrat & Republican could be lain aside until this <u>cruel</u> rebellion is entirely crushed. But I have already written much longer that I expected to. Excuse me & ever believe me your

Friend
A.E. Baker

Good Night!

letter 47

October 20, 1863. Macon City, Mo.
Ben F. Stone. Memphis, Tenn.

Ed Lybarger
My Dear Friend,

I received yours of the 8th Inst. and was realy glad to hear from you. Your letter brought back to me a vivid recollection of some days I passed in Miss. and I can appreciate how "the boys" feel when they loose a little sleep and cook a few rations and all for nothing as we used to think and say, but generally found that there was "something up." I see by the papers that activity is again in the army and fighting must be done, and I am fearful that it will not be a little. Though I was never sanguine of immediate success, and to hear of the loss of a battle and the drawing back of an army is nothing more than what I have all along anticipated, but that does not lessen my confidence in the ability of the government and the final success of our army, the want of success one time or any number of times should only nerve us up until we do have complete success or until the last dollar is expended and every man has enriched the soil of freedom with his blood.

We may sometimes have our feelings dampened, the dishonest purposes of some men may obscure our hopes and ill omened fortune may bear heavy upon us, it will only dissolve our political bickerings and strife and make us forget Sectionalism and unite us together upon the true platform, the Salvation of our country.

Ed, I hardly feel like I was a man. Could I only be with you, my comrades in battles. It looks like cowardice, it makes one feel mean, to be at home, while there is war in the land, while there is an enemy striking at our national existence. I do feel a contempt for those of us who are home with our aches and disabilities, exempting. Well my soldiering is "played out."

I am going to teach school this winter. I hope to excite a noble emulation among the "little ones," to do their duty now and in time to come. I am well and am keeping myself in fine spirits in spite of things. We have plenty of girls here and patriotic ones too. They frequently hymn for me the choral war songs, which clothed in the clear ringing tones of female voices in unison are sweeter than "music on the waters." Well you know I cannot help but love them.

I am pleased at your determination to visit Mo. and better pleased when you promised to visit me. I think I can find you a pretty girl, and I shall pray "that fates spare the surviving boy" until the war is over, and that then you may find somewhere here a beauty who will say "with thee I would love to live, with thee I could cheerfully die." My parents would be very glad for you to visit them, they have a considerable partiality for the Soldiers.

I am in the main very well pleased with your postscript, it shows that you are not an amalgamationist yet. As to the policy of the administration we will not dissolve the Union about that. Administrations are only "for the time" and with themselves their policies do pass away, and in this is a great excellency in the system of our government. The present (negro) policy of the Administration is not in my opinion "a little strong," on the contrary, very week, it is not a pure policy. For where there is white and black there is a blemish, your own theory.

Well I will not trouble your further about this now, but wish you all good luck.

Truly your friend,
Ben F. Stone

Ed Lybarger. Lieut.
Co. K

letter 48

October 23, 1863. Nelsonville, Ohio.
Jennie Hall. Memphis, Tenn.

Nelsonville, Ohio, Oct. 23, 1863

"Hurrah for Brough"
So say I, Friend E.L. Lybarger

How shall I express sufficient thanks for your very kind letter of the 15th and the anxiously looked for shadow? Now if I give my candid opinion don't say that I am flattering. I shall tell you just what I think of it regardless of consequences and if you do not [like] what I say I have no way of convincing you the contrary. I think the picture decidedly handsome and you would not doubt but that I was pleased with it. If you could have been an unseen observer of my countenance as I opened your letter and beheld the "Photo" my eyes certainly did sparkle then with delight. The frank open countenance, the intellectual forehead, the bright expressive eye—how I was going to say—burned my hand, and if, you will allow me the expression, made a complete conquest.

Perhaps though that is saying too much—I am highly pleased with the picture anyhow. It certainly "fills the bill" to perfection of my idea of manly beauty. In conclusion I will say about the shadow that I am much obliged for your kindness in sending it and shall prize it very highly.

Give yourself no uneasiness about my being a married lady. I'm gay, frank, and free yet and have yet to find the one to whom I could safely confide my happiness for life. "I still roam in maiden meditation fancy free."

My circle of friends and acquaintances is very extensive. I have travelled considerable. Some future time I shall give you a synopsis of my history which I think will interest you some.

For my standing in society I refer you to those who can tell you all about your unknown friend. I have acquaintances in all parts of Ohio almost, at least in the principal cities, Cincinnati, Newark, Columbus, Zanesville, and others. If you ever live to return home you will have no trouble of obtaining information of me if you desire it. You may ask me any question you wish and I shall not consider you impertinent either. It would be strange, I think, if you were not curious to know something of your correspondent.

I am sorry there is no "Photo" artist in our Village at this time. I shall however send an Ambrotype. I shall go down in the morning and have one taken. There is something I want to tell you but shall wait until I again hear from you. That "something I want" was the compliments passed on your picture. Are you satisfied with that? If not, what shall I do? I think friend Edwin your picture is sweet enough, and so sweet, that I shall be tempted to . . . k . . . .

Well good night

Pleasant dreams

Wonder if I won't dream of a handsome young officer? Shouldn't wonder. Don't get frightened [if] when you see my ugly visage.

"By By"
Jennie H

Tell me how old you would suppose me to be from my picture? I promise you a longer letter when I have heard from you again. Friday morn.

How provoking that it is just raining in torrents and I cannot have the promised picture taken today. I'll send the letter without though and give you my <u>word</u> that I shall send the picture just as soon as it clears off. Tomorrow if possible.

Please write soon. Jennie.

letter 49

October 24, 1863. Nelsonville, Ohio.
Jennie Hall. Memphis, Tenn.

[Note: This letter was enclosed with that of
October 23 (48).]

Nelsonville, Oct. 24th, 1863

Friend E.L.L.

Enclosed please find the promised shadow. It is not a very good picture although it resembles the original some. We have no good artist in town. Does the shadow resemble the lady you had pictured in your imagination? I'm sure I told you I "was homely."

Cordially yours,
Jennie

💲

letter 50

November 9, 1863. Postmarked Mt. Sterling, Ky.
Lou Riggen. Memphis, Tenn.

Lieut. E.L. Lybarger,

Your novel, singular, and interesting letter excited a variety of interesting and funny thoughts. In reply to my very solicitous inquiries about your welfare after that horrible battle, you merely remark that "you are glad that your correspondent is such a friend to the soldiers." Well—if that isn't cool, I'd like to know what is. Couldn't even tell me whether you were killed or not. I suppose you dislike to be too communicative to a <u>married lady</u> (!)

Now—excuse me sir, it is my turn. You are so excessively suspicious that I suspect to use a hackneyed phrase, that you are judging me by yourself. <u>I guess</u> that you are either an antiquated old "bach" who have persuaded Captain Jack Rogers or some other good looking gentleman to let you have his photo to send to me, or else "the wife you left behind you" is waiting for the letters you ought to send to her instead of to silly girls who have no more sense than to write to married gentlemen, but since you are kind enough, notwithstanding your shrewd suspicions of me, to send your photograph, I can't have the heart to ask you to return the enclosed, which is as good a likeness of myself as I can draw, and since you wish it I am perfectly willing that they <u>should not be returned</u>.

Don't forget the conditions you promised however— "Something sweet" in your next or——O delightful alternative! most condescending young gentleman, most honorable privilege! You will <u>let</u> me kiss you when I see you. I believe I prefer the "something sweet" now lest I should never have an opportunity of <u>demanding</u> the alternative.

I am sorry you accuse me of "Sophistry," as I did not know I had been guilty of false reasoning. If you find any of the same kind in this, please unravel it in your next—and display your progress in logic—of course this letter will be a splendid field for the same.

I fully intended to reciprocate the compliments of Captain Jack Rogers in a previous letter, but was so particularly taken with the rest of your letter that I neglected it. Please give him my compliments and say to him that he can find a correspondent by writing to Miss <u>Irene Livingstone, Mt. Sterling</u>, a young lady who is I think equal to the task of writing to him or "any other man." She is a particular friend of mine, and I hope no "loafer" nor married man will presume to write to her.

Now, Lieutenant Edwin L. Lybarger just write me that you are <u>not</u> a married gentleman and are <u>not</u> having any quantity of fun at my expense and I <u>will</u> send you my photo <u>sure</u> in my next. If you are however you are perfectly welcome to the <u>fun</u>, but not to my shadow.

For myself, I am not married, nor am I anything but what I told you—

Simply—

Lou Riggen

Greenwood, Nov. 9th, 1863.

letter 51

November 10, 1863. Nelsonville, Ohio.
Jennie Hall. Memphis, Tenn.

Nelsonville, Ohio, Nov. 10th, 1863 Evening after tea.
My very interesting friend E.L.L.

Today's mail brought me your favor of the 3rd and very
welcome it was too. Do you doubt that friend E.L.? No, I'm sure you
do not, but before I go any further allow me to return you many,
very many, thanks for the flattering compliments you have so
wordily passed on my shadow. I was not vain enough to imagine you
would admire it for it's only a plain looking picture. However I
intend having a better one taken soon in a different position which
you perhaps will like better. "You say you do know that I am sweet
enough anyhow." You only imagine this of course; but how poor
imagination compares with the real. My darling good brothers have
told me this. "Sister you are awful sweet" after having stolen a kiss
or two. Enough nonsense.

Well I shall tease you no longer about my age—you have
guessed right. I will be 22 this winter. There now—<u>please</u> don't
scold me any more [for] not telling you sooner—and I'll be a <u>real</u>
"good girl."

You say you "are so glad I replied to <u>your</u> advertisment." Thank
you for the compliment again. I too am glad—but I did not dream
that I should be so fortunate in finding so pleasing and interesting
<u>soulder</u> correspondent. As you say there is a <u>great</u> deal said and
written against replying to these army correspondents, and if what
was written were true and the argument plausible it would put the
blush to the faces of we who may have answered the same. I have
thought the matter of [over] a <u>great deal</u> and cannot persuade my
self to believe there is the least harm in the world in it. Perhaps I
may have wrong ideas. If so I wish some one would correct me.
I would be far from wishing to overstep the bounds of female
decorum for I profess to be a lady in <u>every</u> sense of the <u>word</u>! My
reasons for replying to your advertisment were <u>then</u>—I thought

there would be something <u>novel</u> and interesting in corresponding with a gentleman whom I have never met. Another reason—and the main <u>one</u>—to cheer the souldier who has gone forth bravely to fight the battles of this our "beloved country." A gentleman might not in reality form a very exalted opinion of a young lady who would reply to an advertisment but I sincerely hope that no such thoughts have entered your mind during our correspondence which seems to be growing more and more <u>interesting</u>. If by our being entire strangers you might doubt the truth of what I may have told you in my frank candid manner of my self—<u>time</u> will remove them <u>all</u>, rest assured of that if you should live to return <u>home</u>. And that makes me wish more that <u>ever</u> that this "cruel war" <u>was</u> over. Do you blame me?

I feel pretty confident that I shall like you <u>real well</u> after a personal acquaintance, and hope that the time is not far distant when I have the pleasure of seeing my <u>unknown</u> but interesting <u>friend</u>.

I am so fond of singing and I am partial to [the] song "Cruel War." Are you fond of music? If so perhaps I might interest you singing and playing on the Piano or the melodian. Never mind, I shall have learned some pretty pieces by the time we meet if we ever do. Then at home—if you have one—you can again bask in the <u>sunny</u> smiles of <u>loved</u> ones—and spare a smile for your "Blackeyed friend Jennie H."

I promised, I believe in my last, to give you a little of my history, although I do not know that it will interest you <u>very much</u>.

I was born in Urbana, Champain County, Ohio. My father was merchent there. He die when I was <u>small</u>, not old enough to value his <u>love</u> or appreciate his <u>worth</u>. He idolized his wife and family. I being the youngest of ten children was the <u>special</u> pet of the household. Five of the children now only are living—a darling good sister and three kind brothers, all of whom are married and settled in life. My Mother married again, having lived a widow some ten years. I had a kind stepfather, but he too soon died. But I'm getting ahead of my story. After Mother married again she moved to Perry County on a <u>farm</u>. I had not the advantages of an education there in the country that was desired, so my good brother then married and residing in the King City, <u>New York</u>, desired that I should come there and complete my education. I accepted the invitation and bidding adieu to my quiet country home with all its loved surroundings I started to the great metropolis—and there found a happy home with my dear brother, wife and littler cherub, Frankie. ("He is now a little angel") Oh how happy we were there until death came in the "night time" and robbed us of our idol—our treasure. How I loved him—pardon me, I am growing tedious. I entered one of the best schools in the City. My thoughtful brother did not wish me to mingle much in society until I should complete my education. I, like a "good girl," obliged, although he took special pains to show me all the sights, and I at times mingled in the gay whorl of fashionable society for I could not avoid it living with my fashionable brother. I had been there some two years when I was suddenly called home to Ohio to attend the bedside of my Mother who was not expected to live, but God spared her to live, to councel and pray for her children. My stepfather died, and I of course would not leave Mother again—alone. She has now gone to New York to spend the winter with brother. I am staying with Sister. If Mother does not return I shall probably go East next Spring.

You say you are acquainted in Newark. Perhaps you know Old Dr. Hood. He is a cousin of mine, and Mr. Reckinich married a cousin of mine, also Sallie Howard of Zanesville.

Having written you a long letter I will close. Please pardon mistakes, I know there are several—and write me soon as convenient.

Your Friend
Jennie

"Good night"

℥

letter 52

Postmarked November 27, 1863. Millwood, Ohio.
Phrone Rogers. Prospect, Tenn.

Wednesday evening

Friend Ed,

The hour of 8 o'clock finds me seated at the table at your home, all is quiet around save the murmuring of the water. The moon makes the nights so beautiful. The weather is delightfully cool.—but this only tends to sadden me, as it gives me a time for reflection. Ed, I feel grievously disappointed as I am of the oppinion that you have neglected or forgotten me—perhaps both. You have not answered my letter, although I wrote to you so long ago. I know you receive my letters as I correspond regularly with my (friend) Oliver. I received a letter and his picture last week, both which I prize very much. I intend sending him a picture of myself as soon as I can. Please do not repeat to him.

Last Sabbath I went to Pleasant Valley to a Methodist protracted meeting, had a very nice pleasant time. Went to Rob J. Critchfield's home for dinner, met a strange gentleman, a Gambier student. I found him very entertaining, in all quite intelligent if I may consider myself a judge. He thinks he will visit Millwood soon. Then I will have the pleasure of meeting him again. I guess we have plenty of gentlemen now, or at least I am well supplied. I do not know how long it will last. They do admirably to flirt with. I do not expect to be married soon. I intend to wait untill this cruel war is over. Do not become shocked at me, for I can assure you that my head is as near sight[ed] as it ever was.

Your Lizzie White Millis lives just across the street from us. She was at our house the other day and looked at your Photograph, seemed to be very much impressed to see that you had grown so handsome. Ed, I fancy I see you smile at my silly expressions, but never mind them for they are all true, ha! ha!

I intend commencing my school next Monday. O! horror, how I hate it. I would just as soon go to my grave the first week, but then I do not teach any Saturdays so that I can come home every week. Ed, I hope you will not have to leave the place you are now. I read your last letter . . . I must say I admire your way of stealing and I think if you keep on you would be what I would call a scientific thief against you get home, don't think me too complimentary. Ed, I have just written this scribble to inform you that I still exist. I close hoping to receive one of your dear interesting letters soon, very soon.

Phrone

letter 53

November 28, 1863. Postmarked Mt. Vernon, Ohio.
Mollie E. Ward. Memphis, Tenn.

Brandon, Ohio, Nov. 28th

Friend Ed,

For as a friend I now consider you and did I not I would not then address you. It has been now over five weeks since I penned my last to you but I think when I tell you that it was on account of my Mother's severe illness that you will certainly pardon my otherwise seeming neglect. She has been sick over three weeks and the principal part of the care of the household rested upon my shoulders which made it seem anything but pleasant to me. However I have got along with it admirably so far and feel thankful that with the aid of a good physician and good nurses she is partially restored to her former health or at least out of danger. Indeed I feel tired enough at this moment to retire to my own room to seek repose but at the same time I consider it my duty to reply to your long neglected letter. I hardly know where to address [it] so you will be likely to get it now that I am writing. I have not seen any account of your marching to another place but I have been so busy I have scarcely found time for reading the news. There is nothing of importance going on at present I believe.

Oh yes, now that I think of it, the <u>Copperheads</u> are holding a protracted meeting in Brandon at the present time but it is raining so much and has been since the commencement of it that I think it must be poorly attended. I presume the soldiers wonder at the loyal men will permit the copperheads to act as they do in the north. I think myself that it is a shame, a disgrace, for the decent part of [the] community to let those despicable, despised, and degraded creatures rule supreme. But let me tell you that the men here at home are not <u>noble, brave Soldiers</u> like those in the field, but cowards and afraid to defend even themselves. I have heard several of the young men of my acquaintance and those professing to be loyal and true to the flag say what can we do here towards keeping peace in our land; wait untill the soldiers return <u>to help us</u> and then we will quell and rule over them with an iron rod. Such bravery as that does not extend very far with <u>me</u> I can assure you. Such people as that are not worthy of a free country in my estimation. I sometimes wonder what kind of an appearance one of those young gentlemen would make in the front ranks of a bloody battle. There is the place for them so that if either survive the brave may be favored. I suppose of course you have some cowards in the army but I don't believe they excel some of the boys here at home. I do not say they are <u>all</u> cowards here but I <u>know</u> some of them are. However I shall not complain any more about them this time for fear you may think I am inclined to grumble but wait untill you return so that you may see for yourself.

Do you ever think of getting a furlough or is that entirely out of the question nowadays? I suppose it is. Frank Robison is not at home at present nor have I seen her since I recd your last. She is away on a visit to her sisters, I think. I am going to have a small party this week and shall extend her an invitation but do not think she will come as the distance will probably be too great.

If you will excuse this short and poorly written letter I will close untill a more convenient opportunity presents itself or untill time is less precious with me than at present.

I remain as ever your friend and well wisher.

Mollie E. Ward

E.L. Lybarger
    P.S. Write soon and oblige your friend,

Moll

letter 54

Greenwood, Dec. 3d, 1863

Lieut. E.L. Lybarger
My Friend

I received your letter a few days ago. I write this early to let you know that I was pleased to hear from you and shall always be happy to have a word from the 43d either "occasionally" or very often. When we heard that the "Ohio brigade" had positive orders to move I assure you we were all very sorry. It was too bad that our friends from the 43d could not even come over to pay us a parting visit.

For the past few days we have been rejoicing over Braggs defeat. Is not it <u>splendid</u>? The only thing that mars my joy in a great victory <u>for our side</u> is thinking of the many homes and hearts made desolate. I hope that Grant will follow up the great advantage he has gained, then there would be some hopes of this "<u>cruel war</u>" ending <u>some time</u>. Was the "Ohio brigade" in the fight? I did not see the 43d mentioned so concluded it was not in the fight. You know I told you that as soon as the "Ohio brigade" joined that army, that Bragg would be defeated directly. Do I not prophesy well?

What a very long tedious march you had. Poor soldiers, I feel sorry for them and would like very much to do something to help them. I heard from you while at Iuka. Capt. J.C. Hamilton spent a night with us. We were surprised and pleased to see him, as we were not expecting to see any of you so soon.

So Capt. Rhodes actually did take his Guitar with him. I think he deserves a <u>great deal</u> of credit. He has proved that he is indeed a true lover of music. I should like to shake hands with him for it. True, I don't suppose it is very delightful for you to listen at his "continual picking," but hear it patiently Lieut. and comfort yourself with thinking how much it will add to the Captain's charms. I heard Miss Nette Johnson once say, that if any gentleman wanted her to fall in love with him, that he must sing & play for her on the Guitar, that was all that's required. You had better let the Captain know Miss Johnson's sentiments.

Three or four days last week we had very cold weather. I think it must have been nearly as cold as the people enjoy who inhabit the summit of "Greenlands icy mountains." Yesterday the weather greatly moderated, and today has seemed as mild and pleasant as Spring.

Memphis has been turned 'topsy-turvey" for the past week by the last order issued by the military authorities. The order enrolling all citizens, without respect to age into the militia. Father has enrolled but Charley says <u>he</u> will get out of the lines as soon as they begin to enforce the conscription. I suppose he will go out there to die in "the last ditch."

It is a great pity that our musical friends of the 43d have no place to go where they could sing "duets and quartettes." I wish they could come here. I used to enjoy hearing them sing very much, and then you know when they tried to sing a whole book through and got tired, there was always one or two that did not join in the singing to talk to.

I suppose you have left Prospect by this time, as Capt. Hamilton had built him a chimney when you wrote. If I were you and did not want to be constantly on the march, I would not allow him to build chimneys.

I would have no particular objections to sending you my photograph if I had any, but I have not one. I sincerely hope that you will come uninjured out of this war. I feel an interest in all the Union soldiers. God bless them all is my constant prayer. Everyone in the neighborhood with whom you are acquainted is alive and well. Tell me all about your marches and adventures.

Hoping to hear soon that you with all my friends in the 43d are well. I remain your true friend.

M.L. Collins

Direct Rev. C. Collins. There are one or two Irish girls in town named Mary Collins. Mother and Lizzie wish to be especially remembered.

letter 55

December 11, 1863. Millwood, Ohio.
Adelia Shroyer. Prospect, Tenn.

Millwood, Dec. 11th, 1863

My Dear Friend Ed;

I am seated once more for the pleasant task of responding to your very welcome note, which I received a few days ago and read with interest. It came very unexpected as I had neglected to answer your last, for which I cincerely ask your pardon. It was merely neglect. I intended to respond imeadately but waited untill I did not know where to write. I believe I will not make any other excuse. I hope you will have the goodness to pardon me.

You said I still call you my Friend; you <u>can</u> and rest assured that I ever have been a friend and expect to be; I am a Friend of the Soldiers, especially one in whose society I have spent so many pleasant hours, such hours as I have not spent since nor before (but pardon me I am saying too much) as I may be the least among all those you claim as Friends, notwithstanding you may rely upon my Friendship. I often think of the past and of the many pleasures we used to enjoy and sincerely hope you may return home safely and enjoy alike privileges. I suppose you have felt as if you were forgotten by me, but quite to the contrary. In memory I am with you and would much rather you were here tonight than to be writing as I consider my self far inferior concerning penmanship and composition to the <u>one</u> whom I am addressing. I hope you will not take this as flattery, as I am very much opposed to that.

Well, Ed, I hardly know what to write that would interest you. I am aware that you have quite a number of corespondents that will keep you posted. I suppose you are not aware that I have just returned from Adamsville where I stayed some nine weeks visiting my Sisters. I had a very pleasant visit and enjoyed myself finely but nothing could please me better than to have this wicked rebelion and the Soldiers return. I do not enjoy myself as I used to, not by any means. There are too many vacant seats, too many absent ones, ah loved ones.

I am trying to write a Friendship letter, if I should deviate I hope you will consider the source, as I am apt to let my mind run away with me a little sometimes in writing to old Friends. I would love to write some news but there is nothing going on at present that is worthy of notice. I saw your Brother today and told him I received a letter from you; he was very glad to hear from you as it had been some time since he had heard from you. He was afraid that you was in that Battle fought near Chattanooga but I suppose you were not.

I believe I will close for tonight by saying if you wish to corepond with me your letters will be received kindly and read with interest. You have my best regards and

> *kind wishes for your welfare.*
> *Yours ever true*
> *Adelia Shroyer*

Forget me not and thou shalt never be forgotten

> *—Adda*

$

letter 56

December 18, 1863. Mt. Vernon, Ohio.
Edith Welker. Prospect, Tenn.

Sabbath Eve at Home, Dec. 18th/63
Ever Rememberd Friend Edwin

Think [it] not strange of receiving a letter from so unlooked for source, but duty as well as pleasure permits me to the act. I am well and sincerely hope when this reaches you it will find you enjoying the same.

Well, Ed, I expect you will be a little if not greatly surprised on receiving a letter from me, <u>will you not</u>? I answered your letter that you wrote to me immediately on the reception of it. But I addressed it to the Hospital in Kentucky. You remember you were there when you wrote to me. And you told me to direct there and I did so but I heard a little while afterwards that you had joined your Regt. And I suppose you never got it. That has been some two years ago if am not mistaken. I have been making inquiry about you for a long time but could not find out where you were untill a few days ago. And I have come to the conclusion that perhaps a few lines from Eda would not come amiss.

I am going to school this winter. I like to go middling well. I have couple of new studies which keep me pretty busy. I am studying Algebra, Rays Higher Arithmetic, Grammar, and Cornell's Geography, beside my reading and spelling.

We have built a new house this summer and have got moved into it and have been living in it about six weeks. And I like it exceedingly well.

The draft is going off the 5th of next month and the cowards are going daily to Newark to get exemp. I just wish they would not exemp any of them for I think one has just as good a right to help put down this Rebelliene as another. I think it shows how courageous a man is to go and swear to a falsehood to get rid of going. If I was man I would stand my ground. If I died by it I would not expose my cowardice that way <u>anyhow</u>. It makes me so mad when I think about it that I wish I had the power. I'll bet I would make some of the Butternuts pay dearly for some of their big talk. Ed this is my opinion. And am I not right?

But Hark! the clock strikes the hour for retiring and I must bring my uninteresting letter to a close. Hoping to hear from you soon, I will stop. Answer soon.

I ever remain your friend
Eda Welker

Hurrah for Brough
Please send your Photograph and oblige your Friend Eda.
Address Monroe Mills, Knox Co., Ohio

letter 57

December 23, 1863. Postmarked Millwood, Ohio.
Phrone Rogers. Nashville, Tenn.

School room, Dec. 23, 1863

Ever Dear friend Ed.

It is now 8 oclock in the morning and I find an hour in which to answer your two very welcome letters. I had despaired of hearing from you. I was sitting here all alone this morning thinking how swiftly time passed. It is a saddening thought as well as a cheering one, in many respects so much of our life passed that we never have to live over again, so many days of sunshine and tears gone. This is the last letter I will ever have the pleasure of writing you in the year 1863. Oh how many changes have taken place since you left home —even in our feeling and looks I can see it in myself, I cannot say that I am not as happy as in days gone by, but my idea of what constitutes happiness is so different. Ed you seem to be enjoying your self very much and I am very glad. I always like to see my friends happy and my enemys as miserable as they can be not to die. I suppose you think I have a kind heart in me, so I always thought too.

Ed you wanted to know something about your lady friends. I do not know how to begin, but in the first place, who are your friends, but I suppose all the ladies are or ought to be in the light that I see it. John Hammond goes with Ella Rightmire and I think they are engaged, he is very attentive indeed. Lib has no company that I know of. Ike Baker flirts with Mary Hammond, or she with him, I do not know which. Charlotte as you are aware perhaps goes in our society, Lisha Moody is her beau. Karl Hammond with Sallie Peterman everybody supposes are engaged. Your friend Ell has no company. Ed Cook and Het [?] correspond and that is all I know about them. George Baker goes with Kate Moody, and a gentleman by the name of Hunt with Emma. I do not know him personally but from what I hear he does not amount to much. Will Hawn is a very good friend of Amanda Israel—he does not go to Gambles any more. I guess he thought there was too much secession there, this is merely my opinion. I do not know that Whites' girls have any company. Jim McElroy and Fannie Mast are to be married in a few days, I suppose during Christmas and New Years. I also hear that Rob Critchfield and Anna Anderson (a girl that lives at Dr. Mast's) are to be married that same day. Now I guess that I have come to myself, and I am going to tell you the truth. I flirt with all the gentlemen, but most with Dawson Critchfield. He is a collegian as you are aware and suits me very well at present. I will have to stop writing now as it is school time.

Thursday, Dec. 24th

This morning I am seated to finish my letter. I can assure you that I do not feel very bright. I was at a small party at Emma Critchfield's last night and did not get home until two oclock and of course had to rise very early in order to get to school in time. Tonight I am going to a literary society at Cakes school house. I am a member and I intend to rehearse "Bingen on the Rhine." Oh we have such pleasant times. All the young folks around go, and some of the Kenyonites come, there is one in particular that I fancy, he is a Canadian, really intelligent as I think. He often assists in debate. Joss is coming up this afternoon. I think I will show her how to teach a spell. Tomorrow eve I am a going to a party and Saturday eve I am a going to have a small company at home and Sunday eve I expect, if nothing happens to prevent me, I will sleep a wee bit, which rest I think I will need though I can rest all week for I intend to have vacation.

Ed since you speak so highly of Captain Rhodes I think he must be a gentleman and I am very glad that I could change my opinion of him. I did not care anything about him bringing Mary Wolfe to Millwood—but merely wanted you to inform him that I was not of the same character. The note he wrote me shewed for itself that he was not only gentlemanly, but also very intelligent, but enough of the Captain.

Ed your father is as I think very dangerously ill. I do not think you will have a father long. Oh he is so much changed. I notice him failing so much more since I am away from Millwood, as I am a great deal of my time at your house when I am there. Your mother's health is very good now, but she has so much care. My head is aching most tremendously, and I guess I have said all I can think of at present. Oh I had almost forgot to say that your last letter did prove very interesting and all I have to say in reference to it in a critical manner is, that it was too short entirely and it gave me nervous headache to think that I would have to quit reading.

Remember me kindly to Captain A. You may think of me occasionally if you want to. I hope we will not be so unfortunate about our letters any more. I remain you sincere friend.

Phrone

1864 LETTERS

letter 58

January 3, 1864. Nelsonville, Ohio.
Jennie Hall. Pulaski, Tenn.

Nelsonville, Athens Co., Ohio Jan. 3d, 1864

Lieut. E.L. Lybarger

A very Happy New Year to you and many more to follow. I don't know what conclusions you may have come to in regard to your unknown friend Jennie E. Hall—but I imagine that they are not of a very pleasing nature. I shall have to admit that I deserve a good scolding for my long silence; I shall however offer my appologies— then if they are not accepted and you should see proper to chastise me—why I shall accept the same with the best grace possible—only don't be too severe.

Please pardon my <u>long silence</u>. I know you would if you could have been here the last two weeks and known of my engagements and how my time has been occupied—visiting, attending parties, receiving company, etc. I have <u>scarcely</u> had one "wee little hour" <u>all</u> to my self for ten days past. Now Lieut. You know the Bible or some other good book says "Forgiveness is a virtue." You will forgive me, won't you? And now with the imaginary assurance that I have it, I shall proceed.

I am very much obliged for your last kind letter. It was duly appreciated believe me. You must have had a long and tedious march. You speak of my "singing & playing." I never thought to mention it before. I am not a fine performer on any instrument but I sing & play a little on several. I am not acquainted with those pieces you mentioned "Loan rock by the sea" and answer to "Cruel war" but I have just learned three or four very beautiful pieces—not learned—I should have said heard them sung and played—and I am perfectly charmed with them—and think I shall send for the music. One is "Just before the battle, Mother." The sweetest piece I ever heard. I can almost sing it now. Another "Wrap the flag around me, boys" and "Answer to Louisa." Have you ever heard either of those just mentioned? They are new pieces.

I have had the pleasure of becoming acquainted with Surgeon Bell of the 48th. I am intimately acquainted with his wife, but never knew him until recently. He can give you all necessary information concerning your unknown friend—and no doubt he will take pleasure in answering all your questions. He will tell you perhaps that I am a lively and social girl—all true. I shall expect of course that you will keep all my letters strictly confidential. The Dr. returns to his Regiment in a week or two. He seems to have enjoyed his stay at home very much.

We have had bitter cold weather here for a few days past which is favorable in one sense, that is—give us good skating which sport I am extremely fond of.

Please write soon—don't retaliate this time—I shall be glad to learn any piece of music you desire. Yours,

Jennie

letter 59

January 4, 1864. Fort Wayne, Ind.
Calvin A. Anderson. Prospect, Tenn.

Fort Wayne, Ind. Jany. 4, 1864

Dear Cousin;

Some weeks ago Father received a letter from you—and I have been promising myself the pleasure of answering it for sometime back, but never could get seated somehow to do it. My brother and myself belong to the same Rgt. And Company. (Co. "C," 74th Ind. Vols) which is still lying at Chattanooga. I left the Rgt. On the 15 of November last, detailed on the Recruiting Service. I expect to return in about ten days. Gwynne is also at Home on Furlough, he returns to Nashville tomorrow and perhaps will go on to the Rgt. from there. He is detailed as "Clerk" in the Mustering Department. Father and Mother are well. My Sisters, five in number, are all married and doing well. Lydia is living in "Lawrence, Kansas". Sallie is living at Home as is also Resa and Laura, the eldest. Mollie lives some 28 miles from here. Lydia's Husband's name is Shanklin, Sallie's, Evans. Having been sick for some days past, and having a severe headache, I will have to close for the present. I hope I shall have the pleasure of meeting you some time at Chattanooga where we will have a good time if possible. Father & Mother and the Family send love to you.

Good Bye for the present.

Yours truly
Calvin A. Anderson

letter 60

January 4, 1864. Spring Mountain, Ohio.
A. E. Baker. Nashville, Tenn.

Spring Mountain, O, Jan. 4th, '64

Lieut. Lybarger;

I am in a "great hurry"—as usual, but I will write you a "little bit."

Yours of Oct. 28th/63 was duly rec. & let me answer you that I was indeed <u>glad</u> to hear from you <u>once again</u>.

I will remember that I did not in my last letter, ask you to write. The reason of which was that I had been so neglectful in answering <u>your</u> letters. I have no objections whatever to a <u>friendly</u> correspondence with you. Your letters will ever be received thankfully, & if possible I will endeavor to answer them more punctually. I am here studying <u>music</u> only and consequently will have more leisure time than I have had for some time past.

When I started to S.M. some five weeks ago Sister Ada place "Telemaque" in my trunk with a request that I should read it. But heedless of her request it has lain undisturbed. How naturally <u>indolent</u> some people are!

I must confess that I feel quite at a loss to know what to write, for <u>surely</u> Spring Mountain <u>news</u>—even if I had any to communicate, would not be at all interesting to one entirely unacquainted. The Seminary is in a pretty prosperous condition this term. I believe there are between fifty & sixty students in attendance.

But I must not forget to wish you a "happy new year"—'Tisn't too late is it?

Did you <u>enjoy</u> your holiday? I am <u>sure</u> I enjoyed myself. Was at home part of the time. Christmas eve I attended an oyster supper at Danville. The evening was a most beautiful one and we all enjoyed ourselves "hugely." Cousin "Ike" was there. New Years eve I was invited to another oyster supper in S.M. but ther weather was so cold and disagreeable that I declined going. I spent the evening reading the "Widow Bedott." Did you ever read it? It is very entertaining but I fear not very beneficial.

Lieut. Crooks of the 51st Regt. is home recruiting. He took me up to Danville the Thursday before Christmas, & one Friday he went to Mount Vernon to visit his sweet heart, Normanda Sapp— Whose acquaintance he formed the evening of "The" party at Sapp's I'm confident that will make a <u>match</u> if the Lieut. Gets safely through the war. "Sal" Sapp is married.

Well I have written a long letter & nothing much after all. I must close. Adieu.

A.E. Baker

I haven't seen Ellen Gamble since she left school at Danville. I always thought Ell a <u>real</u> good girl.

Have you heard of the marriage of Temp. Darling? <u>Union!</u> <u>preserve the union</u>. Joy be with her!

$

letter 61

January 19, 1864. Nelsonville, Ohio.
Jennie Hall. Mt. Vernon, Ohio.

Nelsonville, Athens Co., Ohio. Jan. 19th, 1864

Lieut. E.L.L.
Friend <u>unknown</u>.

I wrote you a <u>long</u> letter to Tenn. Some time ago—but learning since that the 43rd Reg. are home "on furlough" thought I would drop you a few lines to Mt. Vernon as I understood you to say that place was your home. I have a great deal more to tell you than I can now write.

I <u>almost</u> flatter my self Lieut. That you will honor Nelsonville with a visit on your return south. Dr. Bell is still at home and is one of my best friends.

I'm well and happy as usual, hope you are the same.

Please accept my compliments and favor me with a prompt reply.

The same souldier's
Friend
Jennie E.H.

letter 62

Millwood, Jan. 22nd, 1864

My Dear friend, Ed;

I am at a loss to know why you have not received my letters. I can assure you that I have answered every letter that I ever received from you. I believe I am not in the habit of treating my <u>friends rudely</u>. I haven't much to write to you this time as I gave you <u>all</u> the news in my last, which I suppose you have received ere this time. Just think your last letter was on the road <u>twenty-one days</u>.

Jossie is about well and I think it is about time too as she has some very important business on hand. I wish you could have come home on "Leave of absence" this spring. I think you <u>might</u> come too. I do not believe you care the snap of your finger for <u>any</u> of your friends.

John Hawn starts back to his Reg. I did not know it untill today or I surely would have prepared to have sent you something. Will has just returned from St. Louis; he has been away about six weeks. By the way, we are going to have a dancing party tomorrow evening (given for John Hawn). I do not imagine that I shall enjoy it much if I do not feel brighter than I do today. I am about tired out. We have had splendid sleighing snow for two weeks and I have been improving it. I guess I have gone every night in that time and almost every day. But you better believe this is a dreary day. It has been raining all day. I imagine we will have pleanty of mud now.

Frank is going home to live next week. He stays there part of the time now. Jossie and Mother return you their love. Mother thinks you did right by staying as you have got an easy position as well as a safe one. Jossie requests me to say that she had been saving some canned peaches for you and now that you have disappointed her by not coming home—she will be under the painful necessity of eating them herself.

Ed, write to me soon and as often as you can. There is nothing that affords me greater pleasure than to hear from you. Hoping that you may be able to get home soon, I close.

As ever—

Phrone

$

letter 63

January 23, 1864. Postmarked Mt. Sterling, Ky.
Lou Pearl Riggen. Prospect, Tenn.

Greenwood, Ken. Jany 23d, 1864

Lieutenant Lybarger;

Excuse this empty letter. I have not the slightest doubt that it will be so excessively timid so utterly overcome with its own insignificance that it will occupy just about a month in reaching its destination. I know the poor innocent paper will tremble and flutter at your righteous indignation, because it is not the bearer of that photograph instead of useless apologies—which articles I always did despise.

I think I hear you say "Pshaw! The girl does not intend to redeem her promise." Then you will enter into quite a logical disquisition as follows; No truthful girl breaks her promise. Miss Lou Riggen <u>has</u> broken her promise—and then the <u>inevitable</u> conclusion—<u>Therefore</u>—Now don't. I deny the second proposition. Decidedly! and in a hurry, before you can apply any epithets. <u>Will</u> you believe me when I tell you that. I am out of photographs, that I anticipated no such dilemma when I promised to send one, and that I certainly <u>do</u> intend to keep inviolate and sacred my word? So you won't, because I promised to <u>send</u> "it in my <u>next sure</u>," and here is the "next" minus the photo. Shall I plead "guilty" at last? well— <u>won't you grant an extension of time?</u>

I believe that you make it a point to disbelieve everything I write any how, so I shall not take the trouble to care, and if you persist in believing that I am trying to deceive you, and that I have had your

<u>photo</u> too long. I will return it immediately, but can't send mine in that event, but then that won't do. I must send mine—and will. So don't expect yours just yet. There—I am tired of that and so are you. Shade of L.P.R. rest thee–

O, ye battle! ye wasted sympathies! ye fun at somebody's expense! I didn't, I assure you, think that Chickamauga Creek ran through Main St., Memphis, Tenn., but I did infer from the fact that you wrote you were under marching orders, that you were of the <u>reinforcements</u>.

Nevertheless I acknowledge the sell, and I have to make on request of you—<u>don't</u> on penalty of losing your correspondent (O dreadful deprivation) say anything more about the fearfully good state of your health. I assure you you shall not be bored with sentimental talk about battles again from this source. Battles, indeed! Knoxville, indeed!

I had ceased entirely to expect a letter in answer to my last supposing that you had become quite indignant at my ugly "photo," and was contemplating a very dignified note in which I should with as much easy elegance as I could parade return yours, and therefore, a cessation of hostilities and of letters simultaneously. It came, however, though just "time enough to be too late" as I was away from home and don't know how long it had waited my arrival.

"<u>If you are not a man</u>." How very coolly you do persist in this belief, or rather pretext to persist in it, for I do not believe that you think any such thing. Most profound reasoner! You wrote me that it was only from my chinography that you formed that opinion. Now will you inform me by what mysterious and to me unimaginable chain of reasoning you arrived at this sage conclusion based upon the single accidental circumstance that I make long handled letters or write in too bold a style for a lady. If I make my letters so delicate as to be barely visible to the naked eye I presume you will from the same mode of reasoning conclude that I am <u>undoubtedly a lady</u>. I shan't run the risk, however, of cramping my fingers any further for I know I should make a failure and ere I was aware of it would branch out into the same <u>unbecoming</u> style.

My coolest of compliments to Captain Rogers. Just to think that he should be so devoid of taste! How coolly he writes that he doesn't wish to see another specimen of my drawing—Irene will write soon

I presume if she has not already written.

I don't like this letter. It is too apologetic, it would be far more pleasant just quietly to enclose a photo without saying anything about it. Then I believe you will laugh harder and more of it at the trouble I am taking to write about the wretched old photo (I wish you had it) just as though you cared whether you ever get it or not. Well, I don't care—as I shall not see you laughing, you are as welcome as ever to the fun. <u>Answer this letter</u> so that I can have the exquisite pleasure of proving to you that I can keep a promise, even to a stranger.

Sincerely,
Lou Pearl R—

I am glad that you are not going to delude yourself to the extreme felicity of "<u>Seeing the back of your neck</u>" by advertising for correspondents after you are married. I am also glad you appropriated the compliment I gave your photo for yourself. I knew it was yours but disliked to tell you in so many words that I "really thought you were very handsome indeed."

letter 64

February 21, 1864. Postmarked Millwood, Ohio.
Phrone Rogers. Nashville, Tenn.

Home, Feb. 21st '64

My Dearest Friend,

After a very short delay I seat myself to reply to your very welcome letter.

I have just been wondering where you were, and what you were doing this quiet Sabbath day. You seem to have felt very lonely when you wrote me. You seem always to be looking on the dark side. I had to cry when I read your letter, it made me feel so badly. I hope you will cheer up and remember there is one living for you alone. I feel sure that I will see you again, and am very impatient for the time to come. I never left my room since you left untill last Friday. So you see I have not been having very gay times. I am going up to Kinderhook this eve to commence my school tomorrow and am in hope I will soon be through teaching.

I went down to your home last Friday and stayed all night. Your Mother and I talked nearly all night, but it did not hurt my throat one bit, it rather strengthened it. I think if you were here now that I could talk to you better than I did, but I am afraid that I will not have that privilege for a few months at least.

Rain White was here last night, told me to remember her to you. Give my compliments in return to Capt. Rhodes and tell him that if he can not like me on his own hook that I don't want him to like me at all. As you will remember that you said he remarked that "he liked me because you did." Joss and Mother send their love to you. Mother is a great deal better now. I hope she will be well soon.

With much love I am yours in haste.

Phrone

$

letter 65

February 22, 1864. Bainbridge, Ohio.
Rosa Crum. Prospect, Tenn.

Bainbridge, Ohio, Feb. 22nd, 1864

Dear Cousin;

I received your kind letter Friday evening and was truly glad to hear from you and that you was well. I hope you enjoyed your self while at home although you had much to prevent your happiness. You said you was on your way back to Dixie. I hope you will keep up good spirits and conquer the rebels and soon and return home to live with your friends and be happy once more.

I had not heard from you for a long time until Friday evening although I kept looking for one. Pa sends his love to you and says to put the rebels through and be done with them. I received a letter from Cousin Sallie Foulk Saturday evening, they were all well. Aunt Alcinda and Uncle John are going down to Uncle Strawder's on a visit. You know he has moved back to Missouri. And also received a letter from Aunt Anna. They were all well. I suppose you know Cousin Harrison was married. He has two sons, one is named William Strawder Douglas, the other is named Solomon McClellan Henry. You may perhaps think they have name enough, and so do I.

I am still going to school as_usual. Albert and John also go to school and learn very [quickly] There is a good many soldiers here now on furloughs, they have reenlisted. Some have just enlisted and are going with the old soldiers back.

This is very beautiful weather. I also received Cousin William Louis Foulk's likeness Saturday evening. He looks just like he always did. Well as I have not got much to write this time I will have to close. Excuse this short and uninteresting letter as I have nothing of any importance to communicate this time. Excuse bad writing and mispest words. Papa and the boys send their love to you and I never forgetting to send you a share also. Nothing more. Write soon.

> *from your affectionate cousin*
> *until death.*
> Rosa Crum

☙

letter 66

March 3, 1864. Greenwood, Ky. Lou Riggen. Prospect, Tenn.

Greenwood, Ken., Mch 3rd 1864

Lieutenant E.L. Lybarger

I was agreeably disappointed yesterday afternoon, by the arrival of your letter. I say disappointed because I did not know whether you really wished to continue a correspondence or not, and your long silence decided me in the opinion that you thought it would be a waste of time to write any longer. Some of the staid newspaper writers are animadverting quite freely against the "silly practice" of answering advertisements for correspondence, and pronouncing sentences very decidedly against the either party guilty of such unheard of folly. Well—I know you only as a letter-writer, if you are anything less than a gentleman your letters do not discover the fact to me, and you have the same method of forming an opinion of me. While there is nothing unbecoming in style or sentiment in the letter of either, each can write to the other with impunity.

So much for my defence. I like you as a correspondent, and I wrote to you because you were a soldier. I can easily comply with your request and continue to write during the war (that is if your health permits you to continue a correspondence) and as I have no intention of embarking on the sea of matrimony, shall be glad to have you redeem your promise of coming to see me when the war is over, even if you should marry one of those charming young ladies who "presented arms" and whose weapons doubtless transfixed your heart, that is, if you will bring the lady with you. Don't you think my conditions are the most liberal?

You think I am a good girl, do you? I guess you think I am over-anxious to write away your suspicions concerning me. Perhaps so, but I have no apology to offer for that anxiety.

I owe an apology to Captain Rogers. Miss Irene saw proper to refuse the correspondence, after promising me, as I thought, to take it, and has placed me in a rather unpleasant situation. I guess he need not regret the loss, however, as she has a particular friend in the army to whom I do believe she writes all her ideas and anything she would write to anyone else would be stale. I don't think I am to blame, and Captain R. will I think receive a letter from some one else soon.

That photo—as you perceive—is not enclosed. Being engaged in the delightful employment of teaching school, I am very closely confined, and consequently have had no opportunity of fulfilling my promise yet.

I don't like to write short letters. Please write longer, if it isn't too much trouble.

> *Respectfully*
> *Lou Riggen*

letter 67

March 9, 1864. Nelsonville, Ohio.
Jennie Hall. Prospect, Tenn.

Nelsonville, Ohio, March 9th, 1864

Good morning! Lieutenant!

Were I to say that I was pleased, yes delighted, to receive your kind favor of the 27th of Feb. such words would not express half my meaning. Do you believe me? "<u>Yes</u>" I almost hear you <u>whisper</u>.

This beautiful morning finds me seated on the door step basking in the <u>warm</u> Sunshine of <u>Spring</u>—<u>glorious</u> Spring. I can enjoy the Sunshine and write too. Winter's icy fetters are at last broken and <u>Spring</u>, gentle Spring smiles upon the earth, and gladly do we welcome her, for we are tired of stern winter's storms, cold, ice, and snow, and we sigh for woods, green fields, sweet birds and bright flowers, for <u>they</u> seem to whisper of happiness and <u>Love</u>.

God grant that the sweet restorer of nature's bounties may also bring peace to our <u>beloved land</u>, for then Spring would indeed be beautiful to us, for then we might hope to have the absent dear ones with us to enjoy these pleasures too.

Lieut—I have read your last letter <u>very carefully</u> and I hope you will take no offense if I say—I think you <u>expressed more</u> than you intended, or should have done—for you say "you more than respect —you love me." Now don't think I'm the least offended—but quite the contrary. I feel flattered and <u>honored</u> by your sentiments so freely expressed. And Oh how I admire frankness for without this virtue love cannot exist. I'm sure, Lieut., that I am quite as highly pleased with your (dear letters) and Photo as you could <u>possibly</u> be with <u>mine</u>. Don't you think they have captivated my heart as well as <u>mine</u> have yours? <u>Certainly</u>. There! now—Lieut we are on <u>equal standing</u>. I assure you I'm sincere in all I have or will say.

In regard to Dr. Bell—I'll mention some things but please remember not to mention any thing about it to <u>him</u>. He is only trying to drill or tease you when he says "my eyes are blue," hair brown &c—He told me he intended to tease you if he could so you must be on your gard or not let on you care anything about the

matter. Dr. is a great torment—that is my Picture I sent you most
assuradly—So please pay no attention to what may be told you to
the contrary—

I expect to go to Zanesville, Ohio, to spend the summer. Shall
start in April—and then will have some "Photos" taken there. Will
send you one at your request.

I shall thank you kindly for any music you may see proper to
send me and shall learn to play them expressly for Lieut. E.L.L. So
will that suit you? If you were here this morn we would take
"Moore" my favorite poet—or "Byron" another, and we would
climb yonder lofty hill and seating ourselves while away the hours
reading & conversing. Which Poet is your favorite? I had lately
presented to me a copy of "Moore," Byron, Milton and a Dictionary
of Poets. [sic] I read a great deal. I'll close now by promising you
"more anon."

> *Please write soon to*
> *Jennie*

⚘

letter 68

*March 9, 1864. Postmarked Mt. Vernon, Ohio.
Phrone Rogers. Prospect, Tenn.*

*[Note: letter includes excerpt from Ell Hawn's
final letter (34), p. 166]*

Home, March

Ever Dear Friend;

It has just been two weeks today since I received your letter
which I answered immediately—and as I did not, as I had anticipated,
receive another letter from you today thought I would occupy a part
of this lonely evening by writing to you again. I hope you will not
forget the promise you made me when you left that was to write me
every two weeks, as you are aware that I would not have the pleasure
of hearing from you more than once a month, if you wait to receive
an answer every time from me. I intend writing once every two
weeks wheather I hear from you or not, although I will scold if I do

not hear very often. Now I think that I have lectured you sufficiently on this subject, and will drop it.

Nine more days of teaching and I will be free for a time. I did not find it half as irksome as I expected to when I went back, though I must say I get quite tired of everything.

I hope you have gotten over that fit of melancholy, and feel happy and contented now. And I forgot to say to you, in my last letter that you must not get so deeply in love with Capt. Rhodes as marry him before you return to us again. The boys of the 65th returned home yesterday. They are all looking finally. Charlie Rightmire has not been down to Millwood yet. I would rather see him than any other one of them. Joss saw him, says he has improved very much in his appearance and manner. Perhaps you will think me selfish when I tell you that I did not feel very much pleased when I knew the boys had arrived. I had no particular friend among them. <u>My</u> Critchfield has not been around since you left nor I have not met him out any place. My <u>friend</u> Taylor has not written to me since he went away and I pray that he may not think of it, don't tell him so. Give my compliments to Capt. R—, my love to John Hawn and my best <u>spectacles</u> to Taylor.

I have not read those letters you left at home yet—but hope I may soon have an opportunity. I will get your mother to go away from home and then I will search the house until I find them. I will feast awhile on their contense. For I know your Ma would never give them to me. Here is a Sesech letter, if you have not read it. I think it will prove very interesting—that is if it be really true.

Your mother is well. I was down today. She has not heard from your father since he went to Columbus. I think perhaps they can help him there, if not you will have the satisfaction of knowing that all was done for him that could be done. Mother and Joss send their love.

The provost marshall was down after Leply. I did not find out wheather he got him or not. Alex Graham got off. He said that it was all your fault, that he had but very few enemys in the Co. Said all that you was mad at was because he beat you when he run for Lieut.

"I remain as ever your friend but no longer a lover." Write very soon and oblige your Loving friend Phrone.

letter 69

Macon City, Mo., March 9th, 1864

Dear friend,

Yours of the 28th ult. is at hand. Of course your excuse is sufficient, at any rate the receipt of your letter put me in so good a humor that I am not now in a mood to repeat [?] excuses. I had often thought of you and feared that, like many a noble soul, you had perished in the conflict. I know, Ed, you must have had a jolly time at home. It would have been a real pleasure to me to have been with you. Well, I join with you in wishing this war over. I think we all can then enjoy peace, having suffered so much for the want of it, as we know it is the hungry man that relishes food. We have quite peacible times here in Mo. and it is my opinion that peace will return to all the States in a manner similar to this. The large armies of the enemy will be scattered, guerilla warfare will take the place of systematic war, it and this will be gradually weakened until finally it is altogether broken up; indeed it seems to me, the governmental authorities design that the war should so end. Evidently this manner will best serve the purpose of those who wish to destroy the existence of slavery in the states whose people are in rebellion.

The news here are not startling. The people for the most part are pursuing their ordinary occupations, however there are a great many people making preparations for going to Idaho Territory in search of gold ostensibly; no doubt many of them really to elude an expected, and by some, long dreaded draft. It does seem strange to me how any man can feel himself an honorable man, while seeking to evade plain duty.

We have beautiful weather here now and truly is the springtime delightful. I am enjoying myself first rate and life is passing very agreeably with me. I will visit your uncle so soon as I find a little leisure. I feel confident I shall find him agreeable to me.

I will send you my photograph when I have an opportunity to have it taken which will be soon. I will be much delighted to have yours.

After next week I will have a little recess and a little liberty as my tour will then expire and a few days will be allowed me to regain my wonted spirits, and remove the accumulating dust of five months of patient toil, and breathe again the pure air of freedom.

I would be pleased to have the acquaintance of Capt. Rhodes and hope he will come to this part of the country and I promise that I would be very agreeable, but there are some excellent people here and I think the will to be agreeable is not wanting in me. However, tell him to come along and meet me at my home, I cannot give him the right hand of fellowship, but the left will be tendered with the warmth of the heart in it. Of course you will come along with him to give the introduction. I will probably have selected some fair one to be my companion and there will be a wedding too and my native state will be the home of the brave and the happy. I hope these things are not far off in reality, and will not have to live long in the imagination only. It does me real good to hear of good and true men coming to live in Mo. It revives the hope that one day she may become one of the bright stars in the galaxy of states never to be erased or polluted, continually giving light to all around by her examples of patriotism, intelligence and glory, and in her central position give out the arterial blood that shall give life and energy to the Union of States and render indissoluble the social and political ties that bind us together as a free people.

My father and mother both send their regards to you and hope you good fortune. I hope you catch the Rebs at Decatur, and if you see any of my old "Secesh" friends just send them up to me and I would treat them so well that they would never again wish to revisit their traitor companions in arms. Give them one taste or touch or smell of the blessings of the old government and the old order of things with three grains of reason, and the dreamy fancies of the glories of a Southern Confederacy will vanish from their benighted souls. I do sometimes feel sorry for the miserable beings they are. You boys I guess have the means of administering to them about what they need. I am always glad to hear from you.

Very truly yours,
Ben. F. Stone

P.S. Excuse my awkwardness and carelessness.

B.F.S.

letter 70

March 11, 1864. [Danville, Ohio?] Lib [Annie E. Baker].
[No envelope information]

Home, March 11th/64

Friend Edwin;

"Brevity is the soul of wit" and if that, can make this letter witty it shall be. Please excuse the non appearance of "I embrace &c &c" for I thought the above proper substitute.

I rec. your letter about two weeks ago but haven't time to tell you how glad I was to get it, or recount the various reasons why it was not answered ere this.

I'm so sorry I did not see you while home on furlough. How happy I should have been to have welcomed you & "Ike" at my pleasant mountain home. Would have introduced you to all the prettiest girls in the village. But perhaps that black eyed Millwood "lass" would not have thanked me for doing so. The boys of the 51st from S.M. were home while I was there. You may know we had a "gay" time during their stay. Parties almost every other night. I heard a few days ago that Capt. Will Moore was going to resign & come home. Report says to be married & I shouldn't be very much surprized if it were true. Then won't my "harp be hung on the willows"!! I arrived home from Spring Mt. on the 10th inst, the same day as the close of Ada's school. And of course attended the Exhibition which was rather good. But I shan't enter into any lengthy "retail"—(as I heard a preacher once say) about the performance lest I might break the promise I made in the onset of this letter. I will send you a program & you may judge for yourself as you doubtless know many of the performers. Quite a number of young folk were up from M___ among whom were Jossie Rogers & Frank Israel. There will be no school in D___ next term. Ada is going to Spring Mt. to take charge of that school until Prof. Selby regains his health. The citizens here have procured the lower room of the Masonic Lodge & are going to finish it off for school purposes & so be ready against next term.

I have not decided what I shall do this summer. I'm at present studying at home under my sister—get along finely. George Dawson is taking lessons in Latin also but only recites twice a week. I may go to Delaware in the course of several weeks. Well I declare! I'm nearly at the bottom of the last page & haven't said one word about the Capt. I didn't mean to do so. And now Ed, pardon the familiarity of the term—if you were here I don't know but I might give you a little <u>scolding</u> for the way in which you misrepresented me in giving him my "<u>descriptive roll</u>," for <u>surely</u> he could not have been favorably impressed had you given him a <u>true</u> picture. As regards my Photo I think it would be to my credit not to send it, besides I have none at hand now. Page 1st.

It is true that I never acknowledged the receipt of Capt. R's letter. But I assure you it was not because I did not consider it worthy a reply for his was a <u>good</u> letter. I admired the free & <u>independent</u> air it breathed & under different circumstances I should have been <u>proud</u> to have owned him as a correspondent. But at the time I received the letter I knew him only as Captain of your company & knowing that a nicely written & composed letter is not sufficient proof of a man's respectability I refrained from writing. I have since heard him highly extolled both by yourself & others, & if ever he returns to this region of country I should be highly pleased to form his acquaintance. I have most an <u>awful</u> curiosity to see either him or his <u>Photo</u>. It is Leap Year & I've half a notion of asking you to send both <u>your own</u> and the Capt's. But I must close & I fear this letter is neither witty nor brief. Excuse all & write soon to your friend

Lib

Return compliments to the Capt.
We have a public Singing school next Thursday evening. Can't you come?

letter 71

March 12, 1864. Postmarked Millwood, Ohio.
Phrone Rogers. Nashville, Tenn.

Home, March the 12th, 1864.

Dearest friend Ed,

It has been but a very short time since I wrote you last, but I do
not intend that you shall complain of not hearing from me often
enough. I am going to tell you what has transpired since I last wrote
you. First, the citizens of Boyington town gave a splendid supper for
some of the returned soldiers of the 65th Regt. <u>All</u> my friends
around here were present on the ever memorable occasion. I think
there must have been about seventy or seventy-five present. We had
beautiful weather, gay crowd, and in all a very happy time. You
better think I made use of the time talking to Col. Cassil, and my
dear <u>friend Dawson Critch</u>. It was the first time that I had met him
since you went away. He was not as I had (hoped) expected he would
be offended, seemed to think just as I did that while you were here,
that I lost my heart. To treat so devoted a friend in such a manner as
I treated him. He thinks me cruel indeed. But I have studdied the
whole matter over and can't see it. I told him that I could not have
done differently, as you were a very dear friend of ours (which was
the truth) and of course it would be very natural that I should seek
your very agreeable society. He said he would have been very much
pleased to have known that you enjoyed yourself whilest here, but
did not want you to be gay at his expense or rather loss. I told him
that you had no warmer feeling for me than near friendship, that you
never thought of anything else. I did not see him speak with a girl
there except myself. We prominaded, danced, and talked interesting
talk. I went to the party with Engle, but before I drop the subject of
Daws and myself I am happy to inform you that I am pardoned and
he is <u>again</u> at my service.

I am alone tonight yet not lonely. My thoughts are very pleasant
companions, but my pen is my best friend, for by its means I can
hold sweet conversation with my <u>absent</u> friend. It has been snowing

and raining all day, so that we did not get out of the house and you know how I like to stay in.

Charley Rightmire, Craig Johnson, and Han Mitt [Hen Witt?] and the soldiers have called on us. Some of them have quite sad times. Ella's mother is not expected to live and Joe Critchfield is very sick with the measles. I do not think that he and Mary Hammon will be married while he is home. She seems very down hearted to think that he was so unfortunate as to get sick.

March the 20th, Sabbath eve.

As I quit writing one week ago tonight I thought it about time that I should finish my letter. We have had some very pleasant times within the last week. Went to Amity to a party on Thursday evening with some of the soldiers—had one of the grandest suppers that I ever sat down to eat—had J.D.C. for my partner which reminded me of a good many times and places. <u>Some times</u> which are pleasant to live over again e'en in thoughts. I do not write in this manner because I regret that they are gone. I do not now think that I will ever again have that gentleman as my <u>particular</u> friend, but I always expect to treat him kindly if he will only permit me to. I am invited up to Critch's tomorrow night to a party—hope to have a grand time.

I was all night at Dan Welker's again last Wednesday. My school closed that day, and they had a little company in, for my especial benefit. Mr. & Mrs. Welker told me give their best respect and Edith also told me to remember her to you. Rain White sends her best <u>blue spectacles</u>. I am telling you just the way she expressed it. Jossie sends her love and begs me to say that she does not want you to be so fast in giving Capt. Rhodes information concerning her love affairs, as she might change her mind if she only had an <u>opportunity</u>, and she thinks that perhaps that you are depriving her of this very thing by talking such nonsense to Captain R.—Tell Capt. that I love him "like fun" and remind him that this is leap year.

Joss and Frank are sitting in the room talking but indeed I can not tell you what about. Mother has retired for the night and I expect to follow suit soon as it is already past nine.

Danville had a concert and exhibition which was very good. I saw your friend Lizzie Baker there and a great many other <u>nice</u> people that I knew.

Ed, if you get hold of the "Bonnie blue flag" do send it to me, for I have heard so much about it since you left but cannot get it at the music store in Mt. Vernon. Those slippers you shall have just as soon as I can get them done but not any sooner "as you know of." I hear that you are in possession of Decatur and none hurt. I will close by bidding you good night. Your loving friend Phrone

$

letter 72

March 17, 1864. Columbus, Ohio. Grace Nello. [No envelope]

Columbus, March 17th '64
—"E.L.

Your surprise at receiving a note from me will be fully explained when I inform you that it is through the solicitation of Capt. "Jack Rodgers" that I address you. "Cassie" a very dear friend of mine corresponds with the Captain, and in one of his letters he slyly hinted that a lieutenant "E.L." would like to have some fair unknown write to him. You can do as you please about answering this, but if you conclude to answer me I will try and make my correspondence as interesting as possible.

I am a "Buckeye" girl, and as homely as a "hedge fence." I am 19 years of age, five feet four inches in height, and—and—as I said before, homely! But, notwithstanding all this, I am a true friend of the Soldier, and if a kind word once in a while will afford any pleasure I am satisfied. To me

"Letters are affection's touches
Lighting of Friendship's lamp
Flighting around the heartstrings
Like fireflies in the damp."

I hope we may never be led to regret having commenced this correspondence, but may it prove interesting as well as profitable. I hope you are of that class termed "moral young men." One that neither chews tobacco, drinks liquor, uses profane language, &c. I do not object to an occasional cigar.

Well, I will not waste my time and <u>talent</u> on uncertainties, but if you deem this worthy an [sic] reply I should be happy to hear from you very soon, and believe me to be your true friend.

"Grace"

P.S. Please address Miss Grace Nello
    Box 611, Columbus, Ohio
    "Adieu"

letter 73

March 24, 1864. Millwood, Ohio. T.B. Campbell. Prospect, Tenn.

Millwood, Knox Co., Ohio, March, 24th, 1864
Lieut. E.L. Lybarger.
Dear Friend,

Inclosed you will find permit. I could not send it sooner from the fact that Hildreth neglected to make it out.—

The 65th are home on a regular bender. They have cleaned out all the butternuts in the country.—Hen Witt has a wood chopping today, all the soldiers are there and most of the citizens. I expect we will have a big time in Millwood tonight. Hen bought a keg of ale and I expect we will all get on a regular drunk.

We have had several oyster suppers in town of late. Orange Johnson gave one last night. I see your dearly beloved nearly every day, if I was a young man I might lay see to that pretty little fortress in your abscence. Perhaps you could give me orders to guard it for you. But I have no doubt but that fortress is sufficiently strong to resist all ordinary attacks. You remember she was sick when you left. Somebody had the impudence to say she had the "Lybarger fever."

We have no news of importance. I suppose you can look for some of us down in Dixie about the 25th of April. "So mote it be."

I hope you will soon have an opportunity to put in your petition. If you have a Military Lodge you need no permit from Antioch. I am not certain that the form is exactly right. We had no regular form and it was the best we could do. You will notice that permission is only given you while you are in the army. If you should resign before you are made a Mason your permit would be of no account. I believe that permit does not state that you live within the jurisdiction of Antioch Lodge, but if they should object to it on that account show them this letter.

Well, Ed, I would like to hear from you often. Please write as soon as convenient. Chas. Hawn will send John's permit.

Yours truly,
T.B. Campbell

$

letter 74

March 24, 1864. Bainbridge, Ohio. Rosa Crum. Decatur, Ala.

Bainbridge, Ohio, March 24/64

My Dear Cousin;

Yours of the 11th has been received and I take this opportunity to answer. Well as there are not much news here hardly know what to write. We are all well and hope this may find you still enjoying good health. The weather changes every day; it has been tolerable cold for several days past, but it has changed again and is now very warm and pleasant.

You wished me to give you Cousin Sallie Foulk's address. Direct to Springhill, Livingston Co., Mo. You also said you would like to have Aunt Rachel's. I would accomodate you by telling you if I knew but do not. I received a letter from Mo. last night stating that Electious Jr. was a wandering soldier for his country. I also got a letter from Sallie some time since. They were all well. I received Wm. Louis's likeness. He looks about the same as he always did.

Wm. and John Foulk are going to start to Idaho the first of May. I suppose you have heard of that place; it is the new gold Region.

I am still going to school. School closes in seven weeks, then we are going to have an examination. So just call over.

I also received a letter from Cousin Elijah, they were all well. I suppose you have heard from him before this time, so I need not quote what [he said] about your father. Papa sends his best respects to you.

Well as I have nothing of importance to communicate my letter must needs be short and uninteresting. Excuse bad writing and all mistakes, and John and Albert send their love to you. Well as it is now late bedtime I will draw to a close, hoping to hear from you soon. My love to you will never fail.

Ans. soon.

Your cousin, as ever
Rosa Crum

$

letter 75

April 4, 1864. Postmarked Millwood, Ohio.
Phrone Rogers. Decatur, Ala.

Hawn's Mansion, April 4, 1864

Dearest friend Ed,

Another two weeks have passed since I last wrote you. I am from home as you perceive. Came over here yesterday. We have had some very exciting times, the 65th O.V.I. came home. They have been getting married "with a vengeance." Mollie Hammon and Joe Critchfield were married last Tuesday by Jacob Hammond and at his house, they did not make a wedding, or at least did not invite anyone. I went with the new pair to Rightmires to spend the evening—you better think we had a gay time going in the rain. Lieut. Pealer to Miss Whitney, Andrew Howe to Miss Wallace, Roland Critchfield to Miss Maggie McElroy, and some more out of Co. A that I did not know.

I received about two yards of confiscated lace from a lady friend of yours and mine. I made a collar of it and have worn it to several parties. I have been to eight parties within two weeks. What do you think of it? I have done nothing but run and sleep. I expect now that I will be at home all summer if I am not some place else. I asked Ell Hawn what I should say for her. She said to say that she was on the decline and thinks she is fast going into the consumption. Though she does not know whom I am writing to. It has been raining all day. Well, Ell and I went fishing, came home like so many drounded rats but caught five fish about a half yard or less in length.

You said in your last letter that you often tried to offend me by a certain manner of speaking. You wanted to know if I ever noticed it. I did not, I assure you, if I had ever taken offense you would surely have found it out as I would do just what I told you that I would about correspondents that I wished to discontinue. I would quit and not say one word about it. If you do not whish to write to me often you need not and then I wont write to you at all—

Give my <u>undying love</u> to Capt. Rhodes. Frank Israel was over to Columbus and saw your father. He is declining fastly. He did not know Frank nor remember any of his relatives. He is well cared for. Frank said if he remembered anyone at all it was you, for when Frank mentioned your name he asked where you were.

I have not time to write more now. Answer soon and oblige.

Your <u>loving friend</u>,
Phrone

Compliments to Oliver.

☙

letter 76

April 11, 1864. Postmarked Mt. Vernon, Ohio.
Edith F. Welker. Decatur, Ala.

At Home, April 11th, 1864

Friend E.L. Lybarger

It is with no little pleasure that I seek this leisure moment in addressing you a few lines in compliance with your request. I should have answered sooner but was waiting to have my Photo taken to send to you. I had my negative taken and Mr. Tucker was going to print them and he went to Illinois and did not get them printed, but as soon as I get some taken I will send you one. I hope you will not get angry with me because it was not "my fault"

Times are pretty dull here since the soldiers have gone back. I hear there were only eight of the 65th married while they were at home. They had "gay times" while here, Squire McKee has got home, he was up here last week. He looks very well. Also Frank McGugin arrived home last Saturday eve. I haven't seen him since he came.

I suppose you are aware that Shiply is in the army. He went about five weeks ago. He is at Camp Nelson, Kentuck. Went in the Heavy Artillery. It is very lonely since he went away. I felt very sorry to see him go, although I could not tell him to stay for I think it is a duty of every loyal man to go in defence of "our country." I believe I have written all the news in general. I am well and sincerely hope this may find you the same.

Please respond soon.

I am as ever your true Friend. Eda

My compliments to you.

letter 77

April 18, 1864. Millwood, Ohio. Pat Rightmire. Decatur, Ala.

Millwood, Ohio Aprı1 18th, 1864

My friend Mr. Lybarger;

Your kind letter of March 17th safely found its way to the Old Post Office at Millwood. You said you had given my compliments to Capt. Rhodes and he had formed rather a favorable opinion of me. It is my opinion that Ambrotype of mine is not calculated to leave a very favorable impression with any one, although I might say it is better than the original. You requested me to send you my Photograph. I will grant you your request in order to "satisfy the Captain's curiosity." You said you thought you could procure me a correspondant in Capt. Rhodes. If it is desirable on his part to have a corespondence with me it will be agreeable with me writing his intentions or such as would not be desirable with any one. If he writes to me he will please enclose his Photograph, I will expect you to send me your Photo.

The boys of Co. A 65th Regt. have been home but have gone back to the Regt. We had a very pleasant time while they were home. We had wedings and partys and partys and wedings. It is my opinion that some of the boys of Co. A had a rlaps of their matrimonial fever as you can judge them better than I. I tell you that four of them were maried Joseph Crichfield and Mollie Hammond, Roland Crichfield and Miss McElroy, Lieut. Pealer and Miss Whitny, but the most remarkable weding was that of Andrew How and Miss N. Wallace, but you must not let this discourage you for your love will wait until this cruel war is over.

I seen Capt. Rhodes Photograph last Sabath. I thought it was very good looking. If Captain Rhodes is one of those gay deceptive young gentlemen I do not wish to corespond with him but if he is not I guess I have not any serious objection in having corespondence with him. I might say that I would have written sooner but I did not receive my photo until last evening. My ideas does not range very well for writing a letter today therefore I will close expecting you will become tired of trying to read my scribling. Write soon and forget not your friend.

Pat Rightmire

⚜

letter 78

April 21, 1864. Millwood, Ohio. Phrone Rogers. Decatur, Ala.

[Note: Lybarger's father died in April, 1864; see letter 75.]

Millwood, April 21st, 1864

Friend Ed;

I thought I would occupy my few spare moments by writing you a few lines. I have bought [myself] a piano and am now taking music lessons under Prof. Myers of Spring Mountain—he is such a good teacher I think we cannot help but learn. I practice all day on the instrument and then go to singing school every night. He has about forty scholars. Sings in the Presbyterian Church. So I think I will be able to play for you against you come home—as I can already play several duets with my teacher.

It has been such a short time since I wrote to you that I do not think I have anything now to offer you. Your mother seems cheerful since she has gotten over the first shock of your father's death. She was not very well for a time but is much better now. O dear, I am so tired I can hardly write. I hear that Ike Baker and A . . . Sawyer [Shroyer] are to be married today. He has left Mclouds store. Calvin Winteringer clerks for Millis and boards with him, so you see I run against the rebel often. The singing teacher boards with your mother, (that's the male teacher) and the lady boards with us. Your mother desires me to say that the fence will be finished today and the lumber is in the yard to build the kitchen.

Frank started to Indianapolis yesterday on business, but will be home shortly. Jossie and I had an ambrotype taken to send you, and as she thought you would not know her, she will wait until she goes to town, which will be in two or three weeks, then you shall [have a] picture of her. I am so happy to know that Capt. John loves me so <u>desparatly</u>. Please say to him that I cannot sleep all day for thinking of him. I am so much afraid that he loves some one else from what I can hear. Ask him how he likes Lizzie's photograph?

I have grown a foot and a half since you left and got my hair shingled. What do you think of it? I must close. Please write soon. Am ever your loving friend. Phrone.

$

letter 79

April 22, 1864. Bainbridge, Ohio. Rosa Crum. Decatur, Ala.

Bainbridge, Ohio April 22/64

My Dear Cousin;

I seat myself this morning to acknowledge the receipt of your kind favor which came to hand Monday eve. I assure you that I was very glad indeed to hear from you, but O how sorry to hear the sad news telling of Uncle's death. We deeply sympathize with you in your bereavement and hope He is only separated from us so short time provided it pleases our Savior to receive us into his kingdom.

Papa is out in the country at work. He is well and would like to see you. For two or three days past the weather has been very beautiful but today it is trying to rain a little.

Aunt Sarah and her husband had parted but last evening I got a letter stating that they had made it all up and were again living together. You said you would write to Uncle Strauder and Electious if you knew their address. I would give you Electious address if I knew it. I can give you Uncle Strauders but it will be no use to you for he will not write to you. He was at our house just before he went to Mo. and I read him one of your letters and told him you would [like] to hear from him, but he paid no attention to what I said or read. I also told him if He wished I would write down your address for him and he said he did not need it he guessed. He never liked you nor Elijah very much. Address Strauder Crum, Macon City, Macon County, Missouri. We have never had the scratch of a pen from him since He went to Mo., neither have any of his relatives. We think He has some scheme in his head concerning that farm in Mo. the reason He dont write to any of us. I got a letter from Elijah this week, they are all well.

I am not going to school now school is out in 2 weeks. Albert, John, and Martha go, they all learn very fast, especially Albert. I will not be able to gratify your wish this time but will send you one [photo] the next time I write to you. I have none now but will get some taken. There is nobody here that can [take] a Photograph fit to look at but I will get the best I can.

Well, as nothing of importance has occured here since I last wrote my letter will be uninteresting, excuse mistakes, bad scribbling and mistakes as Cousin Rosa does not profess to be a good scholar. Answer soon. I send my love to you in abundance.

From your Cousin Rosa Crum.

Please write soon. So goodby, take good care of your self and hope the time will soon come when I may be permitted to see your lovely face. I was delighted indeed to get your Photograph as I knew that other one did not look like you with those large eyes. I was so proud to see I had such a handsome cousin, but would [be] better pleased to see the original. So no more.

from your affectionate cousin & friend R. Crum

April 24, 1864. Postmarked Brandon, Ohio.
Mollie Ward. Decatur Junction, Ala.

Apr. 24th 1864

Mr. E.L. Lybarger;
My friend Ed;

Pardon me for neglecting your welcome letter of March 6th so long, but truly I have undergone so much since its receipt that it seems strange to me that I am able to write even now. We have had some sickness in the family and indeed I hardly feel able to sit up today but deeming it a duty to address some of my neglected friends and this being sabbath and as I am unable to get to church I will endeavor to while away part of the time in this manner.

The weather is beautiful here at present and has been for a few days past, notwithstanding it has been very disagreeable the greater part of this month. We have been having lovely times here for the past two weeks. They have been trying to skirmish on a small scale near the town of Brandon or at least have been trying to let some of the copperheads know how it goes to come in contact with "cold lead." One of the boys tested his ingenuity by shooting (he said) the meanest man that was ever let to live in Knox Co. He shot him through the arm, the wound proving quite serious I believe. If they were all served in like manner it would rid the country of the greatest nuissance it possesses at present.

While the soldiers are doing all in their power to restore peace and conquer the enemy in the front let not the rear be overflowing with men that, if it were possible, are doing more towards keeping up the rebellion and the Southern cause than any man there can possibly do. The soldiers seem to have more respect for those who have taken up arms against them than for those who are seemingly too cowardly to fight but who stay at home doing them all the injury they can.

I trust before next year this time the greater part of the army will be enjoying the blessings of home rather than the hardships of the camp. It is the general opinion I believe that the war is about to terminate and I sincerely hope that such is the case.

I presume I have written as much as will be interesting so I will close by wishing the choicest blessings to rest upon the whole U.S. Army.

Respectfully your friend
Mollie E. Ward

P.S. Give my best respects to Jacob Harding[er].

※

letter 81

April 26, 1864. Postmarked Mount Sterling, Ky.
Lou P. Riggen. Decatur, Ala.

Greenwood, Kenty. April 26th, 1864

Lieutenant E.L. Lybarger;

Your very pleasant letter was received with pleasure and I could answer it with equal pleasure were it not that I have a mortal fear of Mrs. Grundy, while a few concientious qualms occasionally arise to remind me that I am "entirely out of sphere." How I wish I had had at least enough sense to refrain from promising to send my photo, how ridiculous do I look enclosing my photograph to a <u>complete stranger</u>. O mother Eve, thy curiousity. I received your photo or <u>some one's else</u> by the promise. If it is yours, I thank you—if it is not—O wouldn't I <u>quit</u>?

Now don't take the trouble to write a page or two of suspicions about the enclosed for it is my veritable shadow, but just send it along-back and I will return yours. Don't put me to the trouble of giving reasons for wishing it returned when they are obvious enough to you. But then it is such a <u>perfect beauty</u> I know you will be so anxious to keep it. "A thing of beauty is a joy forever" you know.

I shall expect you—and the Moon—when this war is over, though I do not like your opinion of a lady as travelling companion —incumbrance indeed. Imagine the rosy cheeked black-eyed girl, or the golden-haired lily looking creature who occupies your soldier dreams—<u>can</u> you imagine how she could be an incumbrance to you? If you can I give you over to hardness of heart.

Has Captain Jack Rogers received no letter yet? I suppose I will be under obligations to <u>write myself</u>! As you know I don't break my promises. I don't know why you italicize the <u>Miss</u> in writing Miss Irene, there was no <u>catch</u> intended—at least on <u>my part</u> nor <u>Irene's</u>, and she does not "consider him presumptious nor impertinent."

I was not wearied, but interested in your description of the boat expedition, and I consider no undertaking "insignificant" in which the lives of human beings depend on the uncertain chances of war, though compared with the gigantic murder, and wholesale bloodshed which are so common, the life of one man is insignificant. O unhappy country, miserable people, and most miserably prosecuted war—

I certainly do not object to the length of your letter, there isn't much pleasure to me in reading letters which begin to quit on the first page. No, I am as fond of writing long letters as of receiving them. So you see I had two objects in asking you to write <u>long</u> letters.

I would like to see the other photo of which you speak and will return both it and the vignette when you return mine.

Write soon, and I will try to answer more promptly.

Respectfully
Lou P. R.

How <u>is</u> your health?

letter 82

April 28, 1864. Millwood, Ohio. Phrone Rogers. Decatur, Ala.

Millwood, April 28th, 1864

My Dear Friend Ed,

As I have gotten your slippers finished I want to know how I shall send them. Mart Hammond says they will be sure to get lost if I send by mail. But if you think it best to send them that way I will do so. Must I direct to Decatur or to Nashville?

I have nothing new to tell you. Our singing school is still going on very prosperously. I guess I am doing very well for a new beginer I do not feel very bright today as I am quite tired. My music teacher and I went over to Louis Critchfield's to spend the afternoon yesterday. Mary Jane and I went all over the farm to gather wild flowers. We had to cross a swamp and I got a cold. I cotch him very bad. My feet were wet and I walked home with them so. And after I came home I found company awaiting me, and of course I did not get to bed till twelve o clock or later. Perhaps you inquire who was he or she? He was Jim Israel, and expects to remain here several days. I expect him to accompany me to and from singing tonight.

Ed I wish you were here. I get so lonely that I wish every day that I was dead and in heaven and had the money for my good clothes.

We are agoing to have a fishing party next week and perhapps a dancing party before the consert There are about a dozzen girls singing in the other room and Mr. Myers is playing. So you can easily imagine how easy it is to think of anything to write to a friend or any other man.

Your folks are well. Please excuse brevity and answer very soon. As ever your loving Phrone.

Jossie sends her love. I do not know to whom.
Compliments to Capt. R____.

$

letter 83

May 5, 1864. Monroe Mills, Ohio.
Fannie Meredith. Decatur, Ala.

Monroe Mills, May 5th, 1864

Ever Remembered Friend Ed,

Some time has elapsed since the reception of your letter, and Photo. I presume you think I am not going to write, or send you my Photo, but that is a mistake. When I received your letter I had none taken and thought I would not write until I got some taken. I went down to M. to get some taken but they were not good at all. Have not had any opportunity of going to Vernon. So I hope you will pardon me for not sending or writing sooner. I am going to Vernon before long to get some taken. Will send you one in my next, <u>that is</u>, if I get an <u>answer</u> to this.

Tonight finds me at Uncle Dan Welker's seated up stairs with Cousin Eda, trying to collect my thoughts together to write you. Eda is writing to Shiply. I presume you have heard he is in the Army.

I feel somewhat tired this evening as I have been teaching school all day. You know that is something new for me. I am teaching in Kinderhook and boarding at Uncle Dan's. I commenced teaching Monday. I like it very well indeed. You better believe Eda and I have some gay times. They are having singing in Millwood now, I have been tending It will be out tomorrow night. We are going to have a concert Saturday night. I wish you could be here and hear us sing. It is only fifteen cents. Can't you come? Mr. Myers from Spring Mt. is teaching. He is a spendid teacher. He has an organ with him, has three taking music lessons, Charlotte Hammon, Emma Gardner, and Frone

It has been very lonely here since the soldiers have all gone back.

Oh! yes I almost forgot to tell about the wedding. Deal and Ike Baker was married last Thursday. He has got a very good wife, and she a good husband. Does it surprize you any or was you expecting it? Also young Charlie Wallace to Miss Martha Ginn all of Knox Co., Ohio.

May peace be with them.

John Tucker buried his little boy Sunday. He was taken sick on Thursday eve, and died Saturday night. Congestion of the brain and lungs was his disease.

It is getting very late, so I will have to stop writing. Hoping to hear from you soon again. Excuse me from writing with a pencil for I had no pen here.

Your True Friend Fannie

Write soon and oblige the absent Fannie.
Direct to Monroe Mills.

letter 84

May 13, 1864. Postmarked Millwood, Ohio.
Phrone Rogers. Nashville, Tenn.

[Note: Letter postmarked May 13, and a penciled note on back of envelope: "received August 23/64; answered Aug. 31/64"]

Home, May 13th, 1864

Ed, I wrote you a note last sabbath and I think it is a good thing that I <u>did</u> change my mind and not send it as I do not think that you would have wanted to have heard from me soon again.

Perhaps as you have changed <u>your</u> mind somewhat you will not want to anyhow. I have heard some things of late that convinces me that I should have asked myself if I could trust even you.

Lizzie Baker was at our house the other day. You seem to think that "it will do me good when I get you" do you? I do not see any point to what you have said perhaps you can see things plainer than Phrone Rogers can. Don't infer from what I am writing that I am offended if you do. Then are you sadly mistaken. All I will say if you think you are capable of flirting me, try it. I think I have had quite as much experience in this matter as you have. It is not good policy sometimes to tell all you know. Perhaps I have already said too much upon this subject.

You told me to get those slippers cut no. nine. I did so, but Mart Hammond has a pair which he says is no. eight and yours are the same length exactly. He may be mistaken in the size. I hope so indeed. I would be very sorry if they were too small. I send you this tape which is the length of them. You can inform me if they will do before I send them.

The concert is over and I can assure you I am glad as I have a very severe cold, therefore do not feel much like singing. We had a picknick and fishing party at the caves this week. I have been <u>dead</u> ever since.

Your mother says you do not receive her letters or if you do, you do not say anything about it. Mr. Myers has gone home, she does not board him longer.

We have had some very hard fighting lately. O, how it makes me shudder to think of it. So many of our soldiers killed. The draft comes off today, four are to go from our township only, and I feel glad of it. My Aunty is here from Illinois. I have some notion of going home with her to stay a few years. O, dear I must close this uninteresting letter. Pardon me if I have trespassed on your time.

Phrone

⚕

letter 85

May 14, 1864. Postmarked Cynthiana, Ky.
Lou Riggen. Millwood, Ohio.

[Note: Letter sent after Lou submits photograph; see letter 81.]

Claysville, Ky. May 14th

Lieut. E.L. Lybarger;
    You "hope I will not deceive myself in regard to <u>your intentions</u>!"
    Thank you. I hope you will attribute to me at least a modicum of common sense.
    That you should be so solicitous for the state of my mind as to devote a whole sheet to the purpose of preventing my being deceived about—I don't know what—is really magnanimous. My gratitude is unbounded. Indeed, I can find no word to express my devout thanks. <u>Therefore</u> I may as well close. I would not have you suffer any uneasiness on my account for anything in the world.
    Then do <u>not</u> I beg you suffer yourself to entertain any more needless apprehensions about

Respectfully
Lou Riggen

letter 86

Millwood, June 1st, 1864

Kindly remembered friend;

I write you again on this first summer day. Mother, Aunty, & Joss have all gone out to spend the afternoon. So you see that I am quite alone. I was just practicing a piece of music and got tired of it and thought I would drop you a few lines in reply to your last, which was received a few days since.

It seems that you have not received my last letter yet. I hope it will go safely through for I am anxious to know whether your foot is too large for your shoe. I sent the measure in my last note to you. If your foot should happen to be too large for the shoe please have some of your longest toes amputated. The opperation will cause but little pain. I suppose you are through fighting before this time, and presume you are not sorry.

I was at a party to the "Caves" a few days ago. The first time that I have been down since you and I were there. It is so beautiful now. I felt like I would like to stay a week, but could not as I had several engagements at Mrs. Rogers that week.

You said that you had been looking for a letter from Frank. He writes to you often and you do not receive his letters. You "do not care whether you receive letters from <u>me</u> or not." I am glad you want to hear from some one here.

Receive my kindest wishes for your safety and believe me your friend.

Phrone

*June 10, 1864. Millwood, Ohio. Phrone Rogers.
Dalton, Ga., via Chattanooga, Tenn.*

Millwood, June 10th '64

Dearest friend Ed;

You seemed very much surprised at the sentiment contained in my last (but one) letter to you. If you are guilty why need it surprise you? If I have done wrong then am I perfectly ignorant of my duty. I will try and tell you a little about it. Lizzie B___ did say some very insulting things to a friend of mine in our house. Said things which if they be true or false shall forever banish all my friendship for her, whatever you may think of her. I do not disbelieve what you have said to me. Then <u>she has lied</u>. So if now you would rather correspond with her than with me you can do so, for as true as I write it you <u>can not</u> under the circumstances write both of us at the same time. I will certainly have confidence in your sincerity if you should for a moment think of doing such a thing. But of course you have this dissision to make yourself. After I had thought the matter over I did not see the point to your treating me in such a manner, when you <u>knew</u> that I was a <u>true</u> friend of yours. I must say that Lizzie must be very deeply interested in my affairs. She was not the only lady friend of yours that told things that you should have said. But nevertheless I will try and think you are as good and noble as I <u>always</u> thought you were. Untill I am truly diseived I care not for the many hints that are given every time I meet some of my relatives for I expected as much from them.

You ask if "I wish to quit corresponding?" I can assure you if that was all, I should have quit and not said a single word about it. I have told you this before, but perhaps you have forgotten all that transpired whilst you were at home. I have not.

But should it be your desire to quit you can do so without even telling me so—this idea never entered my mind before. I want a perfect understanding or none at all. If I said things to hurt your feelings when you did not deserve them, I am very sorry for it. I will hope that I have [not].

That Leply has at last been caught, and made no attempt to kill anyone, but his wife fought. I hope they will treat him as every deserter ought to be treated. I saw that General McPherson has been in another battle, which resulted gloriously, with but few killed and wounded. I think you are seeing hard times enough now.

Your folks are well. I was down to your mother's this morning. I have not been well for a month. I do not know what is the matter, unless I am too lazy to enjoy good health as the saying is. You have not spoken of Capt. J.H.R. for some time. Is he dead? or only sleeping—I think I have written enough. If you will only write this much and as often as I have written to you I will be satisfied. I have not sent the slippers. Excuse mistakes, and believe me—your loving friend

Phrone

$

letter 88

June 12, 1864. Postmarked Danville, Ohio.
Annie E. Baker. Dalton, Ga., via Chattanooga, Tenn.

Hopewell near Gambier O. June 12th/64
Friend "Eddie";
The close of a beautiful Sabbath day finds me engaged in writing you a letter in the answer to the one I rec'd from you several days ago.

I was more than ever glad to hear from you for I had almost feared that you too had met the fate of so many of our brave heroes within the past few weeks. I humbly trust that you are not wholy unmindful of Him who thus kindly preserves your life.

We heard last night that Morgan was intent on making another raid through Ohio. If such should be the case I fear he will not find "Jordan so hard a road to travel" as it was last summer, the National Guard being away—Guess the women will have to "buckle on their armer" & march to the front. But if they should all prove no more brave when in battle, than I thought I did when in Dreamland last night, they would do nothing more than to retreat after the first volley had been fired.

A thousand thanks to you for that splendid Photograph! It is nothing more or less than Edwin——ning. Don't wonder much that Miss Phrone found place in her Album for "three" similar ones. I shant tell you the compliments my Painting teacher past on your "photo," 'twould flatter you too much I fear. I wish that I had a better picture to send you in return. I do not know what sentence you'll pronounce upon it but every person who have [sic] seen them think they do not flatter me in the least. They are deficient in the expression of the countenance as is the case with all the pictures I have ever had taken.

You and the Captain will have your fun over it I know, but then I don't care. I won't hear it—Just so you treat me well to the face— (as I heard a young gentleman say not long since)

I had quite a little visit with Ike Baker & Lady a short time before I left home. They both seem to enjoy themselves, but I rather think it is only feigned—suppose they think they must make the best of it now that it is too late to retreat. O shades of Demosthenes! if Ike would hear what I said! But then he would know I was just joking.

I have been visiting my sister here for the past two weeks, but expect to leave tomorrow for Mt. Vernon where I shall spend a few weeks taking lessons in Oil Painting. Did intend to go to Delaware but the teacher of whom I intended to take lessons unexpectedly left D___ & I had to conclude to go to Vernon though I do not fancy the idea very much. My teacher is the same of whom I took lessons last fall. I must close, it is almost thirteen o'clock. Good Bye— Pleasant dreams—Write soon.

Annie E. Baker

Direct your next letter to Gambier. I'm ashamed to change my address so very often. Kind wishes for Capt. R___   Lib.

letter 89

June 17, 1864. Monroe Mills. Edith Welker. Kingston, Ga.

Monroe Mills, Ohio, June 17, 1864.

Ever Remembered Friend;

I resume my seat, this warm and pleasant morning for the purpose of responding to your last letter which I received about a week ago; will offer no apology for not writing sooner for negligence is all I have to offer. But I hope you will pardon me as I promise to do better in the future.

I have been going to school to Fannie this summer. She makes the scholars walk around about right. She is a very good teacher. I do not believe that I will go any more this summer for I never could content myself in the school House in the summer. I expect you will think that I get lazy. Well, I guess you would think about right for you well know that I am naturally lazy winter or summer.

There is nothing going on around here, at the present. When there is anything going on the crowd merely consists of young Ladies and a few Scattered <u>Homesick</u> cowards, but they do not amount to anything in my eye nor in any young Ladies that has any grit about them, whatever.

Perhaps you will get to see Shiply. He is in the Heavy Artillery; the last we heard from him they were at Cleveland, Tenn. and expected to go on to Atlanta, Ga.

Ed I expect you will be looking for my Photo but indeed I have never had any taken yet. Will Tucker has gone back to Ill, and it is so far to go to Vernon that I haven't had any taken. I think I will have some taken soon and I will send you one immediatly.

I have got an Album since you went away (that is a Photo Album) And you would oblige me very much by sending some Photos to put in it.

I believe I will bring my uninteresting letter to a close by asking you to reply soon.

Your ever true Friend Eda

P.S. Fannie is waiting for an answer to her letter.

letter 90

June 18, 1864. Mount Sterling, Ky. Lou P. Riggen. Dallas, Ga.

Mount Sterling, Ken. June 18th/64

Lieutenant Lybarger

"My friend"

Your most welcome letter was received yesterday evening. You were certainly pardonable in not writing sooner, I did not think strange, of your not writing, as I knew the 43d was engaged <u>this time</u> and was only sorry to have lost my correspondent, which I supposed I had. The suspense you must endure, the fatigue, the privations, the knowledge that you will probably be wounded horribly or killed within the next hour must, it seems to me, be almost unendurable. What a sublime heroism must that be, which inspires men to walk as calmly as though death were not hovering over them to the very mouth of the cannons which are every minute sending violent death and agonizing wounds through their torn and bleeding ranks. The dying brave look their last upon the calm blue sky, thinking with fainting soul, of home and friends, those homes henceforth desolate, those friends henceforth heart-broken, and their comrades pass on to other fields of honor, and glory, and alas death and sorrow. Their graves are green and thick on many a field, and yet they go and fight and die. O, is not this the heroism that should save a nation.

Pardon this gloomy commencement to what I intended should be a more pleasant letter, but I can only write of what is uppermost in my mind and when I think of the wide-spreading gloom which hangs like a pall over all this once happy country and which is deepened by every battle, I <u>cannot</u> control my feelings. I feel that I would be willing to talk and write of nothing else, could I by this means contribute one mite toward the closing of this insatiable war. <u>I</u> indeed, how insignificant—I <u>will</u> forbear and I only hope that if you consider this a useless expenditure of words, you will not trouble yourself to read it.

I presume from your manner of writing that you did me the honor to think my request that you should return "that photo" a wordy nothing.—bosh, to fill blank paper. I really <u>did</u> expect you to return it; true it is nothing but a photograph, and that a very poor one which in itself is of no value to me, <u>but then</u> I disapprove the practice which many ladies have of giving their photographs to gentlemen, do not think it is proper, and never did give my photo to any gentleman—never gave it to you—Now will you return it. <u>I expect that you will</u>. Yes, the neck <u>is</u> crooked, the eyes almost invisible, the mouth horrid, because I was laughing, it <u>looks</u> as though I were <u>crying</u>, the position bad, and the artist was a poor one. I am happy to inform you however that the crook in the neck is the fault of the position, and is <u>not</u> natural. It would <u>not</u> be <u>handsome</u> however with this defect remedied. I thank you however <u>very</u> much for the assurance that you admire it "on account of the original," and assure you that the compliment is appreciated. I can say more of yours, that it is admired for the sake of itself <u>and</u> the original. <u>There</u>!

We have had no mail here for the last two weeks, Morgan having set all eastern Kentucky in an uproar, captured mails, horses, many dry goods and everything comeatable. He fortunately received a decided "whipping" in Mount S. where he first appeared and has kept up a running fight ever since; he must have lost at least half his command, so we have really seen something of "wars alarms." The rebels had the privilege of riding in open daylight where they have not dared appear for months & will not I hope for months again. So we are quite behind the times. (Nothing unusual for me you know) a most distressing state of affairs during the present state of excitement, especially as we have the pleasing knowledge that our letters are perhaps captured—and we cannot even hear from our friends. This of course cannot last long however.

I know you are tired of this and glad to see the end, I can excuse the brevity of your last on condition that you will write longer next time, and if you will excuse the length of this tedious epistle. I will promise you a <u>shorter</u> one next time.

Your friend,
Lou P. Riggen

Should the rebels retreat much farther don't you think the country will be rather warm?

letter 91

June 19, 1864. Bainbridge, Ohio. Rosa Crum.
To Amelia Crum Lybarger, Millwood, Ohio.

[Note: Enclosure, a small 2"x 2" square of material with pattern of very small purple and lavender leaves on finely drawn purple branches. Apparently this letter was sent on to Edwin Lewis Lybarger by his mother, as it was among those in the original collection.]

Bainbridge, Ohio June 19th/64

My Dear Aunt

Your highly interesting letter of June the 12th has been duly received and carefully read. We were very glad indeed to hear from you once more but were sorry to hear that your health was failing. I wish you could come down to see us and stay a while with us, we would be very glad to have you do so. We are all well as common. I have had the whooping cough for 6 weeks but I think it will not be long now until I will be well of it. Aunt Sarah's little Eddie has it too. Aunt Sarah is down to our house now. Little Bell is getting better, think she will get well.

Papa wants to know who Miss Mary Sells is. He says he thinks she is the lady he saw at your house when he was up there and wants you to write and tell him it was her. Papa wants to know if you won't please send him your likeness; he wants it very bad. We got Aunt Alcinda's and Cousin Sallie's pictures the other day; they were all well.

I have not had a letter from Cousin Edwin for about 8 weeks. I dare say he has forgotten me. When you write to him please remind him of me. There is no person I know of that I would rather get a letter from than Cousin Edwin. Please do not forget to remind him of me.

Aunt Sarah is going to go home in the morning. She sends her love to you all. Her and I have just been taking a walk. It is very warm today and I think it will rain soon from all appearances. I hope it will for it is most awful dry. We need rain very bad. Things look very well considering the dry weather as well as could be expected.

We have beets large enough (I mean pretty near large enough) to eat. We have onions as large as the bottom of a glass.

Well as I have written all the news I will close hoping to hear from you soon. Papa wants you to send him your likeness if you please. Uncle Harrison was down this week, they were all well except Jacob. He is in the army and has been sick for some time. John also is in the service. He has been in 14 battles. Uncle Elijah and family are well. Well I close hoping to hear from you soon. Tell Elijah not to forget to answer my letters.

I subscribe myself your affectionate neice
Rosa Crum

Write soon
Here is a peice of my new callico dress. I have just finished it.

Please send us your likeness.

Monday.

Well Aunt as I did not put my letter in the office last evening I will just drop a line or two. We are tolerable well except the whooping cough. Aunt Sarah went home this morning. I have done a large washing and will just call over to you house for a good dinner. Please write soon and send us you likeness. Rosa.

$

letter 92

June 20, 1864. Millwood, Ohio.
Phrone Rogers. Via Chattanooga, Tenn.

[Note: Penciled note on verso of envelope:
"Received June 28/64; Answered July 4/64."]

Millwood, Monday morn., June 20th, 1864
Dearest friend Ed

I will now try and write to you again, that is if "I am able to preserve equilibrium of mind long enough." Your interesting <u>long letter</u> was received a few days ago, and I will just say that I read it over very carefully twice, all at one sitting too. I know you will be surprised to hear this, for I think by the way you write to me, you think I have lost the sense I was born with. Well I must say I <u>had</u> for a time. I felt very indignant towards you and everybody else for a day or two, but all the consolation I offer my loneliness is that you will forgive me and I promise you to think a thing of that kind over two or three times before I write in such a manner to one of the best friends I ever possessed. When I thought the matter over soberly I should not have sent <u>that</u> letter. But what was there left for me to do? Nothing, for the letter was mailed and gone.—Why do you say that you do not know that you will ever hear from me again and perhaps I may never receive another letter from you. How could you be so cruel? When I receive a letter from you I wonder how long I will have to wait to hear from you again. I have never tried to conceal from anyone what I think of you (I must say thought or have thought as you did) for that would convey the idea that I had ceased to think as I had thought of you. I shall never do this untill I cease thinking altogether. O! if I could see you just for one hour how inexpressible would be my joy.

You did not as usual tell me to write you or tell me where to direct. Did you not want to hear from me again?

Miss Emma Critchfield is visiting me now. I enjoy her society very much. She plays the piano and sings beautifully. She and I practice most of the time. We are now learning "Evangeline." Have you ever heard it? I think it perfectly charming. I was at her house one night—last Saturday—had quite a pleasant evening. Mr. Graham & Mr. McNault were there from Gambier. The later gentleman I have spoken of to you before. I expect to go to commencement there this June. I wish you were here to accompany me. What a gay time we would have. I asked Em C_____ what I should say for her, she says say that I am here and send my love but O! You must not say <u>love</u>, say kind regards or something suitable. I told her I thought what she said first was suitable if <u>she</u> thought so. I do not allow any one save myself to <u>love</u> you, but allow every body to <u>respect</u> you as deeply as they please.

You said you were tired, dirty, and <u>hungry</u> for something good to eat. I might relieve your hunger if I were close enough but I am afraid you would have to remain dirty and tired as I could think of no way to rest you and am too lazy to wash clothes. But I can offer my sympathy and say that I am very sorry for you. Mother and Jossie send their love. They know nothing of what has passed between us lately. I hope they will never know. If I ever get mad at you again I will hug you to death—so that I will not be punished for crime. Every body is well.

Ever your loving friend Phrone.

I just directed a letter for your mother. Tell me if you get our letters both at the same time. Your mother is down "sellar" as you used to say now.

Write very soon or as soon as convenient. Phrone.

$

letter 93

June 26, 1864. Millwood, Ohio. Lib Rightmire. Decatur, Ala.

Millwood, Ohio, June 26th/64

Sabath day

Well friend Ed, how are you enjoying this warm summer day? For my part I think it is so warm hear that it is impossible for anyone to realize any enjoyment. I expect that you are beginning to think that I do not intend to answer your letter. I might say that I would have written sooner but I was rather sick with the lung fever the week after I received your letter and have not been able to write since, therefore I hope you will pardon my delay.

I don't know that I have anything very new or interesting to communicate but I will proceed to write something. We have very dry weather hear now. Vegetation appears to be dying, our corn is about two inches high and looks as though it will never be any higher.

I wish you was hear to get some of our Strawberrys if you will come up some evening next week you can have all the Strawberrys and cream you want, and if your Capt. is fond of Strawberrys bring him along. If you think you will come just please send me a note. (But enough of that)

I will have to inform you of the unexpected arrival of C.L. Velandingham. He arrived in Dayton the 18th and proceeded immediately to his residence. He says the assertion of the president that he was arrested because he had labored with some affect to prevent the raising of troops and encouraged desertions from the army and obeyed or failed to council obedience to lawful authority was absolutely false. He denounces order GB [38] under which he was arrested and says it is against the Constitution and laws.

You had better believe the Copperheads are rejoyceing over his return. For my part I would have rejoyced more if I had heard he had gone to the happy land of Canaan[?].

It is reported hear that J.C. Fremont is seeking the nomination for president in the Democratic party and C.L. Velandingham for vice president. For my part they will not get my vote for I intend to vote for <u>Old Abe</u>. What do you say?

I will close for the present, hoping to hear from you soon.

Yours as ever, Lib Rightmire

Excuse poor writing.

letter 94

June 27, 1864. Bainbridge, Ohio. Rosa Crum. Chattanooga, Tenn.

Bainbridge, Ohio, June 27, 1864

My own Dear Cousin;

It is with the greatest of pleasure that I seat myself this very warm Sabbath day to reply to your most welcome letter which it is needless to say I was glad indeed to receive. I had not heard from you for some time. I was affraid that you had met with some misfortune since I could hear nothing from you, but Oh how <u>much</u> was I relieved of mental unasiness when the long desired for letter reached my hand; no one could hardly imagine how I felt. I felt as if I had found a friend that I had never expected to see. I thought a hundred things about you, for says I to myself, if he is living he has certainly forgotten me or he would of written, for you was always very punctual in replying at other times. I would think you had been slain, but never mind the rest, all is right. I feel thankful to the good God who doeth all things well that He has spared you thus far from the many accidents that a soldier's life are liable to. May He ever watch over you and be pleased at last to let you return to that good Mother who is ever thinking about you and praying for your safety. Pray also, dear cousin, that your life may be preserved for I believe in prayer and I believe you do also.

We are all well at this time. I have had the whooping cough but am now getting over it. I tell you it has pulled me down considerable. I was weighed last week and only weighed 123 lbs., 15 lbs. less than I did the last time I was weighed, so you may know how it pulled me down. The weather here is very warm and dry. The crops look as well as can be expected. We have potatoes almost large enough to eat but we have plenty of onions, beets, and radishes. Nothing of any importance has occurred since I last wrote to you more than there is a great amount of sickness accompanied by a great many deaths.

Well I must tell you Uncle Harrison was up last week. They were all well. Jacob is not well. He has not been well since he has been in the service; he is now sick & in the hospital. John Crum is also in the army. He had been in 14 battles when they had last heard from him. We also have heard from Uncle William after a long time. He was living in Kansas and was doing well. I may say he was wealthy until the rebs came and burnt his dwelling houses, took 30 head of his horses, 12 yoke of oxen, 10 cows, beside his other cattle, a great number of hogs leaving him with nothing. Him and his family made their escape but were without a home. Well I close hoping to hear from you soon, answer as soon as possible and I certainly never will forget you. Write often whether you hear from me or not for I will write often. I close by sending my love to you, as ever your truest cousin.

Goodbye, write soon. Rosa Crum.

Please answer soon for it does me more good to hear from you than any one living. I am uneasy all the time when I don't hear from you for you don't seem like a cousin but a Brother.

Pardon my plain speech, but write soon and often.

I your cousin, Rosa.

Well Edwin;

As I did not mail my letter last night I will take the liberty of dropping you a few more lines to tell you of Bell Holliday's illness. She has been sick for 8 weeks but is now on the mend. She is able to go around now. Her disease was the rheumatism at heart connected with other diseases. The doctors all gave her up but she is recovering now very fast. Aunt Sarah was down most of the time and her little Eddie took the hooping cough.

It rained last night and this morning is a very pleasant one. I hope by telling you what I did about Uncle Strauder has by no means made hard feelings; you can write to him though if you wish but my opinion is that he will not reply, from the reason before stated.

I received a letter from Sallie Foulk some few weeks ago, they were well, also her & her Ma's likeness. William Louis and John have gone to Idaho, the last they heard of them they was at Nevada, Kansas. Father is away at work making at the rate of $25 a week. I am very lonesome here by myself, he never comes home only of Saturday evenings. I wish you was near enough to come over and talk a while with me.

There is a young lady in town by the name of Virginia Morrow who sends her best respects to you. She saw you when you was at our house and she also saw your Photograph and says she would like to be acquainted with you for she knows you are all right. She is a nice girl, about the best looking girl in town & has a good Education, has been going to college for a good while. Send your love to her just for a Joke. Write soon.

July 12, 1864. Postmarked Millwood, Ohio.
Phrone Rogers. Chattanooga, Tenn.

[Note: Penciled note on envelope:
"Received July 22nd 64, Answered 31st."]

Home, July 1864

"Dear friend" Ed

I have been gadding about all day and as I do not expect "natures sweet restorer" to visit me for an hour or two thought I would drop you a few lines. Millwood seems to be lively tonight. Every one that has or can get a buggy is out riding. Jossie & I just returned a few moments ago.

I read a letter that Frank received from you last night. It is almost four weeks since I received a letter from you. But I intend doing by you as I heard you told Warner Britten I did by Col. Cassil. I will not tell you anything about it for fear you told the story yourself and therefore would not care about hearing it.

I hear you are having some pretty hard times now. I was at your mother's yesterday afternoon for tea. We were wishing that you were there to participate in the good supper. We thought from your description of what you had to eat you would wish it. Your mother's health is not very good.

What were you doing the 4th of July I would like to know. There was a Butternutt Pick nick at the Caves. I went down to look at the animals for a little while. Was out riding untill twelve oclock and as a natural consequence I was sick all next day. So all my enjoyment was spoiled. I was invited to go down to New Castle to a Picknick but did not go.

I think John Hammond will be married soon, and John Kanukle. I do not know whether that is the way to spell his name or not, to Miss Mary Welker. I should not be surprised if they would be married in a few weeks. I think the engagement must have been a short one. I think it must be John's farm that she admires and not him, not withstanding I think him quite as good as she is. I was up to Rob Critchfield's and stayed a few days, had quite a pleasant visit.

When you last wrote me you did not say anything about your slippers and as your mother sent you a shirt and has heard nothing of it I did not like to send them for fear you would not get them. Your mother got you a pair of kid gloves that she intends to send in the shoes. I guess I will not write more for fear what I have written will not be acceptable as I have not heard from you since the long letter was written. Jossie will have more Photographs printed soon as she does not like the idea of being courtmartialed. I hope to hear from you soon.

Ever your friend Phrone Rog____

How is Oliver Taylor?

Remember me kindly to John Hawn and also to Capt. JH. P.R.

$

letter 96

July 17, 1864. Postmarked Mount Sterling, Ky.
Lou Riggen. Kenesaw Mountain, Ga.

Greenwood, Ken. July 17th, 1864

My friend.

Your kind letter was read with much pleasure, but as I am unfortunately in a profound fit of "the blues" this morning, you need not expect a well arranged nor very interesting letter.

If I were in the army I should congratulate myself on getting into a hospital, or any where else, out of reach of cannon balls. How can you want to go back? A ridiculous question to ask a soldier, I know, but how I would run from a regiment of guns. Do you think "Perhaps I may be killed, but to die for my country is happiness!" or do you rush headlong, with never a thought of death, but with flashing eyes, and thoughts only of <u>destruction death</u> for the base murderers of their country's happiness, thinking not of what you are suffering, but what you are doing. I believe it is said that soldiers after the first fire grow perfectly reckless. By what strange metamorphosis is it that men who at home shudder and shrink at death in its mildest forms, can stand still to be shot down? Can it be mere excitement? If you think it is very dull, answering such silly questions, then don't answer them. You are so much afraid of being considered egotistical that you are always "mum" on the subject. I hope I am not so insensible to the beauties of nature as to consider your description of Look Out "dry stuff." I often wonder why it is that people run off to Europe for sight-seeing, when there is so much grandeur in the scenery of our own country, which cannot be surpassed, and which they do not care to see.

I wish I could believe with you that the close of the war could be effected by "military arbitrament." I hope you'll not call me a "copperhead" for saying so. I love the old flag with all its stars, the Union with no state excluded. I long for the same freedom, the same glorious privileges, the same kindly feeling we once had. "A union of hearts, a union of hands, the American union forever." But I shudder at the awful details of war and cannot but think it inconsistent to try to establish a union by such a method. A union which can only be perpetuated by the consent of the people.

While I abhor the rebellion I yet I shall take care how I dispose of my photos again, and shall not feel much like "forgiving" you when you call it the likeness of your "most interesting correspondent" as however much I might like to be so considered by you. I can't believe it. I think I deserve at least candor from you. If I thought you really prized it "on account of the original" (I know you can't prize it for itself) I would be anxious to send you a better one, but I do not. You remember you wrote some time ago that you did not <u>know</u> who I was which was very true. Do you know anything more now? How can an <u>unknown</u> correspondent be more interesting than your intimate friends. To how many of your unknown correspondents have you written the same thing? I am not proof however against your flattery—if it <u>is</u> flattery.—I will believe you are my friend, whether you are or not. At least I will just now because I don't want to believe anything else. If you knew what it was to be <u>almost</u> friendless you would not laugh so scornfully as I expect you are doing. Just <u>laugh on. You have my full consent.</u> This old letter isn't worth sending but I'll write a better one next time.

Write soon, but don't answer this miserable excuse for a letter. I have not <u>time</u> to write another & will not for 3 weeks or I would not send this. If I don't feel so forlorn next time I'll answer your last letter & next one too. I presume you are in Atlanta by this time. Will direct as you told me, however–

[Lou Riggen]

$

letter 97

July 24, 1864. Danville, Ohio.
Annie E. Baker. Co. K 43d Regt. OVVI

Danville, Ohio July 24th/64

Dear Friend Edwin

I received your letter and as usual was quite glad to hear from you but extremely sorry to learn that you were an inmate of the hospital. But as you said you were not dangerously ill, I have reason to hope that ere this time you are in the full enjoyment of perfect health.

Your description of Look-Out Mountain was <u>not</u> "dry stuff" to me, but was indeed <u>very</u> interesting, although I had heard it described before yet I never tire hearing of <u>such</u> places. How I wish I could "behold it with mine own eyes."!

Well I finished my course of instruction in painting at Mt. Vernon & returned home last Saturday. Shall remain here two weeks longer and am then going to attend school at Spring Mt. Academy, that seminary of learning upon the top of creation, with its romantic scenery, and beautiful surroundings, What, —there! how do you fancy my new method of spelling? I was going to say What a wandering jew I am! I actually believe that I make as many moves as you do in the Army. But never mind. I am going to settle down in peace and harmony when I get all the "book larnin" I want—and <u>when the War is over, you know.</u>

I do not know that Danville can afford any news that would be interesting to you. "Joe" Sapp & "Ed" Cash have joined the Free Masons and Mose Smith the famous letter writer was in town yesterday. By the way, I have been lately honored with a note (as he terms it) from the last named gentleman. But I rather think that journal would be a more suitable term, for it contained no less than sixteen pages, closely written. I have not had the patience to read it through but as near as I can ascertain the main object of his writing was to persuade me to go out riding with him—just whether I loved him or not just to tease some of the other young men. He said "Those who claim you will faint when they hear it, but, never mind that, take a bold stand and let them know you have a mind of your own." He thinks if I would only cultivate his acquaintance I would see the error of my way & that his visit would result in our mutual happiness. Poor foolish man! He has annoyed me so much that I naturally despise him. But I sometimes can't help but feel a small degree of sympathy for him & wish he could find a better half.

When I was in Mt. Vernon I was told by an intimate friend of the Israel family that Frank & Jossie were to be married shortly. I haven't heard anything about it since I came home & scarcely believe it to be true. They surely wouldn't take such an important step on so short an acquaintance.

Oh! I must not forget to say that I have had the pleasure of seeing Capt. R___'s photo. But how, when & where I shall not tell just now. I think him quite a fine looking gentleman but will not "fall in love" with it till I find out whether the original is free from morgage I like lease titles—am not much of a believer in Free Loveism.

So Capt. Crooks appears to know nothing about Normanda Sapp! Oh! Well I've heard of people ta[l]king in that way when the testimony of the other party was quite different.

Ever Your Friend
Annie E.B.

Write soon.

Enclosure: Spring Mountain Academy. Course of Study. June 29, 1864.
Title page states Rev. J.B. Selby, Principal and Miss A. Baker, Assistant.

letter 98

July 31, 1864. Postmarked Millwood, Ohio.
Phrone Rogers. Chattanooga, Tenn.

Home, July 31st, 1864

Dear friend Ed

I will commence by telling you that Jossie has been very dangerously ill for the last ten days. We did not expect her ever to get well. Yesterday and today she is a little better for the first since she was taken sick. Jossie seems too frail a flower for earth and too good I sometimes think. O if she were taken from us what would we want to live for. Life would have no charms for me. The Drs. Campbell and Moffett both say her lungs are both diseased. How hard it is for us to know this.

I received two letters from you not long since and will do my best to answer them. In the first place you were very silly for getting well so soon or at least silly for saying you were well. I think you have fought quite enough to have kept out of those battles before Atlanta. I do not believe that whatever is, is right. You said that in your last letter but one that you "did not remember <u>all</u> you said as your head was buzzing from the affects [sic] [of] Quinine." I suppose the emphasis on all implies that you do remember some things you said—but it matters not whether you remember some things or not—they are written. I hope you will at least grant me the same privilege you wish to enjoy—that is of choosing and using my own words. In one of your letters you asked me several questions—and then answered them yourself. Now please allow <u>me</u> to answer one question you asked. You said if you should have asked me to discontinue any one of my gentlemen correspondents—I would have said "Sir, untill I am under greater obligations to you than at presant I will do as I please." Of course you gave me that for an answer to what I said to <u>you</u>. Now I answer that I would have considered it just under the <u>circumstances</u> to have discontinued.

I had thought never to mention this subject again but I find it necessary. This very day I heard something more that Liz B____ said about our affairs and two weeks ago Amanda Israel told me things she had been saying whilst she was boarding at my friend Kate Andrews which I know are so too. She has been staying three weeks there taking lessons in painting from Miss Pain and Miss Pain told before Amanda what Lizzie said about you and herself. When Miss P___ told Amanda that Liz said you were her beau Amanda told her she "couldn't see it that way." And Lizzie told her cousin that she had written to Captain Rhodes and asked him if you and I were engaged—and you replied to the letter in this way "Phrone is a very good girl but our <u>friendship</u> is very limited." I do not believe that you were the original of these words—but will say in reply to the question you asked in your last—that was if you had said sufficient to satisfy my mind that what I had heard were lies. To satisfy me as to this you will have to cause Miss B to close up her talking and in order to do this I had thought you had better cease your correspondence or else I can not certainly think you the kind of a friend that you have professed to be to me, an understanding between you and me is all I ask and I think there can never be unless you do as I have said.

I have sent the Slippers nine days ago. I do not think that I can "think of you as my own Ed" as you told me to, when some one professes to have the same claim on you. Now this explains, I hope, what I said in one of my letters some time ago. That perhaps you had somewhat changed you mind. I hope after I receive an answer to this letter that this subject may be forever dropt.

Please excuse mistakes as I have been under constant fear and excitement about Jossie ever since she has been sick, and therefore do not feel much like writing. Jossie send her love. With a hope to hear from you soon, I am

as ever Phrone

(come home this fall)

John Hawn wrote home to say to me that he saw my face every day. Did you give that Photo to him?

letter 99

August 15, 1864. Danville, Ohio. Annie E. Baker. [No envelope]

Danville, Ohio Aug. 15th/64

Lieut. Lybarger
My Kind Friend

It is Monday morning and I have seated myself once again to begin a letter, when it will be finished is entirely another matter.

How very many things there are to be done during this short busy life of ours. How many <u>moments</u> there are in our <u>years</u>, and yet when each one is devoted to some particular duty, how few they seem.

We have had company almost constantly since my return from Mt. Vernon. First an Aunt from Louisville, Ky. came and soon after her exit one of my mother's old acquaintances from Cleveland. I have the <u>high</u> honor of playing "Bridget" (an honor however that I would <u>very</u> willingly bestow on someone else) and of course find little time for epistolary duties. But I am answering <u>this</u> letter in <u>two</u> days after its reception. Don't you think I deserve a "credit mark"?

Well I suppose you are aware by this time that I am still at Danville. Yes, I who was <u>determined</u> to attend school at Spring Mt. Seminary. So much for "a <u>fickle wild rose</u>." Think I shall arrive at the "<u>Ne Plus Ultra</u>" of <u>science</u> & <u>literature</u> if I shall continue as faithful to my duty as I have been for the past year.

"But, hear ye, my defense!" I <u>did</u> really expect to go to S.M. [Spring Mountain]. Made no other calculation until the day previous to my starting when the school directors called on me with a request that I should teach the village school for a term of three months. Through <u>their</u> and my mother's earnest entreaties I consented, & will commence my labors about the first of Sept.

Martha and Normanda Sapp have been visiting their friends in & around D_____ for the past two weeks & last Sabbath afternoon, that is, the young people of D_____, what few there are left of us, went on the Ridge some nine miles distant to a singing school. And very unexpectedly I met with a goodly number of my Millwood & Spring Mountain acquaintances. Among the last named was Ex-Captain

Moore. Of course I was <u>very</u> happy to see the honorable gentleman, it being the first sight I had had of him since his return home.

But to my sorrow I learned that the report of his contemplated marriage was but too well founded. At least <u>they say</u> that he is getting a splendid carriage made & I think that a pretty reliable sign, Don't you? Well I guess I shall have to console myself with the thought that there are "as good fish in the sea yet as ever was caught."

Miss Phrone R___ & a Mrs. Stallard from Spring Mt. were to see me last week & there was quite an interesting incident connected with that visit if you were here I might relate to you. But I do not wish to write it with pen and ink for as Mr. Smith says <u>that</u> will <u>stand law</u>.

Ellen Gamble & her brother are coming up to pay Amanda Ellen & myself a visit before long. Oh! wouldn't you like to be here? Ell is a good girl. I love her very much notwithstanding her political principles.

Hadn't you better sheath your sword & come home "quit fighting to free the Niggers" such was a sentence I saw written to a soldier not long since. How ignorant some people are.

Please give my regards to Capt. Rhodes. But I believe I am about <u>half mad</u> at him too for not answering my last letter. Guess I shall have to treat him as Mr. Smith said he would me if I didn't answer his letter, use "Coercion." But I wrote him such a nonsensical letter the last time that I suppose he thinks me a rather unprofitable correspondent. Well! so I am. I do wish I <u>was</u> more dignified, but it's <u>no</u> use to try. I'm Lib Baker and <u>no body</u> else.

Good-bye.

A.E. Baker

Don't forget to write.

letter 100

August 15, 1864. Postmarked Millwood, Ohio.
Fannie M[eredith]. Chattanooga, Tenn.

At Home, Aug. 15th/64

Ever Remembered Friend Ed.

Some time has elapsed since the reception of your <u>very</u> kind letter, and I once more grasp the pen eagerly to trace you a few lines in way of an answer. Ed when I received your letter I had just been to town to have some Photos taken, had to wait a week or two before I got them; thought I would write you as soon as I got them and send you one. And after I got them my school was about to close so I was gone almost every day and night visiting with the scholars. Was going to write directly after my school was out; then came the news that they had a Fight at Atlanta and your Regt. was engaged in it. I did not know but what you were killed or wounded, but heard a few days ago that you had been sick in the Hospital but had gone [back] to the Regt. now. I suppose you were not in the battle were you? I do not know where the Regt. is, but will direct this to Chattanooga.

Ed I am teaching school now in the old Robinson School House. My school was out at Kinderhook three weeks ago. Have been teaching here since. I like it better here than at K., have a great many more scholars. That is such a small district. I have forty-five here on roll, and some coming in every day. I am boarding at home.

Oh! such a beautiful eve. They have all left me to seek the downy pillow of repose and I am alone, no sound disturbs my silent recitations except the <u>Frogs</u> and <u>crickets</u> but I must admit <u>they</u> disturb me a little.

I was down to town yesterday to church. The congregation was quite small. Mr. Jacobs preached. Millwood is <u>very, very</u> dull. I was at Friend Al Critchfield's most all day. She is a <u>splendid girl</u>. She and I are very intimate, but then we always have been. You are aware of that I suppose.

The Draught will come off some time next month I believe. I do wish they would draft enough men and put this war through. I guess a great many of the Butternuts are going to Canada. Do they not think what a disgrace it will be? Why it will be thrown up to them as long as they live.

There is a Gentleman going to preach down to the Rocks Sunday (Peace Meeting). I suppose peace will reign throughout the country after he preaches.

Sister Ell and Royal have just come so I will have to quit writing as they have all gone to bed but me.

Thursday eve.

I again resume my seat for the purpose of finishing your letter. This week brought sorrow to many, many hearts. Ma Erertt's [Everett's?] son was brought home Wednesday dead. We also learned today that you were wounded, and that J. Hawn is taken prisoner; do hope it is not true; if so, hope you are not seriously wounded. O! The destruction of war will it never cease? Do hope it will. What do you think Ed?

I have not heard from Brother John for some two months. Do not know but what he is sick or dead. Ed have you seen him? Please write and tell me if you have. Hen Witt started last Monday. Oh! I do think it was too bad they made him go before he got well. He could go about a little on crutches. I have no doubt but that will be his death.

A great many of the Hundred Day men have died. I suppose they took them too far south, they could not stand the warm weather. They will be home in next month I believe.

This quite a lovely eve. They have all retired but myself. I cannot see the lines on this page as you will perceive. And the Frogs, Katydids and a thousand other insects nearly make the old Brick [house?] ring with their music. It is getting very late and as I have one or two more letters to write tonight I will have to close.

Ed I have a Photo to send to you (according to promise) but as I am not certain about you getting this I will not send until the next letter I write; you must not think that I do not intend to send it for I will most assuredly do as I promised. Would send it this time certain if I knew you would get this.

I will close requesting you to write soon and often. I will be more punctual hereafter.

Write soon and oblige your
Friend, Fannie M.

I know your patience will be wearied after reading this poorly written an uninteresting letter. There isn't anything to write about that would interest you.

Write soon soon.

letter 101

Friday afternoon, Aug. 19, 1864

Friend Lybarger

I again resume my seat for the purpose of addressing you a short letter to know the reason you have not written to me. This is the second letter I have written to you and have received no answer as yet. I cannot conceive the reason. I <u>thought</u> perhaps you did not get my letter—if so I will pardon you. But if <u>Negligence</u> is the reason I do not know whether I would or not.

I should not have written untill I heard from you had I not promised you a Photo and fearing it might come up missing sometime thought I would send it right away. Also to be as good as my word you know I always was.

Ed what do you think of this war? Think you it will close this fall? For my part I think it will very much depend upon the election. If Old Abe is elected I don't think they will make any further resistance and if he is beaten I think they will expect aid from the north—And of course they will get it, don't you think they will? We do not get any war news at the present of importance. I think Richmond and Atlanta will soon be ours.

It is pretty dull around here; scarcely anything going on that amounts to anything at all. You well know <u>Home Cowards</u> amounts to the large sum of nothing any place they are and what few were left here are running off to Canada to get rid of the draft. Quite <u>honorable indeed</u>.

I guess the draft is going to be. I do hope it will take some of the traitorous cowards away from here. I heard Harrison T.P. is making great preparation to resist the draft. If they shew this bravery again like they did at Fort Fizzle, Holmes Co., I <u>think</u> it will be an honor to them as long as they live and forever afterwards.

Well indeed I have written a longer letter than I intended to but if I have intruded in any way I humbly ask pardon.

I will close by asking a reply soon.

Ever remain your
Friend Eda

My Photo is very poor as you will perceive without close examination. It is as good as I can get at the present. The weather is so hot they can't take good ones.

Good Bye

letter 102

August 21, 1864. Millwood, Ohio.
Phrone Rogers. Atlanta, Ga., via Nashville, Tenn.

[Note: Penciled note on envelope:
"Received Sept. 8/64; Answered Spt. lo/64."]

Millwood, Aug. 21st, 1864.

Dearest friend Ed

I was very happy indeed, as I always am, upon receiving another letter from [you]. If you only knew how impatiently I always wait for your letters. I think you would write me oftener. I must congratulate you upon your escape. I think you must have had those "Magical Slippers" on that caused you to escape so miraculously. You would have been amused had you only have seen us when we heard <u>you</u> were taken prisoner. Frank told me that he had bad news for me. Said your Lt. was taken a prisoner. There was not a word spoken by any of us. Then Frank undeceived us by laughing.

It has been raining for several days. In fact this is the only comfortable weather we have had this summer. I have been out several evenings in succession, and consequently have gotten a very severe cold. Jossie is mending slowly but is not able to sit up any yet. She told me to say to you that you did not think or talk of her oftener than she did of you. Your half-brother and his family are visiting your mother now. I like him ever so much. He is quite an intelligent man. I think is a great deal like you, not quite as good.

John Moody is home on a sixty day furlough. He looks better than I ever saw him. I do not see how he managed to get home. I wish some of my friends would play such tricks on the government and get home occasionally. As I have written to you every Sunday for two months and I do not receive one letter from you for three of mine I know you have something else to think of at present but I would be satisfied with a few lines if I could only hear from you often.

Your mother is looking quite well & I think all that prevents her from being perfectly happy is your absence from her. If she was only rid of that little pest Alcinda. She is so self-willed I do not see how your mother has any patience with her at all. Her mother is coming after her soon I believe.

I expect to go to Mt. Vernon as soon as Jossie gets a little better. Mary Zimmerman is to be married next month to Lt. Sam Brent. I am glad Mary is doing so well. I think so much of Sam. I think he is just as good as he <u>can</u> be. I have not written much nor have I written that well. I have to steal time to do my writing in. Please excuse mistakes and write to me very soon.

Ever your loving friend Phrone

letter 103

August 28, 1864. Postmarked Mount Sterling, Ky.
Lou Riggen. Before Atlanta, Ga.

[Note: Penned note on verso of envelope:
"Received Sept. 11th '64, Answered Sept. 17/64."]

Aug. 28th, 1864

Lieut. E. L. Lybarger
My friend

Your tardy letter was quite welcome, and was read with pleasure.

You say you cannot answer all my questions because you might attribute everything to the dealings of Providence. I think <u>that</u> would be the most noble and worthy answer you could give. It seems to me that men constantly in danger of being killed might, as a natural consequence, do see their dependence on the strong right arm of God more clearly than at any other time. If they only would there would be less of absolute horror in our battles; but they <u>don't</u>. They are idle, and therefore, they play cards, and therefore they drink, and then curse and then fight, and inexperienced boys who have known no other influence than that of home, joining the army, coming within such influences, are drawn along, and forgetting their mothers' prayers and warning words, they follow in the steps of the boldest, and when there comes a battle and many of them are killed, their friends remembering them only as they were at home, console themselves with the thought that they have gone to heaven. Perhaps they have. I'm sure I hope they do, but I fear many do not. Do not think I am too sweeping in my strictures. Of course there are numerous exceptions, and of course there is no more excuse for wickedness out of the army than in it. But why should there be so much in the army?

There is another question I never thought about prefacing my questions with my remarks about rudeness or "impertinence" and I expect I would send another brace of them in this letter, but I suppose it is your time next. You ask "if I think it would prove disadvantageous to talk about ourselves occasionally." I never think it disadvantageous to talk of myself, my letters are my thoughts, and my mind is myself so I always feel as if I were writing of myself and I expect I do more than I ought <u>and</u> I like very well to read of yourself. So, I will say No.

I did not intend my last letter for a <u>quiz</u> to find out how many correspondents you had. I could not object you know to your telling each one of your unknown correspondents that she was one of your most interesting correspondents, and don't think I asked you any such silly question. That's all of that. Hoping that your next letter will be from Atlanta, or beyond it, & that you will find time to write it within less than a month, I remain

Your interesting and <u>interested</u> correspondent

Lou P. Riggen

When are you going to return that splendid and <u>beautiful photograph?</u>

✤

letter 104

September 3, 1864. Postmarked Millwood, Ohio.
Phrone Rogers. Via Chattanooga, Tenn.

[Note: Penciled note on verso of envelope:
"Received Sept. [10]/64; Answered [Sept.] 17/64."]

Home, Sept. 3d, 1864

Dearest friend

It is but a short time since I wrote you last. I saw a letter you wrote to Elijah and you said that you were coming home when your time was out. I think your head is quite right only stick to what you have said. I told Mother and Jossie about it. They were both very much pleased to hear it. We do not intend telling any one else any thing about your intentions. Don't tell Elijah that I mentioned it to you for fear that he may not like it. I promised to tell no one except Jossie and Mother. I was very much interested to hear you were so ill. Take good care of yourself and do not be in such a hurry to get back to your company. I think they will do very well without you and if they <u>cannot</u>, stay where you are. Jossie is better, so much so that she sits up in bed to eat. We had Drs. Burr & Pumphrey to see her. I think there is no doubt but what she will recover rapidly as she has not had one of those nervous spasms for about a week.

Gomery Garrett and Barbara Workman were married about two weeks ago. He is seventeen years old and she is twenty-five. And the worst of it is that Garretts were perfectly willing for the match. It is one of awfulest things I ever knew of.

This is another long weary Sunday. I went out to hear Moody this forenoon and expect to go out at five o'clock again. John Moody goes to see Ell H. sometimes. Was there last night. I have known people to feel a great deal worse over <u>small</u> matters than they do over John being a prisoner. Ed I do wish you could have heard an expression they made about you not long since. It was really provoking yet laughable. I will not repeat it here. They <u>do</u> try to taunt me but with poor success I assure you. It has been raining ever since last night and still continues to rain. I stood on the steps in company with two other persons, a gentleman and talking to my friend Dr. Campbell. He was telling me his troubles. He used to come up to our house to play the mandolin [?] while Ella Stall and my music teacher played accompaniments on the piano and the people (that is a certain people) talked wonderfully about it. Said right away that he was in love with Ella. After she went home from here Dr. Cam_____ went away on business to be gone a week, he had not been gone very long before Dr. McMahons and associates circulated it around that Dr. & Ella had eloped. And the people were telling his wife about it and she was I think a little jealous. The people were trying to persuade his wife to leave him. But she waited until the appointed time that he was to be at home, and lo! he came. Dr. said he needed some good friends to help him through safely and he expressed his regrets that you were not here. I can assure you that all that was said about him were lies manufactured by a few individuals who are trying to injure him in his profession. Ella was a very gay lady. Yet she is perfectly virtuous and I think very prudent. I merely rehearsed this to you because he is a friend of yours.

Write soon and often and believe me ever your loving friend

Phrone

$

letter 105

September 25, 1864. Postmarked Millwood, Ohio.
Phrone Rogers. Via Chattanooga, Tenn.

[Note: Penned note on verso of envelope:
"Answered Oct. 24/64."]

Home, Sep. 25th, 1864 Sabbath evening
"Dearest friend"

After having waited some time I received two letters from you. I must congratulate you upon improving so rapidly whilst in the hospital <u>cultivating</u> your <u>temper</u>. I think your first of the last two letters you wrote me shewed signs of a sweet temper. Don't get so cross. It makes me feel very unhappy to receive such letters. I was pleased to hear that you are well again. I sincerely hope that you will not get sick again whilst in the service unless there should be some hard fighting to do. It seems quite a while untill next Feb. although it is not long. Do come home. I want to tell you something. Don't you want to hear it? You say that I can not have another picture or rather Photo of you do you? Well we will see about that. If I can not get those that were taken from me I will go to Mt. Vernon and get one printed from the negative and then I wonder what E.L.L. will do about it, please inform me in your next.

You did not tell me whether you received the handkerchief I sent you or not. If you did receive it—please keep your nose clean. You say you answer every letter you get from me. Darn you. You <u>tell</u> a <u>story</u>. You do not write me as many as I do you, let alone <u>answer</u> them. When you ask me a question I generally answer it, but you do not pay one particle of attention to anything I write you and if you do not quit doing so I will not write you another letter after this year is up.

Jossie is very much better. I think if nothing happens [to] her she will be able to go about against your come home. Now since you refuse to grant some of my requests I will on the other hand refuse to obey some of your commands. Therefore you need not send your love to Mother and Jossie (by me) anymore. For I intend to keep all the love given as sent to me. I must always tell Mother and Joss that you <u>remember them kindly</u>.

I have enjoyed myself gaily for some time. I have had a great many calls and visits and have made several <u>visits</u> myself. You ask "How did you enjoy your visit at Miss Baker's." I hope she has told you all about it and as my powers of discription are very poor perhapps I had not better attempt to tell you anything about it. Another thing we may not tell it just alike. However as you have asked a civil question I will try and answer it——I visited Lizzie under very peculiar circumstances and I suppose I would have enjoyed myself very much if the house had been a little cleaner. Now do not take offense at what I have just said and I will add that I do not think they need a pig pen. You see that I am very lavishing in my terms of praise. Lizzie gave me a very pressing invitation to come and see her at home and set an afternoon that a friend and me should come and as the lady visiting me wanted to go very much and as I had not any particular reason for not going or at least none to give her what was I to do, but to do as I did do. Dan Baker was here to see me one week ago last Saturday evening and spent the <u>whole</u> evening and I must say I found his society very pleasant. He sings very well. He sang several pieces with me while I played. Have you any favorite songs? If so inform me the names of them, and I will try and learn them for you against you come home. Will Knight made us a visit not very long ago. He is just as good as he can be. Maggie will be married in October. Henry was graduated the 3d of this month and was drafted the other day. His honors all came about the same time.

I wish I knew what I was going to do this winter. Perhapps you can help me to decide if I tell you some of the things I was thinking of doing. I thought some of teaching. I can get a good situation in New Castle to teach in the Union school. I can get the primary school and I think it would be very pleasant. And another thing, Proff. Myers talks of teaching music here this winter and as I have an instrument and can practice as much as I please thought perhapps I had better stay at home and practice music while I had such a good chance. I do not want to start to school untill spring. So if I had a teacher this winter I could go right along in music. What do you think of all I have told you about my intentions?

Your mother is well. I go to see her almost every day. She is talking of going to Elijah's to stay this winter. Tell her not to go. I know she will not be down there very long before she will be home sick. It will be so lonesome if she goes away. Please excuse blots and scribling. My hands are so cold I can hardly write. If this letter is too long inform me and I will say less in my next. I remain ever your loving friend Phrone

(Write very soon if you are in a good humor)

I would have liked to have brought up that disgusting subject again but had no room this time. I want you to understand you were the person that should have done the talking and not someone else as you would fain make me believe you understood it . . . e . . . s

letter 106

September 29, 1864. Postmarked Mount Sterling, Ky.
Lou Riggen. Atlanta, Ga.

[Note: Penned note on verso of envelope:
"Answered: Oct. 27/64"]

Lieut. E.L. Lybarger–

Your very welcome little letter of the 15th was received the 26th, and it is answered the 29th of Septr. I congratulate you as a friend for your safety and as a soldier, for the high honor of being one of the many which has achieved such glorious results. May the Stars and Stripes triumph as signally everywhere.

You ask of my parents. My father died when I was quite small. I do not remember him. He was a farmer I believe. Ma has been dead now more than two years. I thank Heaven that I never can forget <u>her</u>. I have one brother and one sister.

Some of your questions are the <u>queerest</u> I ever heard or read about. Music & mince pies, coffee, house-keeping, poetry, history & novels. I presume you brought in the domestic dapartment to see how much "false pride" I had. I confess to some—Kentucky girls don't often boast of their culinary accomplishments—but I <u>have</u> <u>not</u>

enough to keep me from doing any thing which my duty requires. Or perhaps you mentioned this interesting subject in order to prevent my mind from roaming too high in the contemplation of noble themes—leaving this mundane sphere entirely—ahem—some little boats know how to keep near the shore and I'll try and not get lost— But to proceed—"Do you like music?" Yes sir—"Play on the piano?" No Sir—"Can you bake bread?" Yes—Mince pies? No— "Make good coffee?" Yes. "Keep house?" I once kept house for six months to the edification of the whole family except Lou Riggen. My! what an endless task of intricate labor. Brooms, carpets, beds, cobwebs, dinners, suppers, breakfasts, with all their attendant auxiliaries of good butter, sweet milk, done bread & not burnt either. "To be or not to be" good was always the dread question until dinner stood in all its dread array on the table. Sometimes it was and sometimes it wasn't. Don't I know how to boil & bake & fry & stew & roast beef & biscuit & pork & light bread & "season to taste." O . . . I'm so tired . . . & I do hope you are. Why did you ask if you didn't wish to read the answers. If there is any thing "advantageous" in it now I'd like to see it. "Can I eat my share of a dinner?" Could a young lady who ate nothing but white roses & drank the sparkling dew from the delicate morning-glory be guilty of burning her face over a cooking stove or vice versa.

Do I like History, Poetry, or Novels best? I suppose I ought to say History, but I don't like any history except Macauley's & I believe they say it has more style than fact. Biographies are nearly always dull. I can't read about the greatest men nor the most stirring incidents unless I like the author.

You will excuse me for writing here that I like to read novels—not the "yellow back" kind however. "I'm past that" The sensatious stories of hairbreadth escapes & dark caverns & inprisoned fair ones & rescuing knights, or "heroes" I should have said, are not all-absorbing with me. "Emerson Bennett" & "Sylvanus Cobb, Jr." are not my favorite writers in fiction. I don't like Dickens either, notwithstanding it is my duty to do so, as he is so popular. I like his Christmas stories but not his everlasting "Great Expectations." The truth is I hadn't the patience to finish it. I'm telling you whom I don't like, not whom I do. I believe I like the author of "Rutledge" though I don't know who she is. Where there is such a host of writers, & so many literary stars and where there are so many authors whom I have not read, I am a miserable critic. Victor Hugo I believe I like best. You are as tired of this as you were of the house-keeping.

Well I like poetry best. Blank verse better than rhyme. Prentice's "Closing year" is the best thing I think I ever read—sublime. I love to read it, & Poe's "Raven," and—I won't tell you what else. How can I tell my favorite author when there are so many beauties in all? I think of none I like better than Longfellow. His Hyperion has something rare and beautiful on every page, and Hiawatha I dearly love. I haven't read all nor half the American authors and ought to be noncommittal on the subject. I am a member of the Methodist Episcopal Church South.

<u>Well Don't you want to know something else?</u> You are to consider yourself under everlasting obligations to the undersigned for her extreme kindness in replying at such length to your astounding array of questions. You say you will answer my questions truthfully or <u>not at all</u>. <u>Not answer indeed</u>. I shall consider you as in duty bound to answer every question I ask <u>without exception</u>. Consider every question you ask me as having been propounded by myself— <u>all</u> remember & answer them & as many more as you can think of & hold yourself in readiness to answer some real posers—if I can just think of them next time I write.—

Excuse brevity—

Lou P. Riggen

I have a faint recollection of a quotation you gave some time since from which I infer that you like "Waverly" Be sure and tell me whether you have read everything or not & which you like best.

September 30, 1864. Postmarked Millwood, Ohio.
Frank Mared [actually Fannie Meredith]. Chattanooga, Tenn.

[Note: Penned note on verso of envelope: "The scene of
youthful love/ It rules an eve of/ Autumn's Holiest mood."]

At Home, Sept. 30th/64

Kind Friend Ed;

I received your very <u>kind</u> letter last week, was very glad indeed to hear from you, also to hear you were getting better. I was to Uncle Dan's when your letter came, or should have written sooner. My school has been out three weeks today. I haven't been at home any since it was not until this week. Was up to [Mt.] Vernon visiting Sister Ell one week, and to Uncle Dan's one week. This week I am at home. Eda received a letter from you Saturday. She like myself was very glad to hear from you.

Ed since I last wrote to you quite a <u>sad, sad</u> change has taken place. My dear Brother John has killed himself. We received the sad news about four weeks ago. He was standing guard, had his gun upon some boards, it slipped off and he went to replace it, and it went off, shot him through the head. They carried him to the Hospital, he only lived a few minutes. The Capt. wrote such a good letter, also Mr. Fry. They said he was much loved by all his comrades and the officers. If they had Telegraphed to us we would have had him brought home, but I don't suppose he would have looked natural being shot in the face. He told how he was buried, in Soldier Style, told what pieces the Band played.

Oh! can it be that he is dead? my dear Brother. I cannot realize it, that he is no more. So is life, one moment he was doing his duty, the next stretched upon his dying bed. Thus Earth's loved ones pass away. One by one our brightest hopes wither and fade and we learn after years of sorrow and disappointment that there is no true and lasting happiness. Oh! Death is there no power to stay thy rentless hand and snatch the gay, the beautiful, from thy embrace—

Brother Leander was Drafted, he started yesterday. His wife is here. Oh! I do wish this war was over. Some think it will not last longer than this Winter. What is your opinion, Ed?

It has been very sickly here this faul Mrs. Darling lost three children. Sophia Darling is dead. I suppose you knew her, did you not? Clake lost two. Dan McGugin's little girl was buried last week. They all had the <u>Diptheria</u>, it is raging high around here.

I presume you have undoubtedly heard of the weddings. I will mention them. Montgomery Garrett and Barbry Workman. He is very young and she is very old, so I think they will get along. Ed I believe she is the girl you and Len Lehman has a fuss about, had you not? Gum is ahead of you both. But then there is two more. But Ed I would not advise anybody to pitch in there. E. Ann Smith is married to Hen Poults. Hallie is upstairs bothering me so I can scarcely write. She told me to tell you she was not dead yet. Says she has not anything to send you. Says if she had a cake baked she would send it to you. I tell you she is a Captain, there is no end to her talking.

Jake Lybarger came home Wednesday. Charly Rightmire is at Camp Dennison. He is not able for duty, think him and Hen Witt will be discharged. I have written two letters today, one to Maggie Bartlett of Chesterville, the other to Lida Graham of Monroe Mills, perhaps you know her. She is a splendid girl I think. I <u>just love her</u>. Cousin Eda and I are going to Wooster week after next to visit Uncle Mart [?] Welker's. Will stay three or four weeks. I cannot think of anything more to write that would interest you, don't suppose what I have written will interest you any but it is the best I can do under the cirumstances.

Ed I send you an imitation of Fannie. No doubt but what it is better looking than she is, but then it is a very poor picture. Perhaps I will get some more taken before long and I will send you another.

Ed I presume you are tired reading this poorly written and uninteresting letter so I will quit my scribbling by asking you to write soon and often.

Ever your true Friend
Frank Mared

letter 108

October 3, 1864. Postmarked Millwood, Ohio.
Phrone Rogers. Atlanta, Ga.

[Note: Note on verso of envelope: "Answered Oct. 24/64."]

Home, Oct. 3rd, 1864

Dearest friend Ed

Another day has passed and gone and O how much I've enjoyed it and one of my best friends was to see me today, our minister from Washington, Pa., Mr. Breugh. I come as near loving <u>him</u> as I could any man, not to love him. I showed him your Photo, asked him what he thought of your looks. I shant tell you what he said (something good though) I am afraid you would feel flattered and perhaps it would make you vain. It will be long six months before I will have the exquisite pleasure of seeing him again.

It has been raining here for almost two months about every other day and therefore is very disagreeable out, but very agreeable in doors with plenty of good company. You seem to wish to know what some of your friends across the way said about you. If it had been any other kind of an expression from what it was I would have told you long ago, but I'll tell you <u>now</u>. Hett was over spending the afternoon not so very long ago and she was teasing me about you and said if she were in my place she would be afraid that you would go crazy like <u>old Jim</u>, meaning your father. I think I gave her a reply equal to all she said. I told her that I could see no signs of it now and that few men as intelligent as you were and as sound minded in everything were not very likely to become crazed on any subject whatever. Told her also that your father's derangement came from disease and that I had known whole families that naturally had but half sense. With this we dropped the subject, and they have said nothing of the kind to me since. I know you will never let them know anything that I tell you. I told Hett that perhapps you would come home in the spring. She said she would be glad if you would, but that she knew you could not get home when your commission was out. I know how they would be pleased "in a horss sir." We all bear their insults as well as we can. They have treated Joss worse than if she had been a negro. There will be a whole month that not one of the young ladies came to see her. Uncle Gilmor came and that was all. Jossie never did them any harm in her life. Jossie is mending slowly. She does not sit up but very little and has been sick ever since the twentieth of July. I think if it had been me that had layed in bed that long my patience would have been quite exhausted. I was at your house and stayed all night last night. Your mother is well and seems to be very cheerful. I was teasing her not to go down to Elijah's this winter. <u>You</u> advise her not to go and then she will not go. She is having her kitchen built, it will be quite a good sized room. It will make the house so much more convenient.

You said that you did not think you would come home if you got your health again. I hope you will not feel well a day—if that is the way you are coming home. Will says you do not have to stay any longer than this fall, says you can come home when your three years are up, that your time is counted from the day of enlistment. He says there is a new order to that effect. I see you had not received my last letter, when you wrote me last. I do not see why it takes my letters so long to go to you. I believe you tell stories about them so you will not have to answer them so soon, ha! ha! I hope the time has already arrived that you will have nothing to do except "to write letters and read." I will expect a letter from you once a week at least. If you knew how much work I have to do you would not expect me to write any letters at all. Why I hardly have time to draw my breath, only think of it. We are going to have a new hotel in M___ and as I am so well drilled in all kinds of work I am going to try and see if I can not find employment in the "Vaughn House" kitchen. Tom Vaughn bought Peterman's property. He has a whisky shop already and has Captain Howe for clerk. What do you think of the institution? Don't you think it is grand?

You are always talking about writing me long letters. Don't talk so much about it, and write <u>long letters</u>. The kind you spoke of presenting me would be very acceptable from you. But I am afraid you would not have thought of it had I not mentioned it when you were home. It is getting very late and I am anxious to finish a novel that I have been reading. I hope you will be able to read what I have written. I upset my ink bottle and as this is Sabbath evening I could not get any ink.

With much love I am ever your friend Phrone

Write soon and often please. Joss and Mother send their love.

⚜

letter 109

November 6, 1864. Jelloway, Ohio. Rachel Blakeley. Atlanta, Ga.

Home, Jelloway, Nov. 6/1864

Lieut. E.L. Lybarger

I have the pleasure of acknowledging the reception of a kind letter from your hand. It was carefully perused & contense noted. Would say in reply I was glad to hear of your good health, and also to learn that you had been so highly favored as to survive the hardships incidental to the campaign through which you have just passed. I do not attempt to form any idea or have any conception of what the brave boys have endured this summer, from what I have learned through correspondence & the papers, what you have passed through & endured is only known to those that have been able to survive, & never can be painted to our imaginations.—We are under great and lasting obligations to you—Indeed I am under the greatest obligations to the noble defenders of our Government for the peace and quiet that surround our humble dwelling & for the safety I feel this silent hour while attempting to pen a few words to you.

Permit me if you please to address you by the name I was used to call you in our school days, it is awkward for me to say any thing else. I presume you think I am very tardy in responding to your communication. I acknowledge the fact & if it was any body else but a soldier I would not care so much, yours was received a week ago last Wednesday, I have thought of writing every day since, have had an excuse many times and owing to circumstances that was not under my controle have been prevented. Beg your pardon. Edd, you may be assured that I was not a little surprised when your letter came to hand, yet the thought never occurred to me that I was entirely forgotten as I am sure from my own experience, in thinking of the past, we will call to mind occasionally, all we ever mingled with whether we want to or not. Neither did I feel myself neglected as I was pretty well convinced your list of correspondence was long, ere the time I told you we would be glad to hear from you, suficiently lengthy, and made up of names that were more able to interest you & more worthy of occupying a place on that list than either Christie or myself, yet it was a very agreeable surprise, & I can assure you it will always be agreeable whenever you can make it convenient to remember us in the same way (but you remember Christie is much the best correspondent—don't tell her I said so) Christie is now at Millwood, will be home in two weeks more.

I have taken occasion to remind some of the Girls of a remark you made at Millwood last winter "that the soldiers would not need any wives when they got home," gave them your reason for saying so, guess to think from their actions there is some truth in those reasons, consequently three young ladies of our neighborhood have sliped across the line into the state of Matrimony within the last few weeks, as they are mostly strangers to you I will not give their names at present but will say that my brother George was among the number took his wife of the daughter of Old Josephus Tilton, think he has an excelent one not a bit like her brother or his sister that you were acquainted with. _____ Well George, Christie and I had a bid to one of these weddings but it happened to be of the pure Butternut kind, yet we went as a matter of course, it was one of Amos Workman's cousins (you know him as he used to be one of your boys) he was there also, & I was inquiring of you on that occasion he said he had heard from you a short time previous, by way of letter, in short he thought you was an excellent fellow, that was one of <u>The Weddings</u> but I presume he has told you all about it.

I was glad to hear you say you were going to vote for Lincoln & Johnston, that without doubt is the way to vote this time, think you ought to have influence enough over that half of your Regt that does not think with [you] to influence them to vote right, if they don't know any better than to vote in oposition to the way they are fighting. You never need apologise for speaking to me on that subject, as it is my conviction every female should be interested enough in the cause of our Government to keep pretty well posted on politics & every other subject pertaining thereto, at least a little more so than I am.

One of the boys of the 20th Regt arived at home two weeks since to remain with us a while. He (James Waddell) is all the one from our place in that Regt that did not reinlist, says he holds himself in readiness to go again when all have gone that never have went, ___ Had a letter from Henry Saturday, he says all is working well with him in Atlanta, thinks he will make no effort to get Home this winter. If you should be so highly favored as to get back to Knox this winter remember we live 2 1/2 miles west of Brownsville. Your humble friend, Rachel Blakeley

Please Write soon.

letter 110

November 26, 1864. Postmarked North . . . town, [Ky.]
Lou Riggen. Macon, Ga.

Side View, Nov. 26th

Lieutenant E.L. Lybarger

The very decided <u>smile</u> with which I received your letter vanished when I opened it and found that you "hardly knew what to say." There was before my mind a vision of a certain young gentleman looking very much perplexed with a sheet of paper spread out before him, and his pen vibrating between his mouth, where he gnaws the handle, and the inkstand from which he vainly endeavored to fish up ideas. I could not expect you to consider your correspondent other than show, however, when you compared her to an <u>Indian</u> (You are "not Indian enough to read and love" the very book which I love to read. O! O!! how—could—you—be—so—so—"cru—el" boo hoo hoo. Are you not sorry for me? I have been trying so hard to make an <u>impression</u> and now—to find myself compared to an Indian, instead of an angel is provoking. But I will like Hiawatha, the words flow so musically and the thoughts are in such charming unison with them even if you do consider me a savage.

Women's Letters to Edwin Lewis Lybarger

Yes, I like Pollok's Course of Time and Tupper's Proverbial Philosophy, do you? I have read your favorites Sketchbook and some other scattering pieces but they are not animated enough. By your concise and to the point answers I am reminded that I was too rambling and unmethodical in mind. "She scribbled but her heart was good, could she go faster than she could?" If you don't like music you are "fit for <u>treason</u> strategem and spoils—rather dangerous

> "On wonderful streams, is the River of Time
> As it rolls through the realm of tears
> With a faultless rhythm and a
>   musical rhyme
> And a broadening sweep and a surge
>   Sublime
> As it blends with the ocean of Years."

Do you like that and the rest of it? <u>I do, decidedly.</u> The quotation to which I referred is in "Waverly," the first of the Waverly Novels. It is this <u>"As happy as a toad under harrow."</u>

You ask if I don't think the best thing you can do "is to love somebody else's sister." I know no other way by which you can supply the place of a sister, unless it is to love some one who is <u>not</u> a sister to any one and who therefore like yourself has "None to love, None to caress, None to respond to her heart's tenderness." Isn't <u>that</u> the most benevolent manner of dispensing your love!

I voted for McClellan. I am sorry he was not elected. I believe in the Union as it was. You believe in it as it should be. I am for peace, peace, <u>peace</u>. They talk about <u>honorable</u> peace, could it be less honorable than this war. "The tide of blood has long been flowing, alas that it gives no sign of ebbing." You must not call me a rebel, for I won't have it.

Hoping that if the "personal interview" of which you speak would <u>be</u> a pleasure to you, your wishes in regard to it may be realized I close this systematically arranged epistle.

Lou Riggen

Write soon.

"I am well and hope these few lines will find you enjoying the same blessing."

Direct to Claysville, Harrison Co., Kenty. L.

If this isn't directed right it is from my ignorance and your carelessness.

1865 LETTERS

letter III

January 8, 1865. Postmarked Millwood, Ohio.
Phrone Rogers. Via New York with Sherman.

[Note: Postmark reads "Millwood, Jan. 10"; three-cent stamp
was hand cancelled. Addressed "Via Chattanooga, Tennessee";
has been corrected to read "Via New York with Sherman."
Penned note on verso of envelope: "Answered."]

January 8th, 1865

My good friend Ed,

I was delighted upon receiving a letter from you. It seems almost a year since I heard from you. <u>Two months</u> is quite a while to wait for a letter. I was glad to hear that you were safe and well, and hope you may be in a good deal <u>safer</u> place before another month expires. As you have not heard from us lately, you are not aware that Jossie is well enough to "go where she pleases, and stay as long as she wants to." She and I spent a few weeks visiting Mt. Vernon. I enjoyed myself <u>very much</u>, went out to several parties while there. One of them was a <u>dance</u>. I went accompanied by Mr. Ringwalt. You better believe I <u>more</u> than enjoyed it. John Hawn is at home looking better than I ever saw him. His furlough expires the 25th of this month. They (Uncle Gilmins) had quite a large partie last night in honor to John. They certainly had as nice a supper as ever I sat down to. I enjoyed it somewhat—I had fun teasing some folks. I only slept three hours last night so I think it excuse enough for me not writing a better letter. I felt too horrible to hunt my pen and ink, so I did not commence with the intention of writing very much. But I will promise to tell you more in Feb. if I do not loose the use of my tongue, and I can not tell how that will be, for I assure you I use it a good deal. I was agoing to say something else, but I changed my mind.

Dr. Campbell gave an Oyster supper on New Years Eve. We had a good time. Joss, Mother, and Frank were out sleighriding today. Mother stopped at Elijah's to see your mother. Lidia [Elijah's wife] is sick (not dangerously so). Elijah's foot I think will be about well after the draft comes off, as it is improving rapidly. Your mother is looking very well. She does great as I told her she would do, goes ahead with the work, of course they have one hired girl. They also have seven Boarders beside their own folks which makes a great deal to do. Will has not returned from his visit to St. Louis, we miss him so much. We expect him home in a few weeks.

I am too tired to think of any thing, unless it would be a comfortable bed. Therefore I guess I better close. I have been so wicked today, did not attend church, nor read any thing that amounted to a pinch of snuff.

Write soon and oblige

Ever your sincere friend
Phrone

letter 112

January 23, 1865. Macon, Missouri.
Benjamin F. Stone. Savannah, Ga.

Macon, Missouri Jan 23rd 1865.

Dear friend

I have just received yours of the 31st Ult. I was truly glad to hear from you. I had almost lost hopes of hearing from you again. You can scarcely imagine how much pleasure it gave me to hear from you, that you had been one of the sharers of that glorious work that has been performed by Sherman and his army. Allow me to say to you that I feel grateful to you and all the brave boys with you. I feel proud that my country can have such an army. It certainly has astonished the world in what it has accomplished. I think surely the day is beginning to dawn, to our national existence. The hopes of true men are now fast reviving. Certainly we have need of such revival here. I am sorry to tell you that we have had such times here as will forever cast a dark cloud upon the human character. Missouri has been cursed as never a state has been cursed before. Like begets like, the fiendishness of the enemy naturally made men desperate. You know what is the result. I cannot guess of what lies in wait for us. I trust nothing of what has just preceded. There is a general apprehension that there will trouble again next summer. Though our military and civil authorities are using endeavors to avoid it. As you may have noticed, very many of our citisirey are leaving or preparing to leave the state and those parts that were the most populous, enterprising, and wealthy are almost depopulated. Thousands of property are changing hands daily, in some sections large farms are either tenantless or only in care of women and children. The State convention has abolished slavery in the state. From reading the proceedings of that body I see a strong disposition to place the negro on an equal footing [with] the white man. I am of opinion that the sudden elevation of any people from slavery to all the priveligies of a freeman in a republican government will be neither beneficial to the freedman nor to the community in which he lives. I love progress but not in the manner attempted by some. Notwithstanding errors in legislation, when we can have peace in this state we will have prosperity and it is without doubt where a young man can easily earn a competency, and now no one can object to emigrating here on account of slavery and the negro like the indian is fast passing away. I hope you will be spared to come here and live long and happy in free and prosperous Missouri.

Ed guess the cracker business suits you well, you will certainly keep plenty, but I mistake it is RQM instead of RCS. I was thinking how well the latter place would suit you. I guess you have not forgotten Paducah and St. John's Hospital. I am glad you are promoted. We have plenty of pretty girls here but I have not yet been so fortunate as to find one for myself but hope is not gone. I am still studying and am slowly progressing through the tedious labyrinths of human legislation. Hoping you shall meet with the same good success in the future as in the past and that soon our glorious old flag shall wave over the whole country loved and respected by all the people glorying only in one nationality.

I am truly yours,
Ben Stone.

$

letter 113

January 25, 1865. Bainbridge, Ohio.
Rosaltha Crum. Beaufort, S.C.

Bainbridge, Ohio Jan. 25th, 1865

Dear cousin

Yours of the 9th has been mine but a few minutes, and I hail this opportunity for replying. You can <u>imagine</u> better than I can describe how delighted I was to hear from you. It was the first I had received since some time [in] September. I had begun to think I was never going to hear from you again.

We are all well except had colds, bad colds, is the general complaint. Do you have any cold weather or any snow down south? There has been good sleighing snow on the ground ever since before Christmas. There is a very deep snow on the ground at this time, about thirteen or fourteen inches deep. This is about as cold as it was newyear's day a year ago. I am still going to school this winter. We have a very good school and Teachers. I have taken one new study this term. It is <u>Latin</u>. I like the study very much.

We received a letter from Foulks monday evening. They were all well and rejoicing over the freedom of Missouri. Uncle Harrison's family was well last account. Uncle Elijah is in the service but where I am unable to say. Perhaps against I write again I will know. I received a letter from ciz. Elijah not long since, they were all well, but himself, he was a little lame his foot not having got well yet. I suppose you like the service as well as ever, do you not.

Well as this is getting pretty well along to bedtime as I have nothing of interest to write about I guess I might as well draw my epistle to a close. The family all send their love and best wishes to you, and would like to see you. You will always remember my best wishes goes with you. So goodbye, hope to hear from you soon. Write a longer letter next time. Excuse bad writing for I have such a bad cold that my eyes water so bad I can hardly see at all.

As ever your own cousin
Rosa

Ans soon. horrid cold, night this

$

letter 114

February 5, 1865. Spring Mountain, Ohio.
Annie E. Baker. Beaufort, S.C.

Spring Mountain/O Feb. 5th/65

Lieut. E.L. Lybarger

I received your letter about three days ago and to my surprize learned that my letter written last has failed to reach you so I suppose I shall have to bottle up the wrath that I have been in silence pouring down upon your "devoted" head. I met Captain Crooks. You have heard perhaps that he has resigned his position in the Army—at an evening party not long since and he inquired very particularly concerning you, thinking I suppose that I was posted in your doings, and when I told him that I had not heard from you for nearly six months he seemed to doubt the truthfulness of that statement. You may espect to hear from him before long.

Capt. Moore was <u>actually married</u> last Thursday to a lady in Spring Mountain. She is very beautiful and wealthy, but as regards her intelligence I am not prepared to express an opinion having only a passing acquaintance. They go west early in the spring.

O, I have had delightful sleighing for the past few weeks and I have been enjoying it "hugely" and as though I be a student. "Much study is a weariness to the flesh," you know. The school is promising or as much so as we could espect these war times. Our Literary Society which meets every Monday evening is also in a flourishing state. And now while I think of it, we have a literary journal, the "Mountain Echo," and we would be so well pleased to have a contribution occasionally from the "43rd." Will not you be so kind to lend us a helping hand and enrich its columns with something from your ready pen? We will feel very grateful to you, and I will guarantee that the pieces—should you comply with my request—shall be read in such a manner that if you were present you would not feel chagrin.

In three weeks from next Saturday night the "Spring Mountain Glee Club" gives a Concert for the benefit of the Christary C____ missions. Wish you could be here. You would no doubt hear some splendid music, especially from the Alto Class. We are especting some of the good citizens of Millwood & Danville [there?]

I am like "Capt." Crooks I would like to see the "Lieutenant" at home and as Captain Rogers is coming home! I should indeed be very happy to favor his "personal acquaintance." I will spoil all the romance of the affair if I should never see him. But as he has never answered my last letter I suppose he will not put himself to the inconvenience of climbing a <u>Mountain</u> to see me. Write if possible as soon as you receive this. And ever remember me as a <u>true</u> friend.

Annie E. Baker

Lieut. E. I. Lybarger

I was somewhat disappointed to hear of your intention of remaining in the service, another lesson for although how much _____ I have not heard whether Miss Phrone will be here or not. wish that sleighing would last until after that eventful period.

$

letter 115

February 6, 1865. Millwood, Ohio. Phrone Rogers. Beaufort, S.C.

Millwood, February 6th 1865

My good friend Ed

I have been thinking of you so much to day, and I thought I
would drop you a few lines although it has been but a short time
since I <u>last</u> wrote you. The war still <u>goes on</u>. But now I think we can
see the end of it. I was a little disappointed that you did not come
home when you expected to. But then we will only be the more
pleased when you <u>do come</u>. We have had a protracted meeting at the
Me___ Church. The "Camelites" are also having one at the Jeloway
church. I have no doubt but they would like very much to have you
here to <u>ding</u> for them. I would try to tell you something about a
party that went to New Castle. But I know John Hawn will tell you
all about it.

This is Monday eve. I did not have time to write, or rather finish
this last night. We have had a houseful of company all day and you
better believe that I am tired. But amid all the confusion I took Joss
(who "by the way" is almost as well as ever) out riding, and we
drove down to Elijah's and saw your mother. She is looking very
well. I am glad that spring is so near for she will be home to stay
then. I believe she will be glad to get home, I think she has gotten
quite enough of living away from home. We think of moving into
the country this spring—it will suit <u>me</u> "to a Tea" Will and I intend
to make shugar. You better come home and assist us. I think you
would find it more <u>aggreeable</u> than soldiering. Joss is sitting by me
sewing—sends her love—would like to see you. Had some Photos
printed almost on purpose to send you one of them, but they were
such horrid frights that she would not send one. Intends to get some
better ones and then you can have one. Write soon and often.

With much love your friend

Phrone

letter 116

February 14, 1865. Misc. A Valentine.

*[Note: This small piece is on folded lined paper such as used by
Phrone Rogers, Rosa Crum, Lou Riggen, and others. The
embossed emblem in the upper left corner of the first page reads:
"Holyoke Co."[?] The writing has apparently been disguised
and does not resemble any others. No identification.]*

> May the golden beames of
> truth light thy pathway
> through life and the sillken
> chord of Love bind all <u>true</u>
> hearts to thine own.

> *A. Valentine*

letter 117

*Feb. 20, 1865. Postmarked Cynthiana, Ky.
Lou Riggen. Beaufort, S.C.*

Direct to Oddville, Harrison Co. Feb. 20, 1865
Lieut. E.L. Lybarger.

Doubtless you have sighed and looked and sighed & looked
innumerable times for this most important document and doubtless it
will prove most intensely interesting to your expectant eyes. Its pages
so replete with the <u>usual amount of information</u> and interesting
remarks will of course give you any amount of <u>something to write
about</u>. Would that they could. My large and very extensively
<u>cultivated</u> mind however has completely exhausted itself and I find
to my horror that I can neither write anything great nor beautiful for
your edification.

To speak truly however I expect you are tired of your correspondence. The numerous duties of your office render it irksome, besides which the little interest which the novelty gave it, has long since worn off, and you would like to discontinue. Of course I judge from the tone of your letters I did not expect by any means that the correspondence would continue for an indefinite period of time, and if you are in the slightest degree tired of it, I hope you will not scruple to say so, as when it ceases to interest you it will as a natural consequence <u>cease entirely</u> to interest me in the <u>slightest degree</u>.

I do not believe that I ever gave you any ground for "waiting, expecting and looking for that other photo" which you are (of course) so anxious to see. How could I be so inconsistent as to "abandon my present position." You have one photo which belongs to me, and which I expect you to return, and now, to send you another, after writing a half dozen times for that one—beautiful consistency. I wonder what my friends would say, should they see my photograph in your album and know <u>how it ever came there</u>. They would say "Lou Riggen you are a simpleton" to which remark I would be compelled to give my assent. So I have no intention of ever sending another, nor have you any expectation of receiving one.

Pray excuse me for writing so much on so uninteresting a subject.

I don't like Mr. Lincoln's arbitrary dictation of terms, but I am not going to trouble you with my reasons.

Of course you will return my photo when you discontinue your letters, if you discontinue them.

I thought I had answered all your letter, but I find I have omitted a very important item. Your idea of advertising for a wife is a happy one. I have not the slightest doubt that every marriageable "school marm" in Beaufort will respond with alacrity and most gladly agree to support you by their labor—thinking themselves fortunate if they can secure that most desirable article—a husband on <u>any</u> terms. The only trouble will be that you will have so many applicants it will be troublesome selecting, and then so many of the poor forlorn creatures will be disappointed—their brilliant hopes dispelled. Write soon if you wish to.

Respectfully
Lou Riggen

letter 118

February 23, 1865. Postmarked Jelloway, Ohio.
"C.A.B." Via N.Y.

[Note: C.A.B. could be Christie A. Blakely since
Rachel Blakely wrote of her sister Christie,
November 6, 1864, with a postmark from Jelloway, Ohio.]

Shadley Valley, O., Feb. 23, 1865

Mr. E.L. Lybarger

When home the other evening Sister gave me your very welcome letter of Jan. 20th & asked me to reply to it as she expected to be away most of the week and as she is very accommodating some times I did not dare refuse. And so this morning before the scholars commence coming in I shall attempt to scribble a few lines for your perusal. This is a beautiful morning.

Think you enjoy such mornings in camp if it were not for the mud, for it seems almost a task to stay in the house after such a long cold winter as we have had. Long & cold it has been, but not unpleasant for all that. For as you already know we have had excellent sleighing most of the time, which is a treat we do not often get. And I guess they were few who did not enjoy it.

What cheering news we are having from Sherman and his "brave boys." Certainly the Confederacy will not have madness enough to attempt to resist such an army much longer. The people are rejoicing greatly over the good news and seem to think the great success you have been having almost a miracle. The coming draft now so near at hand is making a few of the folks wish they were in Canada, or some place else where Uncle Sam could not find them.

But he must be a traitor or a coward indeed who is unwilling to help bury the country's arch enemy after brave hands have fought the battles.

Have not had a letter from brother Henry for several weeks but trust he is safe & well.

School is almost out and I am not sorry for I am getting almost homesick. It seems too bad to be shut up in the schoolhouse all day these bright days. But guess you know how that goes. It takes somebody that likes teaching better than I to enjoy it much.

24th. Did not get to finish writing yesterday morning and now as I have a chance to send this to the office I must close. It is raining and has been all morning, and O dear, the mud.

Hope you are far enough from swamps this kind of weather. Brother writes "O the detestable swamp."

If you have the time and do not think it too much trouble, shall be glad to hear from you again.

Hoping this may find you well I am

Your friend C.A.B.

$

letter 119

March 11, 1865. Postmarked Monroe Mills, Ohio.
Edith Welker, "Eda." Beaufort, S.C.

At Home, Mar. 11th, 1865

Friend Ed

I presume you think I am not going to answer your letter. But such is not the case. I was taken with diptheria the next day after I rec'd your letter a cuple of weeks; had got able to go around the house when I was again taken with Lung fever and have been sick ever since, am getting better now. It is about six weeks since I was first taken. I know you will pardon me for my long delay for I think I have offered a good excuse for so doing. "Most assuredly I will pardon your long silence." Times are pretty dull around here and news scarce.

Frank Israel and Joss Rogers are married <u>at last</u>. I think <u>they knew</u> each other well enough to get married. I presume Phrone will wait <u>till the war is over</u> before she unites in the "holy bonds of matrimony."

I wish I had a nice dish of the good "fresh Oysters."

Ed what [fair?] fellow is Mr. O. M. Taylor. I have no acquaintance with him; but I have heard a great deal about him. I ask this confidentially and I know you will (as a friend of mine) tell me.

You spoke of coming home on "leave of absence." I should like to see you come and would feel <u>very much</u> slighted did you come and not "call and see me." It would be a pleasure to have you come I assure you. But I am surprised that you have more than <u>one</u> "particular" friend. I thought she lived in M____ well it's no matter where she lives.

Well I believe I have written all the news, will bring my uninteresting scribbling to a close. You will perceive by my writing that my hand is not very steady therefore excuse miserable writing and poor composition. And answer a soon as you can conveniently.

Yours with profound respect
Eda

Are you acquainted with "Charlie Fowler"?

※

letter 120

March 22, 1865. Postmarked Loydsville, Belmont Co., Ohio.
Lizzie Howard. Co. K 43rd Regt. O.V.V.I. via New York.

[Note: The writing in this letter is so pale and faint some words are undecipherable.]

Home, March 22nd, 1865

Kind Sir

One evening week ago when the snow was falling gently, softly as though fearful of disturbing kindred companions already nestling close to mother earth I was seated before a pleasant fire my thoughts playing at random some times amid firm and partially forgotten scenes of other days but were particularly hovering around the present and I then remembered a presentiment I had that I should write to one of our "Country's brave defenders," and strange though it may be a Photo and a name came into my possession about the same time. I had still deferred writing from time to time feeling some diffidence in thus addressing a stranger but on looking on the Photo considered the face was rather an honest looking one and as we were both friends to the same cause I would do as I had been impressed to do. Unfortunately, however, I did not know the address at that time consequently the letter was never sent. Since then I have been so fortunate as to obtain that also and will now for the second time . . . the thoughts this pityable . . . war . . . for truly the breezes are wild today.

My egotism is not sufficient though to make me believe it will prove very interesting for I am but a rustic country girl who always found it pleasant to roam through the grand old forest culling wild flowers for bouquets and listen to the warbling music of the feathered songsters as they were gayly flitting from branch to branch, who always loved the music of the rippling rivulet as it hastened on to mingle its notes with some larger stream.

I have sat and watched the gloaming sunset tinging hill, field, and forest with a beauty unsurpassed by art. With the croak of the frog in the distance and the Goodnight songs of the bird I have thought that nothing inside the brick walls of a city could be half so pleasant.

If I have . . . sentences to drive dull care away for a few moments or while away an hour or so they will not have been written in vain. If you should deem this worthy of an answer Please

Address
Lizzie Howard
Loydsville, Belmont Co., Ohio

❦

letter 121

April 4[?], 1865. Postmarked Millwood, Ohio.
Phrone Rogers. Goldesboro, N.C.

Home, April, 1865 Tuesday evening
Dearest friend Ed

I received another of your ever interesting letters—the first I have heard directly from you, since the first of January. In that short space of time a great many changes have taken place. Jossie has been married over a month. They took a little trip up to the lake, and are now staying at Israels, probably they will go to housekeeping some time this summer, and perhaps not until fall. They intend living on Mr. Israel's farm southwest of Mt. Vernon about a mile. Jossie has very good health for any one so delicate as she naturally is. She and Frank have had some very good Photos printed. But as they are quite large I do not suppose you would care very much about having one of them whilst in camp. Perhaps you have not heard that the soldiers were coming home soon. I believe Jossie intends one of her pictures for you.

We have retired from city life and we now reside in the country. I like it ever so much, it is <u>so</u> <u>much</u> pleasanter up to Will's than where we lived. One thing certain it is not half as much fun as I imagined it would be to move. I never want to move again while I live. We can't find anything at all. I even lost my <u>ink</u> moving and that is the reason that I am writing with pencil. I am sitting in the front door writing. I sent Ella down to Millwood to get me some ink and I see her coming so that I think I will get to finish with a pen.

Osker Welker and Dr. Campbell each had a horse stolen two or three nights ago and have not found them yet. They are both out now hunting for them. Osker had just begun to plow and he can not get another horse easily.

I have been helping to trim the church for the last two days. The "Ladies Union League" of Martinsburg are going to give some kind of an entertainment for the benefit of the sick and wounded soldiers this evening and we all expect to attend although the evening I do not think will be very favorable as it is now five o'clock and drizzling rain.

Your mother is well, has moved home and is getting her house fixed up nicely. Elijah has also moved up to Millwood. He has done very well by buying property as there is quite an excitement about property since they got oil at the Caves. I suppose we will have plenty of oil wells around us soon as almost every one around are leasing their land for the purpose.

Wednesday P.M.

As I did not get to finish my letter last night on account of going out to that entertainment I have already spoken of I thought I would try to finish today—if I could think of all that I wanted to tell you. In the first place I have a notion to scold you. But I will leave you to scold somebody when I give you a little piece of history. Ell Hawn has been mad at me for a good while and I could not imagine what about. But I have finally solved the mistiry She gave me a very good chance herself—accidently. All of those letters that you sent home by Oliver Taylor she has read—among them were some of my letters to you—she therefore knows all about our correspondence for the last year. I hope she had a good time reading my letters. She gained a great deal of very valuable information concerning herself, I have no doubt. Oliver stayed all night over there before he took your letters to your mother. Oliver told your mother that they insisted upon him staying all night to go to church with them. Oliver is perfectly innocent, he does not know their tricks as well as we do. But I have not told you how I came to find this out. I was away in the country spending a week with a friend of mine and while I was gone Rightmires had some company one evening—and Will took Ell down with him—and on the road she asked him "what he would think of a person—say a relative—that would write every little remark someone would make (she did not mention names) to a confidential friend of that person—and then she modified it by saying "friend." She said you very often made remarks that you did not mean any particular harm by making. She has treated mother very cooly too, so when Joss was married she went over to tell the girls about it—and Ell said to Joss that she supposed that Joss thought she (Ell) had treated her cooly by not coming the see her—oftener that she had done of late. But she say "Joss it is not anything that you have done—you have always treated me kindly." But I am ahead of my story. She also said to Will that these things had been seen in black and white and could not be denied (I do not want to deny anything that I may have said about them to you) I knew no one in our family had ever written anything about them except myself—and I never wrote to anyone about them but you. I knew you would never give them a letter of mine to read or never let them get one to read by any other means if you could help it. So I wisely concluded that that they had read some of my letters by some means. I thought I would tell your mother about it and perhaps she could enlighten me on the subject. She surely did too. For although

Oliver Taylor had called on me he did not say anything about bringing your letters home. As soon as I told your mother <u>all</u> about it we could both see through it right away. I will not tire you by writing more about it. I hope you will come home then I could tell you more in a half hour than I could <u>possibly</u> write.

I hope you will be able to read what I have written. This is intended for your eyes alone therefore I hope you will destroy it after you are through reading it. I hope you will excuse all mistakes. I was tired before I commenced writing.

J. Baker has been my escort for a few <u>weeks</u>. I dismissed him <u>honorably</u> last night. You can not imagine what fun I have when in his society he is so odd. My mother says you need not always stay in the army because Joss ate <u>her</u> canned peaches. She says she has some of her own for <u>you</u> and she intends to keep them too untill you do come. I will send you some maple shugar. Mother sends her love. I am agoing to stay all night with your mother tonight. Write soon and often.

With much love
Phrone

letter 122

April 16, 1865. Postmarked Jelloway, Ohio. Christie Blakely.
A. R.Q.M. 43rd O.V.V.I. 17th A.C. via New York.

Home, April 16th 1865

Mr. E.L. Lybarger
Respected friend.

Your very kind and welcome letter of Mar. 20th found its way to its destined point by the last mail and was read with interest & I take this opportunity to acknowledge the favor by scribling a few lines in return. Was glad of your safety after such an arduous campaign. Think you needed rest after such a tramp as that. Guess you accomplished enough that they might afford to let you have a little. From the aspect affairs seem to be taking the grand victories achieved by the union forces. The people here are becoming very hopeful that there will be no need of any more such campaigns. But that peace will soon be restored, and the "brave boys" who have been so fortunate as to outlive every danger, be permitted to return to their homes crowned with the brightest and most enduring honors that America can bestow. That the "great rebellion" is at an end seems almost beyond a doubt. Every body is rejoicing. Southern sympathisers have been suddenly transformed into unionists, and there is a fair prospect for peace at home as well as in "Dixie." And we are heartily glad of it for so much jaring and discord among neighbors and friends is certainly very unpleasant.

Since commencing to write we have the <u>sad, sad</u> intelligence of the murder of our president. What can we say or think. It seems we can do neither, it is so sudden. So awful we hardly comprehend it. How thick the gloom it spreads over the bright light that was dawning.—But we will not be despondent. Believing that the death of <u>no one</u> man in the nation can work our overthrow. Trusting that the God who presides over the destinies of <u>all nations</u> will bring <u>all things</u> to work together for good. Though we may not be so near the end of the great struggle as we were supposing.

The bright face of spring is making all things look glad again. But I suppose in the "sunny south" you welcomed spring long ago, and we are beginning to feel the heats of summer while we are just making garden and trying to get things ready to grow, thinking that summer will be here by and by.

Brother spoke of seeing fruit trees in bloom some weeks ago. Hope if you have to stay in "Dixie" that long that you will get good share of the fruit.

The "Phrenohomeans" about Jelloway are getting very scarce. Had friends visiting us from the west this winter that knew our old teacher Dagmude in his Iowa home. Spoke of him as being a very worthy man commanding the esteem and confidence of all who knew him. Think our little band of students are well represented in "the grand mass" who are so nobly defending our country's honor. But time says quit. So with best wishes and hoping to hear from you again when you have leisure to write to so poor a correspondent I close.

C.A.B.

letter 123

April 22, 1865. Postmarked Claysville, Ky.
Lou Riggen. Goldsboro, N.C.

Woodland Place, April 22nd/65

Lieut. Edwin L. Lybarger

I do think you treated my poor letter so badly. You must have read it backwards, or upside down, at least you contrued its meaning to be <u>just the opposite</u> of that which I intended. I did <u>really</u> fear that you had become tired of writing to me and to be candid, the only thing which induced me to fear this was that you kept telling me you did not "know what to say." <u>That</u> was what gave "<u>tone</u>" to you letters which made me think you did not <u>wish</u> to say anything. If I had wished to quit writing myself, I should have told you so at once but I was silly enough to fear that you perhaps would not be as plain with me but would continue to write merely because I did. Speaking of <u>your</u> being tired, and looking as I supposed from <u>your</u> point of view, I said that the "interest had worn off" and when I said that I did not expect the correspondence to last for an indefinte period of time. I said it in order to show you that I was willing for you to quit if you wished it.

O you are so provoking—You tell me that you "will not hold me to my promise," that you will not "force a disagreeable correspondence on me," that you "will not compel me to read the poor production of your pen," that it is the tone of <u>your</u> letters, "which makes <u>me</u> tired," you don't ask me to write again and even tell me that you don't expect to hear from me more than once, and you don't seem to expect <u>that</u> for you close out your part of the correspondence in a summary manner without hearing what I have to say and all because I thought it my conscientious duty to release you from an irksome task. Now, <u>don't</u> you feel sorry for me? You say that if I "really wish to discontinue the correspondence I must say so in a manner not to be mistaken." I will say that I <u>have always</u> read your letters with <u>very great</u> pleasure, that I consider them <u>very far</u> from being "poor productions" and since you are so kind as to call my letters "very interesting" that I shall be <u>very sorry</u> indeed if you do not continue to write.

I shall not <u>ask</u> to be "released from my promise" to write and as I only proposed to release you on the condition that you wished it, you are by your own confession under obligation to continue writing and I <u>assure</u> you that when you <u>do</u> get tired you may quit without <u>my</u> assistance.

I think I said in my letter that I did not like Mr. Lincoln's <u>terms of peace</u> but "would not trouble you with my reasons." Now let me see, have I any more apologies to make. It is my hard lot to be forever doing something out of the boundless magnanimity of my heart which I would better have left undone. I'll tell you about Irene and Fannie Jerome in my next. <u>Please</u> be good & <u>write soon</u>!

Lou Riggen

✿

letter 124

April 30, 1865. Kokomo, Ind. W. A. Barkalow. R.Q.M.
43rd O.V.V.I. 1st Div. 17th AC. via N.Y.

Kokomo, Ind. April 30th, 1865

Dear Brother

I am in receipt of your most welcome letter of April 5 wich finds us all well truly hoping this small note may find you enjoying the same God's blessing. I also receved your photograph which I am truly happy to see. <u>You</u> spoke of me returning it. Oh, Edwin how could you form an idea that I could be so cruel as to treat such a gift with coldness, on the other hand I shall keep and trasure it as the gift of an absent Brother, hoping to see the original as soon circumstances will permit. I recieved a letter from Brother Elijah about a month ago. He was well at that time. This is Sunday and raining ever since 7 oclock now one. This is a very lonesome day. Every body almost has gone to Indianapolis to see the remains of A. Lincoln ower most Beloved and Esteemed President. It is not necessary for me to write you any war news for you are better posted than we possibly can be. But this much I can write. I have four children, two boys and two girls, the boys being the oldest: Edgar W., Frank, Emma, and J. Emma. I will not brag on my husband or children but if ever you return from the Army come and see for your self and you will never begrudge the trip. We own good property here. This town is improving very fast. We have two Reil Roads passing throe here, the Peru and Indianapolis and Chicago and Cincinnati Air line RR. It was Incorporated a Citty the 15th of this month

This I believe is all the news I can think of at this time, hoping to hear from you soon

I remain your true and beloved Sister till next

W.A. Barkalow

❦

letter 125

May 6, 1865. Bainbridge, Ohio. Rosaltha Crum. R.Q.M. Co. K 43rd O.V.V.I. 1st Division, 17th Array Corps.

Bainbridge, Ohio May 6th, 1865

Cousin Edwin

Yours of the 5th Apr. came to hand yesterday evening. I <u>assure</u> you I was very much gratified indeed to hear from you. I had been looking for a letter so long. I suppose you will soon be at <u>home</u> now as the talk is that the war is about over. <u>I</u> for <u>one</u> am glad. Nothing of any importance has taken place since I last wrote, consequently you will find this a very uninteresting letter as I have nothing interesting to write about. I must (however) tell you about our exhibition. School closed the 27th of last month; in the day we had an exaimation, at night an exhibition. We had a pleasant school and teacher consequently we had a pleasant exhibition. I would of liked very to had you attended. There was a great many present that evening. The church was crowded & every thing went off pleasantly. Your <u>unworthy cousin</u> had the honor of being called the Belle of the exhibition. I say it myself but don't think it flattered me any not at all. I could tell you a great deal of the nice time we had but as I feel very much indisposed at present I will have to desist however. I will send you a programme of the meeting & you can decide for yourself. Several excercises such as the serenades and trip to Columbus were not put in the program. Little Brother Albert has the name of performing better that any of the boys some who were 22 yrs. old.

Uncle Strawder and Harrison were to see us last month. Their families were all well. Uncle Strawder intended going back to Mo. latter part of last month but I don't know whether he has gone yet or not. We have at last heard from Uncle William, he is in Kansas and doing well.

Father sends his respects to you and says when you get home to make arrangements to move out west with him and both of you buy a farm and go to farming. As soon as you get home you and Auntie must come and make us a visit.

I have grown entirely out of you knowledge; four years makes a great change in young folks. I was quite small when you seen me, <u>now</u> as large as any body.

Miss Jennie Morrow returns the compliments and says she would like to see you. Yes, she is very well acquainted with Capt. James Simpson and considers him quite a gentleman.

Perhaps I have wrote enough to tire patience of Job and had better stop. I hope you will be at home against the next time I write. Father and the boys send their love to you. I also send mine, hoping to hear from you soon.

I close remaining as ever your cousin

Rosa

letter 126

May 21, 1865. Postmarked Millwood, Ohio.
Phrone Rogers. R.Q.M. 43rd O.V.V.I., Washington, D.C.

Home, May 21st, 1865 Monday Eve.
Dearest friend Ed

I was rather unfortunate in receiving your last letter & did not get it until today. It came to Millwood Saturday morning, went to Danville, then back to Millwood in the evening. Will got it out of the office and carried it in his packet untill this morning. <u>Then</u> I had the exquisite pleasure of hearing from you again. Was glad to hear that you were marching this direction. Hope you will be home <u>very</u> soon. You Mother is <u>delighted</u> with the idea.

There was quite a sad accident occurred this morning or some time this forenoon. Old Dr. Garrett went down to Biehl's Saw Mill (I guess you know where that is) on the New Castle road near Carpenters. His horses ran away with him and broke his neck. Some of the Carpenter men found him. The wagon head was thrown on him loaded with green lumber that he was getting to finish Gomery's house. I do not know when I have heard anything half so sad. I never saw prople feel so badly.

You seem not to have received my last letter—there was nothing <u>so very</u> important in it. I told you about the letter reading so that it would not be much of a loss after all is said. You must not quit writing because you do not get my letters. I always answer <u>every</u> letter that I receive from you.

I feel quite tired tonight. I have been penned up in the school house with forty scholars. I am teaching the Millwood school this summer. I find it decidedly the pleasantest school I ever taught. I suppose on account of being at home.

I guess I will not write you many more times. I want to write a letter to Amanda Israel to night. She is visiting in Zanesville. She wrote me two weeks ago and expect she thinks it high time that I was answering.

Write very soon, your loving friend Phrone

letter 127

May 22, 1865. Postmarked Belmont, Ohio.
Lizzie Howard. R.Q.M. 43rd Regt. O.V.V.I.
2d Brig. 1st Div. 17th A.C. via New York.

Loydsville, May 22, 1865

Mr. Lybarger

Your letter bearing date April 6th reached me on the 4th of the present month and today thought I would devote a portion of my time in attempting to answer.

Capt. Hamilton and Lady are intimate friends of mine and in supposing he had something to do in the matter you were correct but farther than this your suppositions or suspicions rather were erroneous.

I am truly what I represented myself to be a <u>Country girl</u>, and have not seen Capt. Hamilton nor Lady since my letter was written as they have moved some distance away. In the beginning Jack had something to do with it or I would never have written but if in doing so he went contrary to the wishes of the original of the "Photo" I shall undoubtedly return the picture and retire at once from the scene begging leave to remain "incog."

As to <u>my</u> "Photo" I have none at present, presume I could not induce one to go if I had, as they have a great antipathy of going into the Army.

We are all feeling that Peace is about to assert her gentle reign once more over "The land of the free and the home of the brave."

Your years of civil conflict has taught the people of our country how to appreciate her blessings. What heartfelt joy is in the thought that war is about to cease and those who have so nobly lent a helping hand to our country in her hour of greatest danger "will soon be marching home again with glad and gallant tread." But the joy of the moment will be forgotten when we look at the thinned ranks and look in vain for the manly forms and honest faces of those who went forth with them into battle.

In the beginning of the rebellion I had two noble brothers who obeying the dictates of duty entered the army. One after weary days and months of sickness after almost crossing the dark rolling river of death to the farther shore came back to us. The other met his fate in battle and is numbered with fallen heroes.

The lengthening shadows warn me to lay aside my writing and enjoy the beauty of the evening. It is indeed one of the loveliest of the season. The monarchs of the forest are clothed with the rich foliage and the breeze from their shady depths is fresh and cool, and every where the eye turns is seen the bright green robes of Spring.

I remain

Lizzie Howard

letter 128

May 28, 1865. Brooklyn, N.Y.
Saddie E. Stuns. Washington, D.C.

New York, May 28th, 1865 Washington, D.C.

Lieut. E.L. Lybarger
Co. K, 43rd O V I
My dear Sir

Should this reach you in time, and you intend passing through New York on your way home—and desire to see Miss Jennie Hall formerly of Ohio you may do so by sending her a line soon as you arrive in the city.

Address the note to <u>me</u> and I will see that it reaches her without delay. She desires to see you and explain her long silence that you may have termed "night."

By request

Saddie E. Stuns

P.S. Direct to <u>me</u> No. 810 Park Avenue, Brooklyn , N.Y.
Care Miss E. Alexander
Jennie will be here in a day or two to make a visit. Hope this will reach you in time.

letter 129

June 5, 1865. Postmarked Claysville, Ky.
Lou Riggen. Washington, D.C.

Monday evening June 5th, 1865

Lieut. E.L. Lybarger

Your very welcome letter is answered at my earliest opportunity.
I am glad my last letter was satisfactory as I certainly meant nothing
more nor less in my previous letter than what I told you in my last.

I am also very glad that I have succeeded in making pleasant a
few hours of your last two years of danger, toil and privation. If I
am to believe you are no flatterer, as you say I must, my poor efforts
have been appreciated by you. I am aware of the deficiency of my
letters, they are like their writer—imperfect—but they have fulfilled
their object, that of rendering a little less monotonous the time of a
federal soldier <u>and</u> of bringing interesting replies.

Now, however, <u>peace</u>, beautiful, life—giving, joy inspiring
peace, has <u>returned</u>. I hope and pray to bless the waiting multitudes
who have watched and longed, and fought for it, and as a natural
consequence from our arrangement our correspondence would have
closed, but you propose to continue it. Well, I am aware that, or at
least I expect that I will perhaps weary you with my letters when you
have returned to your home and friends it will be so far different
from what it was in the army, but since you say you wish to continue
and since I am as much interested as ever—I will continue to write.

I expect I ought to quit. As I write, I stop, and think, and I
realize just now, that I am perhaps doing wrong. Then again, what
harm is there in reading your uniformly respectful and agreeable
letters, and answering them? Thus I reason with myself, <u>and</u>
continue to write.

I promised to tell you of Fannie Jerome and Irene L. I did not
write the first note which you received. The young lady who wrote
to you, either could not or would not answer your letter. She insisted
that I should. I was delighted at the idea and wrote the second letter
thinking I would quit when I got ready, <u>but</u> I never <u>got ready</u>! The
letters of course since that have been altogether my own. But for this

mere accident I should I suppose never have had an "unknown correspondent." I was Irene Livingstone but I feared that you and Captain R. would compare letters and discover my identity. Doubtless you <u>would</u> have <u>compared letters</u> indeed, since you would have received them all yourself. Wouldn't that have been funny—I would like so much to see you. I tell you that because you say you were not joking about coming. Should you chance to come, the undersigned would be delighted. I congratulate you sincerely on your return home & happy meeting with friends.

Write soon. Kindly. Lou Riggen

Lest you think this another "hint to quit" I will just tell you now that when I wish to quit I will write quite an <u>elegant</u> farewell.   Lou

$

letter 130

June 6, 1865. Postmarked Loudonville. Christie Blakeley.
A. R.Q.M. 43rd O.V.I. 17th A.C. via New York.

Home, June 6th, 1865

Mr. E.L. Lybarger

Your very kind and welcome letter of May 26th was received last week and read with interest as all "soldier letters" are. Guess we will soon be relieved of the task of writing to the army though it was not an unpleasant one. Don't know as you will stay "down in Dixie" long enough for this to reach you as we have the word that the 43rd is to be mustered out soon. But no matter. Nobody need stay in Dixie land longer than Uncle Sam wants them to to get a letter from me—

But firstly I must tell you how much I prize the flowers you sent me, coming from the place they did. I shall cherish them long in memory of him who gained for us the liberties, the brave of the present generation have had the honor of preserving. I should like much to visit the hallowed spot, but as I <u>cant</u> be a soldier suppose I shall never have that pleasure though I believe all soldiers that might, do not avail themselves of the privilege of looking upon the last resting place of the immortal Washington who <u>fought</u> and <u>won</u> our first great battle in freedom's cause.

The people are all on suspense now and are listening to every whistle of the locomotive to bring back the absent ones. Hope we shall not have to wait long. Your reception at Washington was a grand affair I have no doubt. The papers are full of accounts of the splendor of the day. How thankful every body is for returning peace, but O the sad heart for the "unreturning brave" who are missed now more than ever.

Have not had a letter from brother for several weeks. Suppose he has been thinking he could come home about as soon as the letters and so did not write. But he need not think he will take us by surprise this time for we are expecting him.

But I must not stop to write more just now. Contrary to every expectation I have taken a school again and it is just time to start, board at home this time.

Hoping you will not be disappointed in getting to come home soon.

I remain your friend

C.A.B.

letter 131

June 22, 1865. Postmarked Cynthiana, Ky.
Lou Riggen. Louisville, Ky.

June 22nd, 1865

Lieut. E.L. Lybarger

Your letter was received with the greatest pleasure and I answer it with almost equal pleasure, for I not only like to read your letters, but to answer them.

Those flowers from the grave of Washington I touch them tenderly. I regard them with reverence as my mind reverts to that greatest, best, most glorious man. He has slept peacefully during the years of turmoil and bloodshed, and now that the war is over, these flowers from the tomb of Washington, the noble sublime Washington whose highest ambition was his country's happiness, seem to breathe the very spirit of peace. I shall keep them always in memory of the

Revolutionary Hero, and of the unknown soldier of the late war who sent them to me.

Don't stop at Claysville, because in the first place it is not on or near the railroad, and in the next place, I do not live there. It is my Post Office, that's all. I do not know now where I will be, when you propose to come, as my school is not yet out and I have made no arrangements about where I will spend vacation. I will probably be in Mount Sterling. If I knew just <u>when</u> you expected to come I could tell you more definitely. I know you will think I am the <u>dullest</u>, plain, most unsociable girl you ever saw. My <u>conversational</u> powers are poor. Are you a good talker? I know you will not like your "friend" very much, and wont that be a pity? I am already beginning to feel sorry for myself.

It <u>is</u> "mean" to keep you veterans so long after so much hard fighting. My brother has been writing for the last two months that he expected to be mustered out soon, but still he don't come. It is decidedly vexing.

Friday evening—I have just got home from school. I think I spent just about two hours coming through the woods, for I stopped at every shade I found to look at the depths of shadowy cool green around, and the blue <u>blue</u> sky above, and enjoy my privilege of doing nothing. How I enjoyed being idle! But I don't think it was any harm for I noticed the birds were too lazy to sing and there was not a leaf astir, not a breeze afloat "to cool my burning brow." O! People must always bring in something about their burning brows I believe.—All of which is of course very interesting to you.

Since I commenced this letter I have arrived at the conclusion that I will spend the summer months, at least what remain of them after school is out, with my Cousin near Falmouth because it is a preeminently <u>rural</u> place, and therefore just the place for August, and because the aforesaid Cousin is the best girl in the world. If you write immediately (which you <u>better</u> do) you will direct to Oddville. If not—direct to Falmouth. When you stop at Falmouth any one can direct you to where Rev. H.B. Kavanaugh lives—three or four miles in the country. I mean the place which I shall visit and where you are expected to <u>enjoy</u> your visit and take a <u>fancy</u> to my cousin Anna Poynter. Your friend, Lou Riggen

Monday June 26th—This last is written in a decided hurry—excuse it.

letter 132

June 26, 1865. Bainbridge, Ohio. Rosa Crum. Louisville, Ky.

[Note: Penned note on verso of envelope:
"received June 29/1865."]

Bainbridge, Ohio June 26th/1865

My Dear Cousin

After <u>much long</u> and <u>anxious waiting</u> I received your ever welcome and highly appreciated letter. I was glad to hear you was still well and enjoying yourself so fine. Hope you will have no serious duties to perform any more. Glad you have got as near home as Kentucky. Hope to see you home again. I want to see you so bad. If you come home on leave you must give us a call if possible if not hurry and get home then come down and give us a big long visit. <u>Then perhaps I'll go home with you</u> on a visit.

Father says he thinks it would pay better to buy another farm as <u>half</u> of it Uncle Strawder has already sold. He says for you to go out with him and buy out there and live.

Uncle Elijah has got home from the service, he was to see us last week him and Uncle Harrison, they were well. Uncle Elijah is one of the greatest Union men you ever seen. Got a letter from Cousin Sallie last week, they are all well. She stated her brothers had just got home from Idahoe.

Father is working nine miles from home. He has three large houses to put up down there. They are brick houses but the carpenter work father is doing. The carpenter work of two of them come to $1100 a piece.

I am feeling very much disappointed this evening. I sent to Chillicothe to get me a Photograph album but didn't get it! It was forgotten. I have been waiting a long time for some one to <u>present</u> one to me but alas, I have enough Photos to fill an album but as yet have got none. Edwin I think you might think enough of me to send me one. I would think so much of one from you. I am going to have my negative taken tomorrow and next time I write look out for me. I often come down that way. Went down to Memphis last week and expect to go that way next week again. I got a letter from Louisville the other day (the same evening I got <u>yours</u>) wrote by figures. I am going to send it to you to cipher out. See if you can't read it.

Write soon. from Cousin Rosa

Don't forget to write as soon as you get this. The family all sends their love, of <u>course</u> I do. We had a pleasant rain yesterday, everything looks lovely today. Harvesting is most over. The soldier boys from B___ came home last week, glad to see them.

Don't forget to write soon
and oblige cousin Rosa

letter 133

June 27, 1865. Millwood, Ohio.
Phrone Rogers. Louisville, Ky.

Millwood, June 27th, 1865

Ed. Why don't you answer my letters?

Phrone

letter 134

July 2, 1865. Postmarked Danville, Ohio.
Lib Baker. Louisville, Ky.

Home Lodge, July 2nd, 1865

Lieut. E.L. Lybarger

Your note was duly received and would have been answered immediately but I was so busy preparing for the closing exercises of our school that I could not possibly find time.

Your former epistle was also rec'd and would have been replied to but for two "grand" reasons—one was want of time, the other the brief pages of this letter will not permit me to give you.

With much pleasure do I introduce you to my relatives in Louisville and will guarantee you a cordial reception, but if you are sure of remaining in the city any length of time I would advise you to postpone your call until you hear from me again as two of my cousins are coming to Ohio in a few days and it would doubtless be more pleasant both for you and for them if they were at home. I will write you that you may know when that time will be.

How are you going to spend the <u>fourth</u>? Think you might have done like some of the rest of the boys—got a furlough and spent it with your Ohio friends, though no doubt you will enjoy yourself very well where you are. The citizens of Mt. Vernon and vicinity are intent on having a gay time. I have not decided whether I shall go or not. I am like my friend [?] Mr. Smith, never enjoy myself very well in such large crowds.

By the way I should inform you that I saw that honorable gentleman at Kenyon the other day, the first I had seen of him for a year. He looks as strange and vacant as ever.

Truly your friend
"Lib"

P.S. Don't forget to write.

꠷

letter 135

July 4, 1865. Millwood, Ohio.
M[art?] Hammond. Louisville, Ky.

Millwood, Ohio July 4, 1865

Well Ed.

This is a mighty hot day in this country and an awful big Butternut picnic at the <u>Coves</u>. They came for twenty miles. Some from Fredericktown, Mt. Vernon, Brandon, Warsaw, and almost every place. They are making the biggest of efforts to reorganize their Old Broken rotten Party. They are the Soldiers friends since the War has come about to a close. The Union people have a Grand Soldiers Reception at Mt. Vernon today. Fire Works at night. The Butnuts tried to join and have a big celebration. But when they came together to arrange they could not agree. So each party for its self got up a Fourth of July. Ours is at the Vernon, theirs at the Coves. We heard you were coming home yesterday. The Report is here that the Regement is mustord out. John Turbet got home yesterday from the 121 OVI. He said the 43. will be here soon. The old 65 is gone in they have gone down the River for New Orleans it is a dam Bore they must be dragged about so in funnral march. There will be a nice time when all return to their homes again, then I will be in for a Jubilee that will raise the natives. Your Mother is anxious to see you return and many others almost as much so, give my Respects to all the Boys. We will have a nice Drunk here before ten tonight. Six or Seven Groceries at the Coves to day. They came from Mt. Vernon and other places. Will Hawn & I expect to go to Vernon this evening & have a nice time. Bully for Cox. I will close. Good Bye, hoping to see or hear from you soon.

Yours

M. Hammond

$

letter 136

July 6, 1865. Oddville, Ky. Lou Riggen. Louisville, Ky.

[Note: These two letters were contained in the same envelope, which was postmarked July 11 or 13, 1865, at Cynthiana, Ky.]

Oddville, Ken. July 6th

Lieut. E.L. Lybarger

I have received your letter and am writing immediately to tell you that I am going to Falmouth next week and will, therefore, be at Mr. Kavanaugh's on the 20th. I shall expect you and your friend.

I mentioned my <u>Cousin</u> because I thought after my doleful description of <u>myself</u> you would <u>not</u> come, without some <u>other</u> inducement.

Lou Riggen

Lieut. Lybarger

Your letter of the 2nd came the other day, and surprised as well as disappointed me. I had received your previous letter and answered it, directing as you told me, and was anticipating your visit with any amount of pleasure. I had my best smile and bows in reservation, and was deliberating whether I could talk on that rare and interesting subject, "the weather," or whether I should begin by asking "How is your health?"

Now isn't it too bad to disappoint me in that style. To tell the truth about it I <u>am</u> sorry, but I guess you think I needn't take two pages to tell you what you knew before.

Well, I have answered your little bit of a letter, but don't flatter yourself that I am going to quit just now. I am in a writing mood, though I can't for my life think what subject would interest you most. I will interest myself, and write about the weather. It is raining, the softest, sweetest, most musical of all music, to me is the gentle summer rain. Down it comes, gently, gently, gently, till every blade of grass, every green leaf, every thirsting flower, is "dripping with coolness." I love to listen to its sweet patter and dream, it brings with it a delicious sadness. I love it to drizzle cold and chill on a gloomy November day, and hear it dash and pour in the wild tempest. The rain, the rain it makes me happy.

I <u>know</u> you are thinking "<u>such</u> a poor letter." O yes you are, you needn't deny it, and I am thinking so too. Tell me in your next whether you like to hear it rain or not, and I'll know whether or not there is just the least bit of interest in this.

Direct to Falmouth.

Lou Riggen

letter 137

*July 7, 1865. Postmarked Cynthiana, Ky.
Sallie Anderson. Millwood, Ohio*

*[Note: This letter is written on stained and crumpled paper,
in a stained and torn envelope.]*

There is one indeed, that loves you well
If you wish to know who it is you may know
Search these lines they in silence do tell
I confess the initials do show

> Your Cousin
> Sallie Anderson
> Fort Wayne, Indiana

letter 138

July 8, 1865. Danville, Ohio. A. E. Baker. R.Q.M. 43d O.V.V.I.

Danville, Ohio July 8th, 1865

Lieut. Lybarger

I have learned that the 43d is soon to be disbanded, if so call on Aunt at your earliest convenience.

Cousin "Charley" will not come to Ohio for several weeks yet, his sister is here.

> Yours in haste,
> Lib Baker

P.S. I take it for granted you have rec'd the letter I wrote you several days ago.

> A.E.B.

$

letter 139

August 14, 1865. Postmarked Cynthiana, Ky.
Lou Riggen. Millwood, Ohio

Oddville, Ken. August 14th

Lieut. E.L. Lybarger

Your letter was forwarded to me from Falmouth as I left there sooner than I at first intended. You write "for the purpose of receiving my congratulations on your return home." I should think your happiness on returning home would be so <u>exquisite</u> that all congratulations would be dull and common-place, but for the fact that you say you are lonesome. I always thought that home was the last place on earth at which any one could become lonesome, but I write you this brief note for the purpose of having a returned soldier who has been longing for the pleasures of home tell me how lonesome he is after his arrival there.

If you think it will be worth your while to come, now that you will have no opportunity of falling in love with my cousin, and becoming the hero of a thrilling romance, you will come to Oddville —that is, if I remain here, and I'll tell you in my next whether I will or not, and where I'll be.

Respectfully
Lou Riggen

$

letter 140

August 26, 1865. Louisville, Ky. Mollie B. Millwood, Ohio.

Louisville, Kentucky Aug. 26th, 1865

Mr. Lybarger

I would say that I was surprised and I may say agreeably so when I received your letter for I had never flattered my self with the idea that when you again enjoyed the pleasure of being with so many old friends and relatives from whom you have been so long parted that you would give one thought to your friends here—(and especially me) don't I feel flattered though.

Just seven weeks ago today since you left Louisville though time has past very pleasantly and I have been having a very gay time. When I think of it I can't hardly realize that it has been the short time of two months, for it seems almost one long year to me, and Lonlie. I guess you remember the fuss we made when we bid you good bye, that was nothing compared with the crying after you were gone, in short we like to grieved ourselves to death.

How did you enjoy your trip especially so far as Cinnettie. I imagine you had a gay time, if Lonlie and I didn't have the pleasure of going at that time, though I don't suppose you enjoyed your self so much on the way home as you did after being there a while. Oh how did you spend the time on the day of the excursion? Rather pleasantly I hope, though I suspect not (because the <u>girls annoyed you too much</u>), the poor gentlemen are to be pithed.

Well would you believe it I haven't played cards since I played with you. I know I could not enjoy the game if I were to play thinking of the last time I played, not so much of the time, but of the partner.

I saw Capt. Davis in town not long since he on his way, I don't know where any way, he said some body was going to be married. I am looking for the card every day. Lonlie is now in Cinn . . . she promised to send you news from there.

Col. Parks has visited our city once since he left, paid <u>particular</u> attention to Miss Loncie. Mrs. Cord would send her love if she knew that I were going to write. My respects to Col. Rhoades should you see him and my undying love to Doctor Anderson.

With much respect
Mollie B.

<u>I will make the promise.</u>

letter 141

September 11, 1865. Bainbridge, Ohio.
Rosa Crum. Millwood, Ohio.

Bainbridge, Ross Co. Ohio Sept. 11th, 1865

Dear Cousin,

I believe this morning to be a fitting time for <u>one</u> friend to converse with <u>another</u>, through the silent medium of the pen. Arose from my couch just at the break of day for the purpose of writing you in answer to your very <u>very</u> welcome missive of the 3rd inst. which came to hand on the 8th. I read it with great interest and was glad to hear you were well. Hope you may ever continue to enjoy good health. Mine is excellent. School commences this morning and I will have to stop writing until evening.

Monday evening. I will try to finish my letter this evening though I dont know how well I will succeed as my time is very precious and I have my Latin lesson to learn yet to night. I <u>do</u> <u>not</u> know yet what new studies I will take up but think Botany will be one. Dont you think that would be a nice study for me. I think the winter will close my schooling at Bainbridge and I must improve my time to every advantage. I think of teaching when I go out west. I always had a desire to be a school teacher. I think it would be very pleasant occupation. I will study hard and learn all I can that I may be the better prepared.

Was down to Uncle Elijahs and Harrisons last week all week putting up <u>peaches</u> while we was at Uncle Harrisons. They had a great many peaches this season. But they are about gone. Oh! dear! how warm it is this evening. There appears to be no air at all stirring this evening it is very close. Corn crops are very favorable here this year. The talk is that corn will be twenty cents per bushel.

Received a letter from Cousin Sallie Foulk this evening. They were all well. Uncle Strawder started for Mo. last Monday. I suppose he is at his place of destination ere this. Oh dear I am so warm (after walking from school) I can hardly write I tell you but we have a cross teacher. The boys call him Sideboards. I think you might spend a little time to come and see your <u>best</u> friend. I must cut my communication short as I have six letter to answer and dont know when I'll get them finished for evening and mornings is all the time I have to write letters. Excuse brevity, also all errors and by making an early reply you will greatly accommodate your unworthy Cousin

Rosa

My kind regards to all
Not forgetting my best wishes is always with you,

Rosa

$

letter 142

September 19, 1865. Mount Vernon, Ohio.
Phrone Rogers. Spring Mountain, Ohio.

Mount Vernon, Sep. 19th
Dearest Ed

Notwithstanding all your coldness I address you the same as I always have done. Since it seems you do not believe anything that I have said to you I see no reason why I should tell you the truth. I am aware that I have not much mind, am very changeable, fickle and not at all reliable. But indeed I would like to have credit for what I <u>am</u> and what I <u>do</u>. I had thought you certainly had a little sympathy for one. I find I am either mistaken or else you do not realize my feelings. I am so astonished at your letter that I know not what to say in reply to it. As much reason as you may have for believing the reports concerning my flirtation with Louis Bedellen. They are <u>lies</u>. I have not enough charity for the one or ones that informed you of your so-called <u>facts</u> to say or even think that they were mistaken. My opinion is that a thing of that kind can not be manufactured without something to go on and be anything else than a lie. I have neither seen or heard from Louis Bedellen. You may believe or disbelieve me—just as you please. Now since you need a few facts impressed upon your mind I will just mention another thing. If I wanted to make love to "Charlie" dont flatter yourself that I should insult your preference or opinion about it. I assure you should not do anything of the kind. Whilst I admire Charles mind and think him agreeable and pleasant I am not changed nor was I won by a smile and a few flattering words. You know that nothing compelled me to love you any more than you were compelled to love me. I know I love you for yourself alone and supposed my love was returned the same way. You are not thinking as much of how short months from this time as I am I fear. While it has been (and is) a pleasant (home) anticipation you are making it a doubtful realization. We will now be obliged to give this unpleasant subject up <u>forever</u>. I assure you it will never again be discussed by me. I have made extra efforts to have you trust me and if you will not <u>now</u> I can do no more.

Perhaps you would like to know something about the Fair. I think it was better this year than last. They had . . . for dancing and a very good String Band to play. Besides this there were two Brass Bands. You might not think it any better on this account as you care nothing for music whilst I am particularly fond of it. The fair lasted four days on account of bad weather. I did not attend any day except Wednesday afternoon about two hours time and Amanda went with me. Jim Israel came home last Monday morning a week ago and started back to Chicago yesterday afternoon. He is looking better than I ever saw him. I stayed with Vine last week.

. I am at Jossies now sitting upstairs by the window writing to unworthy Ed. Dont you think me simple for it. I seen our friend Jake Baker last week. He looked about so so without much of a change in his personal appearance. I have been out but very little since I came here. I promised Jake to go around his sisters but did not go. Joss is declining slowly. I am so distressed about her. Nannie has not been well for about two weeks but is a little better now. I am going home tomorrow morning, should have gone today if it had [not] rained so much. I want Mother to come up and stay with Joss as much as she can. I think she will not be with us long. I wish you could be at home two or three days when you come.

I think I have filled your <u>order</u> by writing you a long letter. I only received it about an hour ago. Give me credit for my promptness if you please. I will not request an answer as that would not be so amiable under the circunstances.

I remain as ever your loving Phrone.

letter 143

October 14, 1865. Postmarked Cynthiana, Ky.
Lou Riggen. Millwood, Ohio.

Claysville, Ken. Oct. 14th/65

Lieut. E.L. Lybarger

Now you are going to get married are you? and I am to lose my correspondent. Isn't that vexing? That is to <u>me</u>, of course it isn't to you. I have the magnamimity however, to hope "your girl" will not treat you so badly as to fall in love with some one else, thereby preventing a consummation so devoutly to be wished. I would be sorry to know that you were suffering the pangs of unrequited love, so feelingly portrayed by novel writers. You would be found tearing wildly at your hair wouldn't you, placing your hand theatrically on your heart to still its fearful throbbings, gazing into some pond with fell intent, like Sir Arthur Waldegrave in the Ledger. O, <u>don't</u>. I don't intend to make my "ever interesting letters any longer than yours if you please." <u>Ahem</u>!

It becomes my painful duty to inform you that as I can think of no questions to ask just now and as writing to me is "dull" (I'm so sorry), and above all as I really suppose you are going to marry I say it becomes my painful duty to inform you that this is the last letter you will recieve from Miss Lou P. Riggen. Astounding intelligence! "Interest nowhere, correspondence ceases—ah me—Good bye." "I thank you for your kind attention."

"In the world's broad field of battle" I hope you will always be successful. Imagine a smile—and Good bye.   Lou Riggen

letter 144

November 26, 1865. Bainbridge, Ohio.
Rosa Crum. Millwood, Ohio.

Bainbridge, O., Nov. 26th/65

Dear Cousin Edwin

After waiting <u>very</u> patiently <u>so long</u> a time your welcome favor
has at last been received. I had begun to conclude you had forgotten
there was such a person as I in existence as I never heard from
you anymore. Let me see, It's been almost three months since I
heard from you, hasn't it? Well I will not do as you did and delay
answering so long, but will proceed immediately to acknowledge the
receipt of your welcome favor which I received Friday evening. Was
glad to hear that you were all well. Hope Aunt Amelia is <u>entirely</u>
restored to health by this time. Uncle Elijah and Harrison were to
see us last week. Uncle Harrison has almost recovered from the
<u>wound</u> he received (or did I ever tell you about it?) About six weeks
ago whilst at Uncle Elijah's house in Northunion he was standing on
the grocery porch he was introduced to <u>Ned Henes</u> the Copperhead
who piloted Morgan through Ohio. He remarked when he extended
his hand that he believed he did not care about extending very great
friendship towards Mr. Henes as he believed he was the man, as I
have said above, whereupon <u>another</u> butternut slipped up behind
Uncle Harrison, struck him under the left arm with a scythe blade
which took effect cutting off 3 of his ribs.

Cousin John Crum is here now, he is sitting here reading some
of my school books, he has only been home from the army about 5
weeks. He sends his kind regards to you and says would like to hear
from you. Father and Uncle Elijah and Harrison were talking about
that farm in Mo. wondering what condition it was in &ce. Strawder
has sold his <u>share</u> so he says <u>but</u> I am laboring under the impression
that he sold the whole. He bought him a fine improved farm of 200
acres two miles from Macon City. Where did he get the money from
if he did not sell all the farm. Father thinks some one ought to go
out and see about it. He says he will go if the rest will help pay the

expenses, or if some of the rest will go he will pay his share of the expenses. What do you think about it? When you write let us know. I don't know what Father would have me say concerning the farm as he is away at work & I don't know much about it myself. You can expand what I have said and make as much out of it as you can for indeed I can't.

You wanted to know about Aunt Sarah. She is living with Strain again. I don't know how they are getting along. She was down to see us week before last, brought her <u>four</u> children with her. We received a letter from Uncle William not long since. They were all well. Please write soon and let us know what you have to say concerning the farm. Answer soon. We are all well. I will close hoping to hear from you soon.

I remain

Rosa

$

letter 145

December 11, 1865. Bainbridge, Ohio.
Rosa Crum. Millwood, Ohio.

Bainbridge, Ohio, Dec. 11th, 1865

My Dear Cousin

Always prompt to do my duty I am seated again for the purpose of talking to you a few moments through the silent medium of the pen, but how well I will succeed I cannot say for I cannot get the words to come down through my arm as well as I can my mouth. I suppose though it's best as it is, for if I were with you so that I could converse verbally I would no doubt tire you very much with my talk, but as I am very tired myself this evening I do not feel like writing very much. I have been sewing ever since day light and have at least accomplished my task, which was a pair of pants. Father says he will write to you concerning that Mo. land.

Edwin I almost envy you to think you are teaching school. I wish I was there to help you. I would then be in the occupation I have so long desired. It seems to me nothing would be so pleasant as to be a school maam. But Father does not desire me to commence teaching while so young. I know you have nice times at school. I expect all the girls have fall in love with you. We had a young man for our principal last year, nearly all the large girls was in love with him.

Well Edwin I will tell you Miss Jennie Morrow is married and has gone to Mo. to live. Tomorrow night is our Mite Society. Can't you call over and I will find you a nice and handsome young lady for a partner. Enough of my foolishness, give my love to Aunt and Elijahs family. Oh yes, by the way, I came pretty near forgetting to give you Uncle Williams' address. William E. Crum, Greenwood, Franklin County, Kansas. I have written so much foolishness I had better stop for I know this letter has been growing irksome to you long ere this. From your loving Cousin. Don't forget to write soon.

Rosa

Goodnight, pleasant dreams to you Edwin, say I

Rosa

I received your long letter last Wednesday evening. You know I always appreciate them.

1866 LETTERS

letter 146

January 30, 1866. Postmarked Mt. Vernon.
Phrone Rogers. Millwood, Ohio.

School House, Jan. 30th

Dearest Ed

I am going to write you for the sake of hearing from you. I never remember of being half so lonely in my life. I cryed this morning before I was out of bed and all the way to school. I feel a little better now. I have felt well enough since I came here and have had no trouble with my school. I never had an easier school to govern. I do not believe I can live here two weeks before going home. I had twenty-one scholars yesterday and eighteen today.

Wednesday. Here I am writing by candlelight. I am so sleepy that I almost wish myself dead, or at home. I was out to spelling school last night at Ellen Lybarger's school. Had a real nice sled ride. The night was beautiful. But what did I care about that, I had "noone to love." I find the people very good. The girls are more intelligent than any you will meet at your school and smarter than the majority at Millwood and are all good looking. I have not seen an ugly girl yet. But expect to see Miller's girls tonight. I am invited over there to spend the evening.

I am carrying that old bachelor's watch. What do you think of it? I have not enjoyed this morning yet, but have felt like it mightily. I have not told you why I did not finish this note. Yesterday I had no time. This morning Mr. Adrian is going to Mt. Vernon. I wanted to send with him. There was no ink about the house I thought therefore to finish with pencil. You can excuse if you please and if you do not I'll not feel offended. Write me very soon or I'll die.

Lovingly, Phrone

P.S. Answer on Saturday before the mail goes out and I'll get it on Tuesday.

letter 147

February 11, 1866. Claysville, Ky. Lou Riggen. Millwood, Ohio.

*[Note: This letter is torn on both sides and the signature
is ditto marks, which the editor reads to be Lou Riggen.
There is no envelope.]*

Claysville, Ky.

Lieut. E.L. Lybarger

I cannot drive from my mind the haunting anxiety . . . have
possession of . . . letters I sent you.

Therefore, will you . . . the kindness to . . . them, if they . . . in
existence, and <u>particularly</u> and <u>especially</u> and <u>certainly, the
photograph</u>.

Very respectfully

" " " " " " "

letter 148

*February 14, 1866. Postmarked Martinsburg, Ohio.
Phrone Rogers. Millwood, Ohio.*

School Room, Feb. 14, 1866

"Darling Ed—

I arrived safely at Mr. Adrian's before dark. I retired about
9 o'clock. Slept soundly without dreaming any. When I awoke I did
not feel homesick. Have not cried any since the last time, nor felt like
it. I am boarding at Mr. Reaghs this week. They are very pleasant
people and are members of the Presbyterian church. You wanted
to know whether the Martinsburg school were going to give an
exhibition. They are. In three or four weeks I will be able to tell you
all about it when I see you. I will expect a letter from you tomorrow.

If I am disappointed I shall do something desperately bad. I want you to write to me next Tuesday. I may not get home next week. I will not go home unless someone comes after me on Friday evening. The girls are singing "Home, Home, can I forget thee." I makes me feel a little blue. I get so tired of the noise. I do not feel as if I could live another minute.

Mr. Green closed his writing school last night. I was not feeling very well and did not go. I did not have an opportunity of telling him you wnted him to go over to see you. Don't suppose I shall see him again unless he should succeed in getting another school which I think a little doubtful. Tomorrow evening I expect to spend the evening at Mr. Vance's. I do not know whether I will have a pleasant time or not. I am not acquainted with them.

Why did you not go up to Mrs. Rogers last Sunday as you promised to do. Mother said you should not go away without your breakfast again. Said it was very unhealthy to travel before eating. I am real mad at you for not coming up to dinner. You need not make up an excuse, just tell the truth about it. It is now school time and I will close as I want to send this to the P.O. by Kate Harned [Hand?] I had not much to say to you but thought I must write you a Valentine.

With much love as ever. Phrone

letter 149

March 11, 1866. Postmarked Cynthiana, Ky.
Lou Riggen. Millwood, Ohio.

Claysville, Ken. March 11th, 66

Lieut. E.L. Lybarger

I did think from you letter that you perhaps intended to commit matrimony, but as I do not consider that a crime by any means, I may as well confess that <u>that</u> was not my only reason for wishing to quit so suddenly. There was another point in your letter from which I inferred, well, no matter what. I will bring no more charges. Your last letter dispelled the suspicion which lurked in my mind and which I really believe was an injustice to yourself. Do I not give sufficient proof of this in writing again? I know you think I am gifted with a most fertile imagination to be able to wrest so many unheard of and unthought of ideas from your very good letters, but the truth is, I am sometimes blessed (?) with a rather too morbid temperament I suppose. _____ _____ _____ _____ _____ _____

I was never more astonished than by your failure to send the letters. True, they being such very interesting specimens of literature you are naturally <u>anxious</u> to retain them, but then when you confess that you <u>ought</u> by all means to return them you display a great lack of moral firmness in thus letting your <u>inclination</u> run away with your <u>duty</u>. But considering the temptation is so <u>very</u> great I cannot but consider this a pardonable error. Am not I being an impartial judge, very magnanimous? Why don't you confess that the letters and photo were burnt up on or before the day you received the letter in which I informed you that I would write no more letters. And speaking of the sublime declaration I then made, and looking at this letter which I am deliberately writing reminds me of what a jewel <u>Consistency</u> is said to be.

I hope you told your friend that my letters were just as interesting as usual.

Hoping you will "excuse all bad writing and mistakes" I will close. Have the goodness to send another letter soon to

Your friend
Lou Riggen

letter 150

March 19, 1866. Postmarked Mt. Vernon, Ohio.
Phrone Rogers. Millwood, Ohio.

At Mr. Pumphreys, Sabbath eve., March 19th, 1866
My friend Ed

Since you have advised me not use other (or rather different terms) I am not going to deny receiving a letter from you. What possessed you to think that I would do so? I so very rarely received a letter from you, that when I do I am both ready and willing to acknowledge it. What has come over the spirit of your dreams that you have suddenly grown <u>so cool</u> I do not pretend to <u>understand</u> you. You say you can reply to this if you choose. If you do not there will be no offence given or <u>at least</u> taken. All I hope is that you will not be offended because I have written. I assure you no harm is <u>intended</u>. I suppose I will be obliged to be very careful what I say to you as well as what I write. I am in hope you may yet find some one that will suit your very fastidious taste. While you are trying to injure my feelings you are not hurting any one else.

Nine more <u>weary days</u> and I'll be done teaching. And who knows but what forever. <u>Something good</u> might happen to me yet. O I am so lonely tonight that I want to cease to exist a month and see I would not enjoy life better. I was out to church today. There was Dunkard meeting at Union Grove. It was the first time I ever attended one of their meetings. As the weather has somewhat moderated I suppose you will attend the exhibition at D. Be very careful not to leave the house if the weather is not extremely fine. You might get a cold. I'm so glad that I'm not so delicate as some of my acquaintances. I guess that I am done. I have nothing to tell you. I do not hear anything only when I go home that could interest you.

Good night, darling & except much love from

Phrone

How disgusting I hear you say.
P.S. Tell Mother that I am well and getting along nicely with my school.

letter 151

March 23, 1866. Fredericktown, Ohio.
Ella Gamble. Millwood, Ohio.

Fredericktown, Ohio, March 23d, 1866

Edwin L. Lybarger
Dear Sir:

Your note of the 16th is at hand—while I am not displeased at the liberty you have taken and can say that the pleasure of your company will prove acceptable two weeks from next Saturday evening at home. I shall go home on Friday, that is if I can get any conveyance, and if not I will inform you.

I shall be happy to have you call at my boarding place some Sunday and get acquainted with the folks up here. If these arrangements do not suit you please let me know. I will wait your answer with some anxiety and hope you may reply at your earliest convenience.

I am, Sir, with true esteem

Yours sincerely
Ella Gamble

$

letter 152

April 15, 1866. Bainbridge, Ohio. Rosa Crum. Millwood, Ohio

Bainbridge, pr. 15th/1866

Dear Cousin Edwin

I received your <u>very</u> welcome letter some time since but have neglected to answer it until this late day. I was scolding you the last time I wrote about your negligence, now you have a chance to retaliate but I will ask you to forgive me this once. I have been very busy this spring. I have a great deal of sewing to do and I occupy the greater part of my time in that way.

The boys have quit school. Father thought they were not learning anything and he has placed them under my instruction to see what I can do for them. Will try to learn them all I can and will be delighted in doing so, but it is quite an undertaking I assure you; they would rather play than be kept in the house at their books. We had such a <u>poor excuse</u> of a teacher this term for our principal he wasent a bit account. Oh! how I would be delighted could it only be so. I have longed to come to your house this good while but all in vain. Well I can't expect it until the <u>right time</u> comes. I am placed in a situation that is very confining. I am all Father has to look to and suppose will have to stay home a while longer. He promised me I should visit you this fall if nothing presented, how happy I will be.

Father says no more about going to Mo. next month. He will write to you as soon as he hears from Uncle Elijah. I got a letter from Uncle Harrison's John last week. He stated they were all well and said he was coming soon. Wanted me to come down there and teach school for them & s. John is a very smart young man <u>considering</u> everything his training education & s. & c.

Father's foot is about well, still hurts him a little.

Edwin can't you come and see us. I felt real <u>angry</u> to think we had such bad weather at the time you had a notion of coming down. If you go to Mo. be sure and come this way, we will all be glad to see you. Now don't forget, it won't be out of the way.

Well <u>really</u> I don't know what to write about. I have written three pages and nothing after all but foolishness. If you were acquainted in B. I might tell you something about the weddings that would interest you, about the deaths, fires, and the wedding that <u>is to be</u> before many days. There were two fires last week, one dwelling house and one Tanery the loss of the one about $8000, three young ladies died in one afternoon, one was to be married the Sunday before she died, but she took sick and thus—Well this don't interest you and as I have another letter that <u>must</u> be written I must close this and make haste as it is almost supper time. Excuse bad penmanship & as I am always in a hury Don't forget to write soon to your loving Cousin

Rosa

P.S. forgot just what I wanted to say. Give my love to Aunt <u>Amelia</u>, Elijahs family, and tell them I would like to see them all. Father send his respects to you all. Lovingly

Cousin Rosa

Write soon

$

letter 153

May 22, 1866. Postmarked Millwood, Ohio.
Phrone Rogers. Mt. Vernon, Ohio.

Schoolroom, Monday morning

Dearest Ed.

You cannot imagine how glad I was to hear from you. But I am going to find fault with you. You said you wrote to me only to fulfill your promise. Really you are very kind to even <u>remember</u> your promise—if that be all, you certainly deserve many thanks. I shall wait however till you come home before I bestow them. I came to school early this morning so that I could drop you a line. I did so too for the <u>pleasure</u> of it and not because of any <u>promise</u> to write. I passed yesterday the best I could without you. I was lonesome all day wanting for something or <u>somebody</u> I do not know which. I was out to the M.E. Church in the morning. You know how much I enjoy hearing Mr. Webster. Mother and I were down to your mothers in the afternoon. We went home about six oclock and ate supper and then retired for the night. Charlotte and John were at church. Mr. Hammond invited them home with him which invitation I <u>suppose</u> they gladly accepted. The looked <u>very fine</u> indeed. I am getting along nicely with my school, have had no more trouble. Hesses [?] <u>brats</u> came back. I was not particularly pleased or displeased about it. I suppose you had a pleasant time yesterday with your friend Col. R____ You & <u>Mast</u> were out together. I wish you would come home Friday. I cannot wait untill Saturday to see you. <u>Do come</u>. Please go and see Joss before you come home. Mother has been real uneasy about her. She promised to write us a few lines by

Saturday mail but failed to do so, on some account & Mother thought perhaps she was sick was the reason. Please bring me a pack of envelopes. Some of those narrow white ones. I will be much obliged.

It is school time and I must close. I believe I have written quite as much as I should if I had had more time. Hoping to see you soon, I remain your loving friend　　　Phrone.

letter 154

June 9, 1866. Postmarked Fredericktown, Ohio.
Ella Gamble. Mt. Vernon, Ohio.

W . . . lnr School House, June 9th, 1866

Mr. Lybarger
Sir:

Your note of the 2d reached me duly—and hasten to reply. I am sorry to say that I cannot fulfill my arrangements and can get no opportunity of coming home. You will please excuse me and I will therefore suggest for the present the propriety of your calling on me at my Uncles next Sunday. Then perhaps we can . . . make arrangements a little more convenient. I know I could converse a few hours with you very pleasantly, but will let time and circumstances determine if it be best for us to assume more serious relations to one another than have hitherfore existed. Hoping to see you soon—I am, Sir, with true esteem

Yours sincerely
Ella Gamble

letter 155

July 8, 1866. Claysville, Ky. Lou Riggen. Millwood, Ohio.

Claysville, Ky. July 8th, '66

Lieut. E.L. Lybarger

I hasten to answer your generous letter of June 29th. To explain to you the reason for my style of writing which you so extensively quote, and also for a previous letter would not be at all impossible. But I fear it would all amount to nothing more than this, that your correspondent is morbidly sensitive on some subjects, one of which is unknown correspondence. I admit that it <u>would</u> be extremely ridiculous to "make an unknown enemy of an unknown friend."

You are under no "obligations to me," that I know of, for anything but keeping that old photograph, and your last letter almost cancelled that. I'm glad I thought of the photo. I intended to tell you to "attribute to me <u>only</u> a modicum of common sense," but I won't do it now. I shall reserve the privilege of saying a great many things to balance against that.

Glad to hear that Col. Rhodes remembers his would-be correspondent.

Respectfully
Lou P. Riggen

letter 156

July 8, 1866. No postmark.
Phrone Rogers. Spring Mountain, Ohio

Home, July 8th Monday evening

My Darling Pet

Lizzie Millis will go to Mr. Bakers tomorrow. As I'll have an opportunity of droping you a line I do not know as I have anything to say more that that. I have not been very well since I came from Bakers, picking cherries about finished me. I almost died with the <u>blues</u> that night you went home. Mother wants you to bring her a ham of meat if you have any. Bring Nannie a pair of those little kidd Moroco shoes No. 4. Mother says for you to act the man and not come for me till a week from next Sunday (Do as you please) If this writing is course you must not blame the writer but the moon, it does not give very much light. I am writing on the stone step in the moonlight. With much love and many kisses for my darling—Phrone.

$

letter 157

July 28, 1866. Bainbridge, Ohio.
Rosa Crum. Millwood, Ohio.

Bainbridge, O. July 28th/66

My Dear Cousin

I hail this as the earliest opportunity of acknowledging the receipt of your <u>very</u> welcome letter which I recieved last week. It had been so long since I had heard from you that I had begun to conclude that you had forgotten me but was glad to learn that the long silence was caused by other reasons. You spoke about coming to see us and said you would come about any time the railroad run through our town. I will be glad when that happens if it will be the means of <u>starting you</u> down this way.

You asked me if I had seen Mr. Green (I believe that was his name) It has been some time since he was here, he gave Father that letter of introduction sent by you. He called down to see us and of course we were glad to make the acquaintance of one of your intimate friends. I liked the appearance of Mr. Green <u>very</u> much.

He looks like a young man of good <u>morals</u> and is very interesting in his conversation. Why did you not come along with him?

I received a letter from Cousin Sallie last week, they were all well. She stated that her Pa and Ma had been on a visit down to Uncle Strawders. They left them all in good health. Yes, Uncle Harrison and Aunt Sarah have sold their share of the Mo. farm. I think it time you and father were attending to <u>yours</u> if you are ever going to. Father says he doesent care whether he ever get a cent or not. He wants to be too independent. He says he always has got along with out my help and he can yet but that isent my turn I am for having my share with the rest I would have it if it was but <u>fifty cents</u>. Father says bet you that Uncle Strawder says he got one hundred dollars on shares and the man that bought said he would buy the other shares and $110.00 the same as he gave Uncle Strawder. You see one tells one thing and the other another. There is no telling what Strawder <u>got</u>.

As this is Monday evening and as I have done a large washing today and feel so tired I will close. I did not get to finish this yesterday. Edwin, be sure and come to see us this fall. We have been canning blackberries and making jam for the last three weeks so will have plenty this winter. My love to all, don't forget yourself. Excuse brevity & haste.

Yours affectionately
Rosa Crum

Write soon

⚕

letter 158

August 8th, 1866. Spring Hill, Mo.
Sallie A Foulk. Millwood, Ohio.

Spring hill, Mo. Aug. 8th / 66

My Dear Cousin

It is with much pleasure that I am now writing to you.

I wrote to you when you was in the Army & received no answer but I learned from one you had written to Ma that you did not receive it—this leaves us all enjoying good helth except Ma, she has been puny for some time but she is now recovering. I trust this will find you enjoying good helth.

I had my photograph taken & distributed among my relatives & friends but I will have them taken again & you shall have one.

Women's Letters to Edwin Lewis Lybarger

341

Brother Will talks of going back to Ohio this fall on a visit if he does I will accompany him & then we will see if you will be so kind as to come home with us.

Well Cousin I feel very pious this evening & I hardly know how to write. I have been attending Meeting all weeak. Why should I feel otherwise. Dansing has been banished from my mind and will remain so until I receive another ball ticket. You see I am determined to remain a sinner. Excuse my nonsence.

I received a letter from Brother John a few days ago. He is well & doing well. We had a large celebration here the 4th. We also had quite a nice time. Crops look fine in this part of the country notwithstanding we are needing rain very badly at present. There will be abundance of fruit in our neighborhood this season. Our orchard is just beginning to bare.

Some of my lady friends are very anxious to see you, do not delay to long in making your appearance. Oh you will love them—

Well I will close, hoping to hear from you soon. Give my respects to my Dear Aunt & receive a large portion yourself.

Your Obedient Cousin

Sallie A. Foulk

P.S. Ma requested me to tell you that she could not inform you anything about the township range &c of the farm in Macon but if you cant get word she will write to Uncle Strawder & then let you know.

letter 159

October 11, 1866. Claysville, Ky.
Lou Riggen. Spring Mountain, Ohio.

Claysville, Ken. Oct. 11th /66

Lieut. E.L. Lybarger
Having recovered in some measure from my late disappointment (in not going to Missouri) I think I can perhaps answer your letter. It

was forwarded to this place from Falmouth as I did not go there. Will not go to Missouri before next summer if then. I suppose you have expected two or three letters from me by this time but as I aint going to Missouri I have nothing else of <u>vast</u> importance to write especially when you wont come after so lengthy an invitation.

Your taste is quite orthodox in regard to dress, with this exception. Young gentlemen shouldn't dress to please the ladies, for it is a waste of time and talent as the ladies are so deeply absorbed in their own appearance that they never think of other people's dress.

I can't write tonight and will quit trying. I will try and restrain my volubility long enough to receive your next two letters. I haven't seen that photo.   Truly, Lou Riggen
Direct as usual.

$

letter 160

October 19, 1866. Postmarked Millwood, Ohio.
Phrone Rogers. Spring Mountain, Ohio.

Home, Oct. 19th, 1866

"Thou dearest one of all the earth to me,"

You perceive a sentence in one of my songs. It helped me express a thought. I hope you will not imagine me in earnest. You know that is not my style of writing to you. I suppose you are wondering why I don't say something. I will tell you. I know nothing about anyone except myself. I know you are tired of hearing the same old story. I'll tell you a new one I guess this time. I don't love you any at all. You gave me the Dyphthera. I never had it so badly in my life. I have been in the house ever since you left and part of the time in bed. I have had my throat burnt out six or seven times. I guess I will get along very well now if I do not get cold by going out. I wanted to go and see Joss tomorrow. I do not know whether the Dr. will agree to it or not. I hope these pleasant days will last a while longer. I don't like the idea of losing all this pleasant weather (just on your account too) I think you ought to suffer a little for me to reward me for what I am doing for you. I want you to come over a week from tomorrow. This has been the longest, loneliest week that I ever experienced. I cried once or twice but found it did no good and concluded to quit it. Mrs. Israel was down this week. Joss was about the same as when we saw her. I received a letter from Mrs. Shaw, she was so disappointed because I did not visit her when I expected to. She was expecting her neice Miss Russell from New York. She thought we would have enjoyed a visit together & I know we could. I liked the looks of her picture. But perhaps you would have fallen in love with her then what about <u>poor me</u>? Tell your Mother I did not feel well the morning she left and did not get up early enough to see her off. I did not find out untill noon what was the matter with me. Was she much frightened when crossing the river? I was afraid she would be. I haven't written you anything at all but I don't care a fig if I have not. I want you to write me every mail if you don't I'll die then I guess you won't have any naughty Phrone. Inclosed please find a kiss if you can. I won't be mad at you if you answer this letter verbally. Give my love to your mother & believe me ever your affect

Phrone

§

letter 161

November 2, 1866. Amity, Ohio.
A. E. Baker. Spring Mountain, Ohio.

Amity, Ohio, Nov. 2d, 1866

Friend Lybarger
 It has been said that "there is no friendship in the world." But in defiance of that bold and sweeping declaration I have taken the liberty to address you as my friend, and hope that I may ever have the pleasure of remembering you as much for—

> How much to be prized and esteemed as a friend
> On whom we can always safely depend.
> Our joys when estended will always increase.
> And griefs when divided are hushed into peace.

What practical affirmation! I fear I shall not be able to write anything more. But however will try—

Yours of Oct. 1st was duly received (as letter writers always say) and its contents perused, with no little degree of interest I assure you. Will not appologize for not acknowledging it soon[er] for it is certainly wonderful that I write at all—"without an invitation." Shall not do so again so you can congratulate yourself upon that news.

Was indeed sorry to hear of your woe-begone state of mind. But of what is the use of you talking thus when you know very well that you occupy the first place in that certain person's affections and what more need one desire?

Besides even it had been true that you was supplanted by another, remember that hearts are not always trumps: though really I have no room to talk, for although I was convalessing I most unfortunately took a relapse, and of course am now worse than ever.

I admire your choice of the S.M. girls very much. Miss Moore is certainly a very good girl. By the way, she is a sister to Captain M.____ an old flame of mine.

I have not attended any apple cuttings this fall although I have been invited to quite a number. Was at a wedding in Amity several weeks ago and had the honor of being bride's maid. Had a very nice time indeed. The only thing that marred my happiness was that I had to be only second best.

My school closes on next Friday and taking it all together, I have had a very pleasant term. Would remain during the winter as the people seem to want a school—if it would not interfere too much with some other arrangements I have made. Would like very much to visit your "beautiful, romantic" village during vacation, but as I have partially promised to spend my vacation with my dear friend in Ashland County do not expect I "shall be able to do so."

I heard the question asked the other day whether Morrow County was a Slave State. 'Tis strange indeed that Mr. R____ didn't visit you during September. How unlike him to disappoint!

Don't forget that you are to tell me four weeks before you are to be married. I will not believe all the reports I hear.

With much respect,
A.E.B.

letter 162

November 12, 1866. Postmarked Walhonding, Ohio.
Ella Gamble. Spring Mountain, Ohio.

At Home, Sunday evening Nov. 12th, 1866

My Friend

If you will allow me to call [you] by that name—being lonesome
Thought I would while a few moments away in writing to you—
knowing I could not pass off time more pleasant—Recd your last note
while at Fredericktown (please forgive me for not replying) I would
have replyed immediately—but my school was so near at a close
Thought it hardly necessary—Thinking I would see you at Millwood
as I came home then have the pleasure of replying verbally (which
I prefer all the time) Have been at Millwood ever so often but
circumstances has not thrown us together yet—I think of teaching this
winter where I taught in the summer. I should be very happy to have
you call some time—as I will have a very pleasant boarding place—I
must close my few communications for fear you might think me rude.

If you think this out of place please forgive this error for it is
not intentional. If my letters would be interesting or sensible you
will please reply.—I wish you success in all your undertakings. So
Good Night, Ever a Friend, Ella Gamble

letter 163

December 4, 1866. Claysville, Ky.
Lou Riggen. [No envelope, no postmark]

Claysville, Ky. Dec 4th /66

Lieut. E. L. Lybarger

You want to know why I don't write longer letters. Well, I
always like to interest my readers and consequently dislike to send
letters to any one which are <u>not</u> interesting. What interests me,
might not interest you. So when I have nothing to write I write it as

quickly as possible, and send it along. In other—and your—words, I don't know what to write. Sometimes I am inexpressibly sad—not unhappy, but unavoidably sad. "&a feeling of sadness and longing, that is not akin to pain, But resembles sorrow only as the mist resembles the rain." possesses my soul, and gives a sombre tint to every thought. As I don't care about writing inexpressibly sad things I at such times write inexpressibly silly things. I don't think it's any harm for people to be sad just when it suits them. How can they be forever merry & I would get tired of it. I can't regulate my feelings like I would a watch and I don't care though people <u>do</u> say it's my <u>duty</u> to be cheerful. <u>Duty</u>.

Now tonight there is a pleasure to me in being sad, as I listen to the chill December wind whispering and moaning and whistling in its own exquisitly musical way. I <u>never</u> hear it but that I think of a fair, O how beautiful a face that has faded forever from my sight—a voice that was music which I shall never hear again. May I never cease to dwell with fondness on the memories of those golden days. Howl and shiver cold wind—she sleeps on "nor heeds life's pelting storms." "Who would cease to remember though every recollection be but a pang." If that is too solemn I'll leave the rest until next time.

Now to the rest of your letter. You say "Is it not strange that one of my cast of mind should love anyone or any place?" Well no. I rather think it would be strange if you did not, as to love is a necessity of the human heart and without it "there is ever a void that is yet to be filled."

We are so constituted that our happiness depends on that of others. It is said that "the most devoted attachment in life is that of a woman in love with herself," but that's slander. I don't believe you know much about the "grand passion" for you say you expect to marry someone who will "take pity on you." Pity indeed. How delightful to live in single blessedness forever in preference. Is this letter long enough?

I have been reading some of Tennyson's poems. As I thought it my duty to like so celebrated a poet, read and read, and do like some of them. What common people would call <u>smoke</u> he calls "the warm-blue breathings of a hidden hearth." Isn't that pretty. By all means, wait till you get another photo if you wish it.

Respectfully
Lou Riggen

letter 164

*December 16, 1866. Postmarked Millwood, Ohio.
Phrone Rogers. Spring Mountain, Ohio.*

[Note: This letter is torn and some words are illegible.]

Sabbath evening Dec. 16th, 1866

Dearest Ed

I'm lonely tonight and as you are not here for me to talk to I intend thinking of you as much as I please. I have been busying myself in various ways since you left. Have made several calls since I saw you—one on Mr. Conckel's daughter and an[other] . . . Joe Critchfield. What a dreary day this has been. I have been at home all day reading. Have wished often that you were here. I want to see you sometime if you are so hateful. The installation comes off Christmas night. Will you come? If you could only see my pleading face you would . . .

Dec. 17th

I intend finishing to night. I did not feel like writing and quit. Will arrived from Sim Sapp's shop and reports your slippers on hand. Sim thinks they will be too short. I do not know whether he intends finishing them or not. He could put on them a Morocco toe which would [not] spoil the looks at all.

Mother and I are going to Millwood in a few minutes and I am in a terrible hurry. Fannie McMahon called on me Saturday. Said that Lizzie B. intended starting to Adah to school soon. Suppose she will soon finish her education. Mrs. Earnest's mother was buried today . . . Mr. Riley, Ell Gamble's grandfather . . . Today is Ima [?] Rogers wedding day, rather a bright day. I must close for Mother has got her shawl on to go.

*Good night Your Loving
Phrone*

December 23, 1866. Bainbridge, Ohio.
Rosa Crum. Spring Mountain, Ohio.

Bainbridge, Ohio, Dec. 23rd/66

My Dear Cousin

Once more I am permitted to write you a few lines in answer to your <u>very</u> welcome and <u>always</u> appreciated letter & suppose you was disappointed in looking for a letter last week. I was so very busy that it was almost impossible for me to write. I wrote to you some time since but you say you never received the letter.

Well that is neither of <u>our faults</u> and we can't help it, but I hope it will have better success this time. Father <u>had</u> intended to pay you a visit when he married, but did not hear from you. He changed his mind. He was married last Wednesday evening, and he says tell you he will come some other time now.

Christmas night, ten o'clock.

I have just come from the <u>concert</u> and while all the rest of the family are wraped in sweet repose and perchance having pleasant dreams, I am here this cold still night all alone writing to my cousin with naught to disturb me save the ticking of the old clock. I commenced this letter Sunday but my time is so limited that I was not able to finish it. I am going to school after Christmas and next fall I am going to pay you a visit and I suppose I will have a new Cousin by that time. Edwin <u>do come</u> to see us when you get married I will do all in my power to make your visit pleasant and agreeable too you. You surely can snatch a little time from your business to visit us. I have one of the <u>gayest</u> beaux. He lives in Chillicothe and if you will come I will show him to you. I received a letter from him this evening telling me he was coming up to spend the new years with me. You must write and let me know when you get married. I wish you all the good luck in this world and hope all your pathway be strewn with fortunes fairest flowers. <u>Do try and come and see us.</u>

I enjoyed myself exceedingly at the concert, there is to be another tomorrow night. This was the driest christmas I ever experienced. I have had the blues all day untill this evening, the letter I got revived my spirits.

Father says if you will petition for a division of that Mo. land he will be with you for you might as well get <u>something</u> for it as to have it lay there and do nobody any good. Give my love to Aunt Amelia and don't forget to write soon.

Excuse scribbling, I am in a hurry for I must write another letter before I go to bed, please answer soon.

Ever your cousin
Rosa

$

letter 166

December 31, 1866. A. E. Baker. Spring Mountain, Ohio.
Delivered by favor of D.B.

At Home, Dec. 31st, 1866

E.L. Lybarger
Kind Friend

Your letter containing the unexpected intelligence of your determination to take a "transit from the State of Single Blessedness" into that of—May I say it?—"Double Wretchedness" was received the Saturday before Christmas; and had I not fully expected to see you here at the Installation would have answered by return mail. Why wasn't you here? We had a real nice time. Excellent addresses &c &c But I'll not enter into any "lengthy retail" (as I once heard a preacher say) of the things that transpired in that evening. Will leave that for her whose right and duty it is to write you long letters. Suffice it to say that my friend Mr. Barnes was present. Wish you could have had "a sight" at him. I was earnest in what I told you at S.M. He and I are only friends and will never be any thing more.

Then you have had a letter from our "Mutual" friend Col. Rhodes —and he wishes to be "kindly remembered" By whom? Me? if so tell him I always do try to kindly remember my <u>true</u> friends and of course will not forget <u>him,</u> but should like very much to have an opportunity of pouring out upon his "denoted head" some of the Wrath that I have had bottled up for him for the last ten months. Think it would be highly benficial to myself at least.

Ella Dunlap and I think of going to Columbus next Monday. Will be gone perhaps a week. But if that event of yours will take place before I should be likely to return please let me know as I can very easily postpone my visit there. And here permit me to acknowledge your kindness in remembering your promise and saying I might consider myself "invited." I appreciate such friends and shall always "kindly remember" you and ardently wish for you a life of unsullied (if it were possible) "domestic happiness. The only bliss of Paradise that hath survived the fall."

> *Truly Your Friend*
> *A.E. Baker*

P.S. If you pass through D and have time call and see me.

> *A.E.B.*

1867 LETTERS

letter 167

January 3, 1867. [A. E. Baker.]

[Note: A short letter with no envelope or signature. Attributed to A. E. Baker from the writing and content.]

Jan. 3, 1867

E.L.L.

I have at last found an opportunity of sending this now stale letter. Dan has been going to S.M. every day for the last two weeks and as it takes so long for letters to pass by mail between these two "cities" thought I would prefer sending it by "private conveyance."

I saw you in town yesterday and think you were real mean for not calling, one <u>moment</u> if you even were in a hurry.

Don't tell Rhodes what I said about him in this letter. He may think me too sarcastic and as vengence is not mine I'll not try to repay.

Please answer through Dan.

LOU RIGGEN: THE LAST WORD

$

letter 168

February 26, 1867. Falmouth, Ky.
Lou Riggen. Spring Mountain, Ohio.

Falmouth, Ken., Feb. 26th, 1867

Lieut. E.L. Lybarger

Have you been wondering why I did not write? I suppose you have if not from any desire to hear from me at least because I am usually prompt in writing. I have been sick and have not been able to write until now. If I had a photograph of myself as I look just now I would send it to you. I think it would materially assist you in your efforts to dislike your humble correspondent. I did not suppose you would be writing all this time to one whom you particularly disliked but I am so sorry you like me because you can't help it and since you tried to help it. I am sorry you did not succeed as you say I am "to blame."

Oh, you think I am not selfish because I like to write interesting letters, do you? I am sorry to say it but selfishness is the prime cause of it all. Don't you know that people like to please others because it is a pleasure to please them. Don't you know that people bow politely, and smile affably and talk in their blandest style, because they like to be popular. They turn around after they have dazzled you with their excess of kindness imagining they have won your everlasting friendship by an expenditure of a few words, and if you will just look, you will see that you are as completely out of their minds as if they had never seen you, and if you would suddenly disappear from the world they'd never miss you. I don't think I am of that class though for I am excessively opposed to "maneuvering" that I usually repel instead of inviting friendship, which is about as bad as the opposite extreme. I have seen so much selfishness and so many well-laid schemes lurking in pleasant smiles and beaming radiant glances that I have come to the conclusion that the world is filled with selfish people. Then again that is nothing but human nature. I haven't room on this (as you are glad to see) to write a treatise on human nature, and have run to a point or rather a subject I did not think of touching when I commenced. But as the preachers say "one word and I have done." You think selfishness is an attribute common to all women because you think it doubtful whether you can find one who will marry you—well if ever selfishness is pardonable, it is in regard to matrimony. If I should marry (!) I should want the fortunate gentleman to be most exceedingly selfish, and marry entirely for his own happiness.

Write right soon and if you don't write a longer letter next time won't that be terrible! L.R.

Direct to Falmouth.

Biographical Sketch of Edwin Lewis Lybarger

(SEPTEMBER 29, 1840–JUNE 27, 1924)

E DWIN LEWIS LYBARGER was the great-grandson of Ludwick Lybarger, Sr. (1735–1827), who traveled as a young boy with his family on the ship the *Snow Betsey* from the Rhineland (now southwest Germany) to Philadelphia, one of the many immigrant families responding to William Penn's encouragement to "seek peace and security in the Province of Pennsylvania." Ludwick's seventh child, Andrew Lybarger (1778–1855), married Naomi Thompson and brought the family by covered wagon to the new state of Ohio in 1809, buying farmland near Coshocton and later establishing a tannery in Danville. Andrew and Naomi's oldest son was James Thompson Lybarger (1804–1864), Edwin's father.

James T.'s first wife died in 1830 after a few years of marriage, leaving an infant son, Thompson Lybarger. James T. married Amelia Crum in 1833. Their first son, Elijah, was born in 1838. Edwin Lewis Lybarger was born September 29, 1840, in Blachleyville in Wayne County, Ohio. His middle name came from his maternal grandfather, Lewis Crum, who brought his family from Virginia in 1834 to Highland County, Ohio, where he operated a grist mill.

In 1848, James T. moved his older son Elijah, wife Amelia, and eight-year-old son Edwin to Millwood, Union Township, Knox County, Ohio, managing a hostelry at "The Caves." Edwin attended Millwood

Academy, where from the age of fourteen his lifelong abilities as a public (and patriotic) speaker were first demonstrated in school orations with titles like "History" and "Our Country." He was a serious and handsome young man when he graduated from Millwood Academy in 1858.

His plans to attend Kenyon College in Gambier, Ohio, were apparently thwarted by his wagering all of his college savings ($14) on an unbeatable horse that lost the race. Suspecting trickery he could not prove, Edwin vowed never to gamble again—and never did. He went to work to re-earn his tuition money, possibly as a teacher for a short period. But his schooling was put on hold again when the Civil War broke out in 1861. With friends from Union Township, Edwin enlisted in Millwood resident William Walker's company of volunteers on November 25, 1861, at Camp Andrews in Mount Vernon, Ohio.

Captain Walker's Company K was assigned to the Forty-third Ohio Volunteer Infantry Regiment, commanded by Colonel J. L. Kirby Smith, and departed Camp Andrews on February 21, 1862, joining the Army of the Mississippi in the bombardment and capture of Confederate strongholds at New Madrid, Missouri, and Island No. Ten in the Mississippi River. Brigadier General John Pope assigned four Ohio regiments (the 27th, 39th, 43rd, and 63rd) to Colonel John Fuller's First Division, Second Brigade. Fuller's "Ohio Brigade" earned its impressive reputation in a series of hard-fought Union victories. By April of 1862, Edwin was promoted to second lieutenant. He recorded his experiences in small pocket diaries throughout the war and kept up a steady correspondence with numerous friends and family members.

On the morning of October 4, 1862, in the Battle of Corinth, Mississippi, while defending Battery Robinet, Edwin was wounded in the right knee by a Confederate minié ball. He later recorded in his diary: "The engagement commenced at 4 in the morning. Was wounded about 11 A.M. and left the field. Repulsed the enemy." Edwin's Forty-third Regiment suffered many casualties, including the death of regiment commander Colonel Smith. General Rosecrans praised the courage of the Ohio Brigade as a major reason for the Union victory. Edwin spent the next three months in hospitals in Corinth and Paducah, Kentucky, keeping his leg and regaining the ability to walk.

From the start of 1863, the Ohio Brigade served in the Army of the Tennessee's Seventeenth Corps. On Christmas Eve, 1863, virtually all of the Knox County men of Company K reenlisted for three years or the duration of the war. From November 1864, First Lieutenant Lybarger served as quartermaster of the Forty-third Ohio Regiment during General William Sherman's March to the Sea, also taking temporary command of Company A. He recounts the foraging work during the march, collecting wagonloads of cabbages, potatoes, and other farm produce, along with corn for the horses and mules. In Savannah, Georgia, on New Year's Day, 1865, he recorded in his diary, "Nothing nice to eat and nothing good to drink." But it was a source of pride that while he was quartermaster, the men of the Forty-third Ohio rarely went hungry two days in a row. He ate so much rice when marching through the Carolinas in early 1865 that he would never touch it again, no matter how it was disguised in puddings or other ways. Lybarger declined promotion to captain in order to stay at his post as quartermaster (and first lieutenant rank). In civilian life after the war, however, he was widely known as Captain Lybarger.

On May 24, 1865, Edwin marched with Sherman's Army of the Tennessee in the Grand Review in Washington, D.C., witnessing "[o]ver one hundred thousand citizens crowd[ing] Pennsylvania Avenue, from the Capitol to the White House, to witness the grand pageantry. And the Heroes of Sherman were greeted as never an army was greeted before." The Forty-third Ohio mustered out July 13 in Louisville, and Edwin returned home to Millwood, Ohio, on July 21, 1865, "no more to be disturbed by the sound of the bugle and the clash of arms . . . glad to return to civil life and thankful that my life had been spared whilst hundreds of my comrades had been left in unknown graves." Although he did not bear feelings of hatred for the South, he felt keenly the injustice of the war the South began, and never visited it again. In 1912, he published "Leaves from My Diary," his daily account of Sherman's march and the Carolina campaign.

After leaving the army, Edwin did not attend Kenyon College, needing to support his mother since his father had died in 1864. He read law with William R. Sapp in Mt. Vernon, Ohio, for a short time, although he never practiced law. He received a teacher's certificate in Knox County on November 4, 1865. From 1866 through 1880, he was in partnership in the general merchandising business in Spring Mountain, Coshocton County, with Isaac Baker, a former comrade in the Forty-third Ohio.

He married Sophronia ("Phrone") Warren Rogers on January 27, 1867. Later that year or early the next, they had a son who died as an infant. Theirs was a devoted marriage; on their wedding anniversary in 1876, separated from Phrone, Edwin wrote to her, "I know what a noble, kind hearted, and generous minded woman you are. I thank God that you are mine and that I am yours."

In 1867, Edwin was elected to a three-year term as justice of the peace for Monroe Township. A lifelong Republican, he was first elected to the Ohio State legislature for a two-year term in 1875, and served as a delegate to the Republican National Convention in 1876, nominating Rutherford B. Hayes.

In 1882, Lybarger and Phrone both contracted typhoid fever, and were nursed by his mother Amelia. Although Phrone seemed to recover, she relapsed and died May 13, 1882, while Edwin remained delirious, unaware of her death and unable to attend her funeral. Recovering only to learn of her loss, he entered a deep period of grief, erecting a large monument to her in the Workman Cemetery at Danville, Ohio.

After a two-year courtship, he married Nancy Moore of Spring Mountain, Ohio, on December 10, 1885. Their only son was born in 1888 and named Harry Swayne Lybarger after the Forty-third Ohio commander Edwin greatly admired, Colonel Wager Swayne.

In 1888, Edwin was defeated in his bid for election to the U.S. House of Representatives. He remained in a merchandising partnership with Fifty-first Ohio veteran Sampson McNeal until 1890, when he moved the family to Warsaw, Ohio, and there affiliated with the firm of Wright, Lybarger and Funk. He also built up his land holdings to 700 acres in Monroe Township, raising sheep and selling wool. His interests also turned to banking, and he served as president of the Farmers and Merchants' Bank of Warsaw, as well as vice president and director of the Commercial National Bank of Coshocton.

In 1892, he purchased property on the Walhonding River, where summers thereafter were spent with family and friends living in cabins or roughing it in tents—pleased to be "in camp" again, although the old war injury to his knee required him by this time to use a cane.

He remained active in Republican politics, serving as a delegate to the National Republican Convention in 1884, nominating James G. Blaine. He was reelected to the Ohio State Legislature twice, in 1905 and 1907. The "Lybarger bill" he sponsored helped create Ohio State University as the major pubic university system within Ohio. In 1906 the Speaker of the House appointed Lybarger to a special committee investigating corruption in Cincinnati, citing the "well known rugged honesty of this Coshocton county man."

Throughout this period, while serving on the elected State Board of Public Works, he helped manage Walhonding canals until they were closed after the 1913 floods; during his tenure, the construction of an annex to the State House building resulted in an efficient (and unheard-of) surplus of funds returned to the treasury. As a member of the Horse Department of the State Board of Agriculture, he always made sure that Kentucky war veterans were in charge of judging horses at the Ohio State Fair because "they know more about horseflesh than anyone else." He served as trustee for both the Girls' Industrial School and the Masonic Home in Mansfield, Ohio.

Edwin remained in contact with war comrades throughout his life, and participated in numerous activities of the (veteran) Grand Army of the Republic (GAR), being elected in 1896 as Commander of the Department of Ohio for the annual Grand Encampment. Active in the Masonic Fraternity since shortly after the war, he rose to the rank of grand master of the Grand Lodge of Ohio in 1899–1900. He was also a member of Sons of the American Revolution.

In 1909, Edwin presented his son Harry with a check for $100 on his twenty-first birthday, with the wish that Harry buy an up-to-date dictionary and, at his mother's request, a good pair of gold sleeve buttons. He added, "I hope you will not throw the rest away just because it is a gift and caused no work on your part." Harry, after graduating from Kenyon College and Ohio State University law school, married Ethel Finney in 1913 in Coshocton.

Edwin suffered a stroke in 1916 and was in failing health thereafter. He died at home in Warsaw on June 27, 1924, survived by his wife Nancy, son Harry, and four grandchildren: Nancy, Edwin II, Davida Margaret, and Mary. He was buried in Valley View Cemetery following "one of the largest funerals held in Warsaw."

One contemporary account reported, "His interests are varied, but all along lines of progress and improvement. He is a broad minded man who places a correct valuation upon life, its opportunities and its privileges." A tribute published earlier, to celebrate his seventieth birthday, concluded, "He has lived his life . . . as a deep student of humanity and a leading characteristic has been to make up his mind firmly and then 'stay put.' [We] love his cheery laugh and respect his words of wisdom. Captain, we salute you."

From notes collected by his granddaughter,
Nancy L. Rhoades, 1992,
who remembers him with pleasure.

With additional notes by his great-granddaughter,
Jennifer L. Wilke, 2008

Notes

The chapter epigraph is from p. 347 of Gail Hamilton [Mary Abigail Dodge], "A Call to My Country-Women," *Atlantic Monthly* 11, no. 65 (March 1863): 345–49.

1. *Mount Vernon Democratic Banner* (hereafter cited as *Banner*), November 5, 1861; *Ohio State Journal*, November 12, 1861; Eric Foner, "Ohio and the World: The Civil War Era," in *Ohio and the World, 1753–2053: Essays toward a New History of Ohio*, ed. Geoffrey Parker, Richard Sisson, and William Russell Coil (Columbus: Ohio State University Press, 2005), esp. 79; Frederick H. Dyer, *A Compendium of the War of the Rebellion*, 43rd Ohio (New York: T. Yoseloff, 1908; reprint, Dayton, OH: The Press of Morningside Bookshop, 1979); Frederick N. Lorey, ed., *History of Knox County Ohio, 1876–1976*, 2nd ed. (Mt. Vernon, OH: Knox County Historical Society, 1992), 121. Eugene Roseboom discusses calculations of Ohio troops that vary from 240,514 to 346,326; see Roseboom, *History of the State of Ohio*, vol. 4, *The Civil War Era* (Columbus: Ohio State Archaeological and Historical Society, 1944), 440 (hereafter cited as Roseboom, *Civil War Era*). Lybarger was in Camp Andrews at Mt. Vernon until early 1862.

2. James M. McPherson and William J. Cooper Jr., eds., *Writing the Civil War: The Quest to Understand* (Columbia: University of South Carolina Press, 1998), 2. The terms *Man's War* and *Man's Funeral* are not in quotation marks, because they capture what is by now a common understanding of the war and I have not located authors who may have coined the terms originally.

3. *Banner*, November 26, 1861.

4. James M. McPherson, *Battle Cry of Freedom: The Civil War Era* (New York: Oxford University Press, 1988), ix. For ways in which writers hurried to promote women's war contributions and patriotic symbolism in the postwar years, see Elizabeth D. Leonard, "The Women and the Storytellers after the War," in Leonard, *Yankee Women: Gender Battles in the Civil War*, 159–94 (New York: W. W. Norton, 1994).

5. James M. McPherson introduces these ideas in his foreword to Catherine Clinton and Nina Silber, eds., *Divided Houses: Gender and the Civil War* (New York: Oxford University Press, 1992), xvi. See Gerda Lerner, "Priorities and Challenges in Women's History Research," *Perspectives* 26 (April 1988): 17–20;

M. A. Vinovskis, "Have Social Historians Lost the Civil War? Some Preliminary Demographic Speculations," *Journal of American History* 76, no. 1 (1989): 34–58; Mary Elizabeth Massey, *Bonnet Brigades: American Women and the Civil War* (New York: Knopf, 1966); Agatha Young, *The Women and the Crisis: Women of the North in the Civil War* (New York: McDowell, Obolensky, 1959); Jeanie Attie, *Patriotic Toil: Northern Women and the American Civil War* (Ithaca, NY: Cornell University Press, 1998); Nina Silber, *Daughters of the Union: Northern Women Fight the Civil War* (Cambridge, MA: Harvard University Press, 2005); Drew Gilpin Faust, *Mothers of Invention* (Chapel Hill: University of North Carolina Press, 1996).

6. For examples of such valor, see Karen Rae Mehaffey, "They Called Her Captain: The Amazing Life of Emily Virginia Mason," in *The Journal of Women's Civil War History: From the Home Front to the Front Lines*, ed. Eileen Conklin, 2:74–85 (Gettysburg: Thomas Publications, 2002); and Juanita Leisch, "Who Did What: Women's Roles in the Civil War," in Conklin, *Journal of Women's Civil War History*, 2:160–66. For analysis of the shifting paradigms of U.S. women's history and historians' use of "women worthies," see Manuela Thurner, "Subject to Change: Theories and Paradigms of U.S. Feminist History," *Journal of Women's History* 9 (1997): 122–46.

7. A growing body of work provides examples of such figures and events, including Judith E. Harper's *Women during the Civil War: An Encyclopedia* (New York: Routledge, 2004), Elizabeth D. Leonard's study, *All the Daring of the Soldier: Women of the Civil War Armies* (New York: Penguin, 2001), and Eileen Conklin's edited volumes of the *Journal of Women's Civil War History.* "Behind the scenes" is taken from Leisch, "Women's Roles," in Conklin's *Journal*, 161.

8. James McPherson notes that women's "encouraging letters" from the home front are more often "lost to history" because many collections do not include both sides of communication. See McPherson, *For Cause and Comrades: Why Men Fought in the Civil War* (New York: Oxford University Press, 1997), 134, 139.

9. Faust, *Mothers of Invention;* Harper, *Women during the Civil War,* 88; see also Karen Lystra, *Searching the Heart: Women, Men and Romantic Love in Nineteenth-Century America* (New York: Oxford University Press, 1989).

10. See Reid Mitchell, "Soldiering, Manhood and Coming of Age: A Northern Volunteer," in Clinton and Silber, *Divided Houses,* 44; Gerald F. Linderman, *Embattled Courage: The Experience of Combat in the American Civil War* (New York: Free Press, 1987), 26. McPherson discusses soldier demographics in *Cause and Comrades,* viii.

11. A.E., Annie, Lizzie, and Lib Baker are different names for the same person. I use "Lib Baker" throughout the introduction whether the individual letter is signed Annie, Lizzie, or Lib.

12. Wiley mentions battles, illness, fatal accidents, and executions as common fodder for soldiers' letters; see Bell Irvin Wiley, *The Life of Billy Yank: The Common Soldier of the Union* (Indianapolis: Bobbs-Merrill, 1952; reprint, Baton Rouge: Louisiana State University Press, 1979), 185–87.

13. Velascoe Hildreth was the son of a local merchant and nineteen years old when he volunteered to serve.

14. Lybarger notes his father's death briefly in his diary, a matter-of-fact report that captures another function of letter-writing: "received a letter from home conveying the intelligence of the decease of my father." Family notes and a clipping of letterhead from the Central Ohio Lunatic Asylum indicate that James Lybarger may have suffered from a form of dementia that eventually required care beyond what Amelia Crum Lybarger could provide. Earlier, she cared from him at home with the help of such friends as Phrone Rogers. The death of Lybarger's father may have made other correspondence particularly meaningful.

15. Lou's reference to "long-handled letters" indicates either the looping letters of the alphabet she used in her handwriting or the length of the epistle. Both handwriting and letter length were considered gendered writing expressions. Comments that appear throughout the collection concerning epistle length demonstrate that epistolary convention included attention to length and that writers were aware of this convention. Lou and Phrone frequently disregard this convention, urging Lybarger to write long letters.

16. Wiley remarks on soldiers' and families' volume of writing, *Billy Yank*, 13, and *Johnny Reb*, 192; McPherson and Cooper's edited text, *Writing the Civil War*, details the vast body of writing Americans have produced to explore the meaning of the Civil War—the very act of writing as a quest to understand.

17. The shift in the prominence of oral to written traditions in the nineteenth century was by no means uniform. Certainly, oral traditions continued to be central to the values, practices, and educational initiatives of some cultural groups. Other groups, because of racial discrimination, socioeconomic class disadvantage, and geographical location, could not access print culture and literacy skills to the same extent as middle-class Anglo Americans. See David Tyack and Elizabeth Hansot, *Managers of Virtue: Public School Leadership in America, 1820–1980* (New York: Basic Books, 1982), 32; Henry J. Perkinson, *The Imperfect Panacea: American Faith in Education, 1865–1990* (New

York: McGraw Hill, 1991). Furthermore, the common schools continued to incorporate writing and reading instruction from the classical rhetorical tradition throughout the nineteenth century, including the recitation of oral poetry and the writing of pieces meant to be delivered orally. For additional examples, see James J. Murphy, ed., *A Short History of Writing Instruction from Ancient Greece to Twentieth-Century America* (Davis, CA: Hermagoras Press, 1990).

18. Julia McNair Wright, *The Complete Home* (Philadelphia: J. R. McCurdy and Co., 1879), 199.

19. This phrase is from Hamilton, "Call to My Country-Women."

20. David B. Parker, *A Chautauqua Boy in '61 and After* (Boston: Small, Maynard and Co., 1912), 24, 54.

21. Modern-day psychologists have noted the value of writing for processing difficult life events. Although journals and diaries functioned differently during the nineteenth century, writing may nevertheless have served some individuals in that capacity.

22. One compelling effect of the nexus between print and war historically to consider is that writing letters during the Civil War may have increased literacy, particularly among those who otherwise left few written records. Although some literate soldiers served as writing proxies for others, and writing patterns varied across race and class, the quality of soldiers' and women's 'writing sometimes improved throughout the war. For examples, see Rosa Crum's letters in this collection; David D. Bard, *Friend Alice: The Civil War Letters of Captain David D. Bard, 7th and 104th Regiments, Ohio Volunteer Infantry, 1862–1864*, ed. James T. Brenner (Kent, OH: Scholar of Fortune Publications, 1996); Wiley, *Johnny Reb*, 205, and Wiley, *Billy Yank*, 186.

23. Susan Geary, "The Domestic Novel as Commercial Commodity: Making a Best Seller in the 1850s," *Bibliographical Society of American Papers* 70, no. 3 (1976): 365–95.

24. Mary Ryan, *The Empire of the Mother: American Writing about Domesticity, 1830–1860* (New York: Haworth, 1985), 116.

25. Roseboom reports that Ohio built most of its railroads in the 1850s, with a total mileage of 2,974 in 1860; see Roseboom, *Civil War Era*, 111.

26. Carl E. Kaestle, *Pillars of the Republic: Common Schools and American Society, 1780–1860* (New York: Hill and Wang, 1983), 65.

27. *Banner*, October 10, 1862; Eighth Census, 103.

28. Wright, *Complete Home*, 206. See Burton Bledstein, *The Culture of Professionalism: The Middle Class and the Development of Higher Education in America* (New York: W. W. Norton, 1976), for ways in which middle-class identity became imbricated in the development of "professionalism" and its

various apparatuses, including correct grammar and speech, in the nineteenth century.

29. See Theodora Penny Martin, *The Sound of Our Own Voices: Women's Study Clubs, 1860–1910* (Boston: Beacon Press, 1987).

30. As part of their home away from home, soldiers sometimes set up libraries and had Bible study and discussion groups on important social questions. Reid Mitchell discusses this as an extension of the soldiers' home communities and of the culture of nineteenth-century volunteerism; see *The Vacant Chair: The Northern Soldier Leaves Home* (New York: Oxford University Press, 1993), 23. Wiley discusses spelling bees, theater, and orations as part of soldiers' efforts to stay "gay and happy" in *Billy Yank*, 152–91. Lybarger's diary notes that he participated in a literary study in December 1863.

31. *Banner*, November 26, 1861.

32. See William J. Reese, *The Origins of the American High School* (New Haven, CT: Yale University Press, 1995), 104–5.

33. S. Michael Halloran, "From Rhetoric to Composition: The Teaching of Writing in America to 1900," in Murphy, *Short History*, 163–64.

34. Reese, *Origins*, 142; George Franklin Smythe, *Kenyon College: Its First Century* (New Haven, CT: Yale University Press, 1924), 171. For more on educational legislation in Ohio, see Nelson L. Bossing, "The History of Educational Legislation in Ohio from 1851 to 1925" in *Ohio History* 39, no. 1 (1930): 78–219.

35. Laurence Van Buskirk to Daniel Van Buskirk, 1855, Van Buskirk Family Papers, MSS 690, Box 1, Folder 2, Ohio Historical Society (hereafter referred to as OHS), Columbus, Ohio.

36. Daniel Van Buskirk to Laurence V. Hartwell, February 15, 1849, Van Buskirk Family Papers, MSS 690, OHS.

37. Foner, "Ohio and the World," 78, quoted in McPherson, *Cause and Comrades*, 149.

38. For examples of debates over variations in white identity, see Matthew Frye Jacobson, *Whiteness of a Different Color: European Immigrants and the Alchemy of Race* (Cambridge, MA: Harvard University Press, 1998).

39. Lawmakers at times turned to public understanding of "race" to make determinations of citizenship. See Jacobson, *Whiteness;* and Ian F. Haney-Lopez, *White by Law: The Legal Construction of Race* (New York: New York University, 1996).

40. John Higham's classic study, *Strangers in the Land: Patterns of American Nativism, 1860–1925* (New Brunswick, NJ: Rutgers University Press, 1955), is useful here; in 1860, the populations of foreign-born in the cities were higher

than they have been ever since (Higham, *Strangers*, 15). Anti-Catholic texts were printed across the next two decades, following patterns of nativism and Protestant xenophobia that resurfaced in the post–Civil War years; see Ray Allen Billington, *The Protestant Crusade, 1800–1860: A Study of the Origins of American Nativism* (New York: Peter Smith, 1938). For an example of an anti-Catholic treatise published by Cincinnati presses, see Julia McNair Wright's *Priest and Nun* (Cincinnati: Western Tract Society, 1869). Cincinnati was a publishing hub in the 1840s and 1850s but faded in influence after the Civil War; see Roseboom, *Civil War Era*, 147–50; for uniting power of war, see Higham, 12–14.

41. Many women who belonged to this wave of writers were white, middle class, of New England origin, and of Protestant faith. For detailed treatment of these characteristics of women writers and their products, see Nina Baym's overview of nineteenth-century writing, *Woman's Fiction: A Guide to Novels by and about Women in America, 1820–1870* (Champaign: University of Illinois Press, 1993); and Nina Baym, *American Women Writers and the Work of History, 1790–1860* (New Brunswick, NJ: Rutgers University Press, 1995). For lengthier treatment of the ideas in these three paragraphs and their racial implications, see Lucy E. Bailey, "Wright-ing White: The Construction of Race in Women's 19th Century Didactic Texts," *Journal of Thought* 41, no. 4 (Winter 2006): 65–81.

42. Baym, *Woman's Fiction*, 11.

43. Geary, "Domestic Novel," 366–67. Key factors in the nineteenth-century context contributed to this popularity: changes in publishing practices, marketing strategies, literacy rates, and the symbolic power of middle-class discourses of professionalism. Sales figures must always be read with caution, however, as they were often difficult to pinpoint, were sometimes inflated, and were used to market books. JoAnne McFarland, "Those Scribbling Women: A Cultural Study of Mid-Nineteenth Century Popular American Romances by Women," *Journal of Communication Inquiry* 9, no. 2 (1985): 33–49, esp. 38; see Bailey, "Wright-ing White," 66.

44. Lewis Rowe to Father, April 26, 1862, Hamburg, Hardin Co., Tennessee, private collection. Thank you to Mary Hitz for these resources.

45. Mitchell, *The Vacant Chair*, 21, and Reid Mitchell, "The Northern Soldier and His Community," in *Toward a Social History of the American Civil War*, ed. M. A. Vinovskis (Cambridge: Cambridge University Press, 1990), 78–92.

46. Many writers stressed the significance of correspondence. For an example, see Lois E. Myers, *Letters by Lamplight: A Woman's View of Everyday Life in South Texas, 1873–1883* (Waco, TX: Baylor University Press, 1991), 34.

47. Although this text focuses on Northern women's letters, correspondence was significant for women during the Civil War era overall. Mail cost was particularly prohibitive for Confederates as prices rose throughout the war and paper and print became increasingly scarce. Mary Chesnut notes spending $12.00 on paper and envelopes in 1864, compared with $10.00 on a concert ticket. Paper shortages were common in the South, and women used anything they could find to compose letters and diaries. These "adversity covers" took a variety of forms: maps, pages torn from books, even wallpaper. Mary Boykin Miller Chesnut, *Mary Chesnut's Civil War*, ed. C. Vann Woodward (New Haven, CT: Yale University Press, 1981), 688. Also see Faust, *Mothers of Invention*, 116.

48. The *Banner* refers to a paper shortage in Knox County, November 29, 1862; "Paper Rags," *Banner*, December 13, 1862.

49. Shirley A. Leckie, *The Colonel's Lady on the Western Frontier: The Correspondence of Alice Kirk Grierson* (Lincoln: University of Nebraska Press, 1989).

50. Myers, *Letters by Lamplight*, 11.

51. Carroll Smith-Rosenberg, "The Female World of Love and Ritual: Relations between Women in Nineteenth-Century America," *Signs* 1, no. 1 (Autumn 1975): 1–29. More recently, Joyce A. Walker has examined a group of women's letters, including her own, suggesting their foundational role in sustaining friendships over time and exploring the meaning of events in women's lives; see Walker, "Letters in the Attic: Private Reflections of Women, Wives and Mothers," in *The Methods and Methodologies of Qualitative Family Research*, ed. Marvin B. Sussman and Jane F. Gilgun, 9–40 (New York: Haworth, 1996).

52. Van Buskirk Family Papers, February 23, 1849, MSS 690, OHS.

53. For more information on the ways in which women used correspondence as a form of spiritual support, see Mary Morrissey and Gillian Wright, "Piety and Sociability in Early Modern Women's Letters," *Women's Writing* 13, no. 1 (March 2006): 44–59; for soldiers and community, see Mitchell, "Northern Soldier," 83–85.

54. See *New Family Manual or Ladies Indispensable Assistant* (New York, 1852) as an example.

55. Halloran, "From Rhetoric to Composition," 153–57, and Don Paul Abbott, "Reading and Writing in Renaissance Europe and England," in Murphy, *Short History*, 114–15.

56. Daniel Van Buskirk to Laurence Van Buskirk, November 22, 1855, Van Buskirk Family Papers, MSS 690, Box 1, Folder 2, OHS.

57. Myers, *Letters by Lamplight*, 29–31.

58. Wiley, *Billy Yank*, 184.

59. Wiley, *Billy Yank*, 183–84.

60. Lewis Rowe (Twenty-seventh Ohio) to Father, April 26, 1862, In the Camp in the Woods, Hamburg, Hardin Co., Tennessee, private collection.

61. Charles N. Hughey to John M. Rowe, December 4, 1861, Sedalia, Pettus Co., Missouri, private collection. Charles F. Finsley mentions that poor lighting rather than poor skills may sometimes explain variations in writing quality; see Finsley, ed., *Hannah's Letters: The Civil War Letters of Isaac E. Blauvelt, Friends, and Other Suitors* (Cedar Hill, TX: Kings Creek Press, 1997).

62. Although some scholars note the performative function inherent to letters, Byrd Gibbens suggests that spontaneity in women's letter writing indicates an escape from rhetorical and epistolary constraints and most approximates the writer's inner voice. In this view, the "spontaneous writing" and breaks from convention evident in the Lybarger letters may indicate the perceived closeness and comfort between writers. See Gibbens, ed., *This Is a Strange Country: Letters of a Westering Family, 1880–1906* (Albuquerque: University of New Mexico Press, 1988).

63. The quotation used in the subheading is from letter 129, written by Lou Riggen. The reference to letters as "emblematic" of the private realm is from Sally L. Kitch, *This Strange Society of Women: Reading the Letters and Lives of the Woman's Commonwealth* (Columbus: Ohio State University Press, 1993), 21, and Elizabeth Heckendorn Cook, *Epistolary Bodies: Gender and Genre in the Eighteenth-Century Republic of Letters* (Stanford: Stanford University Press, 1996), 6.

64. This reference to "women's consciousness" is from Nancy Cott, *The Bonds of Womanhood* (New Haven, CT: Yale University Press, 1977), 17.

65. Primarily literate, middle-class women's lives.

66. See Olga Kenyon, ed., *800 Years of Women's Letters* (New York: Penguin Books, 1992). Carolyn Steedman suggests that "the woman writing a letter" has acquired almost mythological status in offering a new origin story of the modern, Western, private subject; see Steedman, "A Woman Writing a Letter," in *Epistolary Selves: Letters and Letter-Writers, 1600–1945*, ed. Rebecca Earle, 111–33 (Brookfield, VT: Ashgate, 1999), 119.

67. Kitch, *Strange Society*, 21.

68. Ruth Perry, *Women, Letters and the Novel* (New York: AMS Press, 1980), 69.

69. See Margaret A. Hogan and C. James Taylor, eds., *My Dearest Friend: Letters of Abigail and John Adams* (Cambridge, MA: Belknap Press,

2007); Virginia Woolf, *Woman and Fiction*, reprinted in *Collected Essays: Virginia Woolf*, ed. Leonard Woolf (London: Hogarth, 1966), 2:141; Dale Spender and Lynne Spender also cite Woolf in *Scribbling Sisters* (Norman: University of Oklahoma Press, 1987), 9.

70. Kitch, *Strange Society*, 241.

71. See Ruth Miller, "The Missionary Narrative as Coercive Interrogation: Seduction, Confession and Self-Presentation in Women's 'Letters Home,'" *Women's History Review* 15, no. 5 (November 2006): 751–71.

72. See Michèle Farrell's intriguing treatment of this unusually comprehensive collection of women's seventeenth-century letters, *Performing Motherhood: The Sévigné Correspondence* (Hanover, NH: University Press of New England, 1991).

73. For examples of letters' varied roles, see Perry, *Women, Letters, and the Novel*; Kitch, *Strange Society*; and Linda S. Kauffman, *Discourses of Desire: Gender, Genre and Epistolary Fiction* (Ithaca: Cornell University Press, 1986). Baym is also cautious with claims of "public" and "private," recognizing that these terms were metaphors used to denote labor patterns and broader social changes. Baym, *American Women Writers*, 5–6.

74. The content of men's letters was indeed often audience specific. For example, this excerpt from one soldier's letter to his friend includes sexualized content. Soldier Jos Cox writes boldly to "Friend Milt [Rowe]" on May 2, 1863, that he "fell in love with . . . three or fore . . . good looking ladyes. . . . I think I am man a nuf for that many what do you think." Corinth, Missisippi, private collection. Rowe served in the Twenty-seventh Ohio; see Charles H. Smith, *History of Fuller's Ohio Brigade, 1861–1865: Its Great March, with Roster Portraits, Battle Maps and Biographies* (Cleveland: Higginson Book Co., 1909), 478.

75. Wiley, *Billy Yank*, 185.

76. Perry, *Women, Letters and the Novel*, 71; Kitch, *Strange Society*, 23.

77. Edward FitzGerald, trans., *The Rubaiyat of Omar Khayyam of Naishapur*, 4th ed. (New York: Doxey's, 1879, 1900), 88.

78. Reported in *Banner*, November 1, 1862.

79. *Mt. Vernon Republican*, May 7, 1863.

80. Massey, *Bonnet Brigades*, x.

81. Wiley, *Billy Yank*, 183; Wiley, *Johnny Reb*, 201.

82. Wiley, *Billy Yank*, 64–65.

83. Ohio Roster Commission, comp., *Official Roster of the Soldiers of the State of Ohio in the War on the Rebellion, 1861–1866* (Akron: Werner Co., 1886–95), vol. 4; Taylor was a member of Company K. He enlisted shortly after Lybarger on December 5, 1861, and was mustered out on January 29,

1865, at the end of his service. Lybarger's letters may have been transported home at that time, although the first reference to the collection does not appear until April 1865 (letter 121).

84. For more on the ways letters facilitated community, see Mitchell, "Northern Soldier," 78–92; Wiley, *Billy Yank*, 189–91; Bard, *Friend Alice* [1862], 10, 30; Edwin L. Lybarger, *Leaves from My Diary: Being a Transcript of the Daily Record I Kept during Sherman's March to the Sea and to the End of the War* (Coshocton, OH, 1910), no page numbers.

85. Ohio Roster Commission, *Official Roster*, vol. 4; Smith, *Fuller's Ohio Brigade*, 572–82, 138; Ohio Adjutant General's Dept., *Civil War Muster In and Muster Out Rolls, State Series 2440, Regiment 43*, OVI, part 2, muster-in roll of Captain J. H. Rhodes, Company K, January 1, 1864, OHS.

86. Adelia is spelled "Deliah" in the 1860 Census, Union Township, Millwood, p. 19. For Newton, see Ohio Roster Commission, *Official Roster*, 4:756. Washington Shroyer, the eldest son, served as a Squirrel Hunter during the Confederate threat to Ohio in 1862; see Gerald M. Petty, *Index of the Ohio Squirrel Hunters Roster* (Columbus, OH: Petty's Press, 1984), 85.

87. *A paper read by Captain E. L. Lybarger, Forty-third Ohio Volunteer Infantry, at a reunion of Fuller's Ohio Brigade, held at Marietta, Ohio*, September 10, 1885; Smith, *Fuller's Ohio Brigade*, 84–100.

88. McPherson, *Battle Cry*, 523–24; Reid, *Ohio in the War*, 273–74. Smith offers different numbers, reporting 38,000 Confederates and 18,000 Union men, with 20,000 charging the Ohio Brigade; *Fuller's Ohio Brigade*, 90.

89. Statistics in Smith, *Fuller's Ohio Brigade*, 90; Lybarger, *A paper*, 1885.

90. John W. Fuller, *"Our Kirby Smith": A Paper Read before the Ohio Commandery of the Military Order of the Loyal Legion of the United States, March 2, 1887* (Cincinnati: H. C. Sherick and Company, 1887); Smith, *Fuller's Ohio Brigade*, 86–87, 437.

91. *Banner*, October 18, 1862. Reports of battle losses vary. Lybarger reports 97 dead in the Forty-third Regiment. Smith, *Fuller's Ohio Brigade*, 106, reports 16 casualties and 74 wounded, five days after the battle. The 1860 census indicates that Samuel and Sarah Shrimplin had ten children ranging from one to twenty-two in age, including four sons of service age: Van Buren, Johnson, Allen, and Bruce. Allen enlisted with his brother Van Buren in Company K and died May 29, 1862, in Millwood of illness; Smith, *Fuller's Ohio Brigade*, 581; 1860 census, Union Township, Millwood, p. 7. Letter 23 suggests that Sam Shrimplin sympathized with the Rebel cause.

92. The quotation in the subheading is from letter 72, written by Grace Nello.

93. The ads, in order of appearance, were published in *Licking Record*, Newark, Ohio, November 29, 1864; unknown source; *Aledo Weekly Record* (Mercer County, Illinois), April 5, 1864, Abraham Lincoln Presidential Library. ("Seeing the elephant" was a common phrase soldiers used to refer to the fact that they had experienced battle); unknown source; unknown source.

94. Private collection, original source unknown.

95. Of course, Lybarger may have substituted for a friend who advertised as Frank Wharton, just as Lou claimed she substituted for her friend. My search for Lybarger's original ad in county newspapers in the areas where his correspondents lived was unsuccessful. No Frank Wharton is listed in Company K or book 4 of the roster of Ohio soldiers. "Jack Rogers" also seems to have been a pseudonym for Captain J. H. Rhodes (see letters 50, 72).

96. See Mitchell, "A Northern Volunteer," 51–52, for soldiers' use of the family metaphor. The handwriting on letters 31 and 40, both signed "Fannie Jerome," differs. This indicates that Lou's friend may have indeed written the first "Fannie" letter as Lou confesses (129). However, because letter writing is a performative act, "the truth" of which "Fannie" originally wrote to the soldier is less significant than the circuitous machinations constitutive of letter-writing relationships the women's plotting reveals.

97. Wiley, *Johnny Reb*, 209–10; Mitchell, "Northern Soldier," 86, 89–90; McPherson, For Cause and Comrades, 134, 139.

98. For example, see ads in the *Banner*, December 13, 1861.

99. Quotations are from Hamilton, "Call to My Country-Women," 345–49. She is likely the original visionary of Civil War letters as war work.

100. Lieutenant Colonel Dawes, Marietta, Ohio, March 13, 1863. See Rufus R. Dawes and Alan T. Nolan, *A Full Blown Yankee of the Iron Brigade: Service with the Sixth Wisconsin Volunteers* (Lincoln: University of Nebraska Press, 1999), 27.

101. Quotations are from Hamilton, "Call to My Country-Women," 345–49.

102. Mitchell, "Northern Soldier," 83.

103. For an overview of both these and other notable and less-known women during the war years, see Harper, *Women during the Civil War*, esp. 34–40; Elizabeth Brown Pryor, *Clara Barton: Professional Angel* (Philadelphia: University of Pennsylvania Press, 1987); Conklin, *Journal of Women's Civil War History*; Peter F. Stevens, *Rebels in Blue: The Story of Keith and Malinda*

Blalock (Dallas, TX: Taylor Publishing, 2000); Leonard, *All the Daring;* Young, *Women and the Crisis;* and Massey, *Bonnet Brigades.*

104. See Ella Forbes, *African American Women during the Civil War* (New York: Garland, 1998) for a detailed discussion of women's varied activist efforts, forms of resistance, and contributions during the war years —including survival (p. 159). Forbes attends to key differences among women—slave/free status, socioeconomic class, geographic location, skill set—to provide a more complex understanding of women's roles during the war. She also discusses the connotations of the term *contraband* in reference to fugitives from slavery and the federal government's exploitation of the labor of newly freed African Americans in ways that resembled that of slaveholders (pp. 9–13). See Susie King Taylor, *A Black Woman's Civil War Memoirs* (Princeton, NJ: Markus Wiener, 1995) for insight into a black woman's experiences on the war front and perspective on black soldiers. See also Dorothy Sterling, *We Are Your Sisters: Black Women in the Nineteenth Century* (New York: W. W. Norton, 1984).

105. *Banner,* September 16, 1862; October 23, 1862; October 24, 1862; November 5, 1861.

106. Young, *Women and the Crisis,* 69.

107. Young, *Women and the Crisis,* 113; *Banner,* "The Ladies Still at Work," September 16, 1862. Similar reports pepper the *Ohio State Journal* and *Mt. Vernon Republican* throughout the first years of the war.

108. See LeeAnn Whites, "The Civil War as a Crisis in Gender," in Clinton and Silber, *Divided Houses,* 6–19. Whites discusses how women were often described with both masculine and feminine qualities—both "heroic" and "self-sacrificing"—as the war progressed. Some women were forced into these roles in men's absence, whereas others embraced them.

109. Whites, "Civil War," 17.

110. Young, *Women and the Crisis,* 69–71; Faust, *Mothers of Invention,* 196–219.

111. Jane E. Schultz, *Women at the Front: Hospital Workers in Civil War America* (Chapel Hill: University of North Carolina Press), 173–79. For more on female medical practitioners, see Mercedes Graf, "Against All Odds: Women Doctors Who Served in the Civil War," in Conklin, *Journal of Women's Civil War History,* 2:7–32; Leonard, *Yankee Women,* chap. 3; Harper, *Women during the Civil War,* 119–21.

112. Quoted in Schultz, *Women at the Front,* 107.

113. Schultz, *Women at the Front,* 80.

114. Mitchell, "Northern Soldier," 86.

115. Other collections likewise contain references to this writing genre: "I find the Brimfield ladies not behind any others in their war correspondence," wrote Private David D. Bard to Friend Alice, November 25, 1862, in Bard, *Friend Alice*, 35, OHS.

116. The quotation in the subheading is from letter 32, written by Mollie E. Ward.

117. For more information on families settling Knox County whose descendants' names appear in these letters, see Norman Newell Hill, comp., *History of Knox County, Ohio, Its Past and Present* . . . (Mt. Vernon, OH: A. A. Graham and Co., 1881), OHS.

118. *Banner*, October 10, 1862.

119. See Mitchell, "A Northern Volunteer," for a discussion of masculinity and war service.

120. Fuller's Brigade was engaged at Decatur, Alabama, on March 8, 1864; at Sugar Valley, near Resaca, on May 9; at Resaca, Georgia, May 9–16 (at the Oostenaula River Bridge on May 13, with the battle of Resaca spanning May 14–15). The advance on Dallas, Georgia, occurred May 18–25, with battles about Dallas, New Hope Church, and Allatoona Hills, lasting from May 25 to June 5, 1864. See Dyer's *Compendium*, part 3, Ohio 43rd Regiment Infantry; Smith, *Fuller's Ohio Brigade*, 449–50; Lybarger, *Leaves from My Diary*, no page numbers.

121. The term "kinship work" is anthropologist Micaela di Leonardo's; she uses it to capture the often invisible work of tracking birthdays, planning family reunions, writing letters, and calling distant relatives that women perform to maintain families and communities. See di Leonardo, "The Female World of Cards and Holidays: Women, Families, and the Work of Kinship," *Signs* 12, no. 3 (Spring 1987): 440–53.

122. A similar idea is expressed in David Blight, "No Desperate Hero," in Clinton and Silber, *Divided Houses*, 60.

123. Mitchell, "Northern Soldier," 83.

124. The muster-in rolls for the Forty-third Ohio in January 1864 in Prospect, Tennessee, show at least nine Millwood area men reenlisting in Company K, as well as men from Butler Township; Smith, *Fuller's Ohio Brigade*, 437.

125. Ohio Roster Commission, *Official Roster*, 4:284. William Mitchell was appointed as captain July 21, 1862, and resigned March 3, 1863.

126. *Banner*, November 26, 1861; November 12, 1861.

127. Josephine Rogers, Phrone's older sister, married Frank Israel during the war. Israel was a local milliner from a well-known family that resided in Mt. Vernon. The 1860 census lists the value of his real estate and personal es-

tate as \$14,500, the highest value listed by any Millwood resident and well above the majority. Frank's father, Samuel, was an attorney who improved the mill in Knox County, put in a dam, and advertised his legal services and rental properties frequently in the *Banner;* for examples, see January 7, 1862; November 12, 1862; and May 6, 1865. He served as the auditor for the Knox County Agricultural Society and was a member of the military committee formed to help prepare and arm troops for war; see *Banner,* September 9, 1862. Republicans called him a "butternut"; see *Banner,* June 17, 1865. At the time of the 1860 census, the Israels had five children living at home (Amanda, Sarah, Sanera, James, and Samuel), several of whom are mentioned in the letters, as well as a domestic named M. Hofu. *Eighth Census,* Mt. Vernon, Ohio, 5th Ward, 65–66, OHS.

128. Smith, *Fuller's Ohio Brigade,* 578.

129. McPherson, *Cause and Comrades,* 131–39; Mitchell, "Northern Soldier," 86.

130. Wiley claims that most soldiers were "compelled by circumstances to do considerable courting work through correspondence"; Wiley, *Johnny Reb,* 281; Harper, *Women during the Civil War,* 86.

131. "Fair Knitter," *Banner,* January 14, 1862; "Union of Hearts," *Banner,* November 29, 1862.

132. See Harper, *Women during the Civil War,* 86–91; American war losses are from McPherson, *Battle Cry,* 854; Ohio's from Foner, "Ohio and the World," 80. Whitelaw Reid's figures are lower: 11,237 lost in battle, 13,354 through disease. See Reid, *Ohio in the War,* 2:5.

133. For more on the significance that men's absence and potential loss had for young Southern women's lives and their changing desires, expectations, and goals see Faust, *Mothers of Invention,* 139–52; Harper, *Women during the Civil War,* 88.

134. *Banner,* October 14, 1862; May 27, 1865. The Southern percentage is from Faust, *Mothers of Invention,* 141.

135. Faust, *Mothers of Invention,* 139–41. For an example of a heterosexual homesteading woman who chooses to remain single despite opportunities for marriage, see Philip L. Gerber, ed., *Bachelor Bess: The Homesteading Letters of Elizabeth Corey, 1909–1919* (Iowa City: University of Iowa Press, 1990).

136. Faust addresses women's relationships with other women in *Mothers of Invention* (142–45), as does Smith-Rosenberg in "Female World."

137. The quotation in the subheading is from letter 25, written by Emma Peterman. For more on nineteenth-century love letters and the ideal of romantic love that encouraged introspection, self-revelation, and identification

between amours, see Karen Lystra, *Searching the Heart: Women, Men and Romantic Love in Nineteenth-Century America* (New York: Oxford University Press, 1989), esp. 28–35. Also see 276–79 for a summary of scholarship on nineteenth-century sexuality.

138. Harper, *Women during the Civil War*, 87; Faust, *Mothers of Invention*, 118.

139. Lystra, *Searching the Heart*, 25–27.

140. David D. Bard to Alice and Clemmie, *Friend Alice*, 24, OHS.

141. *Mary Chesnut's Civil War*, 690 and 565; see Mitchell, "Northern Volunteer," 45, for other examples.

142. Wiley argues that differences in the patriotic intensity of Yankee and Rebel letters speak to varying motivations and investments in the war. He suggests that Northern soldiers often fought because of the pay. Clinton and Silber's collection, *Divided Houses*, demonstrates more-particular motivations for involvement based on class and sex, such as yeoman farmers who put aside their differences with their planter neighbors to rally for the Confederate cause in defending their rights as masters of their own modest households. See Stephanie McCurry, "The Politics of Yeoman Households in South Carolina," in Clinton and Silber, *Divided Houses*, 22–38. Similarly, Whites argues that Confederate women's support of the war included the defense of their elite positions in the household, protected through the contrasting institution of slavery; see Whites, "Civil War," esp. 5–6.

143. Samuel P. Williams enlisted November 13, 1861, and died September 2, 1864, at Rome, Georgia; Smith, *Fuller's Ohio Brigade*, 582.

144. Letter 4 is likely misdated. It bears the date of October 27, 1862, but is more likely to have been written on October 27, 1863. It was directed to Memphis, where the Forty-third was encamped in the fall of 1863; references a visit from Captain Rhodes and Mary Wolf (also discussed in September 1863; see letter 42); and includes references to the election of Ohio governor John Brough, who reemerged in the political spotlight only in 1863 to claim a key Union victory over Vallandigham. See Roseboom, *Civil War Era*, 417, 421.

145. Kitch, *Strange Society*, 23.

146. *Banner*, September 9, 1862.

147. Wiley mentions that illiterate Rebels relied on friends to write letters for them, which adds another layer to the public nature and circulation of Civil War letters; Wiley, *Johnny Reb*, 284.

148. Quoted in Lystra, *Searching the Heart*, 23.

149. Women became photographers in increasing numbers during the Civil War. According to Tracey Baker, half of the photographers listed in

directories in larger cities in Minnesota during the 1860s were women; see Baker, "Nineteenth-Century Minnesota Women Photographers," *Journal of the West* 28, no. 1 (January 1989): 15–23.

150. Faust, *Mothers of Invention*, 311.

151. Shawn Michelle Smith, *American Archives: Gender, Race and Class in Visual Culture* (Princeton, NJ: Princeton University Press, 1999), 6. The phrase "imagined visual community" draws from Benedict Anderson's well-known concept of "imagined community" in the political work of forging ideas of nation and community through the work of print.

152. This section draws from Smith's arguments about images; the gendered, racial, and sexual meanings of the photographic portraits she explores are relevant to the Lybarger letters but lie outside the scope of the current project. All content and quotations in this section not from letters are drawn from Smith, *American Archives*, esp. 6, 51.

153. This phrase is Walter Benjamin's, quoted in Smith, *American Archives*, 51–53. Smith's larger argument is that visual paradigms, of which photography is one, influenced the development of new white middle-class subjectivities over the course of the nineteenth century and the spread of, and resistance to, white nationalism. This argument is relevant to women's Civil War letters but lies outside the scope of the current project.

154. Fannie Gordon to General John Gordon, quoted in Faust, *Mothers of Invention*, 117.

155. Smith, *American Archives*, 51.

156. *Godey's Lady's Book*, August 1848, 111–12.

157. Wiley, *Johnny Reb*, 272.

158. The term Grace uses, *hedge fence*, refers to farmers' use of the Osage orange tree—an unusual tree with dense thorns and striking, wrinkled fruit—planted in millions during the nineteenth century to mark property lines and contain livestock. Some still use the fruit today to fend off insects. Thanks to Professor Dyanne Tracy for this connection.

159. In recent years, historians of education have critiqued the "grand narrative of emancipation" in which women's emergence as professional teachers has often been cast. Stories such as Phrone's help in this mission. Even though the public opportunities that teaching offered women in the nineteenth century have often been characterized in romantic terms with women as teaching heroes of sorts, teaching, like other professions, has been both a beloved and a despised occupation. Marjorie Theobald argues that expanding attention to teaching experiences that contradict the "pleasurable melodrama" some women experienced is necessary for enriching our understanding of women's varied relation-

ships with this profession. A key point, she insists, is acknowledging that the history of teaching has "largely been written by women who do not wish to be school teachers" ("Teachers," 20–21). See Theobald's essay, "Teachers, Memory and Oral History," and others in *Telling Women's Lives: Narrative Inquiries in the History of Education,* ed. Kathleen Weiler and Sue Middleton, 9–24 (Buckingham, UK: Open University Press, 1999).

160. Theobald suggests that the common phrase used to describe this time period, "feminization of teaching," is misleading and would be better replaced with the "masculinization of administration," given the parallel rise of school bureaucracy and male administrators. Jackie Blount addresses this phenomenon in *Destined to Rule the Schools: Women and the Superintendency, 1873–1995* (Albany: State University of New York Press, 1998); Blount also provides an overview of forces influencing and reactions to women's emergence as teachers. Significantly, since this period, women have remained the majority of schoolteachers in America's public school system. Women's entrée into professional positions in higher education in the nineteenth century was far more incremental than for their counterparts in the common schools, yet women moved into teaching roles at every level of U.S. colleges and universities. The U.S. Department of Education reports that in 2003, women made up 38 percent of college faculty with full-time jobs and 48 percent of part-time workers. Of full-time faculty, women made up 24 percent of full professors, 38 percent of associate professors, and 46 percent of assistant professors. Among non–tenure track teachers, women constituted 48 percent of instructors and 53 percent of lecturers. While women's presence in higher education is by now well established, these percentages indicate that women are concentrated in the lower levels of teaching, with limited change from their status in the nineteenth century.

161. Ohio State Teachers Association, *A History of Education in the State of Ohio: A Centennial Volume* (Columbus, OH: Gazette Printing House, 1876), 448.

162. Schultz, *Women at the Front,* 183.

163. The larger argument referenced here, women's shifting sense of self forged through the demands of the home front, emerges in Faust, *Mothers of Invention;* Leonard, *Yankee Women*; Clinton and Silber, *Divided Houses*; and Attie, *Patriotic Toil.* Similar arguments have been made in relation to women's factory labor during World War II; see Rosalyn Baxandall, Linda Gordon, and Susan Reverby, eds., *America's Working Women: A Documentary History—1600 to the Present* (New York: Vintage Books, 1976; revised ed., New York: W.W. Norton, 1995).

164. "Elizabeth" from Knox County, *Ohio Cultivator*, February 15, 1850, 62, quoted in Amy H. Clifford, "Feminism in Ohio, 1848–1857" (master's thesis, Kent State University, 1972), 16.

165. Compiled from Union Township, Millwood census, 1–28 (218 households, 132 farmers). Van Shrimplin's mother, Sarah, and Henry McElroy's mother were among those listed as unable to read or write; *Eighth Census*, 112–17. From 1853 through 1873, the category "school-age" included youths ages 5–21; Ohio State Teachers Association, *History of Education*, 446.

166. The quotation in the subheading is from letter 161, written by Lib Baker.

167. Clifford, "Feminism in Ohio," 16; *Banner*, October 29, 1861; *Godey's Lady's Book*, August 1848, 111–12.

168. Laurence Van Buskirk to Daniel Van Buskirk, January 1849, Van Buskirk Family Papers, MSS 690, OHS.

169. For more on educational initiatives in Ohio, see Roseboom, *Civil War Era*, 175–97. Also see Bossing, "History of Educational Legislation," for full discussion of legislative initiatives, ideological and political differences among Ohioans, school control, and teacher training. The idea of tax-supported schools was still contentious in the 1830s; see Smythe, *Kenyon College*, 73; "School Teachers," *Banner*, April 9, 1861. Temperance Darling, perhaps one of Lybarger's early love interests (letter 41), was one of nine children in a female-headed household in Butler Township and was eighteen years old when she received her certificate.

170. Laurence Van Buskirk to Brother, Van Buskirk Family Papers, MSS 690, OHS; Roseboom, *Civil War Era*.

171. *Ohio School Journal*, December 30, 1851. This figure does not include the "German-English" and "Colored" schools; Ohio State Teachers Association, *History of Education*, 447. See Bossing for discussion of conflicts in school control, 100–102.

172. Ohio State Teachers Association, *History of Education*, 447.

173. Commissioner of Statistics, *Annual Report, 1859*, 82–83, 133–34, quoted in Roseboom, *Civil War Era*, 182, 179.

174. For an overview of Ohio women's educational and cultural pursuits throughout the nineteenth century, see Stephanie Elise Booth, *Buckeye Women: The History of Ohio's Daughters* (Athens: Ohio University Press, 2001), 151–85.

175. Lorey, *History of Knox County*, 321–24; Ohio State Teachers Association, *History of Education*, 445. High schools in Ohio were mainly urban; see Bossing, "History of Educational Legislation," 101.

176. Roseboom, *Civil War Era*, 179; Reese, *Origins*, 222–24. One Ohio source cites females exceeding male graduates in Dayton, Toledo, and Sandusky by the 1870s; see Ohio State Teachers Association, *History of Education*, 159–77.

177. Foner, "Ohio and the World," 76.

178. See Robert Samuel Fletcher, *A History of Oberlin College: From Its Foundation through the Civil War*, 2 vols. (Oberlin, OH: Oberlin College, 1943); James Oliver Horton, "Race and Region: Ohio, America's Middle Ground," in Parker, Sisson, and Coil, *Ohio and the World*, 63–64.

179. Clifford, "Feminism in Ohio," 22.

180. Clifford, "Feminism in Ohio," 22–26; Eleanor Flexner, *A Century of Struggle: The Woman's Rights Movement in the United States* (Cambridge, MA: Belknap Press, 1977), 29–30, 69.

181. Roseboom, *Civil War Era*, 181; Ohio State Teachers Association, *History of Education*, 122. Stoddard's arithmetic series, Mitchell's *Geography*, and McGuffey's readers were among those the Knox County School Board recommended in October 1853; Knox County, Ohio, Board of Education, Clinton Township Minutes, 1853–1896, State Series 3228, OHS, 1861 and 1862. Ray's *Arithmetic*, Cornell's *Physical Geography*, Harvey's *Grammar*, and McGuffey's readers were used in Guernsey County until graded schools were instituted there; Early School Book Committee, *Early Schools of Guernsey County* (Dallas, TX: Taylor Publishing, 1987).

182. *Banner*, October 29, 1861.

183. Financial need may have inspired Amelia to take in a boarder; Lybarger sent portions of his pay home throughout the war, but the amounts of $10.00 and $50.00 earlier in his service jumped to $360.00 in November 1864. Payment of $50.00 to Lybarger's father is shown for September 1, 1863. Auditor, Knox County, Ohio, *Record of Money Sent Home by Soldiers, 1862–1865*, State Series 3255, OHS. Mrs. Lybarger and Widow Lybarger of Union Township are shown to have received payments multiple times from Knox County commissioners for the relief of families serving in the Civil War. Ohio Auditor, *Statement of Amounts of Funds Received and Distributed for Relief of Soldiers' Families, 1861–66*, State Series 2982, Knox County, OHS.

184. A. Banning Norton, *A History of Knox County, Ohio, from 1779 to 1862 . . .* (Columbus, OH: R. Nevins, 1862), 322, 389.

185. Roseboom, *Civil War Era*, 188.

186. The quotation in the subheading is from letter 145, written by Rosa Crum.

187. For more on the history of teaching standards and preparation, see James W. Fraser, *Preparing America's Teachers: A History* (New York: Teachers College Press, 2007).

188. Ohio State Teachers Association, *History of Education*, 448; the "prosper" quotation is from Reese, *Origins*, 123.

189. See Massey, *Bonnet Brigades*, 108–30, for an overview of regional differences and Kathryn Kish Sklar's work for other differences, in *Catharine Beecher: A Study in American Domesticity* (New Haven, CT: Yale University Press, 1973).

190. This phrase is from historian Thomas Woody; quoted in Blount, *Destined to Rule the Schools*, 10.

191. Lowell, Massachusetts, was one of the earliest mill areas in the country. Factory owners began hiring women in 1823. Lowell is also the site of historic industrial strikes in the 1830s and 1840s in which workers protested factory owners' decisions to cut wages and require longer hours when the economy faltered. Women, whose wages were already lower than men's, participated in the strikes and contributed to some of the first public hearings in the country on factory working conditions. See "The First Official Investigation of Labor Conditions in Massachusetts," in *A Documentary History of American Industrial Society*, ed. John R. Commons, Ulrich B. Phillips, Eugene A. Gilmore, Helen L. Sumner, and John B. Andrews (Cleveland: Arthur H. Clark, 1910), 130–42; Philip S. Foner, ed., *The Factory Girls: A Collection of Writings* . . . (Urbana: University of Illinois Press, 1977).

192. Massey, *Bonnet Brigades*, 5; *Eighth Census*, quoted in Booth, *Buckeye Women*, 20. Information on the increase in female printers, merchants, bookkeepers, and postmistresses in Ohio can be found in Clifford, "Feminism in Ohio," 231–37. Teaching statistics are in Ohio State Teachers Association, *History of Education*, 448.

193. Cited in Blount, *Destined to Rule the Schools*, 17. See Sklar, *Catharine Beecher*, chap. 12; Catharine Beecher, *The Evils Suffered by American Women and American Children: The Causes and the Remedy* (New York: Harper and Bros., 1846), 11–14.

194. Quoted in Bledstein, *Culture*, 119. Ohio women express similar sentiments in the 1850s; see Clifford, "Feminism in Ohio," 14.

195. For details on this phenomenon, see Bledstein, *Culture*.

196. For the reference to the Knox and Muskingum County Board of Education, see Roseboom, *Civil War Era*, 186. For information on the development of teaching training in Ohio, see Ohio State Teachers Association,

History of Education, chap. 4; Roseboom, *Civil War Era*, 187–89; and Bossing, "History of Educational Legislation," 314.

197. The quotation in the subheading is from letter 97, written by Lib Baker.

198. This extemporaneous speech was apparently given in response to women's rights opponents at a convention in 1851 and was recorded by Frances Gage almost ten years later. See Miriam Schneir, ed., *Feminism: The Essential Historical Writings* (New York: Random House, 1972); scholars refer to the speech both as "Arn't I a Woman" and as "Ain't I a Woman." Nell Irvin Painter, *Sojourner Truth: A Life, a Symbol* (New York: W. W. Norton, 1997), argues that women's rights activists used Truth as a symbol and that she may never have given this speech at all, 77–78.

199. Flexner, *Century of Struggle;* Clifford, "Feminism in Ohio," 69, 94, 100, 107. Clifford discusses varied restrictive Ohio laws that were changed to better serve women in the nineteenth century and reports that northern Ohio men were more likely than southern Ohioans to support the removal of the word *male* from the Ohio constitution. "Feminism in Ohio," 137; Booth, *Buckeye Women*, 60.

200. Seneca Falls Convention, Declaration of Sentiments, 1848; Clifford, "Feminism in Ohio," 100; Booth, *Buckeye Women*, chap. 3.

201. *Banner*, November 12, 1861. For an example of sensationalist tales of women discovered to be men surfacing during this time, see "A Man Woman," *Banner*, May 27, 1865.

202. *Banner*, May 27, 1865.

203. William T. Sherman, *Home Letters of General Sherman*, ed. M. A. Dewolfe Howe (New York: Charles Scribner's Sons, 1909), 335.

204. *Mary Chesnut's Civil War*, 672, 650.

205. Leonard, *Yankee Women*; Schultz, *Women at the Front*, 107.

206. *Mary Chesnut's Civil War*, 181.

207. For examples of changing gender roles, see Leonard, *Yankee Women*, and Faust, *Mothers of Invention*; for an example of the resiliency of gender norms in the postwar South, see Schultz, *Women at the Front*, 151–54.

208. The quotation in the subheading is from letter 94, written by Rosa Crum.

209. Blount, *Destined to Rule*, 19–21; see chap. 1 for arguments for and against women teaching. Also see Nancy Hoffman, *Women's "True" Profession: Voices from the History of Teaching* (Cambridge, MA: Harvard Education Publishing Group, 2003) for more information on this gendered history.

210. Thomas Woody, *A History of Women's Education in the United States* (New York: Science Press, 1929), 490–99. The board awarded teaching certificates to 60 women and 13 men in March 1861 (*Banner*, April 9, 1861) and to 41 women and 5 men in April 1862 (*Banner*, May 5, 1862). Data on Ohio teacher salaries are from Ohio State Teachers Association, *History of Education*, 448–49; Knox County Board of Education, *Clinton Township Minutes, 1861 and 1862*, State Series 3228, OHS; and Roseboom, *Civil War Era*, 184.

211. In the South, women's earnings ranged from $200 a year in some areas to as much as $600, although teachers were sometimes paid in Confederate scrip, which became equivalent to pennies by Appomattox. During the war, the cost of living rose 100 percent while in some cases teachers' wages rose only 20 percent and in other cases were cut. See Massey, *Bonnet Brigades*, esp. 120–22. Roseboom reports 10 percent salary reductions for some Ohio teachers by 1862; see *Civil War Era*, 184.

212. Fraser, *Preparing America's Teachers*, 33.

213. School changes and teaching statistics cited in Roseboom, *Civil War Era*, 184, 191. See State Commissioner of Common Schools, *Annual Report*, 1862, 3–4. Also see Emerson E. White and Thomas W. Harvey, *A History of Education in the State of Ohio* (Columbus, OH: Gazette Printing, 1876).

214. McPherson, *Battle Cry*, 569, 570–72.

215. See Frances Ferguson, "Interpreting the Self through Letters," *Centrum* 1, no. 2 (Fall 1981): 107–12.

216. Wiley, *Billy Yank*, 186.

217. The title of this section is drawn from Christine Dee, ed., *Ohio's War* (Athens: Ohio University Press, 2007). The quotation is from Roseboom, *Civil War Era*, 426; see also 397–98, 423–26. See Frank L. Klement, *Dark Lanterns: Secret Political Societies, Conspiracies, and Treason Trials in the Civil War* (Baton Rouge: Louisiana State University Press, 1984), 27–28; *Banner*, September 2, 1862; Luther M. Feeger, *Copperhead Agitation in Wayne County, Indiana and General Morgan's Raid through Southern Indiana* (Richmond, IN: Palladium-Item, 1955).

218. Roseboom, *Civil War Era*, 397–98; *Banner*, September 16, 1862.

219. Gerald M. Petty, *Index of the Ohio Squirrel Hunters Roster* (Columbus, OH: Petty's Press, 1984); *Banner*, September 9 and 16, 1862.

220. Quotations from Ohioans in McPherson, *Cause and Comrades*, 16. Ohio implemented the draft in many locations, particularly in 1864, though as many as 18,000 deserted in Ohio; Reid, *Ohio in the War*, 1:208–20; Roseboom, *Civil War Era*, 388–95, 428; Lorey, *History*, 121.

221. The quotation in the subheading is from letter 63, written by Lou Riggen.

222. Lincoln's quotation is from Roseboom, *Civil War Era*, 421, although some historians doubt that the message was ever sent. See Klement, *Limits of Dissent*, 252. The alleged telegram has nevertheless achieved a place in Ohio lore. For statistics, see Roseboom, *Civil War Era*, 371, 435, 437.

223. Quotation from McPherson, *Cause and Comrades*, 133. He mentions, as does Wiley, that women's letters from the home front often lamented the difficulties that men's absences caused. Gail Hamilton's letter responds to this tendency in the North.

224. *Banner*, November 12 and 26, 1861.

225. This letter (June 23, 1863) is likely misdated by one month, as Morgan moved into Indiana after July 8, then into Ohio, before his surrender on July 26.

226. Roseboom, *Civil War Era*, 409.

227. The quotation in the subheading is from letter 22, written by Ella Hawn.

228. Phrone calls Campbell a "secesh" in letter 14, which contrasts with his prowar and Unionist sentiments in letter 23. The discrepancy indicates that he may have wavered in his political convictions, that Phrone was in error, or that he intentionally expressed political opinions he believed his long-time friend on the front lines would want to read.

229. Klement, *Dark Lanterns*, 7–33; *Limits of Dissent*, 111, 148.

230. Ohio Adjutant General, *Civil War Muster Rolls, Regiment 43*, Company K, Roll 3, "Statement of Discharge," October 10, 1872 (Butts); "Statement of Service," May 1, 1888 (Baker).

231. Roseboom, *Civil War Era*, 421; Klement, *Limits of Dissent*, 2, 149; *Banner*, September 2, 1862; Roseboom, *Civil War Era*, 411–14.

232. Klement, *Limits of Dissent*, 178–84; Roseboom, *Civil War Era*, 411–14, 421–23.

233. C. L. Vallandigham, *The Record of Hon. C. L. Vallandigham on Abolition, the Union, and the Civil War* (Columbus, OH: J. Walter and Co., 1863); McPherson, *Battle Cry*, 600, 608, 601, 610, 600; Klement, *Limits of Dissent*, 131–32.

234. Roseboom, *Civil War Era*, 410; Smith, *Fuller's Ohio Brigade*, 418–19; Wood Gray, *The Hidden Civil War: The Story of the Copperheads* (New York: Viking, 1942), 94; Horton, "Race and Region," 67.

235. *Banner*, December 20, 1862.

236. McPherson, *Battle Cry*, 688.

237. *Banner*, December 20, 1862; September 2, 1862.

238. The statistics are from Lorey, *History*, 111–12; the quotation is in McPherson, *Battle Cry*, 565.

239. Roseboom, *Civil War Era*, 7; Horton, "Race and Region," 43–45, 67-68; for more on the racial history of Ohio, see chapters in Parker, Sisson, and Coil, *Ohio and the World*, and documents in Dee, *Ohio's War*. Noah Andre Trudeau, *Like Men of War: Black Troops in the Civil War, 1862–1865* (New Jersey: Castle Books, 2002), includes a bibliography on black regiments.

240. *Banner*, September 23, 1862, emphasis in original; for an exploration of gender in African-American enlistment, see Jim Cullen, "'I's a man now:' Gender and African American Men," in Clinton and Silber, *Divided Houses*, 76-91.

241. *Banner*, January 28, 1862.

242. See Jacobson, *Whiteness of a Different Color* and Noel Ignatiev, *How the Irish Became White* (New York: Routledge, 1995).

243. Although race is rarely explicit in the collection, it is nevertheless a constitutive element of letter writing and the middle-class norms of letter production, and a worthy topic to explore in greater detail elsewhere. The racialized and racist elements of white women's nineteenth-century writing—produced amid colonialism, social Darwinism, and immigration—have been well theorized in a variety of genres. For examples of the ways in which whiteness can function as an unmarked but potent presence in a writer's imaginary, see Toni Morrison, *Playing in the Dark: Whiteness and the Literary Imagination* (New York: Vintage Press, 1992) and Bailey, "Wright-ing White." Also see Vron Ware, *Beyond the Pale: White Women, Racism and History* (London: Verso, 1992) for a historical perspective.

244. *Mt. Vernon Republican*, April 9, 1863.

245. *Mt. Vernon Republican*, April 16, 1863.

246. Mary Chesnut's famous line is "god forgive us but ours is a monstrous system and wrong and iniquity," March 18, 1861, *Mary Chesnut's Civil War*, 29.

247. *Banner*, September 23, 1862.

248. McPherson, *Cause and Comrades*, 21; *Banner*, September 9, 1862; and Foner, *Ohio in the World*, 86.

249. *Banner*, June 17, 1865, *Republican*, June 6, 1865.

250. As this text was in its final stages of publication, I discovered two texts that I would have liked to consider during research. I include them here

for others' reference: Patricia L. Richard, *Busy Hands: Images of the Family in the Northern Civil War Effort* (New York: Fordham University Press, 2003); and Jennifer L. Weber, *Copperheads: The Rise and Fall of Lincoln's Opponents in the North* (Oxford University Press, 2006). In one chapter, Pritchard explores the phenomenon of soldier correspondence ads and their moral and romantic elements; we note similar themes and come to some common conclusions. Weber's text extends Klement's work on this powerful antiwar force that was prominent in these letter writers' lives.

Bibliography

Abbott, Don Paul. "Rhetoric and Writing in Renaissance Europe and England." In *A Short History of Writing Instruction*, edited by James J. Murphy, 95–120. Davis, CA: Hermagoras Press, 1990.

Abbott, Virginia Clark. *The History of Woman Suffrage and the League of Women Voters in Cuyahoga County, 1911–1945.* Cleveland: 1949.

Adjutant General to the Governor of the State of Ohio. *Annual Report.* Columbus: Richard Nevins, State Printer, 1866.

Aledo Weekly Record, (Mercer County, Illinois). Abraham Lincoln Presidential Library.

Attie, Jeanie. *Patriotic Toil: Northern Women and the American Civil War.* Ithaca, NY: Cornell University Press, 1998.

Auditor, Knox County, Ohio. *Record of Money Sent Home by Soldiers, 1862–1865.* State Series 3255, OHS.

———. *Reports of the School Treasurers, 1864–1888.* State Series 3757, OHS.

Bailey, Lucy E. "Wright-ing White: The Construction of Race in Women's 19th Century Didactic Texts." *Journal of Thought* 41, no. 4 (Winter 2006): 65–81.

Baker, Tracey. "Nineteenth-Century Minnesota Women Photographers." *Journal of the West* 28, no. 1 (January 1989): 15–23.

Bard, David D. *Friend Alice: The Civil War Letters of Captain David D. Bard, 7th and 104th Regiments, Ohio Volunteer Infantry, 1862–1864.* Edited by James T. Brenner. Kent, OH: Scholar of Fortune Publications, 1996. OHS.

Baxandall, Rosalyn, Linda Gordon, and Susan Reverby, eds. *America's Working Women: A Documentary History—1600 to the Present.* New York: Vintage Books, 1976. Revised ed., New York: W.W. Norton, 1995.

Baym, Nina. *American Women Writers and the Work of History, 1790–1860.* New Brunswick, NJ: Rutgers University Press, 1995.

———. *Novels, Readers, and Reviewers: Responses to Fiction in Antebellum America.* Ithaca, NY: Cornell University Press, 1984.

———. *Woman's Fiction: A Guide to Novels by and about Women in America, 1820–1870.* Champaign: University of Illinois Press, 1993.

Beauchamp, Virginia Walcott, ed. *A Private War: Letters and Diaries of Madge Preston, 1862–1867*. New Brunswick, NJ: Rutgers University Press, 1987.

Beecher, Catharine. *The Evils Suffered by American Women and American Children: The Causes and the Remedy*. New York: Harper and Bros., 1846.

Billington, Ray Allen. *The Protestant Crusade, 1800–1860: A Study of the Origins of American Nativism*. New York: Peter Smith, 1938.

Bledstein, Burton. *The Culture of Professionalism: The Middle Class and the Development of Higher Education in America*. New York: W. W. Norton, 1976.

Blight, David W. "No Desperate Hero: Manhood and Freedom in a Union Soldier's Experience." In *Divided Houses: Gender and the Civil War*, edited by Catherine Clinton and Nina Silber, 55–75. New York: Oxford University Press, 1992.

Blount, Jackie. *Destined to Rule the Schools: Women and the Superintendency, 1873–1995*. Albany: State University of New York Press, 1998.

———. *Fit to Teach: Same-sex Desire, Gender and School Work in the Twentieth Century*. Albany: State University of New York Press, 2005.

Booth, Stephane Elise. *Buckeye Women: The History of Ohio's Daughters*. Athens: Ohio University Press, 2001.

Bosch, Mineke. "Gossipy Letters in the Context of International Feminism." In *Current Issues in Women's History*, edited by Arina Angerman, Geerte Binnema, Annemieke Keunen, Vefie Poels, and Jacqueline Zirkzee, 131–52. London: Routledge, 1989.

Bossing, Nelson L. "The History of Educational Legislation in Ohio from 1851–1925." *Ohio History* 39, no. 1 (1930): 78–219.

Chesnut, Mary Boykin Miller. *Mary Chesnut's Civil War*. Edited by C. Vann Woodward. New Haven, CT: Yale University Press, 1981.

Clifford, Amy H. "Feminism in Ohio, 1848–1857." Master's thesis, Kent State University, Kent, Ohio, 1972.

Clinton, Catherine, and Nina Silber, eds. *Divided Houses: Gender and the Civil War*. New York: Oxford University Press, 1992.

Conklin, Eileen, ed. *The Journal of Women's Civil War History: From the Home Front to the Front Lines*. 2 vols. Gettysburg: Thomas Publications, 2001, 2002.

Cook, Elizabeth Heckendorn. *Epistolary Bodies: Gender and Genre in the Eighteenth-Century Republic of Letters*. Stanford: Stanford University Press, 1996.

Cott, Nancy. *The Bonds of Womanhood*. New Haven, CT: Yale University Press, 1977.

Cozzens, Peter. *The Darkest Days of the War: The Battles of Iuka and Corinth.* Chapel Hill: University of North Carolina Press, 2006.

Cullen, Jim. "'I's a man now': Gender and African American Men." In *Divided Houses: Gender and the Civil War,* edited by Catherine Clinton and Nina Silber, 76–91. New York: Oxford University Press.

Dawes, Rufus R. and Alan T. Nolan. *A Full Blown Yankee of the Iron Brigade: Service with the Sixth Wisconsin Volunteers.* Lincoln: University of Nebraska Press, 1999.

Dee, Christine, ed. *Ohio's War.* Athens: Ohio University Press, 2007.

Di Leonardo, Micaela. "The Female World of Cards and Holidays: Women, Families, and the Work of Kinship." *Signs* 12, no. 3 (Spring 1987), 440–53.

Dyer, Frederick H. *A Compendium of the War of the Rebellion.* New York: T. Yoseloff, 1908. Reprint, Dayton, OH: The Press of Morningside Bookshop, 1979.

Early School Book Committee. *Early Schools of Guernsey County.* Dallas, TX: Taylor Publishing, 1987.

Eighth Census of the United States, 1860 Federal Population Census Index.

Eisenmann, L. *Historical Dictionary of Women's Education in the United States.* Westport, CT: Greenwood Press, 1998.

Farrell, Michèle. *Performing Motherhood: The Sévigné Correspondence.* Hanover, NH: University Press of New England, 1991.

Faust, Drew Gilpin. *Mothers of Invention: Women of the Slaveholding South in the American Civil War.* Chapel Hill: University of North Carolina Press, 1996.

Feeger, Luther M. *Copperhead Agitation in Wayne County, Indiana and General Morgan's Raid through Southern Indiana.* Richmond, IN: Palladium-Item, 1955.

Ferguson, Frances. "Interpreting the Self through Letters." *Centrum* 1, no. 2 (Fall 1981): 107–12.

Finsley, Charles F., ed. *Hannah's Letters: The Civil War Letters of Isaac E. Blauvelt, Friends, and Other Suitors.* Cedar Hill, TX: Kings Creek Press, 1997.

"First Official Investigation of Labor Conditions in Massachusetts, The." In *A Documentary History of American Industrial Society,* edited by John R. Commons, Ulrich B. Phillips, Eugene A. Gilmore, Helen L. Sumner, and John B. Andrews. Cleveland: Arthur H. Clark, 1910.

FitzGerald, Edward, trans. *The Rubaiyat of Omar Khayyam of Naishapur.* 4th ed. New York: Doxey's, 1879, 1900.

Fletcher, Robert Samuel. *A History of Oberlin College: From Its Foundation through the Civil War.* 2 vols. Oberlin, OH: Oberlin College, 1943.

Flexner, Eleanor. *A Century of Struggle: The Woman's Rights Movement in the United States.* Cambridge, MA: Belknap Press, 1977.

Foner, Eric. "Ohio and the World: The Civil War Era." In *Ohio and the World, 1753–2053: Essays toward a New History of Ohio,* edited by Geoffrey Parker, Richard Sisson, and William Russell Coil, 73–94. Columbus: Ohio State University Press, 2005.

———. *A Short History of Reconstruction, 1863–1877.* New York: Harper and Row, 1990.

Foner, Philip S., ed. *The Factory Girls: A Collection of Writings on Life and Struggles in the New England Factories of the 1840s by the Factory Girls Themselves, and the Story, in Their Own Words, of the First Trade Unions of Women Workers in the U.S.* Urbana: University of Illinois Press, 1977.

Forbes, Ella. *African American Women during the Civil War.* New York: Garland, 1998.

Fraser, James W. *Preparing America's Teachers: A History.* New York: Teachers College Press, 2007.

Fuller, John W. *"Our Kirby Smith": A Paper Read before the Ohio Commandery of the Military Order of the Loyal Legion of the United States, March 2, 1887.* Cincinnati, OH: H. C. Sherick and Company, 1887.

Fuller, Michael J. *Ohio and the World.* Oxford, OH: School of Education and Allied Professions, Miami University, 1980.

Geary, Susan. "The Domestic Novel as Commercial Commodity: Making a Best Seller in the 1850s." *Bibliographical Society of American Papers* 70, no. 3 (1976): 365–95.

Gerber, Philip L., ed. *Bachelor Bess: The Homesteading Letters of Elizabeth Corey, 1909–1919.* Iowa City: University of Iowa Press, 1990.

Gibbens, Byrd. *This Is a Strange Country: Letters of a Westering Family, 1880–1906.* Albuquerque: University of New Mexico Press, 1988.

Ginzberg, Lori D. "'Moral Suasion Is Moral Balderdash': Women, Politics, and Social Activism in the 1850s." *Journal of American History* 73, no. 3 (December 1986): 601–22.

Godey's Lady's Book, 1848.

Graf, Mercedes. "Against All Odds: Women Doctors Who Served in the Civil War." In *The Journal of Women's Civil War History: From the Home Front to the Front Lines,* edited by Eileen Conklin, 2:74–85. Gettysburg: Thomas Publications, 2002.

Gray, Wood. *The Hidden Civil War: The Story of the Copperheads.* New York: Viking, 1942.

Halloran, S. Michael. "From Rhetoric to Composition: The Teaching of Writing in America to 1900." In *A Short History of Writing Instruction*, edited by James J. Murphy, 151–82. Davis, CA: Hermagoras Press, 1990.

Hamilton, Gail [Mary Abigail Dodge]. "A Call to My Country-Women." *Atlantic Monthly* 11, no. 65 (March 1863): 345–49.

Haney-Lopez, Ian F. *White by Law: The Legal Construction of Race*. New York: New York University, 1996.

Harper, Judith E. *Women during the Civil War: An Encyclopedia*. New York: Routledge, 2004.

Higham, John. *Strangers in the Land: Patterns of American Nativism, 1860–1925*. New Brunswick, NJ: Rutgers University Press, 1955.

Hill, Norman Newell, comp. *History of Knox County, Ohio, Its Past and Present, Containing a Condensed, Comprehensive History of Ohio, Including an Outline History of the Northwest; a Complete History of Knox County . . . a Record of Its Soldiers in the Late War; Portraits of Its Early Settlers and Prominent Men . . . Biographies and Histories of Pioneer Families*. Mt. Vernon, OH: A. A. Graham and Co., 1881.

Hoffman, Nancy. *Women's "True" Profession: Voices from the History of Teaching*. Cambridge, MA: Harvard Education Publishing Group, 2003.

Hogan, Margaret A., and C. James Taylor, eds. *My Dearest Friend: Letters of Abigail and John Adams*. Cambridge, MA: Belknap Press, 2007.

Horton, James Oliver. "Race and Region: Ohio, America's Middle Ground." In *Ohio and the World, 1753–2053: Essays Toward a New History of Ohio*, edited by Geoffrey Parker, Richard Sisson, and William Russell Coil, 43–72. Columbus: Ohio State University Press, 2005.

Howe, M. A. DeWolf, ed. *Home Letters of General Sherman*. New York: Charles Scribner's Sons, 1909.

Ignatiev, Noel. *How the Irish Became White*. New York: Routledge, 1995.

Jacobson, Matthew Frye. *Whiteness of a Different Color: European Immigrants and the Alchemy of Race*. Cambridge, MA: Harvard University Press, 1998.

James, Peggie Seitz. *Knox County, Ohio, 1860 Federal Population Census Index (Heads of Families)*. Munroe Falls, OH, 1973. OHS.

Jolly, Margaretta. "Confidantes, Co-Workers and Correspondents: Feminist Discourses of Letter-Writing from 1970 to the Present." *Journal of European Studies* 32 (2002): 267–82.

Kaestle, Carl E. *Pillars of the Republic: Common Schools and American Society, 1780–1860*. New York: Hill and Wang, 1983.

Kauffman, Linda S. *Discourses of Desire: Gender, Genre and Epistolary Fiction.* Ithaca, NY: Cornell University Press, 1986.

Kennedy, Joseph. *Population of the United States: Compiled from the Original Returns of the Eighth Census, U.S. Census Office.* Washington, DC: Government Printing Office, 1864.

Kenyon, Olga, ed. *800 Years of Women's Letters.* New York: Penguin Books, 1992.

Kenyon College. Circleville, OH: Press of the Union-Herald, 1880.

Kerber, Linda K., and Jane Sherron De Hart, eds. *Women's America: Refocusing the Past.* New York: Oxford University Press, 2004.

Kitch, Sally L. *This Strange Society of Women: Reading the Letters and Lives of the Woman's Commonwealth.* Columbus: Ohio State University Press, 1993.

Klement, Frank L. *Dark Lanterns: Secret Political Societies, Conspiracies, and Treason Trials in the Civil War.* Baton Rouge: Louisiana State University Press, 1984.

———. *The Limits of Dissent: Clement L. Vallandigham and the Civil War.* Lexington: University Press of Kentucky, 1970.

Knox County (Ohio) Board of Education, Clinton Township Minutes, 1853–1896. State Series 3228, OHS.

Knox County, Ohio, Clerk of Courts, *Justice of the Peace Civil Docket, 1847–1899.* State Archives Series 3240. Columbus: Ohio Historical Archives.

Ladies Indispensable Assistant. New York, 1852.

Leckie, Shirley A. *The Colonel's Lady on the Western Frontier: The Correspondence of Alice Kirk Grierson.* Lincoln: University of Nebraska Press, 1989.

Leisch, Juanita. "Who Did What: Women's Roles in the Civil War." In *The Journal of Women's Civil War History: From the Home Front to the Front Lines,* edited by Eileen Conklin, 2:160–66. Gettysburg: Thomas Publications, 2002.

Leonard, Elizabeth D. *All the Daring of the Soldier: Women of the Civil War Armies.* New York: Penguin, 2001.

———. *Yankee Women: Gender Battles in the Civil War.* New York: W. W. Norton, 1994.

Lerner, Gerda. "Priorities and Challenges in Women's History Research." *Perspectives* 26 (April 1988): 17–20.

Licking Record. Newark, Ohio.

Linderman, Gerald F. *Embattled Courage: The Experience of Combat in the American Civil War.* New York: Free Press, 1987.

Lorey, Frederick N., ed. *History of Knox County, Ohio, 1876–1976.* 2nd ed. Mt. Vernon, OH: Knox County Historical Society, 1992.

Lybarger, Donald Fisher. *History of the Lybarger Family.* Trenton, NJ: Lybarger Memorial Association, 1988.

Lybarger, Edwin L. *Leaves from My Diary: Being a Transcript of the Daily Record I Kept during Sherman's March to the Sea and to the End of the War.* N.P. Coshocton, OH, 1910.

———. *A paper read by Capt. E. L. Lybarger, Forty-third Ohio Vol. Infantry, at a reunion of Fuller's Ohio Brigade, held at Marietta, Ohio, September 10, 1885.* OHS.

Lystra, Karen. *Searching the Heart: Women, Men and Romantic Love in Nineteenth-Century America.* New York: Oxford University Press, 1989.

Martin, Theodora Penny. *The Sound of Our Own Voices: Women's Study Clubs, 1860–1910.* Boston: Beacon Press, 1987.

Massey, Mary Elizabeth. *Bonnet Brigades: American Women and the Civil War.* New York: Knopf, 1966.

McCurry, Stephanie. "The Politics of Yeoman Households in South Carolina." In *Divided Houses: Gender and the Civil War,* edited by Catherine Clinton and Nina Silber, 22–42. New York: Oxford University Press, 1992.

McFarland, JoAnne. "Those Scribbling Women: A Cultural Study of Mid-Nineteenth Century Popular American Romances by Women." *Journal of Communication Inquiry* 9, no. 2 (1985): 33–49.

McPherson, James M. *Battle Cry of Freedom: The Civil War Era.* New York: Oxford University Press, 1988.

———. *For Cause and Comrades: Why Men Fought in the Civil War.* New York: Oxford University Press, 1997.

McPherson, James M., and William J. Cooper Jr., eds. *Writing the Civil War: The Quest to Understand.* Columbia: University of South Carolina Press, 1998.

Mehaffey, Karen Rae. "They Called Her Captain: The Amazing Life of Emily Virginia Mason." In *The Journal of Women's Civil War History: From the Home Front to the Front Lines,* edited by Eileen Conklin, 2:74–85. Gettysburg: Thomas Publications, 2002.

Miller, Ruth. "The Missionary Narrative as Coercive Interrogation: Seduction, Confession and Self-Presentation in Women's 'Letters Home.'" *Women's History Review* 15, no. 5 (November 2006): 751–71.

Mitchell, Reid. "The Northern Soldier and His Community." In *Toward a Social History of the American Civil War,* edited by M. A. Vinovskis, 78–92. Cambridge: Cambridge University Press, 1990.

————. "Soldiering, Manhood and Coming of Age: A Northern Volunteer." In *Divided Houses: Gender and the Civil War*, edited by Catherine Clinton and Nina Silber, 43–75. New York: Oxford University Press, 1992.

————. *The Vacant Chair: The Northern Soldier Leaves Home.* New York: Oxford University Press, 1993.

Morrison, Toni. *Playing in the Dark: Whiteness and the Literary Imagination.* New York: Vintage, 1992.

Morrissey, Mary, and Gillian Wright. "Piety and Sociability in Early Modern Women's Letters." *Women's Writing* 13, no. 1 (March 2006): 44–59.

Mount Vernon Democratic Banner. Mt. Vernon, Knox County, Ohio.

Mount Vernon Republican, Knox County, Ohio.

Murphy, James J., ed. *A Short History of Writing Instruction from Ancient Greece to Twentieth-Century America.* Davis, CA: Hermagoras Press, 1990.

Myers, Lois E., *Letters by Lamplight: A Woman's View of Everyday Life in South Texas, 1873–1883.* Waco, TX: Baylor University Press, 1991.

Norton, A. Banning. *A History of Knox County, Ohio, from 1779 to 1862 Inclusive: Comprising Biographical Sketches, Anecdotes and Incidents of Men Connected with the County from its First Settlement . . . and a Sketch of Kenyon College, and Other Institutions of Learning and Religion within the County.* Columbus, OH: R. Nevins, 1862.

Ohio Adjutant General's Dept. *Civil War Muster in and Muster out Rolls, State Series 2440, Regiment 43.* Columbus: Ohio Historical Society.

Ohio Auditor. *Statement of Amounts of Funds Received and Distributed for Relief of Soldiers' Families, 1861–1866.* State Series 2982, Knox County, OHS.

Ohio Dept. of Education, Annual Report of the State Commissioner of Common Schools, Ohio Docs 33 v. 8–11 (1862–1863). Ohio Historical Society, Columbus, Ohio.

Ohio Roster Commission, comp. *Official Roster of the Soldiers of the State of Ohio in the War of the Rebellion, 1861–1866.* Akron, OH: Werner Co., 1886–95. Columbus: Ohio Historical Society.

Ohio School Journal, 1851.

Ohio State Teachers Association. *A History of Education in the State of Ohio: A Centennial Volume.* Columbus, OH: The Gazette Printing House, 1876.

Painter, Nell Irvin. *Sojourner Truth: A Life, a Symbol.* New York: W. W. Norton, 1997.

Parker, David B. *A Chautauqua Boy in '61 and After.* Boston: Small, Maynard, 1912.

Parker, Geoffrey, Richard Sisson, and William Russell Coil, eds. *Ohio and the World, 1753–2053: Essays Toward a New History of Ohio.* Columbus: Ohio State University Press, 2005.

Perkinson, Henry J. *The Imperfect Panacea: American Faith in Education, 1865–1990.* New York: McGraw Hill, 1991.

Perry, Ruth. *Women, Letters and the Novel.* New York: AMS Press, 1980.

Petty, Gerald M. *Index of the Ohio Squirrel Hunters Roster.* Columbus, OH: Petty's Press, 1984.

Pryor, Elizabeth Brown. *Clara Barton: Professional Angel.* Philadelphia: University of Pennsylvania Press, 1987.

Reese, William J. *The Origins of the American High School.* New Haven, CT: Yale University Press, 1995.

Reid, Whitelaw. *Ohio in the War: Her Statesmen, Generals, and Soldiers.* 2 vols. Cincinnati, OH: Moore, Wilstach, and Baldwin, 1868.

Roseboom, Eugene Holloway. *History of the State of Ohio,* vol. 4, *The Civil War Era, 1850–1873.* Columbus: Ohio State Archaeological and Historical Society, 1944.

Rowe family letters, 1861–1865, private collection.

Rury, John L. *Education and Women's Work: Female Schooling and the Division of Labor in Urban America, 1870–1930.* Albany: State University of New York Press, 1991.

Ryan, Mary P. *The Empire of the Mother: American Writing about Domesticity, 1830–1860.* New York: Haworth, 1985.

Schneir, Miriam, ed. *Feminism: The Essential Historical Writings.* New York: Random House, 1972.

Schultz, Jane E. *Women at the Front: Hospital Workers in Civil War America.* Chapel Hill: University of North Carolina Press, 2004.

Scott, Joan W. *Gender and the Politics of History.* New York: Columbia University Press, 1988.

Silber, Nina. *Daughters of the Union: Northern Women Fight the Civil War.* Cambridge, MA: Harvard University Press, 2005.

Silbey, Joel H. *A Respectable Minority: The Democratic Party in the Civil War Era, 1860–1868.* 1st ed. New York: Norton, 1977.

Sklar, Kathryn Kish. *Catharine Beecher: A Study in American Domesticity.* New Haven, CT: Yale University Press, 1973.

Smith, Charles H. *History of Fuller's Ohio Brigade, 1861–1865: Its Great March, with Roster Portraits, Battle Maps and Biographies.* Cleveland: Higginson Book Co., 1909.

Smith, George Winston, and Charles B. Judah. *Life in the North during the Civil War: A Source History.* 1st ed. Albuquerque: University of New Mexico Press, 1966.

Smith, Shawn Michelle. *American Archives: Gender, Race and Class in Visual Culture.* Princeton, NJ: Princeton University Press, 1999.

Smith-Rosenberg, Carroll. "The Female World of Love and Ritual: Relations between Women in Nineteenth-Century America." *Signs* 1, no. 1 (Autumn 1975): 1–29.

Smythe, George Franklin. *Kenyon College: Its First Century.* New Haven, CT: Yale University Press, 1924.

Solomon, Barbara Miller. *In the Company of Educated Women: A History of Women and Higher Education in America.* New Haven, CT: Yale University Press, 1985.

Spender, Dale, and Lynne Spender. *Scribbling Sisters.* Norman: University of Oklahoma Press, 1987.

Steedman, Carolyn. "A Woman Writing a Letter." In *Epistolary Selves: Letters and Letter-writers, 1600–1945,* edited by Rebecca Earle, 111–33. Brookfield, VT: Ashgate, 1999.

Sterling, Dorothy. *We Are Your Sisters: Black Women in the Nineteenth Century.* New York: W. W. Norton, 1984.

Stevens, Peter F. *Rebels in Blue: The Story of Keith and Malinda Blalock.* Dallas, TX: Taylor Trade Publishing, 2000.

Taylor, Susie King. *A Black Woman's Civil War Memoirs.* Edited by Patricia W. Romero and Willie Lee Rose. Princeton, NJ: Markus Wiener, 1988.

Theobald, M. R. "Teachers, Memory and Oral History." In *Telling Women's Lives: Narrative Inquiries in the History of Education,* edited by Kathleen Weiler and Sue Middleton, 9–24. Buckingham, UK: Open University Press, 1999.

Thurner, Manuela. "Subject to Change: Theories and Paradigms of U.S. Feminist History." *Journal of Women's History* 9 (1997): 122–46.

Trudeau, Noah Andre. *Like Men of War: Black Troops in the Civil War, 1862–1865.* New Jersey: Castle Books, 2002.

Tyack, David B., and Elizabeth Hansot. *Managers of Virtue: Public School Leadership in America, 1820–1980.* New York: Basic Books, 1982.

Vallandigham, Clement Laird. *The Record of Hon. C. L. Vallandigham on Abolition, the Union, and the Civil War.* Columbus, OH: J. Walter and Co., 1863.

Van Buskirk Family Papers, 1817–1897, MSS 690, Ohio Historical Society, Columbus, Ohio. 1847, 1849, 1855.

Vinovskis, M. A. "Have Social Historians Lost the Civil War? Some Preliminary Demographic Speculations." *Journal of American History* 76, no. 1 (1989): 34–58.

———, ed. *Toward a Social History of the American Civil War.* Cambridge: Cambridge University Press, 1990.

Walker, Joyce A. "Letters in the Attic: Private Reflections of Women, Wives and Mothers." In *The Methods and Methodologies of Qualitative Family Research*, edited by Marvin B. Sussman and Jane F. Gilgun, 9–40. New York: Haworth, 1996.

Ware, Vron. *Beyond the Pale: White Women, Racism and History.* London: Verso, 1992.

Warren, Donald, ed. *American Teachers: History of a Profession at Work.* New York: Macmillan, 1989.

Washburn, Carl D. "The Rise of the High School in Ohio." Ph.D. dissertation, Ohio State University, 1932.

Weiler, Kathleen, and Sue Middleton. *Telling Women's Lives: Narrative Inquiries in the History of Women's Education.* Buckingham, UK: Open University Press, 1999.

White, Emerson E., and Thomas W. Harvey, eds. *A History of Education in the State of Ohio.* Columbus, OH: Gazette, 1876.

Whites, LeeAnn. "The Civil War as a Crisis in Gender." In *Divided Houses: Gender and the Civil War*, edited by Catherine Clinton and Nina Silber, 3–21. New York: Oxford University Press, 1992.

Wiley, Bell Irvin. *The Life of Billy Yank: The Common Soldier of the Union.* Indianapolis: Bobbs-Merrill, 1952. Reprint, Baton Rouge: Louisiana State University Press, 1979.

———. *The Life of Johnny Reb: The Common Soldier of the Confederacy.* 1943. Reprint, Baton Rouge: Louisiana State University Press, 1978.

Woody, Thomas. *A History of Women's Education in the United States.* New York: Science Press, 1929.

Woolf, Virginia. *Woman and Fiction.* In *Collected Essays: Virginia Woolf*, edited by Leonard Woolf, 2:141–48. London: Hogarth, 1966.

Wright, Julia McNair. *The Complete Home.* Philadelphia: J. R. McCurdy and Co., 1879.

———. *Priest and Nun.* Cincinnati: Western Tract Society, 1869.

Young, Agatha. *The Women and the Crisis: Women of the North in the Civil War.* New York: McDowell, Obolensky, 1959.

Index of Correspondents

General Index

letters (*cont.*)
 as harmless pleasure, 36
 as kinship work, 19–20, 30, 43–44, 47–50
 public function of, 24–26, 28, 38, 47–49,
  59
 published, 28–29, 45, 139, 145
 as romantic work, 34–37, 50–64, 126–27,
  133–35, 138–39, 147–48, 154–55, 157,
  165–67, 172–73, 182–83, 189–90,
  191, 193–95, 199, 204–5, 206–7, 210,
  214–15, 217, 218–20, 225, 251–53,
  260–61, 284, 292, 321, 339–40, 344,
  346, 350 (*see also* Rogers, Phrone, in
  Index of Correspondents)
 and reputation, 61–62, 205
 and silences between, 32, 44–45, 47–48,
  49, 59, 61, 127, 133, 142, 155, 166, 182,
  186, 196, 206, 209, 211, 215, 220, 239,
  241, 243, 247, 249, 252, 253, 254–55,
  257, 259–60, 268, 269–70, 282, 287,
  292, 315, 316, 333–34
 and tracking receipt of, 29–30, 33–34
letter-writing manuals, 20–22
Lexington, KY, 96, 120
Lincoln, Abraham, 13, 87, 91, 97, 98–99,
  101, 107, 113, 119, 169, 254, 268, 284,
  295, 303, 305
Lincoln, Mary Todd, 40
Livermore, Mary Rice, 40
Livingstone, Irene (pseud. for friend of Lou
  Riggen), 37, 192, 213, 217, 238, 305,
  311–12
Lonlie/Loncie, 322
Lookout Mountain, TN, 260
Loudonville, OH, 312
Louisville, KY, 31, 125, 133, 264, 313, 315,
  316, 317, 318, 321, 322
Lybarger, Aaron, 118, 132
Lybarger, Amelia Crum (mother of E. L.
  Lybarger), 30, 47–48, 68, 81, 119,
  122–23, 125, 129, 130, 135–36, 142, 145,
  151, 155, 164, 169, 175, 180, 205, 215,
  220, 234, 241, 245, 250, 253, 257, 258,
  270, 276, 282, 288, 293, 300, 301, 302,
  308, 318, 327, 329, 337, 342, 344, 350,
  355, 358
Lybarger, Andrew, 355
Lybarger, Elijah Crum (brother of E. L.
  Lybarger), 48, 119, 130, 202, 229, 235,
  251, 272, 276, 282, 288, 290–91, 293,
  300, 329, 337, 355
Lybarger, Ellen, 330
Lybarger, Harry Swayne, 358
Lybarger, Jake, 280
Lybarger, James Thompson (father of E. L.
  Lybarger), 30, 47–48, 81, 119, 122,

130, 131, 136, 142, 151, 155, 166, 169,
  176, 180, 205, 220, 231, 234, 281, 355
Lybarger, Ludwick, Sr., 355
Lybarger, Lydia Winterringer, 288
Lybarger, Sophronia Rogers. *See* Rogers,
  Phrone (Sophronia)
Lybarger, Thompson (half-brother of E. L.
  Lybarger), 270, 355
Lybarger, Upton Flenner, 130
Lydic, Mae, 79, 118
Lydic, Rance, 151
Lystra, Karen, 55, 64

Macon, GA, 285
Macon/Macon City, MO, 143, 158, 187, 221,
  235, 288, 327, 342
Malhouse, 134
Mann, Horace, 82
Mared [Meredith?], Ell, 279
Mared, Frank [Fannie Meredith?], 279
Mared [Meredith?], Hallie, 280
Mared [Meredith?], John, 279
Mared [Meredith?], Leander, 280
Marion (Grant County), IN, 169–70
marriages, mention of, 116, 122, 128, 134,
  137, 164, 179, 205, 210, 230, 233, 234,
  240, 261, 270, 273, 280, 297
Martinsburg School, 81, 331
Massey, Mary, 29
Mast, Emanuel (Dr.), 96, 137, 205, 337
Mast, Frances E. (Fannie), 204
May, Ida, 36
McClellan, George Brinton, 91, 98, 102, 286
McElroy, Henry, 81, 138
McElroy, James (Jim), 96, 205
McElroy, Maggie, 230, 233
McGugin, 97
McGugin, Dan, 280
McGugin, Frank, 233
McKee, Squire, 232
McCloud, Robert, 234
McLoud's Store, 234
McMahon, Fannie, 348
McMahon, Dr. (William), 273
McNault, Mr., 252
McPherson, James, 50, 108, 113
McPherson, James B., 245
Memphis, TN, 57, 59, 67, 121, 125, 143, 144,
  146, 147, 148, 152, 156, 157, 160, 161,
  162, 163, 165, 167, 169, 170, 172, 174,
  177, 178, 184, 185, 191, 192, 193, 197,
  199–200
Meredith, Ell, 267, 279
Meredith, Fannie, 22, 31, 32, 52, 79, 81, 96,
  97, 117–18, 124, 239–40, 247, 266–68,
  279, 280

General Index